James Hogg
A Life

James Hogg
A Life

Gillian Hughes

EDINBURGH UNIVERSITY PRESS
2007

© Edinburgh University Press, 2007

Edinburgh University Press
22 George Square
Edinburgh
EH8 9LF

Typeset at the University of Stirling
Printed and bound in England by
Antony Rowe Ltd, Chippenham, Wiltshire

ISBN 978 0 7486 1639 8

A CIP record for this book is available from the British Library

Acknowledgements

My first thanks must go to David Sweet, without whom this book might never have been started and would certainly not have been completed. This biography has its roots in an interest in James Hogg going back more than thirty years, so that a very old debt is to the teachers with whom I first studied Hogg's writing, Tony Dyson at the University of East Anglia and Ian Campbell at the University of Edinburgh. Douglas Mack first suggested that I should undertake a biography of James Hogg, whose work he has studied and written about for many years.

Peter Garside is well-known for his generosity to other scholars, and has always been supportive of my work on James Hogg, here and elsewhere. I am indebted to Karl Miller, not only for the committed scholarship of his own book on Hogg, *Electric Shepherd*, but for the many suggestive and illuminating comments he has made. I would also like to thank Richard Jackson and John Ballantyne for the generosity with which they have put their detailed knowledge of various Scottish archives at my disposal and indicated several promising avenues for further exploration.

Among my former colleagues at the University of Stirling I should like to thank Susan Dryburgh and the staff of the Department of English Studies Office for their moral and secretarial support. I must also thank Suzanne Gilbert and Janette Currie, both Hogg scholars of the Department of English Studies, for their help. I thank Helen Beardsley and Gordon Willis of Stirling University Library for meeting my requests for access to rare books and manuscript material, and for promptly and patiently answering varied pleas for advice and practical assistance, sometimes at very short notice.

Throughout the writing of this book I have been conscious of my debt to the various editors and researchers of the Stirling/South Carolina Research Edition of the Collected Works of James Hogg. My task has been made easier by their dedicated scholarship and I am grateful to all those engaged in this project under Douglas Mack's leadership.

Any biography must owe a tremendous debt to many librarians and archivists, and this one is no exception. I am grateful to the many librarians with whom I have had dealings in the course of my research for this volume, but would like to express my particular gratitude to Paul Barnaby, Jocelyn Chalmers, Janet Horncy, Mike Kelly, Donald Kerr, Sheila Mackenzie, Sheila Noble, Julian Pooley,

Virginia Murray, and Tessa Spencer. The staff of the Edinburgh Room, Edinburgh Central Library, the National Library of Scotland, and the National Archives of Scotland have smoothed my path on numerous occasions.

The writing and research of this biography has been supported by a major research grant awarded by the United Kingdom's Arts and Humanities Research Board. I have been able to look at letters and other archival material in North America and New Zealand because of generous grants made by the Carnegie Trust for the Universities of Scotland and the Bibliographical Society, and was privileged during October 2001 to be the Frederick A. & Marion S. Pottle visiting research fellow at the Beinecke Rare Book and Manuscript Library, Yale University. An honorary research fellowship at the University of Manchester has allowed me to access the resources of the John Rylands University Library of Manchester.

The support of Hogg's descendants has been essential for this volume, and I am grateful to Chris Gilkison, Margaret Gilkison, Liz and Alan Milne, and David Parr in particular. The James Hogg Society has been a wonderful focal point for the study of Hogg's life and writings for more than thirty years now. Current and former staff at Edinburgh University Press have been generous with their time and trouble, particularly Ian Davidson, Wendy Gardiner, Jackie Jones, Máiréad McElligott, and Douglas McNaughton.

I would also like to thank the following friends and fellow-enthusiasts (by no means mutually exclusive categories): Jim Barcus, Val Bold, Ian Duncan, Penny Fielding, Gillian Garside, Alan Grant, Hans de Groot, Wendy Hunter, Peter Jackson, Willie Johnstone, Judy King, Bill Lawson, Kirsteen McCue, Wilma Mack, Liz MacLachlan, Robin MacLachlan, Susan Manning, Jane Millgate, Jean Moffatt, Meiko O'Halloran, Elaine Petrie, Murray Pittock, Sharon Ragaz, David Reid, Tom Richardson, Patrick Scott, Deirdre Shepherd, Judy Steel, and Graham Tulloch. This biography is also greatly indebted to the pioneering scholarship of David Groves, particularly to his study, *James Hogg and the St Ronan's Border Games*.

I wish to thank the following institutions and individuals for permission to cite manuscript materials in their care: Alexander Turnbull Library, Wellington, New Zealand; Mr John Ballantyne; The Beinecke Rare Book and Manuscript Library, Yale University; The Bodleian Library, University of Oxford; The British Library Board; The Duke of Buccleuch and the Buccleuch Heritage Trust; Directors of the Canterbury Caledonian Society; The Trustees of the Chevening Trust; Cornwall Record Office; Edinburgh University Library, Department of Special Collections; Glasgow University Library, Department of Special Collections; The Historical Society of Pennsylvania, Philadelphia (HSP); The Huntington Library, San Marino, California; The John Rylands University Library, The University of Manchester; Special Collections and Digital Programs, University of Kentucky Libraries; Liverpool Record Office, Liverpool Libraries and Information Services; the Longman Collection at Reading University Library; Sir Maxwell McLeod, Bart.; Mrs Doreen Mitchell; National Archives of Scotland; The Trustees of the National Library of Scotland; The Trustees of the National Museums of Scotland; National Register of Archives for Scotland; The Trustees of the National Galleries of Scotland; Northumberland Record Office; the Trustees of Sir Francis Ogilvy, of Inverquharity, Bart.; Pearson Education Limited; Queens University Archives, Kingston, Ontario; Department of Rare Books & Special Collections, University of Rochester Library; The Royal Company of Archers; the Royal Highland and Agricultural Society of Scotland; permission was kindly granted by the Royal Literary Fund; Savings Bank Museum, Ruthwell; Scottish Borders Council Museums and Galleries Service; Courtesy of the Society of Antiquaries of Newcastle-upon-Tyne; the Society of Antiquaries of Scotland; Rare Books & Special Collections, Thomas Cooper Library, University of South Carolina; Stirling University Library; Department of Special Collections, Charles E. Young Research Library, UCLA; James Hogg Collection, Special Collections, University of Otago Library, Dunedin, New Zealand; University of Washington Libraries, Special Collections; The Wordsworth Trust.

Hogg's letter to Andrew Picken of 16 [January–March 1832] in the Nichols Archive Project is cited by kind permission of the owner. For further details of the Nichols Archive Project see www.le.ac.uk/elh/staff/jpa.html. Hogg's letter to James Cochrane of 1 March 1834 is quoted by permission of the Houghton Library, Harvard University. Hogg's letters to an unknown correspondent of 21 April 1834 is published with permision of the Princeton University Library. Hogg's letter to the Duke of Buccleuch of 7 December 1832 is published with grateful thanks to the Ogilvie family, of Chesters.

The illustrations to this volume have been reproduced courtesy of the Trustees of the National Galleries of Scotland and Edinburgh Central Library, and from volumes owned by myself.

Every effort has been made to trace copyright holders, but if any have been inadvertently overlooked the publisher will be pleased to make the necessary acknowledgement at the first opportunity.

Contents

Illustrations

x

James Hogg
A Life

CHAPTER ONE

The Days of Vision

James Hogg was born in the modest farmhouse of Ettrickhall in Selkirkshire in Scotland, a humble dwelling within a stone's-throw of Ettrick parish church. The spot was a remote one, tucked away between hills in a sheep-farming district, about 19 miles from the county town of Selkirk and 16 miles from the nearest market-town of Moffat by roads that were 'almost impassable'. There were few bridges over Ettrick Water and in the winter heavy snowfalls occurred.[1] In later life Hogg himself insisted that he was born on 25 January 1772, sharing a birthday with Robert Burns, but the available evidence suggests that he was born instead towards the end of November 1770. Alexander Laidlaw thought that Hogg's mother had told him as much, while Hogg's baptism is recorded in the parish register for 9 December 1770.[2] Ettrickhall was a single storey, clay-built cottage, typical of the older houses of the district, thatched with straw and containing an outer room and inner room known in Scotland as a but and ben. In later life Hogg recorded that it had at one time been used by a local landowner as an occasional stable. This man, an Anderson of Tushielaw, was the subject of a comminatory prophecy in the district, because in order to create a fine mansion and grounds he had ejected a whole community of cottagers from the land:

> Ettrickhall stands on yon plain
> Right sore exposed to wind and rain
> And on it the sun shines never at morn
> Because it was built in the Widow's corn
> And its foundations can never be sure
> Because it was built on the ruin of the poor
> And or an age is comed and gone
> Or the trees o'er the chimlay top grow green
> We winna ken where the house has been[3]

It was thus a fitting birthplace for a writer who made the resilience of the ordinary people of Scotland, despite oppression and change, a recurring theme of his work.

The family of James Hogg's father, Robert Hogg, had been Border shepherds and small tenant farmers for generations past. Robert later told his son James that the Hogg family had farmed the lands of

Fauldshope in Ettrick Forest for several ages as tenants of the Scotts of Harden, until one of them, William Hogg, the laird's champion and nicknamed 'The Great Boar of Fauldshope', had lost his master's favour by leading him into a jeopardy which almost cost him his life. Hogg later associated the jeopardy with the tale of how the young Scott of Harden had been captured by Sir Gideon Murray of Elibank and forced to marry his ugly daughter, 'Mickle-mou'd Meg', a legend relating to a marriage that took place in 1611. Even further back it was reputed that another Hogg ancestor, a notorious witch as well as wife to a local farmer, had challenged the power of, and been defeated by, the thirteenth-century wizard, Michael Scott of Aikwood.[4] Both of these Hogg forebears were duly celebrated in their descendant's written work.

Robert himself, born in 1729, was a much less exciting person. He was the third of the five children of William Hogg, and his wife, Euphame Brown, who lived firstly at Broadmeadows and later at Newark in Selkirkshire. William Hogg died in middle age and left his widow to bring up her family of four sons and a daughter alone, which is perhaps why none of them had any formal schooling. Robert's elder brother George settled at Melrose in Roxburghshire; his elder sister Janet married a man named Robert Bryden and settled to the south of Selkirk at Ashkirk; another son was named Walter; and the youngest of the family, James Hogg, seems to have settled at Kelso. Robert Hogg's own children had more than a dozen surviving first cousins born in those places. Robert himself learned to read the Bible, being particularly fond of the major prophets, Isaiah, Jeremiah, and Ezekiel, and could also relish poetry with a devotional or religious theme such as James Hervey's *Meditations and Contemplations* (1746–47). In later life he became an elder of the established, presbyterian church of Ettrick—indeed when the Rev. Robert Russell was inducted as minister in September 1791 he was the only parish elder.[5] Learning beyond what was helpful to either business or religion was regarded by Robert Hogg with some suspicion, and the few surviving reports of his sayings and doings confirm his taciturn and prudent character. Visitors calling at the house in search of ballads found that Robert Hogg had absented himself, 'doubtless considering us crazy fools'. On another occasion when suspicion of necromantic practices was cast upon a shepherd's debating society he 'did not say much either the one way or the other, but bit his lip, and remarked that "fo'k wad find it was an ill thing to hae to do wi' *the Enemy*"'. He married relatively late in life, on 27 May 1765 at the age of thirty-six, so that his own children were younger than most of their cousins.[6] At the time of his marriage he was a shepherd at Mount Bengerhope, and the event took place only after he had saved enough from his wages to lease and stock the small farms of Ettrickhouse and Ettrickhall. His bride was of a similar age to himself.

Hogg's mother, Margaret Laidlaw, seems to have been a much livelier personality, a woman with a witty, pithy manner of speaking, a fondness for conversation and society, and a 'memory stored with tales and songs of spectres, Ghosts, Faries, Brownies, voices &c.'. She once told a discontented man, 'ye look at a' things as ye coudna help it', and when on another occasion her opponent in an argument started to sing an anti-Jacobite song she drowned his voice with her own rendering of the famous Jacobite song of 'Johnnie Cope'. Her house seems to have been a port-of-call for anyone with a story to tell, whether a life-history, a fantastic tale, or the product of tradition, and one such visitant approvingly described her as 'your father's bairn yet'.[7] That father, William Laidlaw, was a well-known character in the district, a shepherd noted for his athleticism and for having been the last man in the district to have conversed with the fairies. For many years he had lived in a remote corner of Ettrick parish called Upper Phaup. He and his wife, Bessie Scott, had seven children. Margaret, the third and the eldest girl, was born in 1730. Regular education for the children was impossible in such a place, which could at times seem as gloomy as it was isolated:

> Nothing was to be seen but long tracts of Heath & on the tops of the Hills frequently was a dark and thick mist. Nothing was to be heard but the howl of the winds and dash of waters. The sound of these only varied by the increase or diminution of their force; which indeed was perpetually changing, but still the sound was doleful & uninterrupted & engendered gloomy Ideas.[8]

Will's own humour and his illicitly-distilled whisky, however, could draw people about him even in this apparently desolate corner. He had a stock of ballads, learned from the elders of his own day, and a fund of amusing stories drawn from his own experiences and those of his neighbours. Periods of isolation must have been broken on many occasions by social calls and lively evenings, and although his children did not attend school Will saw that their minds were stored with 'a good system of Christian Religion' as well as the wild tales told by himself and his visitors. Margaret's mother died in 1752, when she was not much over twenty and when her youngest sister

Janet was only eleven years old. As usual in such cases she appears to have taken her mother's place as housekeeper, firstly for her father and then for her brother, until her own relatively late marriage in 1765. Her children had at least seventeen first cousins.[9] James Hogg and his brothers must have been much more conscious of their Laidlaw than their Hogg connections, since their Laidlaw cousins were closer to them in age and (being baptised in Ettrick parish) lived much closer too.

To begin with, however, James Hogg's world was the small world of most young children, largely confined to his immediate family and their daily visitors, and to the neighbourhood of home. In his subsequent poem, 'Farewell to Ettrick', Hogg recalled his earliest impression that the place was the 'very centre of the world', a largely self-contained cup formation:

> I thought the hills were sharp as knives,
>   An' the braed lift lay whomel'd on them,
> An' glowr'd wi' wonder at the wives
>   That spak o' ither hills ayon' them.[10]

For the rest of his life a natural landscape was a hilly landscape, and (like Wordsworth) he felt uneasy and uncomfortable in a flat country with an extensive open prospect.

Hogg's elder brother, born in 1767, had been named William after his grandfathers and Hogg's own birth was followed by that of two more boys, David in 1773 and Robert in 1776. There may also have been other children who died at birth or in early infancy. By 1776 the small cottage farmhouse would have been crowded, Margaret Laidlaw caring for four young children, the eldest of whom was only nine years of age, as well as her own aged father. Will o' Phaup had been born in 1691, and though famous for his physical vigour and agility, was now well into his eighties and long past going out with the sheep. James Hogg remembered him only as 'old, and full of days', and his stories about his grandfather all seem to have been taken from other family members, with the exception of one highly significant personal recollection. Privacy must have been impossible at Ettrickhall, and Hogg recalled that Will was 'the first human being whom I saw depart from this stage of existence'. The Ettrick Parish Register records the death of 'William Laidlaw late of Ettrickhall' on 17 September 1778 when Hogg would be only seven years old. In his later genre-piece 'A Peasant's Funeral' one of the children who witnesses his father's death in a similar farmhouse is terrified out of his wits:

> The beds face towards each other, you know, and little John, who was lying awake, was so much shocked by a view which he got of the altered visage of his deceased parent, that he sprung from his bed in a frenzy of horror, and ran naked into the fields, uttering the most piercing and distracted cries.[11]

Hogg's own shock at his first youthful experience of death was probably similar.

In reasonable weather the older children would be mostly out of doors, while their mother was occupied with her household tasks and the younger children. It is easy to imagine Hogg tagging along with his elder brother through 'the meadow, among the hay', by the streams where 'the grey trout lies asleep', and on the hillside like 'Billy and me' of 'A Boy's Song'. James and William Hogg became friends as well as brothers, the four boys falling naturally into pairs of brothers as they grew older. The older two enjoyed reading and writing and reaching for wider horizons, while the younger two seem to have been more content to acquire a purely local reputation as dependable shepherds and farmers. (Robert and David later married sisters, which must have increased the bond between the younger pair.) Occasionally the childhood ramblings of the Hogg boys about the immediate countryside would lead to trouble, as the land was farming land as well as a natural playground, and they would be confronted with the damage they had caused and punished for it, as William later recalled:

> In our excursions for diversion, we were often wasting growing corns, &c or otherways wasting the implements of agriculture; and for these we were called to a strict account. James generally plead our cause with great openness and simplicity, stood often beside his accuser as if unconscious of any crime, but the moment he was seized for punishment he became perfectly frantic and used every method to extricate himself from their grips.[12]

Hogg's open and confiding temper was one of the most attractive parts of his character, a willingness to believe that others regarded him with indulgence so strong that he (rather than his elder brother) acted as advocate on such occasions. The sudden loss of emotional control is another notable feature of his character.

When bad weather or the darkness of the long winter evenings meant that all her boys were indoors and getting underfoot, Margaret Laidlaw kept them from being troublesome by entertaining them herself. This was a suitable time for religious instruction and for training their memories, and she repeated aloud favourites among the metrical psalms of the Church of Scotland so often that before he was of a suitable age to go to school James knew several of them by heart. If her children grew too boisterous and over-excited she would also sober them by fearful tales and songs of the supernatural, how the fairies would trip along the bottom of a lonely dell, how deadlights or a shapeless contorted appearance would announce the death of some near relative, and how the spirit of the gathering storm was heard to shriek through the air. Children love to be frightened and to have their minds filled with dreadful apprehensions, but after hearing their mother's tales both William and James were afraid to step outside after dark, as William recalled, 'without one to protect us and even this had to be one whom we supposed to be more powerfull than the spirit whom we thought lingered without the walls of the house and watched an opportunity to catch us'.

The two elder boys were duly sent to school, a seasonal rather than year-round event in most agricultural societies almost within living memory. In the winter children would be regular attenders at school, but during the summer when there was so much more farmwork to be done their labour was too useful to their parents—herding cows, running errands for the harvesters, and generally assististing the regular farm-workers. William Hogg accordingly speaks of his next brother as going to school for 'only three or four winters' from 'when he was about 6 years old', and describes his progress in terms which suggest it was respectable rather than remarkable. James was probably at school for even less time than his brother recalled, since the parish schoolmaster could not remember his having been a pupil, and he himself recollected only attending for 'two or three months', probably a single winter. In that time he had learned to read, using the more straightforward parts of the devotional books generally available, the Shorter Catechism and the Proverbs of Solomon. The outdoor life the boys led was a healthy one and James became a sturdy and active child, 'forward at every diversion that required agility and vigour'. One day when the children were enjoying their school playtime a neighbouring shepherd organised some races for them and James was an eager competitor, despite his flying shirt-tail which 'was over his breeches & spread almost half round him, when he ran it floated very large behind'. His clothes were in bad repair, and he had trouble keeping his trousers up, as his 'left hand generally held up his breeches and he had nothing but his right for all the operations of the day'.[13] Despite these badges of poverty and a limited education this childhood was clearly a very happy one, with sufficient food, the emotional security of a close family, and plenty of freedom and time to exercise the imagination. From a child's point of view its combination of freedom and adventure with a sufficient measure of safety and companionship seems idyllic.

The world of Hogg's early childhood was soon to be disrupted by trouble, however. Robert Hogg's very moderately prosperous circumstances changed sharply for the worse, and he became bankrupt, an event both his elder sons remembered vividly. William wrote guardedly that 'by once engaging in a business of which he had no previous knowledge he involved his private affairs in confusion: & that at a time when his family was both small and helpless'. Robert Hogg was no doubt a good practical shepherd, well up to the work of the two small farms he leased in Ettrick, but he had clearly tried to improve his income by dealing in sheep. By Hogg's own account he lacked perspicuity in knowing whom to trust at a time of falling prices:

> He then commenced dealing in sheep—bought up great numbers, and drove them both to the English and Scottish markets; but, at length, owing to a great fall in the price of sheep, and the absconding of his principal debtor, he was ruined, became bankrupt, every thing was sold by auction, and my parents were turned out of doors without a farthing in the world. I was then in the sixth year of my age, and remember well the distressed and destitute condition that we were in.[14]

Hogg's uncertainty about his date of birth makes his dating of this event uncertain too, though it probably took place shortly after 1776. The Ettrick parish register describes Robert Hogg as a tenant rather than as a herd for the baptism of all four Hogg brothers, but William Hogg's description of the family as 'small and helpless' when the bankruptcy occurred implies that some of the children were so young as to be unable to fend for themselves in the slightest respect.

Self-pity was not a feeling Hogg chose to indulge, and he says no more about this experience in his autobiography, but there is no doubt that it conditioned his life-long identification with the dispossessed and the oppressed, and in various forms was transmuted into his subsequent writing. The sufferings experienced by Mr Adamson of Laverhope in the story of the same name, for example, appear to follow on his pursuing a modest debt owed by a struggling neighbour named Irvine. Irvine, like Robert Hogg, loses not only his farm but all his worldly goods, and his family are rendered homeless, as the Hoggs had been. Mrs Irvine comes to Adamson with a child in her arms, begging him to put off the enforced sale for a month to give her time to appeal to her friends for assistance, and bitterly asks him, 'Will ye hae the face to kneel afore your Maker the night, and pray for a blessing on you and yours, and that He will forgive you your debts as you forgive your debtors?'[15] Hogg's later sympathy with groups at the opposite ends of the political and religious spectrum, the Highlanders after the Jacobite defeat at Culloden in 1745 and the Covenanters in hiding in the 1680s is less inconsistent than it seems. Both groups have this in common, that they have been dispossessed and are consequently suffering cruelly both in mind and body. It seems that the Hoggs were not homeless for long, since Hogg records that a kindly neighbour, Walter Bryden of Crosslee, provided them with a home by renting the farm of Ettrickhouse himself and employing Robert Hogg as his shepherd. But the child's sense of being the centre of his universe, his faith in his parents' omnipotent protection, was nevertheless abruptly shattered. The young Charles Dickens working among the blacking bottles was astonished that he could be so cast away, so removed from every brighter prospect in life, and Hogg too was made painfully conscious of his vulnerability at a very young age.

In the reduced circumstances of the family even the pitiful financial gains from sending the older children out as farm servants was helpful, though this amounted to little more than saving the cost of feeding them at home. James Hogg accordingly 'being only seven years of age, was hired by a farmer in the neighbourhood to herd a few cows; my wages for the half year being a ewe lamb and a pair of new shoes'. From being a farmer's son, stravaiging the countryside in summer with his elder brother, he had become a herd-boy, the lowest category of rural worker. To begin with, Hogg would only be employed during the period each year between the Scottish Quarterdays of Whitsunday and Martinmass, roughly mid-May to mid-November, when the cows were out at pasture: in the colder winter months they would be kept close and no herd was needed. During the winter following his first such summer Hogg returned to his home and his parents sent him to a teacher, not the parish schoolmaster William Beattie this time, but 'a young lad called William Ker, who was teaching a neighbouring farmer's children'. During this winter he learned to write a little as well as to read, 'and had horribly defiled several sheets of paper with copy-lines, every letter of which was nearly an inch in length'. Despite Hogg's self-mockery, he had made good use of the only two brief spells of formal schooling he ever received, and the use of paper for his writing practice suggests that he was one of William Ker's more advanced students.

Paper was expensive, and children normally began by tracing letters in a sand-tray or writing on a slate that could be wiped and reused— only the best were trusted with the precious sheets of paper. Hogg's hand-eye co-ordination must have been remarkable for him to have learned to write so well in such a brief period of schooling, just as it was still unusually good even in old age. His adult handwriting is confident, plain, firm, and well-spaced, defying every conventional preconception about the writing of a peasant poet. The rest of his education was self-education, improving his reading and writing skills by comparing ballads and psalms he had by heart with the printed characters in chap-books and his Bible, and imitating the shapes of the letters by copying what he saw onto an old slate.[16]

One measure of Hogg's shock at the family's temporary home-lessness is the honour in which he held and continued to hold their rescuer, Walter Bryden, 'the best friend that we had in the world' as he termed him many years afterwards. When the farmer of Crosslee was killed in a freak accident in March 1799 by the fall of a tree on him at Newark, Hogg wrote his elegy, describing him by that 'no-blest name, the FRIEND OF MAN' and significantly praying, 'Do thou, kind Heav'n, his children bless, | Nor let the widow's heart despair'. Hogg may have had the comforting words of Psalm 37. 25 in mind here, 'I have been young, and now am old; yet have I not seen the righteous forsaken, nor his seed begging bread'. In his old age he was shaken when Bryden's own children were oppressed by a domi-neering creditor ('My heart is like to break about the Brydens of Crosslee'), arguing that 'Such a curse hanging over a good man's family is a thing that can hardly be contemplated with resignation'.[17]

Many of the stories Hogg set in the traditional farming commu-nity of the Scottish Borders depict the vulnerable condition of a child whose parents are not at hand to protect and defend him. It was in many ways a hard society, where justice was often rough justice, where great and real kindness was not always shown to best effect, and where acts of cruelty could go unchecked for lengthy periods. In 'Rob Dods' a young lad working as a shepherd's assistant dies of exhaustion and hunger brought on by his master's cruelty, and there is retribution but not protection. In 'Mr Adamson of Laverhope' an orphan's only friend, his faithful colley dog, is struck unconscious by his master in a momentary fit of temper and when the boy com-plains he is beaten himself and is only shielded from further perse-cution by a young shepherd named Robert Johnston. Hogg witnessed one such scene of brutality while a farm servant himself:

I once served with a master, an old gentleman, who had a

blackguard son that had broken as a wine-merchant, and came home to his father's house destitute; and his father, to give him some employ, set him over us all. [...] A young shepherd, having supped his own share of the paritch at breakfast time, set down the allotted remainder to his colley, a little spotted very valuable animal. Mr. Robert, our tyrant, had a large beautiful English setter, a very fine animal, and valuable in its way; and as her master had nothing in the world beside, she was with him a great pet. No sooner had the lad set down the paritch to his little colley, than the setter seized it by the throat and shook it like a clout. The poor fellow ran to save his friend, and in separating them he struck the setter with the ramhorn spoon that he had in his hand—that was all. On which Mr. Robert knocked him down; and not content with that, he seized the kitchen tongs and knocked the colley dead. But there was a shepherd present named Andrew Tait, a tremendously strong fellow, and when put into a rage scarcely like other people, anger always throwing him into a state of derangement. He sprung from beyond the table where he was sitting, seized the setter by the cuff of the neck, and in less than two seconds wrung her nether jaws off, and flung them in her master's face. A fierce battle began; but Mr. Robert, though a powerful man, was a babe to Tait, who thrashed him to his heart's content. It was a bloody morning, for both dogs were killed and both combatants wounded.[18]

It must have been terrifying to witness such scenes, and Hogg was occasionally ill-treated himself. 'From some of my masters,' he recalled, 'I received very hard usage; in particular, while with one shepherd, I was often nearly exhausted with hunger and fatigue'.

Hogg must also, to begin with at least, have greatly missed the companionship of his elder brother, William. His own recollections of his earliest days in service are of his solitary and imaginative reconstruction of the social sports he enjoyed so much throughout his life. In the absence of companions he created a world from his own imagination:

I was wont to strip off my clothes, and run races against time, or rather against myself; and, in the course of these exploits, which I accomplished much to my own admiration, I first lost my plaid, then my bonnet, then my coat, and, finally, my hosen; for, as for shoes, I had none. In that naked state did I herd for several days, till a shepherd and maid-servant were sent to the hills to look for them, and found them all.

He must have missed his mother too, a kindly older servant-girl no doubt acting in some degree as a maternal surrogate. Hogg recalled that during his second summer's service as a herd when he was only eight years old he formed an attachment to a girl of marriageable age named Betty. He herded her new-weaned lambs for her, they ate their lunch together every day, and then he slept for a while with his head on her lap, silently weeping when he heard her pity him and say to herself, 'Poor little laddie! he's joost tired to death'. In his fantasies, his young master would marry Betty and he would continue to be her little favourite, just as in the adult Hogg's story of 'The Wool-Gatherer' the ragged servant-boy Barnaby becomes the young laird's steward after his marriage to Jane, whom Barnaby has protected and defended in ill-fortune. As Hogg said, 'I have liked the women a great deal better than the men ever since I remember'.[19]

Hogg's occupation as a cow-herd would also throw him into the company of the old men of the district, since a man whose strength was gradually failing him in old age would be just as incapable of the more arduous duties of the farm as a child who had not yet achieved his full strength. His open and ingenuous look and frankness of temper were combined with a certain imaginative credulity that made him an attentive listener to the odd experiences and all kinds of legends and stories they told him. Many of his later tales had their origin in the long days when his elderly companions told him stories to pass the time on the hillside. One of them named David Proudfoot, he recalled, 'was a very old man, herding cows, when I was a tiny boy at the same occupation. He would often sit with the snuff-mill in his hand, and tell me old tales for hours together; and this was one among the rest'. David preferred stories in which he was an actor to some degree, and Hogg affectionately tells his tale of 'Tibbie Johnston's Wraith' very much 'as David told it', in the first person and concluding with his address to his young companion, 'When ye come to my time o' life, ye may be telling it to somebody; and, if they should misbelieve it, you may say that you heard it from auld Davie Proudfoot's ain mouth, and he was never kend for a liar'.[20]

He was also attentive to the odd and out-of-the-way characters of the district, such as William Dodds, who recounted Jacobite songs in the eccentric mock sermons, 'which he was accustomed to deliver to the boys and lasses in the winter evenings, to their infinite amusement, in the style and manner of a fervent preacher'. Another recounter of Jacobite traditions was an old woman named Betty

Cameron from Lochaber, 'a well-known character over a great part of the Lowlands' for the sixty years before her death in 1819, although her base was Edinburgh. She possessed 'an abundant store of information and anecdote concerning the principal families of Scotland, as well as of the young Chevalier, whom she had seen in her youth. She talked with enthusiasm of the deeds of Highland valour, and preserved to the last all the prejudices of clanship'. According to Hogg she never mentioned the sufferings of those who were out in the Jacobite Rising of 1745 without tears, and her stories were the foundation of his early poems 'Glengyle' and 'The Happy Swains'. The itinerant traders of the district would also sing songs or tell tales in order to improve the welcome they received in the houses they visited on their rounds. Hogg's supernatural tale 'A Sea Story', for example, is referred to a yarn-merchant named John Robson, 'a great favourite with the wives' who willingly bartered with him and gave him overnight lodging in return for his 'long romantic stories of battles and perils by land and water'.[21]

Gradually as his strength increased Hogg became capable of harder and better-paid work. By the time he was fifteen years of age he had on this account served a dozen masters. Though considering him a 'soft actionless boy', they generally liked him 'for the general fidelity of his conduct and for the candid & sprightly manner of acknowledging his errors when any piece of business had misfortuned with him'. He was observant, could express himself aptly, and with 'an immediate fervour of spirits'. Sometimes he would work at harvesting, threshing, and with horses, and at others acted as a shepherd's assistant, gradually acquiring the experience that would fit him to become a shepherd himself. His boyhood masters included Robin Grieve, shepherd of the Craigyrigg in Yarrow (who may have been the master who ill-treated him), and Ebenezer Stuart, whose wife was skilled in the use of medicinal herbs and cured animals belonging to the farmers of Hyndhope and Gilmanscleuch while Hogg was living in the family. The boy would watch his elders, and learn the appearances of herbs such as 'the healing-leaf', the places where they were likely to be found, and how to prepare medicines from them. Hogg had what he termed 'a quick eye in observing the operations of nature', and all the time he was in service he was learning natural history. In his future profession of shepherd he must know the characteristics and behaviour of the wild animals and birds about him, and how to care for and treat the illnesses of farm animals. When he was minding a large herd of lambs and passing the time by knitting stockings he was troubled by 'sturdies', or sheep with water on the brain, attracted by the lambs' bleating. If Hogg cured their affliction they would leave him alone, so he used his knitting needle to pierce the sacks of water by thrusting it up the nostrils of the afflicted animal—this he found was often effective, though it was not a remedy to be advertised, since if the animal died he might be held responsible by the owner for his loss.[22]

The natural world was a source of entertainment and wonder as well an object of professional study. As a child Hogg was excited by rather than afraid of the commotion of a summer thunderstorm, 'entranced with delight' indeed, and 'always loved to watch the lightning and listen to the thunder'. The sky-lark was 'an inmate of the wilds, and the companion of my boyhood', and Hogg recollected he had often lain 'in the grey of the morning and tried in vain to discover him from his notes on high, until the rising sun revealed him to me like a little musical star on the breast of heaven'. He learned to imitate the cries of the moorfowl so exactly as to be able to call numbers of the birds around him on the hill in the early morning, and to interpret the different cries and actions of sheep. Closest of all to him, inevitably, were his various dogs. As he later recalled, 'My dog was always my companion. I conversed with him the whole day—I shared every meal with him, and my plaid in the time of a shower; the consequence was, that I generally had the best dogs in all the country'. Wonderful stories were related of the sagacity of the Border sheepdog. John Hoy, the husband of Hogg's maternal aunt Agnes Laidlaw, for instance, could listen to a field-preacher as darkness fell and leave his dog with only rudimentary instruction to gather in his sheep for him. And in service on Ettrick Water as a boy Hogg had witnessed the marvellous exploit of Chieftain, a dog belonging to John Graham, the tenant of Ashiestiel, in finding within half an hour a lost sheep simply on being taken in the dark to the spot on which a neighbour had last seen her on the hillside. The trusty dog 'brought the individual lost sheep to our very feet [...] John called him all the ill names he could invent, which the other seemed to take in very good part. Such language seemed to be John's flattery to his dog. For my part, I went home fancying I had seen a miracle [...]'.[23]

As Hogg's earnings gradually increased he was allowed by his parents to keep a little money for his own use. One of his first purchases was an old violin for which he paid five shillings, a considerable outlay for a fourteen-year-old farm servant. Hogg loved music, singing, and dancing, and among the highlights of the year were the times when the itinerant fiddler appeared at the farmhouses where he worked—at the sheep-shearing, at the harvest-supper, at the end of the year, and at seed-time in the spring. The neighbours would be invited and the night spent gaily in singing and dancing. Every man who attended the dance would pay the fiddler sixpence and the farmer would give a present in kind, a fleece at the shearing, for example, and a lippie (or quarter-peck measure) of oats at seed-time. It was natural that as an adolescent Hogg should wish to be such another welcome guest and entertainer, but remarkable that with little leisure time and no tuition he should have become an accomplished fiddler within a year or two. He practised at night after his day's work was done in the stable or byre where his bed was placed and where, as there was straw about, no open flame could be permitted. He had to learn the fingering in the dark, judging by ear rather than seeing when his hand was in the correct position to make the note intended. A beginner on the violin makes an excruciating racket, and unsurprisingly Hogg's fellow-servants sometimes complained—nevertheless he persisted, sawing over the old tunes he knew again and again until he had mastered them, taking his fiddle with him when he moved from one service to another. One of his friends in later life declared that Hogg was fonder of music than of poetry.[24]

It was probably at Martinmass 1785 that Hogg transferred himself and violin to Singlee on Ettrick Water. His master, William Scott, paid five hundred pounds a year in rents and had some fifteen children. He had farmed Singlee at least as early as 1772 when his eldest son Robert was born there and continued to hold it until his death in November 1814, when he was succeeded by his son Gideon. Other children were set up with farms or in various professions, his third son, Henry, becoming a partner in a prosperous Edinburgh hatters business. At his death William Scott left an annuity to his second wife, and sums ranging from £400 to £1,000 to his younger children, apart from the inheritance of his eldest son Robert.[25] Looking back in old age at the world of his youth Hogg felt that master and servant then lived together intimately with little distinction of rank. The farmer sat at the head of his kitchen table sharing the servants' meals, he directed communal religious worship, and 'conversed with all his servants familiarly, and consulted what was best to be done for the day'. This was probably true of the smaller households in which Hogg served, but at Singlee there appears to have been a greater distance between master and servants. The old ways were already being abandoned by some farmers even in Hogg's adolescence and a prosperous man like Scott can have paid little attention to the young James Hogg or to the conversation of his other servants if he was unaware of Hogg's constant (and often extremely

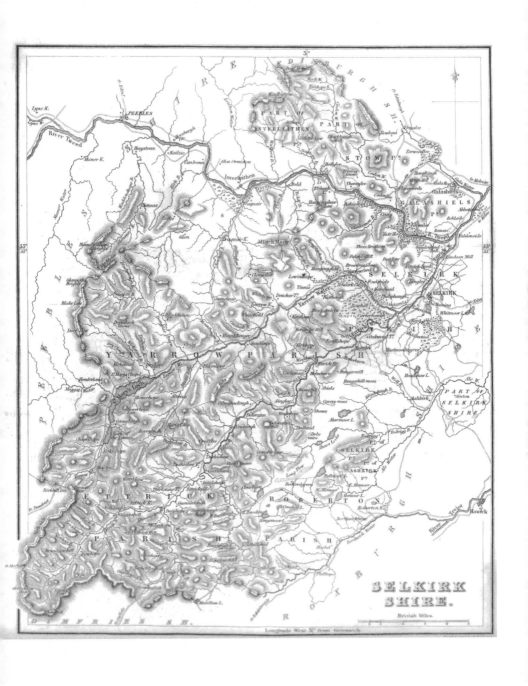

SELKIRK SHIRE.

British Miles

Longitude West 3° from Greenwich

irritating) fiddle practice. His attention was drawn to it one night, however, in a rather dramatic fashion, when arriving home late he decided to stable his horse for himself rather than disturb any other member of the household. On entering the stable he heard such fearful noises that 'he run into the house with the greatest precipitation, crying that he believed the devil was in the stable'. When Scott held a dance at Singlee some time later it seems to have been for the benefit of his family, their friends and neighbours, James Hogg (and presumably the other servants) being present only as spectators. Of course the lad paid great attention to the music and 'on the company breaking up, I retired to my stable-loft, and fell to essaying some of the tunes to which I had been listening'. The musician, who had come outside to urinate, heard that

> [...] the tunes which he had lately been playing with such skill, were now murdered by some invisible being hard by him. Such a circumstance, at that dead hour of the night, and when he was unable to discern from what quarter the sounds proceeded, convinced him all at once that it was a delusion of the devil; and, suspecting his intentions from so much familiarity, he fled precipitately into the hall, with disordered garments, and in the utmost horror, to the no small mirth of Mr Scott, who declared, that he had lately been considerably stunned himself by the same discordant sounds.

Fortunately for his fellow-servants, Hogg's playing gradually improved, to the point where they 'at last began to discern harmony in his performances, and expressed their approbation by listening and sometimes dancing'. No doubt his repertoire included some of the well-known tunes he mentions in 'Geordie Fa's Dirge'.[26]

Hogg's next period of service, probably for eighteen months from Martinmass 1786, was at Elibank, a farm near Clovenfords bordered by the River Tweed that he afterwards described as 'the most quiet and sequestered place in Scotland'. It was an excellent pasture farm well stocked with Cheviot sheep, and Hogg must have got on well there since he not only stayed for a half-year longer than usual but his next position, with his master's father, was the longed-for promotion to become a shepherd in his own right.

A shepherd was the aristocrat of rural hired labour, the best-paid servant on a farm, his wages being about one-fifth more than those of a ploughman. His duties and responsibilities were considerable, particularly when he had charge of a large flock in an extensive pasture:

He must go through his flock early in the morning and late at
night, and at other times during the day, and count his flock
once a-day; he must keep them clean from scab, maggots,
and other filth; he must watch the ewes at the lambing-sea-
son night and day, and castrate the tup lambs; he must wash
the sheep and clip the wool, and bath them for turnip-feeding
in winter; he must be able to slaughter sheep and pigs neatly;
and he must give such general assistance in harvest as his
time permits [...].

Of course some of the most arduous tasks were seasonal ones only.
Particular attention was required, for example, at rutting time, to
ensure that the tup mated with as many ewes as possible. Afterwards when the lambs were born the shepherd must make sure the
mother gave suck to her offspring and try to pair up a ewe whose
lamb had died with a motherless lamb. One way of doing this was to
tie the dead lamb's skin to the living one and shut mother and baby
up in a dark place until feeding was well established. After suckling
for between three and four months the lambs would need to be
weaned, which meant keeping them in a group for two or three weeks
away from the sight and sound of the dams they were eager to rejoin
until they were accustomed to feed heartily on grass. This meant
round-the-clock supervision to begin with, and often one of the maidservants from the farm would be sent out to keep watch so that the
shepherd could steal a few hours' sleep. If the shepherd was young
and the girl attractive he might prefer to court her rather than take a
nap, and such an occasion Hogg later made the subject of one of his
most delightful songs of rural courtship, 'I'll Ne'er Wake Wi' Annie'.[27]

The shearing of the fleeces generally took place in June, and was
another time when the shepherd had a female helper. In 'Mr Adamson
of Laverhope' Hogg portrays a scene in which he must often have
participated:

It is the business of the lasses to take the ewes, and carry
them from the fold to the clippers; and now might be seen
every young shepherd's sweetheart, or favourite, tending on
him, helping him to clip, or holding the ewes by the hind legs
to make them lie easy, a great matter for the furtherance of
the operator. Others again, who thought themselves slighted,
or loved a joke, would continue to act in the reverse way, and
plague the youths by bringing such sheep to them as it was
next to impossible to clip.

Hogg describes every pair as 'being engaged according to their biasses, and after their kind—some settling the knotty points of divinity; others telling auld warld stories about persecutions, forays, and fairy raids; and some whispering, in half-sentences, the soft breathings of pastoral love'.[28] Late October brought a task that was without such social pleasures and was even more laborious, the smearing of the sheep with a mixture of tar and either oil or butter to protect the animal against ticks and maggots. The fleece would have to be parted at regular intervals and the mixture rubbed well in, an operation which Hogg subsequently described as an 'eident and naseous business [...] which continues every lawfull night until a late hour'.

One way and another the shepherd had many responsibilities and was entrusted with a considerable portion of his master's wealth. He was expected to be a man of excellent character, and to be sober in an age of hard-drinking. Hogg himself said that his youthful habits were regular, and that so far as his consumption of whisky was concerned 'as long as I remained at my pastoral employment, I could not calculate on more than a bottle in the year at an average', and this seems likely to be true. He could not afford to get the reputation of an habitual drinker who might neglect his flock. 'A shepherd' Hogg remarked 'is rarely if ever, in this part of the world at least, found in the public-house, excepting once or twice a-year, at the great fairs, when they "tak a rouse wi' ane anither, an' wi' the lasses"'. The shepherd's attention to his flock was often secured by the custom of allowing him the keep of eight ewes of his own, summer and winter. A prudent shepherd could improve the stock of his own sheep along with those of his master, and add a useful sum to his income by selling the lambs.[29]

Willenslee is a hill farm in Innerleithen parish on the verges of Midlothian, described by Hogg as 'wild and bare'. His bed was in a stable that stood in front of the Willenslee Burn and after the quietness of Elibank he could not sleep at first for the loud roaring noise made by the water, and instead cat-napped during the day, wrapped in his plaid among the heather. Laidlaw was probably an elderly man, since by 1805 he was dead. He was presumably a kind enough master, since Hogg stayed with him two years, despite the loneliness of the situation. The sheep he had charge of were the hardy old black-faced breed best suited to such an exposed location. Hogg remembered that one of the winters he served at Willenslee was a particularly hard one, when the sheep lost weight towards the spring and 'there was a severe blast of snow came on by night about the latter end of April, which destroyed several scores of our lambs'. He was touched by the devotion of this breed towards their young. The ewes would try to let the lambs suckle when unable to stand, and follow the bodies of their dead lambs wherever Hogg trailed them, even into the house and among the people and dogs gathered about the fireside. One ewe stood over the body of her dead lamb until it decayed away almost entirely. In such weather the shepherd would need to predict the direction of the wind so that he could place his sheep in a sheltered situation, and Hogg himself believed that his dreams helped him:

> When I was a shepherd, and all the comforts of my life so much depending on good or ill weather, the first thing I did every morning was strictly to overhaul the dreams of the night, and I found that I could better calculate from them than from the appearance and changes of the sky.

A wrong decision could mean a night out on the hillside in a snow-storm, trying to dig the sheep out of a drift and get them moved to safer ground. This was dangerous as well as unpleasant, for occasionally shepherds died of exposure. Among Hogg's weather observations in his youth were some odd atmospheric conditions that produced optical effects designed to terrify a young man brought up on tales and legends of the supernatural. In 1785, for instance he had seen himself accompanied by two shadows.[30]

Stories of far-off times and distant places came even to remote Willenslee from time to time. An itinerant worker named Alexander Stewart, or Boig, told Hogg stories of his service as a Highland soldier in America and Gibraltar and of the supernatural hauntings he had witnessed in his youth. The other servants were sceptical, but Hogg on his own confession 'swallowed them all as genuine truth; and if they were not so, they certainly told very like them'. Occasional social events also broke the monotony. Folk gathered from far and wide to the annual church sacraments in a parish, and to the district's fairs where sheep and cattle were bought and sold, servants hired, and necessaries bought. A young shepherd would transact business for his master then enjoy a drink with his cronies, and take a pretty girl to one of the numerous merchant's stalls to buy her a 'fairing' of ribbons, a new comb, or a length of dress material. There were the kirns at the end of harvest, with singing and dancing, and meetings almost every week in some farmhouse or cottage to prepare flax for the weaving of linen. At these 'lint-swinglings' song was the chief amusement.[31]

At Whitsunday 1790 Hogg left Willenslee for another isolated farm, that of Blackhouse in the Yarrow valley where he stayed for ten years, a period that was one of the most important as it was one of the happiest of his entire life. When Hogg arrived at Blackhouse he was in the flush of youth:

> [...] when Hogg was nineteen years of age, his face was fair, round, and ruddy, with big blue eyes that beamed with humour, gaiety, and glee. And he was not only then, but throughout his chequered life, blessed with strong health, and the most exuberant animal spirits. His height was a little above the average size, his form at that period was of faultless symmetry, which nature had endowed with almost unequalled agility and swiftness of foot. His head was covered with a singular profusion of light brown hair, which he usually wore coiled up under his hat. When he used to enter church on Sunday (of which he was at all times a regular attendant), after lifting his hat, he used to raise his right hand to his hair to assist a shake of his head, when his long hair fell over his loins, and every female eye at least was turned upon him as with a light step he ascended to the gallery, where he usually sat.

Hogg described himself as possessing an 'ardent disposition'. He was highly-sexed and extremely attractive to women, and later wrote up many thinly-disguised amorous adventures of his own youth in his story, 'Love Adventures of Mr George Cochrane'. This youngster lies all day in the heather waiting for the night to come so that he can court a local farmer's daughter behind her father's back, and ends up leaving the premises by a fall from an upstairs window.[32] But his ardent disposition was also intellectual.

As a shepherd Hogg was already among the aristocracy of rural labour, and the next step in his career would be to save for years in order to purchase stock and lease a farm for himself, moving up into the class of tenant-farmer as his own father had done previous to his late marriage. Hogg's energy and ambition, however, required a wider outlet. The routine life of a sheep-farmer he felt was monotonous in the extreme with 'no stirring, no animation', the same 'from generation to generation'. He was bored by the great sheep-farming debate of the day, the wisdom or otherwise of the gradual displacement around 1785 of the old hardy black-faced sheep of the Borders by the delicate Cheviot breed that demanded more intensive labour from the shepherd. Hogg referred to the endless contentions on the subject as 'that everlasting drawback on the community of Ettrick Forest'.[33] He was greatly amused by the violence of the old shepherds' objections to the new and fashionable breed, viewed as 'white-faced shilpit-like wretches crawling about the laiggins of the hills, all attended to as if they had been fine ladies', and relished the eccentric prayers that were sent up to heaven against 'the ghosts of sheep; and whey-faced b–hes' by old shepherds such as Watie Brydon. He also had his own view of the question, regarding the enthusiasm for the new breed as 'little better than the tulipo-mania that once seized on the Dutch'.[34] But his mind could never be fully occupied by such questions.

During his previous service at Willenslee Hogg had begun to read whatever printed works were available to him, limited though these clearly were and though as a reader he was amusingly undiscriminating. His master's wife had lent him the newspaper which he 'pored on with great earnestness–beginning at the date, and reading straight on, through advertisements of houses and lands, balm of Gilead, and every thing'. He later described himself as 'much in the same predicament with the man of Eskdalemuir, who had borrowed Bailey's Dictionary from his neighbour' and attempting to read it as a narrative found it 'the most confused book that ever I saw in my life!'. The theological works loaned to him were disturbing and rousing to his emotions if not to his intelligence, one work about the end of the world generating apocalyptic scenes of 'the stars in horror, and the world in flames' that affected his thoughts by day and his dreams by night much as Gil-Martin's later theological arguments sunk into the very being of the receptive Robert Wringhim. More intelligible were the adventures and patriotic achievements of the Scottish hero Sir William Wallace, as recounted in Blind Harry's poem paraphrased for the eighteenth-century by William Hamilton of Gilbertfield, while Ramsay's play of *The Gentle Shepherd* linked Hogg's own experiences with the foreign realm of polite literature. He learned this latter work by heart, and would often repeat it, 'names, songs, and scenes just as they lay in their order'.[35]

So far Hogg had lacked an environment that would foster his intellectual development. His parents, by William Hogg's account, saw little virtue in his incipient bookishness: 'Our parents doubting that reading too much would induce to a neglect of his business dissuaded him powerfully from the perusal of every book that was not some religious tract or other'. His former masters were similarly concerned only with his efficiency as an employee. Hogg's new master, James Laidlaw of Blackhouse, was different, his kindness being 'much more like that of a father than a master'. The farm was situated on some of the highest ground in Selkirkshire, where winter set in early and the snow continued long on the ground, in the immediate vicinity of the Douglas Burn, but the occupiers were warm-hearted and intelligent people. James Laidlaw clearly lived on terms of intimacy with his household, servants as well as his immediate family, and as he 'had a natural desire for acquiring useful knowledge even separate from that which constituted him master of his own profession, he did not discourage James from reading–And this of itself was sufficient to give the powers of his mind a new impulse'. James Laidlaw and his wife Catherine Ballantyne had three young sons, who were cousins by their mother to one of Hogg's other early friends, John Grieve, son of the retired minister of the Reformed Presbyterian Church, living at Cacrabank in Ettrick. Hogg (always kind to and popular with his juniors) is supposed to have taught the younger Laidlaw boys their letters. The eldest son, William, was sent by his father to the Grammar School in Peebles, and it may have been he who introduced Hogg to the circulating library kept in the town by a local printer and bookseller, Alexander Elder, a very modest establishment where a cow quietly chewed her cud behind the bookshelves and where the principal books for sale consisted of catechisms, spelling-books, school Bibles and Testaments, half-penny coloured prints produced by the firm of James Lumsden of Glasgow, and 'penny chap-books of an extraordinary coarseness of language'. Elder's circulating library consisted of aged copies of the literature of a previous age, such as 'the comicalities of Gulliver, Don Quixote, and Peregrine Pickle', the poetry of Pope and Goldsmith, and 'books of travel and adventure [...] scarcely less attractive than the works of pure imagination'. Hogg may well have come across translations of Greek and Latin classics here, since the collection included Pope's translation of the *Iliad* and Gavin Douglas's translation of Virgil's *Aeneid*, as well as the rougher verses of Walter Scott of Satchell's rhyming history of the local Scott clan.[36] William Laidlaw was only ten years old when Hogg first came to Blackhouse, but it was the start of a lifelong friendship between them.

James Laidlaw enabled Hogg to attend the meetings of a local debating society, by taking charge of his sheep for a day and a night every now and then. The members, mostly fellow-shepherds and farmers' sons, met at one another's houses in the evening and read the essays they had composed on a set subject, the following general discussion and criticism often lasting all the following night. John MacQueen has argued that in the Scotland of 1794 'a more or less secret meeting of agricultural labourers probably included several freemasons in its number; equally probably, the agenda included the forbidden subject of radical politics and the need for reform, if not revolution', referring to Hogg's description of the 'flaming bombastical essay' prepared for one particular meeting. Very little is known of the nature of their debates and essays, however. The one recorded meeting is recounted by a servant girl who takes little or no interest in it, and she can only report the subject as the vaguely metaphysical one of 'the fitness o' things', and the scandalous declaration by Jamie Fletcher that 'there was nae deil ava'. A challenge to orthodox Calvinism seems more likely perhaps than a challenge to the state of Great Britain, and far from being secret the existence of the society was clearly well known to Hogg's parents, the local gossips, and to Hogg's master. When a storm centred on the society's meeting-place they were universally blamed for it, on the grounds that they must have summoned up the devil. Some self-mockery in Hogg's account cannot hide his excitement and pleasure in this society, the members of which included his brother William and several cousins and friends—'indeed' he later remarked, 'I looked on the whole fraternity as my brethren, and considered myself involved in all their transactions'.[37]

Besides this large fraternity Hogg also had a bosom friend in Alexander Laidlaw of Bowerhope on the shores of St Mary's Loch in Yarrow, who fondly recalled that 'Mr Hogg and I were in our youthful days almost inseparable companions'. While Laidlaw shared Hogg's literary tastes he was also a natural scientist. Hogg is now so firmly established as a literary figure that his scientific proclivities are often overlooked. To some extent they were professional, since a shepherd to a great degree acted as his own veterinary surgeon, and could gain an important local reputation for skill with animals. Ignorance of the common diseases of sheep made a shepherd a laughing stock, as in the following ludicrous anecdote of a man who misinterpreted his sheep's intoxication from feeding on broom for symptoms of fatal illness:

> I knew a shepherd of Traquair, who, one day, coming to a number of his hirsel intoxicated this way, and thinking they were at the point of death, that their flesh might not be lost, cut the throats of four of them, cursing and crying all the while; and was proceeding in haste to dispatch more of them, if his master had not arrived and prevented him. The different passions, which then swayed each of them, were not a little amusing. His master asked him, in a rage, 'How would you like, if people were always to cut your throat when you are drunk?'

Hogg may have slept in the byre-loft at Blackhouse with his dog in the hay-nook below, but he was also entrusted with a considerable portion of his master's wealth, taking charge of seven hundred lambs at weaning-time when James Laidlaw kept only about two thousand sheep.[38] It is clear from many passages of Hogg's later handbook *The Shepherd's Guide*, for instance, that he was accustomed to dissect animals in order to determine the causes of death and to learn about common diseases. On various occasions in his later life Hogg also engaged in scientific experiment, marking the tails of fish for instance in an attempt to see whether the par was the fry of the salmon or not. His friend Alexander Laidlaw kept a journal of weather records and similar observations over many years, and built model sheep-stells. He is almost certainly the author of a letter of 19 June 1802 sent from Yarrow and signed 'A Herd' that appeared in the *Edinburgh Weekly Journal* of 30 June 1802. This concerns 'a very destructive worm' that made its appearance on several farms in the vicinity of St Mary's Loch about the middle of May that year, and of which the writer was 'carrying on a course of observations'. Laidlaw's investigations are mentioned some thirty years later by Rev. Robert Russell in his account of 'the *wormy* year' in Yarrow parish in the 1845 *Statistical Account of Scotland*. Laidlaw kept specimens in a bottle until they formed into chrysalids and eventually hatched as butterflies. He was a friend of the explorer Mungo Park, with whom Hogg was also acquainted in his years at Blackhouse before Park's first expedition to Africa in the summer of 1795.[39]

At this time Hogg himself kept a notebook, recording unusual experiences of his own, and those he had read about in books and newspapers. One fine summer morning, for example, while coming along the Hawkshaw rigg at Blackhouse Hogg saw a phantom drove of Highland cattle on the other side of the Douglas Burn, and even called on his fellow-shepherd Robert Borthwick and his master's sons William and George to turn the intruders from the farm's pastureland. On another occasion Hogg recorded that he saw a 'huge dark semblance of the human figure, which stood at a very small distance from me, and at first appeared to my affrighted imagination as he enemy of mankind. Without taking a moment to consider, I rushed from the spot, and never drew breath till I had got safe amongst the ewe-milkers'. Only on the following day did he realise that he had seen his own shadow. Another impressive optical illusion was perhaps the result of anxiety and physical exhaustion on returning from a night spent looking for his sheep in a snow-storm, when he saw trees overhead in a place where he thought no trees could be and at first feared they were the product of enchantment until he realised that he was in a different place from the one where he thought he was and seeing actual trees.

> So that after all they were trees that I saw and trees of no great magnitude neither but their appearance to my eyes it is impossible to describe. They flourished abroad not for miles but for hundreds of miles to the utmost verges of the visible heavens.

During the same night Hogg had observed that James Laidlaw fell into a sort of exhausted trance where he had spoken to his companions and taken food and drink without afterwards having any recollection of a single circumstance that had occurred.

On another occasion he noted how the defences of the mind were relaxed in sleep—sheltering amorously under his plaid on a rainy day a girl dozed off and, talking in her sleep, 'addressing me as another man, revealed a secret of her own which she ought not to have done. When she began to speak, I was frightened, for her voice was so much altered, that I thought it was not hers, but that of a spirit speaking through her'. Hogg noted generally that sleep-talk always related to 'those circumstances of life that lie nearest the heart', even though it sometimes seemed to be 'perfectly consistent and regular' and sometimes incoherent. Hogg's account of his own reactions here is revealing, his scientific interest coming as a defence against the instinctive superstitiousness inculcated by his upbringing and by those stories told by his mother which made him afraid to venture out after dark. He was perfectly capable of experiencing superstitious fears and horrors himself and of playing upon those fears in others. Once when he thought the Blackhouse servant-maids were foolish to be going out after dark to a distance, for instance, he caused them to change their minds by simulating the effect of the warning dead-bell, running his finger around the rim of a wet glass in their hearing but safely out of sight.[40] He was conducting a psychological experiment and an artful piece of manipulation, while also sharing in local beliefs in dreams and omens.

Hogg's efforts to work out the mental processes of animals are most clearly revealed in his accounts of the various dogs with whom he lived, worked and slept. The first of these animals was named Sirrah, and had been bought by Hogg out of pity. It is not too far-fetched to suspect that in the ill-treated and neglected but intelligent-looking animal he bought for a guinea from a careless stranger he saw another homeless and dispossessed being such as he had become himself in childhood. In Sirrah Hogg detected 'expedients of the moment that bespoke a great share of the reasoning faculty'. When Sirrah refused to let a sheep go after bringing it home from Stanhope in Peebles with great difficulty and trouble, for example, Hogg concluded that the dog wanted him to take the ewe home and kill her. For many years afterwards Hogg kept a dog descended from Sirrah, though always preferring to a more capable sheepdog one of eccentric ways, and with 'estimable qualities of sociality and humour'.[41]

Hogg's literary progress during his ten years' residence at Blackhouse was significant. His earliest efforts at literary composition were probably made in in 1793 or 1794, since his first published poem 'The Mistakes of a Night' appeared in the October 1794 issue of the *Scots Magazine*, a slight but attractive Scots poem about a man who courts his girl's mother in the dark and, when she falls pregnant, is obliged to marry her. Hogg's expertise as a fiddler and his familiarity with Scottish folk tunes would naturally incline him to make up words to his own music for communal performance by local friends and acquaintances, and many of his other early compositions were songs. He was delighted to hear them sung by the local girls in chorus, and to be dubbed 'Jamie the poeter'. In sharp contrast to the local informality of his songs, he also wrote some stultifyingly formal and derivative poems in response to his reading of standard eighteenth-century works. An early poetical epistle to a friendly student of divinity he later described as 'mostly composed of borrowed lines and sentences from Dryden's Virgil, and Harvey's Life of Bruce'. 'The Happy Swains', a four-part pastoral founded on Betty Cameron's Jacobite legends of 1745, filled over a hundred and fifty pages in Hogg's hand and must surely have been inspired by Ramsay's Jacobite pastoral of *The Gentle Shepherd.* Hogg's poetic voice seems to have fallen at this stage into two opposed modes—one was essentially literary, derived from his reading of the eighteenth-century classics he borrowed from James Laidlaw or from Mr Elder's Peebles circulating library, and the other was more demotic, describing local incidents and personalities. A comedy of 1795 was clearly a local production:

> In 1795, I began *The Scotch Gentleman,* a comedy, in five long acts; after having been summoned to Selkirk, as a witness against some persons suspected of fishing in close-time. This piece [...] is, in fact, full of faults; yet, on reading it to an Ettrick audience, which I have several times done, it never fails to produce the most extraordinary convulsions of laughter.[42]

The piece was the outcome of George Rodger, the Selkirk procurator fiscal, bringing a series of prosecutions against Yarrow men, including James Laidlaw of Blackhouse and his eldest son, for salmon-fishing during the prohibited close season between April and July 1795.[43] It featured Hogg's own reluctant appearance as a witness against an acquaintance, and one act was taken up with the examination of the fishermen in court. In Hogg's account there is a certain puzzlement that only a local audience, familiar with the originals of his characters, should find this comedy amusing. He had not yet learned how to generalise the local to appeal to a wider audience.

On the other hand his more formal pieces now seem hopelessly derivative, as if literature was a realm quite distinct from that in which he lived. Hogg's expansion of Psalm 117, for instance, lacks specificity in the most barren tradition of hymn-writing:

> Ye straggling sons of Greenland's rigid wilds,
> Y' inhabitants of Asia's distant isles,
> With all between, make this your final aim,
> Your great Creator's goodness to proclaim.

The titles of the poems produced as entries in a poetical contest between Hogg, his brother William, Alexander Laidlaw, and another shepherd are revealing–'Urania's Tour', 'Astronomical Thoughts', and 'Reflections on a view of the Nocturnal Heavens'. Surviving lines from Hogg's own entry demonstrate his reading of Edward Young's *Night Thoughts* (1742–45) and James Hervey's *Meditations and Contemplations* (1746–47).[44] Harvey's work indeed included a template 'Contemplations on the Starry Heavens'.

Hogg's endless reiteration in his later years of the need for originality was perhaps a natural reaction to his being in thrall to such poets at the start of his career, and it is in this context that his discovery of Burns came to be viewed as an almost religious revelation. Hearing 'Tam o' Shanter' recited in 1797 had the effect of a thunderclap. A half-daft man, John Scott, had taken a liking to Hogg and sometimes travelled five or six miles to the heights at Blackhouse to tell him 'songs and stories of all sorts'. It was impossible, Hogg said, 'to describe the delight and amusement that I experienced. I made Jock sit down and repeat it over and over to me until I learned it by heart'. Hogg was not only delighted but ravished, for here was a living poetic voice which could recount the doings of local characters and humorous incident while also controlling and using the literary moralising mode of eighteenth-century verse. Here was an energetic and brilliant fusion of two positions Hogg had only been able to hold separately and derivatively, verse that related to the village and to the whole reading world simultaneously. This poet could draw his reader into an archaic world of witchcraft and superstition while simultaneously lightly ironizing it from a rational Enlightenment perspective. Other labouring-class poets, such as John Younger the cobbler poet of Kelso, also found their first encounter with Burns 'an electrifier' that made them feel 'as I suppose people will feel when going crazy'.[45] If a ploughman from Ayrshire could do it, then so could other labouring men. Hogg began during his Blackhouse years to build up a portfolio of his own work, continuing each year to add numbers of smaller pieces of poetry and songs to his collection. His flocks demanded constant vigilance while allowing him unpredictable bouts of leisure during the summer months, and he carried a few sheets of paper stitched together and a vial of ink to the hillside with him, to write down his thoughts as they arose. His poems, however, he composed and corrected in his head before he ever put pen to paper. Hogg's pride in his early publications in periodicals was tremendous. 'It was when engaged in *smearing* sheep at Blackhouse that the publication containing the first prose article of his which had the honour of appearing in print was handed to him by his master'. Though he tried to conceal his emotion from his fellow workers, Hogg recalled, 'they found it out for all that, to their cost; for I was proud o' the thing, and they found, at least for a' that day, for ance that they had nae chance o' keeping up wi' me'. (The article probably appeared anonymously and cannot now be identified, unfortunately.) Hogg's confidant was William Laidlaw, his master's son, a teenager who was no doubt inclined to look up to the kindly and energetic shepherd ten years his senior and so much more a man of the world. The youth showed Hogg's compositions 'to every person, whose capacity he supposed adequate to judge of their merits; but it was all to no purpose; he could make no proselytes to his opinion of any note [...]'.[46]

It was during his years as a shepherd at Blackhouse that Hogg began to travel within Scotland, professionally at first to markets and fairs both near and distant since James Laidlaw would on occasion wish to sell some part of his flocks and buy other sheep that would improve the quality of his breed. Hogg certainly visited Edinburgh, his business centring on the bughts in the Grassmarket beneath the shadow of Edinburgh Castle, at the heart of the city's Old Town district. By this time the medieval city, with its backbone of volcanic rock stretching from the castle high in the west downhill to Holyrood Palace a mile or so eastwards, was only just beginning to be deserted by the gentry and aristocracy who made their living or spent the winters sociably in the Scottish capital. A network of bridges crossed the ravines that surrounded it and enabled the building of more modern and elegant houses for the affluent, firstly on the south side of the city where George Square had been constructed in 1766, and subsequently in the first Georgian New Town. This was laid out to the north in the 1780s, though Charlotte Square was not designed until 1792. The old city was still, however, the commercial and social hub of Edinburgh at this time. Hogg would almost certainly have lodged in one of the inns surrounding the Grassmarket, perhaps even the same one that he favoured in later years an old and oddly-constructed building near the Cowgate Port called the Harrow Inn. Often such places drew their clientele from specific country districts, as Hogg's later story 'The Lasses' reveals. Coming into town from Selkirkshire his lovers arrange to meet their friends at 'the Golden Harrow, in the Candlemaker-Row' and evade them by going unexpectedly to an inn in the Canongate instead.[47] Although a small town by modern standards Edinburgh would be lively enough to a young man from the country. If Hogg's business was concluded promptly, or if he had to wait a day or two from the conclusion of one day's market to the next a couple of days later, he would have time to wander about the streets and amuse himself. He might spend his money perhaps on a book or magazine from one of the booksellers' shops on the High Street or even attend the Theatre Royal in Shakespeare Square, strategically placed at the junction of the city's Old Town and New Town.

Hogg's brother William related that it was while he was in the service of James Laidlaw of Blackhouse that Hogg 'was sent to help home a flock of sheep to some part in Argyle-shire—This induced him to make several subsequent journeys into that noted country'. Hogg's enounter with the Scottish Highlands provided the culture shock of a language he did not understand and a history and set of traditions sharply distinguished from those of Ettrick Forest. Here Hogg listened to singing of the original Gaelic songs James Macpherson had drawn upon for his celebrated works of Ossian, for instance, and since he did not understand them his 'fancy got leave to revel free'. The highland performers were not so different from the singers among his own family and friends in Ettrick, and evidence of the viciousness of government attempts to stamp out Highland culture after the Jacobite Rising of 1745 not so different from that of persecution of the Covenanters in the Borders. Hogg could not identify entirely with the Protestant and lowland ascendancy, which both feared and despised the barbarian Highlanders, his childhood memories of dispossession fuelling an immense anger at Highland persecutions and impelling him 'to say things I should not say'. Almost until the time of his marriage in 1820 Hogg was in the habit of taking a summer walking tour either alone or with a chosen friend or two into some part of the Highlands or Islands of Scotland and he wrote and published journals of the tours he made in the opening years of the nineteenth-century. There is no formal record of his earliest Highland excursions, however, but only scattered hints and allusions in his subsequently-published writings. Hogg mentions that around 1792 he passed through Stirlingshire, Breadalbane and Glenorchy. He also seems to have made a tour of Invernesshire and Rosshire on horseback in 1798 or 1799, and had the terrifying experience of stumbling across the body of a murdered man named Hector Kennedy. Travelling at night through a wood on the way to Tomantoul, Hogg's horse refused to go on:

> I was driven desperate, and knew not what to do; and after calling out several times and receiving no answer, I was obliged to fasten my mare to a bush, and go forward and reconnoitre. I had not gone far till I perceived a dead man, lying at full length across the road. Yes! a dead man, and a murdered one! I went up and looked at the body—called, but got no answer—laid my ear to his face, to hear if there was any breathing; but there was none. [...] I mounted, galloped to Tomantoul, told the people what I had seen, and proffered to accompany them to the place; but they refused, and said, "It was as fitter to let sleeping togs lie." And they informed me further, that there was a gang of gipsies lurking about their woods, who took every thing they could get, and they had no doubt that they had murdered the gentleman. I could sleep none that morning, and mounting at an early hour I rode straight for the Lowlands; for I had a sort of lurking dread that I might be taken up for the murderer.[48]

The Highlands were fascinating, but also wild and dangerous, even uncanny.

Besides more or less falling over a corpse on one of his summer excursions, Hogg experienced a near-death experience during his years at Blackhouse. He had suffered from time to time from a violent pain in his bowels and in November 1798 while he was visiting a neighbouring farm to help with the smearing of the sheep the pain increased to an inflammation of which he nearly died. He later recalled that he saw the old woman who watched over him fall into a swoon 'from a supposition that she saw my *wraith*:–a spirit which, the vulgar suppose, haunts the abodes of such as are instantly to die, in order to carry off the soul as soon as it is disengaged from the body: and, next morning, I overheard a consultation about borrow-ing sheets to lay me in at my decease'. However, he not only recov-ered but the illness never recurred again.[49]

Again and again in his writings Hogg reverts to the years when he was a shepherd at Blackhouse, and in his 'Memoir' he remarked that he might not improbably have been at Blackhouse still but for the fact that his aged parents in Ettrick needed his help. Robert Hogg was now tenanting Ettrickhouse but was too old and infirm to do the work of the little farm, and his eldest son William had lived with the old couple and managed the place for their support. At the end of December 1798, however, William had married Mary Beattie, the daughter of the Ettrick schoolmaster, and the couple had recently produced a little daughter, christened Margaret on 4 May 1800. It was evident that the tiny holding could not support both William's aged parents and his own family, which might be expected to in-crease rapidly during the next few years. William, Mary, and their baby moved to a shepherd's cottage at Mukra on the edge of the parish, and at Whitsunday 1800 James Hogg took over as manager of the little farm on his father's behalf.[50]

His time was probably less occupied at Ettrickhouse than it had been during his years as shepherd at Blackhouse, since the farm was clearly only just large enough to support Hogg and his aged parents. Effectively Hogg was now his own master. At first he decided to improve his income and use some of his leisure time by engaging in sheep-dealing, and this perhaps led to his forming a friendship with the young Adam Bryden of Aberlosk, the son of a prosperous if eccentric tenant-farmer in Eskdalemuir. Hogg recorded of the father that 'he was the first who introduced the draining of sheep pasture', but 'in all other things he made a point of letting them remain as God made them. He castrated no males, weaned no lambs, and bap-tized no children'. Bryden's introduction of drains enabled the pro-duction of hay on his farm to feed sheep during the winter, and he was clearly a prosperous man, though notably old-fashioned, being 'clothed in a coat of the family's providing, and always as it comes off the sheep's back, for ordinary, gray; and all the rest of his apparel is like unto it, and he lived in a house like a dung hill'. His son Adam was a few years older than Hogg, and when his father grew too old to manage the farm cut a more dashing figure with 'a coat of superfine cloth, and all the rest of his apparel like unto it, and he hath made a house with a slate roof, and furnished it conformably'. He was thought to excel his father in the management of affairs and was 'well-beloved with all around him', besides by Hogg's account being a careless, light-hearted and witty fellow. Hogg pictures him at a country wedding, joking about his Cameronian pony, drinking toasts, and as full of daffing and fun as of whisky. Hogg relates how Aedie once banished an adversary by pitchforking dung from the midden at him, and how in the spring of 1806 he sent a personal letter to George III accompanying his outstanding taxes.[51] Aedie o' Aberlosk as the central figure of 'a number of curious and extravagant stories' is not so different from that side of Hogg's nature that was later to be exaggerated into the Shepherd of the *Noctes Ambrosianae*. As the well-dressed son of one of the most prosperous farmers of the district Bryden was a cut above Hogg socially and probably to some degree a role model.

One of Hogg's earliest surviving letters, of 1 July [1800], is an attempt to interest Aedie o' Aberlosk in a sheep-dealing venture planned in partnership with Robert Borthwick, the other shepherd of Blackhouse during Hogg's engagement there. Hogg offered to market Bryden's lambs for him, on generous terms:

> [...] I will regularly on my return settle accounts with you and pay you down every penny that I get for them bating my expenses which shall be moderate; and as I do not want to make any thing of them but merely for a beginning, I will leave it entirely to yourself as to my recompence; and then I will take them away at what time or in what quantity you please; neither by this plan can any of us lose much, because if you be not pleased with the prices that I get you can stop when you please.

Hogg was no more likely to succeed as a sheep-dealer than his father had been, since he was far from focused on money-getting and his temperament open and unsuspecting. In fact, Hogg probably acted as a dealer for only a very short time. Although he occasionally attended the various markets 'he saw, that to succeed this way the utmost diligence and circumspection were requisite; and being naturally of an open, unsuspicious character, he was also too liable to be imposed upon by artful and designing men. These considerations, with his natural propensity to literary pursuits, induced him to give it up entirely'.[52]

Some of his new leisure was undoubtedly spent in pursuing the girls, if the confessedly autobiographical 'Love Adventures of Mr George Cochrane' are anything to go by. Music also continued to occupy spare time, when Hogg's mother would form an admiring and occasionally critical audience for the Scottish tunes he played during the long winter evenings. On one such occasion hearing him play the strathspey 'Athol Cummers' she inquired if there were any words to it, and being told that there were not, replied, 'O man, it's a shame to hear sic a good tune an' nae words till't. Gae away ben the house, like a good lad, and mak' me a verse till't.' The request was immediately complied with. The outré behaviour of Hogg's dog Hector was also a source of entertainment, particularly his dislike of the family cat which he followed about and pointed whenever he was indoors, so that Hogg accounted for this outrageous behaviour at the end of the evening devotions on the supposition that he interpreted the praying posture of the family as a similar pointing of the cat. Hector it was who spoiled Hogg's attempts to deputise for the precentor at the Sunday services in Ettrick church by joining at the top of his voice in the line of psalm given out until the 'shepherds hid their heads, and laid them down on the backs of the seats rowed in their plaids, and the lasses looked down to the ground and laughed till their faces grew red'.[53]

Besides helping his parents, trying a new line of work as a sheep-dealer, and providing both public and private entertainment, Hogg also pursued his literary ambitions seriously on his return to Ettrick. To work on more sustained compositions Hogg visited his friend Alexander Laidlaw's home at Bowerhope, sometimes staying with him for a fortnight at a time.[54] Some of his productions were essays on the diseases of sheep which he entered for premiums advertised by the Highland Society of Scotland in the Edinburgh newspapers. On 10 February 1802 the *Edinburgh Weekly Journal* reported that the sum of three guineas had been awarded 'To James Hogg, at Ettrick House [...] for his Communication on the diseases of Sheep, their causes, cure, and prevention', while a year later the *Edinburgh Evening Courant* of 29 January 1803 noted that his essay on braxy and other diseases of sheep, signed 'Arcadus', had been awarded '*A Gold Medal, or Piece of Plate of Ten Guineas value*'. Perhaps this professional distinction reconciled Hogg's parents to his other writings? For Hogg was gradually assembling a manuscript collection of his poetry, discussing the individual poems contained in it with friends such as Alexander Laidlaw, William Laidlaw, and the Selkirk doctor, Ebenezer Clarkson. Hogg probably now had publication in mind, and when an opportunity occurred he took it. As he recollected a few years later

> Having attended the Edinburgh market on Monday, with a
> number of sheep for sale; and being unable to sell them all, I
> put them into a park until the market on Wednesday. Not
> knowing how to pass the interim, it came into my head that I
> would write a poem or two from my memory, and have them
> printed. The thought had no sooner struck me, than I put it
> in practice; when I was obliged to select, not the best, but
> those that I remembered best. I wrote as many as I could
> during my short stay, and gave them to a man to print at my
> expence; and having sold off my sheep on Wednesday morn-
> ing, I returned into the Forest, and saw no more of my poems
> until I received word that there were one thousand copies of
> them thrown off. I knew no more about publishing than the
> man of the moon; and the only motive that influenced me
> was the gratification of my vanity, by seeing my works in
> print.

Hogg's printer, John Taylor, had premises 'opposite Buchts' (i.e.
sheep-pens) in the Grassmarket, and it seems likely that he was essentially a stationer who also printed the odd pamphlet and sale-bill,
allowing his customers the use of his premises for writing letters on
paper purchased from him. Hogg seems to have written out his poems in the shop in the autumn of 1800. He was given or sent a 'proof
sheet', probably a sample of Taylor's work since this included a mock-
up of the title-page, and the work was also advertised as 'This day is
published' in the *Edinburgh Evening Courant* of 5 February 1801. Essentially, though, *Scottish Pastorals* was vanity publishing, as Elaine
Petrie has confirmed. As the printing of the thousand copies cost ten
pounds and each copy sold for a shilling, Hogg cannot have intended
to make any money by the publication. He had no patron and no
publisher. *Scottish Pastorals* is accurately described by Petrie as looking like a chap-book, its sixty-two pages being 'a plain workaday bit
of printing' on low-quality paper, with some alterations being made
to the text in the course of printing. The inclusion of a list of errata,
some of which appear to be authorial, confirms that Hogg had seen
some of the work at the proof stage, especially 'A Dialogue in a Country Church-Yard', a poem written to commemorate the death of his
family's benefactor, Walter Bryden of Crosslee. Later in life, when
he was an established professional author, Hogg was somewhat
ashamed of this amateur production.[55]

Since the intended audience for *Scottish Pastorals* consisted of Hogg's peers, his friends and country neighbours, the naïve 'peasant poet' persona designed to appeal to a genteel middle-class readership was largely irrelevant and while Hogg measures himself against traditional tale-tellers ('The Death of Sir Niel Stuart and Donald M'Vane, Esq.') he also places himself alongside Gray and Young ('A Dialogue in a Country Church-Yard') as well as Burns and Allan Ramsay. The seven poems of *Scottish Pastorals* show the influence of Hogg's reading in the eighteenth-century British classics of poetry as clearly as his folklore background. The lack of the kind of editorial control exercised by a book-trade printer or a publisher (as Petrie notes) also means that Hogg's frank treatment of sexual matters and his graphic use of Scots come over unmodified, and the author expresses himself confidently as one who sees his Borders homeland as 'this modern Parnassus'. While the author declares in ringing tones that 'Constancy an' perseverance | Ever will rewarded be', he is also free to express 'the frustrations and anxieties of common folk in times of war and high taxation'.[56] Biographically the most interesting poem in *Scottish Pastorals* is 'Dusty, or, Watie an' Geordie's Review of Politics; An Eclogue', a conversation between two shepherds which embodies several of Hogg's own experiences and describes what living through the French Revolutionary War period was like for Borders folk.

From the memorable meeting of the States General of France in May 1789 monarchy had been gradually exposed as a failure in France and was succeeded from 1792 by more radical experiments of republican government. The influence of these on Scotland had been clearly shown in the King's Birthday Riots in Edinburgh in 1792, and in demonstrations later that year of public discontent with the established political order headed by leading Tory Scottish politician Henry Dundas. A month after the execution of Louis XVI in January 1793 Britain was at war with France, and Scotland's citizens were being taxed to pay for a continental war while at the same time finding their political liberties threatened at home. The year in which 'Dusty' is set, 1798, was a crisis year within Britain, with naval mutinies at the Nore and Spithead and riots throughout Scotland in protest against the Militia Act, although shortly afterwards identification of France with the championship of popular liberty diminished as Napoleon effectively established first a military dictatorship and then an empire there.

Watie and Geordie view the state of the nation from the perspective of Hogg's friends and neighbours. Both agree that the French would be 'kittle masters', but Geordie expresses real dissatisfaction with the country's political rulers who are imposing taxes on

> Our hats, our claes, our drink, our meat,
> Our snuff, our baca, shoon o'ur feet,
> Our candles, watches, horses, even
> The very blessed light o' heaven;

Watie admits that the twelve shillings he pays each year is dear and that he wishes for peace as much as his friend, but retorts that 'In gen'ral ilka thrifty man | Is richer than when it began', with agricultural prices greatly stimulated by a booming wartime economy. Furthermore, he argues, the scene of conflict was outside Britain altogether and little British blood was being spilt, while British naval supremacy was being established and significant territorial gains made in the colonies. Both shepherds agree that the hardest part of their wartime lot is the five-shilling dog-tax, and their grief at being obliged to part with their faithful companions, Watie's Springkell and Geordie's old dog Dusty. This reflects Hogg's personal experience, since he had felt obliged to get rid of his old dog Sirrah because of the dog-tax, a betrayal of the faithful animal he had rescued from a cruel master some years previously and who had repaid him by devoted adherence ever since. After he sold Sirrah to a neighbour for three guineas and the dog realised he would not be returned to his master, he refused to acknowledge a new master or to work for him, returning from time to time for months afterwards to visit Hogg. The three guineas were duly refunded and Sirrah found a comfortable home until his death with the father of the lad who had bought him. Hogg resolved never to sell another dog.[57]

The publication of *Scottish Pastorals* proved a disappointing experience for Hogg. As soon as the work was advertised, he received a letter from his two Laidlaw friends objecting to the advertisement's description of him as 'Tenant in Ettrick' (when his father was the tenant) and to an allusion in 'Dusty' to the circulation of a radical newspaper, the *Kelso Chronicle* by a local landowner, Lord Napier. His friends clearly advised him to reprint the volume, eliminating this reference, for Hogg retorted that while it 'might indeed be an easy matter for you or Clarkson to do that' he could only wish he had 'the one paid that is printed'. Public notice of the volume was slight, perhaps confined to the republication of 'Willie an' Keatie' in the *Scots Magazine* for January 1801, published towards the end of February. Hogg had clearly expected better things, commenting in July 1801 that 'a liberal publick hath not given' him his deserts and in December 1803 that the pamphlet was 'never known unless to a few friends'.[58] It seems unlikely that Hogg recouped very much of his ten pound outlay from sales, and copies of the work are now extremely rare.

At this point Hogg needed to learn about the mechanics and finances of the world of authorship and publishing. Fortunately, he was about to meet a canny operator in that world who would help him to negotiate with it over many years to come.

CHAPTER TWO

The Broken Ground

During Hogg's time at Ettrickhouse his path was converging with that of a young Edinburgh lawyer named Walter Scott, then engaged in collecting traditional ballads for his *Minstrelsy of the Scottish Border.* Andrew Mercer, a portrait-painter and would-be literary man, was in Selkirk in the summer of 1801 and collecting legendary lore 'in compliance with a request which Mr Scott made me'.[1] During that summer, as Peter Garside has indicated, Hogg received a transcript of Mercer's from Laidlaw in connection with Scott's work. During 1802 Hogg submitted a sheet of songs and a separate poem to Ruthven's *Edinburgh Magazine*, of which Mercer was an important contributor and supporter. Mercer was enthusiastic about the poem, 'Sandy Tod', which was published in the *Edinburgh Magazine* for May 1802, writing to Laidlaw on 5 June 1802 to ask Hogg to write and give him 'an account of the pieces he has written since he published his collection last year'. If Hogg would send him copies of some of them, he was prepared to suggest corrections with a view to further magazine publication.[2] Hogg's promising connection with the *Edinburgh Magazine* was short-lived, since Mercer defected to Archibald Constable's *Scots Magazine* at about this time, and the periodical itself merged with Constable's publication at the end of 1803, but Hogg's connection with Mercer did serve to bring him within Scott's orbit. The first two volumes of Scott's *Minstrelsy* had been published in February 1802, but Scott was still avidly collecting for a supplementary third volume.[3] Laidlaw had a manuscript of the ballad of 'Auld Maitland' supplied by Hogg from the recitation of his uncle William Laidlaw corroborated by his mother, and in April that year when Scott called on him at Blackhouse along with John Leyden Laidlaw gave it to him. At the same time Laidlaw described Hogg enthusiastically to Scott, who took a note of his address.[4]

Hogg's first meeting with Scott is one of the great moments of Romantic myth-making, founded on the dramatic account of a supposedly initial encounter given by Hogg himself many years later, but in fact their acquaintance appears to have developed gradually. It is possible that Scott invited Hogg to call on him in Edinburgh that spring or summer, since in Hogg's first surviving letter to Scott of 30 June 1802 he refers to him as a person he had 'seen and conversed with'. When Hogg left Ettrick on a Highland tour on 22 July he was

certainly acquainted with Scott, for he called briefly on him in Edinburgh and received at least one useful letter of introduction from
him.[5] Although Scott was not yet the colossus of Scotland's literature
that he was shortly to become, he was regarded with a great deal of
deference in Selkirkshire as the Sheriff of the county and an Edinburgh professional man with good connections among the local gentry. Hogg must have been keen to impress but not sure that he had
made the desired impact before the key meeting in his native Ettrick
in late August or early September 1802. The two men then spent a
substantial amount of time in each other's company, and were also
very much on Hogg's home-ground, with Scott the ballad-seeker
ssuccessfully hunting down his informant James Hogg.[6]

The two surviving accounts of this encounter, by Hogg himself
and by William Laidlaw, were both written many years after the
event and are not entirely consistent.[7] Hogg places the encounter at
Ettrickhouse itself, seemingly eliding an after-dinner call on Scott at
Ramseycleuch farm and a visit by Scott to Ettrickhouse on the following day, while Laidlaw in remarking that Scott was 'pleased &
even surprised at Hoggs appearance' mistakenly implies that Scott
had not met Hogg previously. Invited to tea by Laidlaw's Bryden
cousins at Ramseycleuch, Hogg arrived with 'a M. S. of some size' to
find himself 'the chief object of the sheriffs notice & flattering attention'. Each man clearly exerted himself to please and to charm the
other and the rest of the company, and Laidlaw recorded that he
never again spent such a night of merriment:

> The qualities of Hogg came out every instant & his unaf-
> fected simplicity & 'fearless frankness' both surprised &
> charmed The Sheriff. They were both very good mimics &
> each of them born & bred story tellers & when Scott took to
> employ his dramatic talent he soon found he had us all in his
> power: for every one of us possessed a quick sense of the
> ludicrous & perhaps of humour of all kinds. I well recollect
> how the tears ran down the cheeks of my cousin George &
> although Walters laugh was more quiet it was easy to see it
> came from his heart & Hogg & I were unbounded laughers
> when the occasion was very good. I mentioned that Hogg
> was a good mimic & when the Brydens & I requested him to
> bear a hand like as if a song in his turn & although we were
> amused as usual we soon discovered that Hoggs subjects were
> too local & perhaps likewise of too low a caste, and doubtless
> the best proof of our enjoyment of the evening was that Hogg
> never sung a song that blessed night & it was between two &

three o'clock when we went to sleep

On the following day Scott and Laidlaw called at Ettrickhouse to meet Hogg's mother and hear her sing 'Auld Maitland'. Hogg was aware that 'Mr. Scott had some dread of a part being forged, that had been the cause of his journey into the wilds of Ettrick. When he heard my mother sing it he was quite satisfied'. In his poem commemorating the visit, Hogg portrays his mother as 'the ancient Minstreless', whose performance causes tears to stand on Scott's 'nut-brown cheek', while his 'fist made all the table ring,– | "By –, Sir, but that is the thing!"'. Old Margaret Laidlaw then turned the tables on her guest, accusing him of failing the test of authentic transmission with which she and her son had been confronted:

> "[…] But mair nor that, except George Warton and James Steward, there was never ane o' my sangs prentit till ye prentit them yoursell, an' ye hae spoilt them a'thegither. They war made for singing, and no' for reading; and they're nouther right spelled nor right setten down."
> "Heh–heh–heh! Take ye that, Mr. Scott," said Laidlaw.
> Mr. Scott answered by a hearty laugh, and the recital of a verse, but I have forgot what it was, and my mother gave him a rap on the knee with her open hand, and said "It is true enough, for a' that."[8]

Hogg, Laidlaw, and Scott set off for Rankleburn to search for traces of the early Scotts of Buccleuch in the highest possible spirits, according to Laidlaw, with Scott imagining himself leading a cavalry charge and Hogg running behind the two horsemen laughing while Scott shouted out 'Slaughten. Mienen Kinder Slaughten!' ('Slaughter, my children, slaughter'). Hogg's account of the expedition emphasises the local and down to earth, since the Brydens come too and Scott's daring horsemanship is mocked, 'the maddest deil of a beast I ever saw' plunging with him 'out o' ae lair intil another'. Scott's leap of imagination in the old ruined churchyard is just as amusing, transforming 'one half of a small pot, encrusted thick with rust' into 'an ancient consecrated helmet':

> Laidlaw, however, scratching it minutely out, found it covered with a layer of pitch inside, and then said, 'Ay, the truth is, sir, it is neither mair nor less than a piece of a tar pat that some o' the farmers hae been buisting their sheep out o', i' the auld kirk langsyne.' Sir Walter's shaggy eyebrows dipped deep over his eyes, and suppressing a smile, he turned and

strode away as fast as he could, saying, that 'we had just rode
all the way to see that there was nothing to *be* seen.'[9]

Hogg, writing up the episode years afterwards, portrayed it as a
parallel to the fictional Jonathan Oldbuck's identification of a contemporary dike as the Kaim of Kinprunes in Scott's novel, *The Antiquary*. Hogg's immense respect for Scott never prevented his teasing
him.

Hogg himself was an attractive figure at the age of thirty-one, an
athlete who by his own account 'for speed had not my marrow |
Thro' Teviot, Ettrick, Tweed, and Yarrow, | Strang, straight, and swift
like ony arrow'. He was able to run and catch a sheep that went
wrong when a flock was being shed, or separated, just like his maternal grandfather Will Laidlaw, and was a formidable competitor at
the Border Games held in Eskdalemuir, where he had won prizes in
the most difficult contests of leaping and running and been commemorated in a local rhyme as 'a clifty, clever chiel', beaten by only
'half a heel' by a rival named Jamie Battie. Hogg was five feet ten
and a half inches tall with a well-proportioned figure, and of a neat
appearance. His long auburn hair was tied neatly behind with a black
ribbon and as an adult (in contrast to the raggedness of his boyhood) he was notably clean and well-dressed for his rank in life.
Although he disliked any approach to foppery his clothes were usu-
ally of good quality, as a surviving pair of his gloves in the Otago
Museum bears witness. These are of plain leather, but supple and
well-stitched, and noticeably small and neat for those of a man, giving the lie to the later Blackwoodian image of an appropriate peasant grossness. In all there was a 'brightness of [...] personal appearance' about Hogg that was extremely attractive and engaging. A keen
sense of humour made him appreciative of out-of-the-way characters and comical incidents. Once, for instance, he was with a party in
a changehouse when a dispute arose between his cousin, James
Laidlaw, and Walter Bryden, known as 'Cow Wat', about the nature
of hell. His cousin's prayer for Cow Wat mentioned that Wat had
cheated fellow-shepherds financially and deserted his wife for another woman, and Hogg was convulsed with laughter at Wat's una-
vailing rage.[10] Perhaps this was the kind of local comic incident with
which he tried to entertain Scott at Ramseycleuch.

When Scott published his third volume of the *Minstrelsy* in May
1803, Hogg was sent a full set of the work on Scott's instructions.
His assistance had been considerable with ballads such as 'The Battle of Otterburn', 'The Gay Goss Hawk', and 'The Dowy Houms o'
Yarrow'. Hogg's surviving manuscripts are carefully prepared with

stanzas neatly written and numbered, and notes giving background information on the localities and events concerned.[11] Scott had made good use of these in his published work, often transferring Hogg's words more or less intact. Hogg had written of 'The Dowy Houms o' Yarrow', for example:

> The Hero of the ballad is said to have been of the name of Scott and is called a knight of great bravery. he lived in Ettrick some say Oakwood others Kirkhope but was treacherously slain by his brother in law as related in the ballad who had him at ill will because his father had parted with the half of all his goods and gear to his sister on her marriage with such a respectable man The name of the murderer is said to be Annand a name I believe merely conjectural from the name of the place where they are said both to be buried which at this day is called Annan's Treat a low muir lying to the west of Yarrow church where two huge tall stones are erected below which the least child that can walk the road will tell you the two lords are buried that were slain in a duel.

Scott's note to the ballad, called 'The Dowy Dens of Yarrow', in the second edition of his *Minstresy* is as follows:

> The hero of the ballad was a knight, of great bravery, called Scott, who is said to have resided at Kirkhope or Oakwood castle, and is, in tradition, termed the baron of Oakwood.[...]
>
> Tradition affirms, that the hero of the song (be he who he may) was murdered by the brother, either of his wife, or betrothed bride. The alledged cause of malice was, the lady's father having proposed to endow her with half of his property, upon her marriage with a warrior of such renown. The name of the murderer is said to have been Annan, and the place of combat is still called Annan's Treat. It is a low moor, on the banks of the Yarrow, lying to the west of Yarrow kirk. Two tall unhewn masses of stone are erected, about eighty yards distant from each other; and the least child, that can herd a cow, will tell the passenger, that there lie "the two lords, who were slain in single combat".[12]

In this particular case James Hogg has somehow disappeared after functioning as a filter between Scott and tradition, but elsewhere Scott referred handsomely to 'my correspondent, James Hogg', not only mentioning Hogg's mother as his source for 'Auld Maitland' but quoting a passage from Hogg's letter to him of 30 June 1802 in support of its authenticity despite the introduction of some modern words and phrases.[13] The James Hogg readers would have encountered in the *Minstrelsy* is partly a source of tradition and partly a fellow-antiquary, the 'Jacobus Porcus' of the American James Kirk Paulding's satirical *Lay of the Scottish Fiddle* (1813) reflecting this positioning accurately enough. Hogg had plainly wanted to appear in the work as a fellow-poet too, for his letter to Scott of 10 September 1802 included a copy of his own song 'By a Bush' as well as of 'The Battle of Otterburn' and the instruction, 'You may give it what title you chuse: if you introduce it to the public as a song which indeed I intended it it sings to the tune of the Maid that tends the goats'.[14] Although it boosted Hogg's self-confidence in other respects, in this the third volume of the *Minstrelsy* must have disappointed him.

Grateful for Hogg's assistance and well-disposed towards him personally, Scott was naturally eager to promote Hogg's literary schemes in turn. Between 22 July and 17 August 1802 Hogg had travelled northwards through Perth, Dunkeld, and Pitlochry as far as Dalnacardoch in Rosshire, ostensibly to look for a suitable farm to lease. Robert Hogg's tenancy of Ettrickhouse was due to expire at Whitsunday 1803, and Hogg was already beginning to cast about for another home for his aged parents and himself, possibly a Highland sheep-farm. He had hoped for the company of William Laidlaw or of Andrew Mercer, who had received his poem 'Sandy Tod' so enthusiastically. Hogg had been particularly excited at the prospect of traversing 'the wild romantic scenery of Athol, Badenoch, and Ross-shire' in company with 'a man about my own age, who was a painter, a poet, and a philosopher', but in the end had been obliged to set out alone. Scott now encouraged Hogg to write up an account of his journey for the readers of the *Scots Magazine*, and instalments appeared there between October 1802 and June 1803, the first of these being ushered in by a recommendatory letter from Scott himself. Several of the instalments were sent to Scott as they were written. On 10 September Hogg promised to send 'the first letter you will recieve from me giving an account of my northern jaunt' very shortly, another instalment accompanied his letter to Scott of 1 January 1803, and on 7 January Hogg regretted being 'behind with my Journal'. Under the circumstances 'A Journey Through the Highlands of Scotland, in the Months of July and August 1802' concerns itself very much with the Edinburgh literary scene and Scott features prominently as its author's patron. Having been thrust from his 'little patrimonial farm', Hogg tells his reader,

[...] my heart exulted in the thought, of finding amongst the

Grampian mountains a cheap and quiet retreat in the bosom
of some sequestered glen, where unawed by the proud, or
unenvied by any, I would nourish and increase my fleecy
store, and awaken, with the pipe and violin, echoes which
had slept for a thousand years, unless aroused to a transient
hum by the voice of the hunter, or the savage howl of the
wild beast of the desart.

As Hogg knew perfectly well, the Highland glens were far from
empty and the Lowland farmers who leased parts of them as sheep-
walks often dispossessed the native Gaelic-speaking population. As
someone who was himself about to be dispossessed by a wealthier
neighbour Hogg was naturally sympathetic to the Highlanders' plight
despite the object of his journey: on the Duke of Athol's lands, for
instance, he conversed with a man, 'one of nineteen farmers who
were removed from the Duke's land to make way for one man, who
now possessed the whole of what they, with their families, lived hap-
pily upon'. He also noted with some satisfaction the plight of Mack-
intosh of Dalmunzie, who had chased his people off the land 'but
their curses had fallen heavy on him, for he never hath had the power
to let it since'.[15]

Hogg's narrative, drawn from the 1791–99 *Statistical Account of Scotland* as well as his own recollections, focuses on the kind of historical and literary associations that might be appreciated by the *Scots
Magazine*'s readers as much as on the land's capability for farming,
with comments on inns, churches, notable landscape features, and
literary and legendary landmarks and reflections. The first instalment gives an account of Ettrick Forest, and the second describes
Peebles before settling Hogg at his Candlemaker Row inn in Edinburgh. Having arrived in Edinburgh the narrative is reluctant to
leave it, and gives a detailed account of two performances at the
Theatre Royal, of *The Heir at Law* and of *Hamlet*, and of the annual
Leith Races. Only half-way through the third of the six published
instalments does Hogg reach the Highlands at all. Arrived there, he
notices a stone chair said to mitigate the pains of childbirth, and
retails legends of fairies and of a large-headed little monster called
Phaam. There are Ossianic allusions to the hunting that terminated
in the death of Diarmid and to the stream where Fingal lost his
consort, a meditation over the grave of Claverhouse at Killiecrankie,
a speculation as to the modern woods at Birnam growing out of the
stumps of those cut down by Shakespeare's Macbeth, and a reflec-
tion on the imprisonment of Mary, Queen of Scots at Lochleven. In
one notable passage Hogg takes a guided walk over the ground that

was reputed to have seen the battle of Loncarty in about 980, during which a mighty peasant named Hay and his two sons rallied their countrymen successfully against the onslaught of Danish invaders thus establishing the family of the Earls of Errol.[16]

Hogg's newly-acquired friend and mentor Walter Scott is very much the tutelary genius of the published account, 'my guardian angel' as Hogg termed him. Ensconced for the night in a rude inn at Dalnacardoch in Perthshire, Hogg told Scott, he began to reflect on the possible dangers of his situation, alone in this strange country of the highlanders. Thinking of turning homewards once more he had a curious dream:

> I thought I was sitting in my chamber at Dalnacardoch by a window that looked toward the south, and writing to you of mountains and plains of unspeakable grandeur and beauty, when you suddenly entered behind me. I held you out the letter, telling you that was the way you sometimes did with me; but without making me any answer to that purpose, you began to upbraid me for my irresolution, and wondered how I could so soon relinquish an enterprise of which I seemed so fond. I then went over the above arguments with some warmth, which you quite disregarded, and were busy all the while adjusting something about your dress, which was much more magnificent than ever I had before seen it; yea, so *braw* were you, that had it not been for your voice and gait I could not have recognized you. No sooner had I finished than you left the room, telling me peremptorily to proceed, and depend on your promise that I never should repent it.[17]

Hogg's window looks south to Edinburgh, where Scott had persuaded him to embark on this Highland journey, so that the account of the dream served (when given to Scott before publication) as a reminder that Hogg had put himself to some personal inconvenience to write it on the promise of obtaining Scott's patronage. There is also perhaps a faint foreshadowing of the relationship between the hapless Robert Wringhim and the stern and authoritative potentate Gil-Martin, who is also magnificent in dress and peremptory in stifling any objections made by the actor of his plans. Scott's magnificent clothing signifies the wealth and status to which Hogg was aspiring by means of the written paper that he hands to Scott.

Publication of Hogg's account of his 1802 Highland Journey ceased abruptly with the instalment in the *Scots Magazine* for June 1803, probably because Hogg had by that time set off on a second and more extensive trip which would take him as far as Harris and last from the end of May until well into August 1803. Hogg had an 'edition of the letters' previously suggested by Scott in his mind, no doubt, and thought that another journey, 'through the west Highlands', with more letters of introduction to landowners there, would prove useful.[18] Scott's friend Colin Mackenzie had provided introductions, and perhaps he might use his influence to secure the patronage of the Highland Society of Scotland for the resulting volume.

Hogg's letters of introduction and his own relatively humble social position made for some startling juxtapositions during this trip. He spent one night, for instance, bedded down on the floor of a shepherd's cottage at the back of Ben Vorlich with the family of a cousin, 'with four or five cows, and as many dogs, the hens preferring the joists above us', and on the following day he was entertained, thanks to Scott's letter of introduction, 'in the splendid dining-room in the Castle of Inverary', the guest of the Duke of Argyll. On this journey, however, Hogg intended to make definite arrangements to undertake the tenancy of a farm, since the lease of Ettrickhouse had now formally expired. Even though Hogg was still dating his letters from there at the end of the year and the new farmer perhaps had another house to live in, he and his parents could not continue to live at Ettrickhouse indefinitely.

Although Hogg's object was to lease a Highland sheep-farm, he did not necessarily view his actions as helping to depopulate the Highlands. On the contrary, he believed that a woollen manufactory would help to stop emigration to North America and proclaimed 'that men, sheep, and fish, are the great staple commodities of Scotland'. When Mackenzie of Dundonnel asked for a valuation of the income of his estate let as sheep-walks, and realised that he might have an annual income of two thousand rather than seven hundred pounds, Hogg reminded him that at present he enjoyed absolute sway over his people, greater even than Bonaparte's in France. 'I saw him call two men from their labour a full mile, to carry us through the water', Hogg noted. 'I told him he must not expect to be served thus by the shepherds if once he had given them possession'. Nor was Hogg unsympathetic to Highland Catholicism. He felt a deep religious awe on wandering over the ruins of the Virgin's chapel and its burying-ground at St Mary's Isle on Loch Maree, and declared that he would never esteem a man the less because he differed from himself in religion but on the contrary thought each should adhere to the religion in which he had been brought up.[19]

Hogg's business trip was by no means free of adventure and excitement. Scrambling over rocks and precipices on his way from Letterewe in company with a Highland minister's daughter Hogg was worried that the wind, catching at the clothes of this elegantly-dressed lady, 'would carry her off, and looked back several times with terror for fear that I should see her flying headlong toward the lake like a swan'. Travelling by ship to Stornaway and wrapped in his plaid on deck reading Shakespeare, Hogg was alarmed by the appearance of a huge whale alongside the ship: 'I once called to one of the sailors to come and see how he rubbed sides with the ship. "Eh!" said he, "he pe wanting one of us to breakfast with him!"'. Arrived safely in Stornaway, Hogg hired a lad called Malcolm as a guide and travelled northwards to explore the Isle of Lewis. By 21 June, the longest day in the year, he had reached Barvas in the north-west, where 'owing to the bright sky in the north, and the moon in the south, beaming on the ocean, *there was no night there*'. Entranced by the phenomenon of the 'white nights' Hogg made an excursion along the shores of the northern ocean to view the Butt of Lewis itself, the northernmost point of the island.[20]

Before mid-July, however, he had come southwards to Harris, and was in close communication with the tacksman of Luskintyre (*Losgaintir* in Gaelic), William Macleod, about leasing a farm at Shelibost (*Seilibost*). This was fertile, attractive land on the machair, a coastal district whose lime-rich land was covered with pulverised sea-shells deposited by the Atlantic ocean, and Hogg's farm would be an extensive one. The Luskintyre tack was virtually the whole of south Harris, from a line from Horgabost to the head of Loch Stockinsh to the isthmus at Tarbet. Hogg's sublet appears to have been the part from Seilibost village on the west to Meavag village on Loch Diraclett on the east, up to Tarbet but excluding the arable land of Luskintyre itself. A tack drafted by Hogg himself of 13 July 1803, duly signed and witnessed by the two parties, has detailed provisions covering kelp production, the grazing of horses and cat-tle, the payment of duties, and responsibilities towards those living as cottagers on the property. Hogg was to enter on the farm on 26 May 1804 and to have possession for seven years at an annual rent of a hundred and fifty pounds. The rent was due at Martinmass (11 November) 1804, as was customary in the Highlands, although the Borders farmers normally paid their year's rent at the end of their year's farming. Hogg commented on the custom subsequently as one that, on top of the cost of stocking the farm, put a severe strain on the capital of the incoming tenant. In addition to this, he also bound himself to provide a legal obligation before 'Martinmass first'

from the bankers William Forbes and Company in Edinburgh that
the money was ready to be paid when due, an arrangement clearly
designed to protect Luskintyre against a possible default by someone who was, after all, a stranger: before Hogg ever took control of
the land Macleod could be certain of receiving his first year's rent.
Hogg, though, must hand over the money (or equivalent securities)
to the well-known Edinburgh banker a year before the rent was due,
and eighteen months before custom would have dictated its payment in the Borders. The tack also included a penalty clause of thirty
pounds, binding on either side, for breach of contract.[21] The land
was actually owned not by Luskintyre but by his landlord Alexander Hume, son to the Alexander Macleod who had bought the island of Harris in 1779 and died in 1790. The son had adoped his
mother's family name, and unlike his father (who was very much an
improving landlord) lived mainly in England and India, managing
his estates in Harris with the help of factors. Macleod was simply
the tacksman, holding a lease as the husband of Isabella the eldest
daughter of the former tacksman, Alexander Macleod of Luskintyre.[22]

After spending several weeks on Harris, familiarising himself with
local farming methods and places, Hogg left for Ettrick sometime in
August with the feeling that his future was now secure. His plans,
however, were threatened almost at once when, coming into the
Sound of Mull on the voyage back to Greenock, the ship in which he
sailed fell into the path of a Royal Navy cutter carrying a press-
gang:

> [...] the Sailors immediately betook themselves to the boat
> and fled to the mountains of Mull, and by some unaccount-
> able neglect proceeding from pride, I refused to accompany
> them, but had reason to repent of my temerity. The boat was
> scarcely returned when the cutter appeared and came streight
> upon us and to such particulars which can do no honour to
> me nor any concerned. Suffice it to say that I got an ugly
> fright, and shall never be as near hauled a board a man of
> War untill I go altogether. Indeed I have often wondered
> since that they suffered me to escape considering the limited
> Time that had for making up their quota however escape I
> did & my heart in a few hours gradually receded from the
> rapidity of motion to which the presence of a press gang had
> raised it[23]

Had Hogg been pressed into the Royal Navy during the Napoleonic
conflict, his literary works might never have been written. It might

also have been months, or even years, before his poor old parents in Ettrick learned of his fate.

Hogg's choice of Harris as his future home seems an extraordinary one for a man who was trying to establish a literary reputation. During the following autumn he was much occupied with literary plans that could be executed well enough forty miles from Edinburgh, but would have been impracticable from there. If Hogg could afford to pay an annual rent of £150 he could surely have leased a farm much closer to home. Did he expect his elderly parents, Ettrick Forest folk from birth like himself, to uproot themselves from all their early associations and family connections to live in what was certainly in some respects a foreign country? Perhaps he was unduly drawn to a myth of exile, taken from the career of his idol Robert Burns. Hogg's projected move to Harris undoubtedly parallels Burns's plans to go to Jamaica when he was unable to continue farming in his native Ayrshire, and 'Jamie's Farewell to Ettrick', published in the *Scots Magazine* for May 1804, shortly before Hogg's departure for Harris, is equivalent to 'On a Scotch Bard Gone to the West Indies', besides containing other Burnsian allusions:

> My happy days wi' you are past!
> An' wae's my heart! will ne'er return!
> The brightest day will overcast!
> An man was made *at times* to mourn.[24]

Hogg's poem laments Ettrick with no sense of pleasure in his Harris prospects, and his true commitment to them seems doubtful.

Hogg's literary reputation was spreading that year. His Ettrick friend John Grieve, now in business in Alloa, brought an Alloa friend, the timber merchant and amateur poet Alexander Bald, to visit Hogg in Selkirkshire in 1803. Bald was a fellow-contributor to the poetry section of the *Scots Magazine*, where several of Hogg's songs were beginning to appear. Hogg had performed his topical and probably newly-composed 'Donald Macdonald' in honour of his Macdonald host in a social party at Barrisdale on his way to Harris, and it had been so highly applauded there that he sang it often during the rest of his journey and perhaps realised what a huge popularity it was shortly to enjoy. Furthermore, at Greenock on his way home he had been surprised to be hailed as a poet, and invited to dine at the town's Tontine Hotel with no less than thirty gentlemen, including James Park and the future novelist John Galt, then a 'tall thin young man, with something a little dandyish in his appearance'.[25]

Towards the end of the year, Hogg spent an evening with Scott

and his wife in Castle Street in Edinburgh, a visit notoriously caricatured by Lockhart (nine years old at the time and completely unknown to Scott) as the occasion when Hogg had stretched out at full
length, dirty boots and all, on Mrs Scott's sofa and had addressed his
host and hostess as 'Wattie' and 'Charlotte'. Hogg himself owned to
being 'at least half-seas over' and his memory of the evening confused, though he did remember that Scott had cautioned him on parting 'against being insnared by the loose women in town'. Hogg's
recent journey through the Highlands had obviously been discussed
and he proposed to Scott 'a volume of letters to you on my journey
thro' the Highlands', but he also wanted Scott's support for a volume
of his popular songs. Hogg's own account of his life, written at
Ettrickhouse, might be ghosted by Scott himself as a preface, 'putting
He for I', and the volume could be dedicated either to Scott or to the
Countess of Dalkeith, the young and intelligent daughter-in-law of
the Duke of Buccleuch. Hogg planned to work hard at this volume
over the winter and thought that it might be ready for publication 'in
a month or two at the furthest'.[26]

Hogg's attempt to emigrate to Harris in 1804 failed, and was probably a half-hearted one though the details remain obscure. His characteristic reluctance to recall 'bygone affairs which had been vexatious to thought or disagreeable to feeling' was exemplified by his
unwillingness to discuss the Harris episode with his friends or to
provide details in his 'Memoir'. Given that his date of entry to
Seilibost was 26 May Hogg set out from Ettrick remarkably late on
21 May 1804, taking with him not sheep and agricultural implements
but his two friends William Laidlaw and John Grieve, who were
probably accompanying him partly as a holiday. In his written account of the trip Hogg denominated this 'the *unfortunate journey*', in
which the three travellers' usual state was to be 'drenched to the
skin and mud to the knees'. The weather was against them, they
took wrong roads, they were nearly ship-wrecked, and Hogg's companions were seasick. He manages to project a real sense of being
ill-fated, that the outcome was never to be a positive one. (His tone
contrasts sharply with that of the narrative of his 1803 journey, itself
by no means free of dangers and hardships.) When the party finally
arrived in Luskintyre they spent only three days there. Grieve and
Laidlaw were vexed and weary and wanted to go home, and incredibly Hogg preferred to return with them rather than remain on Harris
alone. He left even though a messenger arrived at Luskintyre requesting him to visit the owner of the land, Mr Hume, and his factor,
Angus Campbell of Ensay. There is something curiously wilful about

Hogg's actions, as if he was determined on one level to have his plans for settling on Harris frustrated, or was trying to establish that his settlement there had been prevented by providential means. Once Hogg has failed to discuss his future with the island's landowner and his factor and is on his way back to Selkirkshire, difficulties melt away and the party are home a mere five days later.[27] When it came down to it, did he really want to move to Harris at all?

It seems likely that Hume and Campbell of Ensay intended to inform Hogg of a dispute with William Macleod over the terms on which he held Luskintyre from the estate. Hogg had realised when he saw him in Harris in June that Luskintyre was nervous about having exceeded the proportion of the land he was allowed to sub-set by his landlord, since he wanted Hogg if challenged to pretend to 'hold it of him in steelbow to save his head'. (Steelbow is a form of tenancy where the stock belongs to the person leasing the land and is provided by him for the tenant's use during the term of the lease.) During the following summer, Hume did apply to the Court of Session in Edinburgh to have Macleod removed from Luskintyre, and it is possible that the legal process was at least under discussion a year earlier. An early account of Hogg's life tends to confirm this, stating that Hogg had been informed of the dispute as early as July 1804. After returning home to Ettrick from his Harris trip

> [...] he purchased a good many sheep, with which, when he was finally setting out for Harris, about the middle of July, he received notice that the tacksman's right to the subject was called in question, and a plea entered at the Court of Session accordingly. Thinking it unsafe to venture himself with so much property in a distant island, where the proprietor was likely to become his enemy, he immediately resolved on that step to which least apparent danger was attached.[28]

By the provisions of the tack Hogg and Luskintyre had signed Hogg would have forfeited only the agreed £30 penalty by not proceeding to Seilibost, but if the tack itself was *ultra vires* each of its provisions would be equally outside the law. Hogg's subsequent letters to Scott imply that Luskintyre had somehow got hold of the £150 Hogg had deposited as his first years' rent with William Forbes, or at least that the banking house had refused to refund it to Hogg because Luskintyre had claimed it. It was presumably at Scott's suggestion that the Edinburgh solicitor Joseph Gillon had been employed to resolve the matter, for Hogg asked him to

> [...] speak to Gillon and see what can be done about the

recovery of the £150.– – from Sir William Forbes. I will need
it much shortly. [...] I am certainly informed that he [i.e.
Luskintyre] stocked the farm himself that same year for which
my money was lodged as rent. Certainly sir there is no reason that I should lose that money. though I believe that had I
gone I might have got my sheep upon the ground for one
year but no more neither could I have kept his beasts from
abusing it wholly that same year: but he broached so many
new laws as inherent in the island on my second visit that it
was visible he was resolved I should never go there and I
now see that the retention of the £150 was his sole aim.

The matter seems eventually to have gone to arbitration, and
Luskintyre retained the money.[29] Hogg was certainly angry about
the financial loss, but easily resigned to not settling in Harris. He
was inclined to be fatalistic.

Hogg's return to Ettrick in July 1804 involved 'a great many disagreeable questions and explanations'. He had to explain why his
much-vaunted tenancy of a large Harris farm had failed to materialise, and to dispose of the sheep he had intended to stock it with.
Worst of all, he had let his old parents down. Robert Hogg and
Margaret Laidlaw clearly moved into a cottage at Craig-Douglas in
Yarrow, the neighbouring farm to Blackhouse, which was also tenanted by Hogg's old master James Laidlaw at some point. Writing a
letter from Blackhouse on 1 December 1804 Hogg requests that the
reply should be sent to him at 'Douglas-Craig by Selkirk', while the
1806 edition of Scott's *Minstrelsy of the Scottish Border* mentions that
Hogg's mother 'at present resides at Craig of Douglas, in
Selkirkshire'.[30] Hogg's father was presumably still there in 1814, when
Hogg used the pseudonym 'J. H. Craig of Douglas' for *The Hunting
of Badlewe*.

Unable to face the Ettrick folk in the summer of 1804, Hogg
promptly set off on his travels again, this time southwards into England. He may have intended to see the mountains of North Wales,
but if so he got no further than Lancaster. By his own account he was
daunted by the number of people condemned at the local assizes
and decided to turn back 'for Scotland by the Lakes of Westmoreland
and Cumberland', places already beginning to be associated with
the Lake Poets, Wordsworth, Coleridge, and Southey. In Lancaster
his wounded pride and self-respect must have been considerably
revived by an episode which suggested that his literary prospects
were brighter than his farming ones. He had attended the theatre
and heard one of the actors, a Scotsman named M'Rae, sing two of

his own patriotic songs in the course of the performance, 'Caledonia' and 'Donald Macdonald'. The second was wildly successful:

> It took exceedingly well, and was three times encored, and
> there was I sitting in the gallery, applauding as much as any
> body. My vanity prompted me to tell a jolly Yorkshire manu-
> facturer that night, that I was the author of the song. He laughed
> excessively at my assumption, and told the landlady that he
> took me for a half-crazed Scots pedlar.

Hogg seems to have passed about a month at Keswick, though without introducing himself to any of the Lake poets, getting to know
'every scene almost in Cumberland'.[31] He then returned home to
Ettrick Forest hoping to restore his fortune by the use of his pen.

Hogg spent the autumn and winter of 1804–05 in Ettrick Forest.
Though considered an irresponsible fool by many, his real friends
stood by him and he paid visits to Alexander Laidlaw at Bowerhope
and to the Laidlaws at Blackhouse. Walter Scott continued his willingness to help Hogg too and tried to find him employment. Scott
had been looking for a summer residence in Selkirkshire, firstly at
Broadmeadows and then more successfully at Ashiestiel. During the
greater part of the year, however, he would need to live in Edinburgh. Perhaps Hogg could act as manager of his country home and
look after it during his absence? Through Mrs Scott of Harden Scott
was also able to offer Hogg a situation as bailiff or chief shepherd to
the lady's nephew, Lord Porchester. The exact details are unclear,
but in his letter to Scott of 16 January 1805 Hogg describes the offer
as 'poor'. The salary was probably £20 a year with 'a riding horse,
house and small farm free of rent', but on condition that Hogg was
to put his 'poetical talent under lock and key for ever'. Hogg, consol-
ing himself for his financial losses with hopes of literary achievement, expected Scott to sympathise. Bitterly hurt by the estimate of
his talent implied in Scott's communication of Lord Porchester's offer, Hogg wrote years afterwards in *The Queen's Wake*, 'But sure, a
bard might well have known | Another's feelings by his own!'.[32] Such
lack of faith in his future literary career was a bitter humiliation.

Nevertheless Hogg worked hard at his writing that winter, no
doubt cheered by the continuing success of his song of 'Donald
Macdonald' which was highly topical that year, expressing widespread Scottish defiance of a threatened invasion from Napoleonic
France. Beacons had been prepared across the country as an invasion signal, and on 2 February 1804 the watchman at Home Castle
had misinterpreted an accidental fire in Northumberland and lit his

own beacon, triggering a chain of alarm across the Scottish Borders. The Selkirkshire Yeomanry mustered at Dalkeith, for example, 'though the roads were in a bad state, and many of the troopers must have ridden forty or fifty miles without drawing bridle', as Scott recounted many years later with conspicuous local pride.[33] On a visit to Edinburgh that November Hogg offered 'Donald Macdonald' for publication to his fellow-Borderer Andrew Mercer, now editor of the *North British Magazine*. When Mercer heard Hogg sing it over their dinner at a Fleshmarket Close chop-house, he thought it deserved a wider popularity and arranged for Thomas Oliver, one of the best singers in Scotland, to sing it on 30 November at the St Andrews Day Freemasons' meeting of the Grand Lodge of Scotland. On that occasion 'it was received with rapturous applause. The walls of the Grand Lodge literally shook with the acclamations'. The Earl of Dalhousie, the Grand Master that year, on hearing it was composed by 'a shepherd lad in Ettrick' offered to take fifty copies if the song was published. Single copies of the song were printed by the Edinburgh music teacher and publisher John Hamilton, of 24 North Bridge Street, and sold at sixpence each, but informally it circulated far more widely. Hogg later recalled that it was 'perhaps, the most popular song that ever was written'. A General M'Donald, for example, who was probably the Lieutenant-Governor of Fort William, believed that it was written in his honour and delighted in having it sung every day at his mess.[34]

Hogg may fleetingly have considered publishing the account of his 1803 Highland Journey in the *North British Magazine* too, for the notices 'To Correspondents' in the first issue for January 1804 had stated, 'We daily expect to be favoured with the account of a *Shepherd's Tour*'. By the autumn, however, Hogg had plainly decided to publish his Highland Journeys together in volume form. At the beginning of December he sent Scott a long essay designed as a supplement and entitled 'An Essay on the Utility of Encouraging the System of Sheep-Farming in Some Districts of the Highlands, and Population in Others. Addressed to the Honourable President and Members of the Highland Society'. Hogg hoped to publish by subscription with the support of the Highland Society, and the essay was designed to shift the focus of the work more towards an agricultural report. He had also written up his experiences and observations during his most recent Highland trip in May 1804 to supplement those of 1802 and 1803. Some idea of the proposed publication may be gained from a notice in the 'Scottish Literary Intelligence' section of the *Scots Magazine* for August 1805:

> Mr Hogg (the Ettrick Shepherd) with whose poetry our read-
> ers have been so often and so highly gratified, is about to
> publish, by subscription, a Collection of Letters, written dur-
> ing his journies through the Northern and Western High-
> lands and Islands of Scotland, in the summers of 1802, 1803,
> and 1804. Describing the scenery, manners, and rural
> economy of each district; the local advantages and disadvan-
> tages attached to each; with suggestions on the best probable
> means of their improvement, adventures, anecdotes, &c. To
> which will be added *a Supplement*, addressed to the Highland
> Society, on the utility of encouraging the system of Sheep-
> farming in some districts, and Population in others.[35]

Hogg was also working towards another volume publication, of
his songs and ballads prefaced by an account of his life in the shape
of a series of letters addressed to Walter Scott. He hoped, with Scott's
assistance, to persuade Archibald Constable to publish it. Hogg had
felt that the ballad imitations in the third volume of the *Minstrelsy of the
Scottish Border* were less than satisfactory, and had been busy writing
his own. By the start of December 1804 he informed Scott, 'I am well
advanced in Gilmanscleuch and have finished Sir David Graham'.
His ballads of 'The Death of Douglas, Lord of Liddesdale' and 'The
Pedlar' (published in the *Scots Magazine* for May and November 1804
respectively) were both 'in Imitation of the Ancients'. 'Sir David
Graham. A Border Ballad' was shortly followed by 'The Fray of
Elibank'. Two of these poems relate the doings of the Scotts of Harden,
from whom Scott was proud (inordinately proud, Hogg later declared) to be descended.[36] In 'Gilmanscleuch' (a particular favourite
of Scott's), one of the sons of Scott of Harden had been killed by the
brother of a girl whom he had made pregnant, and Harden had
revenged himself and feathered his own nest simultaneously by getting the king to make him a grant of the offender's lands. The Scotts,
once the baby has grown to manhood, accept him as their nephew
and grant him the farm of Gilmanscleuch, since 'A Scott shou'd ay
support a Scott'. The forced marriage between young Walter Scott
of Harden and Meg Murray in 'The Fray of Elibank' turns out well,
Meg's wide mouth being accurately interpreted by her reluctant bridegroom as a favourable omen that she will have plenty of food to put
into it. Their descendants (such as Scott himself), it is slyly insinu-
ated, have inherited this feature and 'rather have a' a good luck for
their meat'. Hogg's own ancestor, William Hogg 'the Boar of
Fauldshope', fares less well in the poem since the 'unequalled strength,
courage, and ferocity' which led to the exploit lost him his master's

favour.[37] In both poems Hogg portrays Scott's ancestors as canny, thriving people sure to succeed materially, perhaps indirectly expressing some envy of his mentor. Walter Scott, Sheriff of Selkirkshire, had a fine house in Edinburgh's New Town and a newly-acquired summer home at Ashiestiel near Selkirk, while Hogg had nothing.

Though Hogg had plenty of time for writing that winter he had no money, and remarked ruefully, 'It is plain that I must always have something to complain of, I have often complained of having too much employment now I am vexed at having so little'. He certainly could not continue to 'lye idle thus' in Yarrow, he told Scott on 16 January, adding 'if I cannot be employed in my own proffession I will be forced to enlist into the army'. Nor could he afford frequent trips to Edinburgh to forward his publications, though fortunately his old Ettrick friend John Grieve had left Alloa in 1804 for Edinburgh, where he entered into partnership with a hat-manufacturer named Chalmers Izett. Grieve would be willing to act as Hogg's Edinburgh agent. Hogg was occupied in writing for the *Scots Magazine*, songs such as 'Bauldy Fraser's Description of the Battle of Culloden' appearing there as well as his ballads. Scott did his best to keep Hogg's spirits up. For one thing he gave him a copy of James Grahame's new poem, *The Sabbath*. A fresh book was a real treat to Hogg, who had read most of the volume within twenty-four hours of receiving it and uttered the pithy verdict that 'the Cameronian hath had more in his head than hair'. Brought up in the same tradition of reverence for the Covenanting past of the Scottish church and the simplicity of its worship, Hogg was perhaps Grahame's ideal reader. Scott also repeated praise of some of Hogg's Highland letters by various Edinburgh friends to whom he had shown them. Hogg made light of Scott's suggestion that some anecdotes and personal names should be removed from the Highland Journeys book, however, reminding him that it was a rule 'of the Highland society that in all essays communicated to them they may be *authenticated by proper references*'. Hogg seems to have felt optimistic enough at this point to get some subscription papers for this work printed at Hawick, 'in order that the people may be taken while they are moved by the spirit', but the book was never published as Hogg then envisaged it.[38] He had also prepared an essay on the diseases of Sheep in response to an advertised premium of forty guineas offered by the Highland Society of Scotland. By the closing date of 20 November 1804 Hogg's brother William and the new tenant of Ettrickhouse farm had also submitted entries along with many others. There was no single winner, a digest of thirteen of the best entries being eventually prepared by Dr Andrew Duncan for publication in the *Prize Essays and Transactions of the Highland Society of Scotland*.[39] It is possible, however, that the authors of the thirteen chosen essays were paid something, and Hogg would find it useful to be thus distinguished in his profession.

Whitsunday 1805 was now looming, one of the Scottish Quarter Days when farm workers began a new term of service, and Hogg knew that he must find a position as a shepherd again—his time for devoting himself exclusively to writing was running out. Impatiently he told Scott on 16 January 1805, 'I am living in utter ignorance what is going on, but it is a great loss for me that the subscriptions have not been set on foot long ago as I must of necessity have the book published betwixt this and Whitsunday, whilst I am otherwise unemployed'. A few weeks afterwards he reported, 'I have not been able as yet to do any thing anent establishing myself in the world. I am perswaded *something has said against it.* whether for my good or ill is hard to say'.[40] But by Whitsunday he was once again employed as a shepherd, though in Dumfriesshire rather than his native district, by a Mr Harkness of Mitchelslacks farm in Closeburn parish.

Perhaps Hogg was regarded as such a ne'er-do-well in Selkirkshire that he was unable to find employment among the Ettrick and Yarrow farmers, or perhaps he was simply reluctant to go back to shepherding in a district where he had been his own master. His removal to Dumfriesshire was an unfortunate one, however, insofar as it took him even further from the publishing centre of Edinburgh. Perhaps Hogg's choice of Dumfriesshire (like his earlier choice of Harris) was partly influenced by his devotion to Robert Burns? Burns had spent his final years in Dumfries itself, some twelve miles away from Closeburn, and Hogg was obviously fascinated by every aspect of his life. Hogg sometimes attended church in Dumfries where he sat in the next seat to Burns's middle-aged widow and decided that in her youth she must have been pretty as she was then 'smartly dressed, had fine eyes, and looked very well', besides being rumoured to have several wooers. He also sought out those who remembered Burns, such as the old farm servant Saunders Proudfoot who had drunk with Burns at a Thornhill fair, and disputed with him about original sin. 'What did he say about it, Saunders?' enquired Hogg eagerly. Proudfoot could not remember the details of the debate, but related how, sharing a room with Burns one night, he involuntarily witnessed his private devotions, and his intense repentance for blasphemy. Hogg's new master, James Harkness, had also seen Burns, but did not share Hogg's devotion to his memory, considering him 'a low blackguard-looking fellow'.[41]

The Harknesses of Mitchelslacks and the adjoining farm of Locherben were honoured in the neighbourhood for their support of the Covenanters in the 1680s, and had lived in Closeburn parish for perhaps three hundred years when Hogg arrived there. James and Thomas Harkness had played a part in the Enterkin Pass rescue of 1684, when a band of Dumfriesshire men had successfully ambushed a party of soldiers taking Covenanting prisoners to Edinburgh for trial and execution. Thomas was subsequently executed for it in the Grassmarket on 5 August 1684, his 'plain and natural Testimony' being printed and highly commended by Robert Wodrow in his *History of the Sufferings of the Church of Scotland.* James survived and died at Locherben in 1723 at the age of seventy-two. He was buried with other members of the Harkness family in Dalgarnoch kirkyard, the inscription on his tombstone celebrating his escape through God's providence from Claverhouse and his endurance of twenty-eight years persecution, all because

> [...] he would not give up
> With Christ his glorious King,
> And swear allegiance to that beast,
> The Duke of York, I mean.
> In spite of all their hellish rage
> A natural death he died,
> In full assurance of his rest
> With Christ ieternalie.[42]

A place called 'Red Tam's Gutter' marks the spot where James Harkness shot a dragoon who was pursuing him, and where the ground is supposed to have run red with blood for two or three days afterwards. Hogg later adapted the legend into his own 'A Tale of the Martyrs', in which 'Red Tam Harkness' is bayoneted at that spot ('a kind of slough east from the farm-house of Locherben') by the persecutors before he can reveal the fate of her husband, John Weir, to the goodwife of Garrick.[43] Besides listening to anecdotes of Burns during the long winter evenings at Mitchelslacks, Hogg undoubtedly heard a great deal about the local exploits of the Covenanters, no doubt a more welcome subject of discourse in the Harkness household. Hogg is not often considered to be a Dumfriesshire writer, but many of his tales have Dumfriesshire settings and are surely based on what he heard at this time.

Mitchelslacks is a remote hill-farm on the north-eastern boundary of Closeburn parish, looking shadowed and bleak on days of mist and rain even in summer. Part of the sheep-walk was along the slopes of the great hill of Queensberry, rising to a height of over two thousand feet above sea-level. The present square two-storey stone house was built after Hogg's time and would have replaced one of the more primitive dwellings described by the parish minister in 1834 as formerly characteristic of the parish:

> Half a century ago the farm-houses of this parish were cot-tages built of rough stone and clay mortar, and containing generally two, sometimes three apartments, one of which was the kitchen. The floors were paved with mud, and the roofs destitute of ceiling. [...] The cottages of the peasantry are, with scarcely an exception, superior to the dwelling-houses fifty years ago, on farms now let at L. 500 a-year.

The old-fashioned wooden 'lang-settle', however, on which Hogg is supposed to have rested himself in the farm kitchen at the end of his day's work, was preserved in the modern farmhouse at least until 1901. This traditional house and household would be utterly famil-iar to Hogg, and the parish minister, the Rev. Andrew Yorstoun, was a hard-working, kindly pastor of the old sort who visited the farms in turn to catechise the inhabitants. Hogg later recollected with some amusement that on one such occasion after explaining 'who were our superiors and whom we were to regard as our equals' he asked a Mitchelslacks lad named William Haining who were his inferiors. When Will replied 'The tinklers', the minister 'was obliged to raise both his hands to cover his face and laugh'.[44]

But although Hogg reckoned his master, Mr Harkness, as 'a good worthy man' he was 'void of any taste as to literary things', a very different master from the sympathetic James Laidlaw of Blackhouse. At Mitchelslacks too Hogg was one servant among others, a consid-erable change from being his own master at Ettrickhouse. His time was more fully occupied by shepherding than it had been for some years past.

> [...] my flocks take up the whole of my attention so that I have not a moment to think of my favourite studies neither have I any convenience farther than writing on my knee upon the hill so that my poetical effusions as well as every thing else of that nature are at an end for some time. I am not unhappy far from it but I am somwhat vexed—not for being obliged to [eol] to toil hard a whole year for such a small pittance but for the sake of that same small pittance to be obliged to forego all my favourite studies, the more so as I have been long convinced that if ever I rise above or even to

a mediocrity it is to be by my writings.

He asked Scott rhetorically 'how would you like to write as I do now amongst a housefull of brutal noisy servants but I have no other alternative but the fields'.[45]

Hogg was understandably eager to see some of the work he had accomplished during his winter of unemployment in Ettrick moving rapidly towards publication. The 'Scottish Literary Intelligence' of the *Scots Magazine* for August 1805 announced that he had his poetry volume, *The Mountain Bard*, 'ready for the press, and will publish immediately', though it was not in fact published until 1807. Constable, who was to be the publisher, was far from enthusiastic and did not reply to Hogg's letters. 'Pray dear Sir' Hogg wrote to Scott, 'would you be so good as to thresh his skin I would be a jill in your debt [...] Constable is like the fool at herding cows he is *below it*'. It was difficult for Hogg to get to Edinburgh since he would have to arrange for a suitable substitute shepherd to take care of his flock, but he managed nevertheless to wait upon Constable, accompanied by Scott himself. Constable, Hogg later recollected,

> [...] received me very kindly, but told me frankly that my poetry would not sell. I said I thought it was as good as any body's I had seen. He said that might be, but that nobody's poetry would sell; it was the worst stuff that came to market, and that he found; but, as I appeared to be a gay queer chiel, if I would procure him two hundred subscribers he would publish my work for me, and give me as much for it as he could. I did not like the subscribers much; but, having no alternative, I accepted the conditions. Before the work was ready for publication I had got above five hundred subscribers; and Mr. Constable, who, by that time, had conceived a better opinion of the work, gave me half-guinea copies for all my subscribers, and a letter for a small sum over and above.

Scott was a powerful backer. *The Lay of the Last Minstrel*, published in January 1805, had undoubtedly increased the value of his recommendations to Edinburgh publishers. At a time when Hogg felt more remote from the literary centre than before Scott had become a national poet. At much this time, Hogg visited Andrew Livingston at Airds near Castle-Douglas, hoping to rent a farm from him. He was not successful, but did enjoy a long conversation with Livingston about Scott's ballad collection and *The Lay of the Last Minstrel*. Livingston wrote to Scott on 28 April 1806 to say that 'John Hogg the Etterick Shepherd' had told him that Scott would like a copy of the ballad of the Pentland hills, and enclosed one from the recitation of his own servant, subsequently included by Scott in future editions of the *Minstrelsy*.[46]

Hogg wanted to regain a measure of independence and a quiet space for his writing, and at first he hoped that it might be possible for him to lease and stock a farm again at the end of his year's service at Mitchelslacks. But for this he needed a good deal more cash than his shepherd's wages for the year. His hopes of publishing a book of his Highland Journeys had faded by March 1806, and although he seems not to have abandoned the hope of reclaiming the £150 he had paid out as advance rent for Seilibost until December 1806, his best chance of obtaining the necessary funds undoubtedly lay in the successful publication of *The Mountain Bard*. During his time at Mitchelslacks Hogg had cultivated the Countess of Dalkeith as a potential patron and dedicatee for the work, making a presentation copy of his ballad 'Gilmanscleuch' for her on 26 August 1805. In March 1806 he approached her unsuccessfully to ask if he might rent a farm at Canonbie in Dumfriesshire from the Buccleuch estate too. Things were moving forward for his publication but not fast enough. It was 11 March before Hogg was able to close with a definite offer from Archibald Constable, of ninety pounds for a sale edition of 750 copies with another 250 copies on fine paper of *The Mountain Bard*, and Whitsunday was looming. Scott, meanwhile, had written from London sending cheering news of Royal patronage. When the Princess of Wales had asked him at Montagu House to recite some verses of his own, he gave her instead 'a short account of the Ettrick Shepherd, and repeated one of the ballads of the *Mountain Bard*', and she had responded with a request that her name might be placed on the subscription list.[47] Hogg gratefully replied on 17 March 1806, 'I fear my thoughts would have been otherwise employed'. Scott was clearly thriving, with the birth of a second son and the confirmation of his employment as a Clerk of Session. His prosperity was certainly well deserved, yet Hogg, the Mitchelslacks shepherd, could not suppress a wistful if not an envious note: 'It is a d–d thing that no body has ever to congratulate me on any thing only that *such a thing might hae been waur*'. By 18 April Hogg had reluctantly engaged to serve another year as a shepherd at Mitchelslacks.[48]

On 3 April 1806 Hogg had proudly sent Scott his manuscript for *The Mountain Bard*, which he described as 'my first born legitimate infant son [...] whom I commit to your tuition with as sanguine hopes and joyfull expectations as ever parent committed his heir to a preceptor and sent him abroad in quest of adventures'. As the famous

author of *The Lay of the Last Minstrel* Scott could help an authentic
minstrel, the Bard of the Mountains, to achieve literary success. He
duly suggested subjects for ballads to Hogg, revised the poems he
wrote, organised the proposed contents of the volume, obtained a
printer and a publisher as well as many subscribers for it, and was
the person to whom it was dedicated. Hogg's attitude to his powerful mentor was not entirely uncritical, however, and while he was
duly grateful for Scott's revisions to his work they were sometimes
also resented as undue interference. He referred to one letter of
Scott's as being 'brimfull of Criticisms, articles which I mortally ab-
hor', stating that he would rather exclude a piece from the volume
altogether than have his train of ideas spoiled by the hated alterations. Scott was wrong in wishing to refine place-names in the ballad of 'Mess John', and only the actual rape of a country girl could
justify the death of the priest who lusted after and persecuted her. It
was Hogg himself who 'must abide by the consequences' of the publication and therefore he expected 'a considerable sway in the publication'.[49]

In describing the ballad 'Willie Wilkin' as 'an abridgement of Mr
Michael Scott' and 'a second edition of Michael Scott on a smaller
type and coarser paper' Hogg both acknowledged and resented the
influence of the supernaturalism of *The Lay of the Last Minstrel*. On
reading Scott's poem Hogg had criticised the 'terrible parade of fetch-
ing Michael Scott's black book from the tomb' as superfluous to the
plot. 'Willie Wilkin' also concerns a wizard and a magical book, but
makes the book the immediate cause of a vile treachery. Wilkin's
pious mother hopes to protect him from demonic influence by se-
creting a bible about his horse, and when the fiends resent it asks
them to spare her son's life and take her own. Wilkin responds to
this selfless love by calling out, 'Take her, and spare thy friend!', and
Hogg forces the details of her subsequent dismemberment on the
reader's flinching attention. This undead wizard, as Hogg's notes
make clear, manifests himself at his own will and not at that of others up to the present day. He is frequently heard curling on the loch
in Closeburn parish 'to the great terror and annoyance of the neighbourhood, not much regarding whether the loch be frozen or not.
[...] every one allows it to be a dangerous place, and a place where
very many have been affrighted [...]'. (Indeed, as late as 1826 a newspaper report of the embankment giving way at the loch jocularly
supported Hogg's claim of supernatural malevolence by noting, 'It is
even said, that when the embankment burst, every hill and glen re-
sounded the demoniac cry–"Weel dune, Wilkin, now's the hour!"')[50]

It seems likely that Hogg envisaged *The Mountain Bard* as much more of a vehicle for his songs and other contemporary poems than Scott was prepared for. Hogg's best-known work to date was his song of 'Donald Macdonald', after all, while 'Sandy Tod', he felt, had gained him more 'encomiums as a poet and more correspondents than any thing I ever published'. He had been disappointed that Scott did not include 'By a Bush' in *The Minstrelsy of the Scottish Border* and in April 1806, when Scott was preparing a new edition, Hogg thought that 'surely the song which you proposed publishing before and neglected would form no bad supplement to the Minstrelsy'. *The Mountain Bard* included a section of 'Songs Adapted to the Times' as well as its 'Ballads in Imitation of the Ancients', and, as Peter Garside has commented, Hogg in a series of letters to Scott during the autumn of 1806 'is found [...] endeavouring to impress on Scott the availability of such materials, and recommending John Grieve as the custodian and best judge of his "modern" pieces'. Hogg had mentioned Grieve to Scott in April 1806 as someone who was prepared to act as his agent in Edinburgh, and in October he repeated his assurances that Grieve's 'desires to further every thing that can be of service to me are boundless'. Grieve held many of Hogg's 'modern pieces' in manuscript and was 'a good judge better acquainted with them all than you are'. Early the following year he introduced Grieve at Scott's Edinburgh home in Castle Street.[51]

'Songs Adapted to the Times' was eventually expanded to occupy fifty pages of *The Mountain Bard*, four items being added even after the initial printing of the volume had been completed, possibly when Hogg found himself unable to provide a list of his subscribers in the volume and suggested 'an additional song or two in place of the names'.[52] This emphasised Hogg's recent work for the *Scots Magazine*, where he had come to prominence as a shepherd-poet. A Burnsian note was struck with Hogg's verse epistle 'To Mr T. M. C.' and his 'Farewell to Ettrick'. Hogg's role as the patriotic commemorator of national events was also signalled, with the inclusion of 'Scotia's Glens' and 'Donald Macdonald', even though his shepherd's dialogue on the death of Nelson, 'Jock and Samuel', was not reprinted there.

The *Mountain Bard* sequence of the 'Memoir' of Hogg's life, 'Ballads, in Imitation of the Antients' and 'Songs Adapted to the Times' emphasised that he was a tradition-bearer and a peasant poet, the successor to James Beattie's *The Minstrel*. The *Scots Magazine* no doubt had such as *The Farmer's Boy* in mind when hoping that Hogg's poem would be 'found fully equal to several, which in England have in similar circumstances experienced the most lavish patronage'.[53]

The Mountain Bard emphasises the importance to Hogg of Scott's friendship during the two years he served as a shepherd at Mitchelslacks, but naturally there were other significant friendships at this time. It was while herding his sheep on Queensberry hill that Hogg became acquainted with Allan Cunningham and his elder brother James, then living and working as stone-masons only a few miles away at Dalswinton. Their father, John Cunningham, had been factor to the local landowner, Patrick Miller, from 1786 until his death in 1800 and on good terms with Hogg's idol Robert Burns. Hogg himself had formed a connection with another Cunningham brother, Thomas Mounsey Cunningham, through the pages of the *Scots Magazine*. 'To Mr T. M. C. London' in the *Scots Magazine* for August 1805 expressed Hogg's admiration for Cunningham's magazine contributions and speculated on the unknown writer's motives for living in London (' a dang'rous hole for poets!'), urging him as a Scots poet to 'Come back an' live an' die amang us' and 'Let baith our buoyant brains combine, | To raise our country's Magazine'. Cunningham's reply in the issue for March 1806, written 'Frae mang the wa's o' auld Gomorrah', gives a brief account of his Scots education and commercial experience in London, complaining 'O Scotland, Scotland, sair ye wrang'd me, | Like onie stepmither ye bang'd me'. He and Hogg are 'just twa pigs o' the same stye', he remarks, and eschewing mutual envy should 'brither like, gae hand in hand, | Singing our lov'd, our native land'. When Cunningham published two songs commemorating his lost love Julia Curtis in the *Scots Magazine* for June 1807 they were prefaced by an address to 'J– H–' as 'my dearest Jamie', 'Son of the song'.[54]

Allan and James Cunningham called on Hogg in the autumn of 1806 while he was out with his sheep. Allan, Hogg thought, looked like Burns, being a dark ungainly youth with a well-developed frame for his age and strong, manly features.

> The eldest came up and addressed me frankly, asking me if I was Mr. Harkness's shepherd, and if my name was James Hogg? to both of which queries I answered cautiously in the affirmative, for I was afraid they were come to look after me with an accusation regarding some of the lasses. The younger stood at a respectful distance, as if I had been the Duke of Queensberry, instead of a ragged servant lad herding sheep. The other seized my hand, and said, "Well, then, sir, I am glad to see you. There is not a man in Scotland whose hand I am prouder to hold."

As it was a rainy day the three men retired into a little shelter on the hill, as Cunningham recalled many years subsequently: 'The little sodded shealing where we sought shelter rises now on my sight—your two dogs—old Hector was one lie at our feet—the Lay of the Last Minstrel is in my hand for the first time to be twice read over after sermon as it really was—poetry—nothing but poetry is our talk and we are supremely happy'. This was the companionship of equals. Hogg visited the brothers at Dalswinton and subsequently kept up a correspondence with James Cunningham for many years. Thomas, in distant London, was appealed to for songs to fill sixteen pages of Hogg's 1810 song collection, *The Forest Minstrel*, and gave Hogg permission to make use of his contributions to the *Scots Magazine*.[55]

Another friend made in the course of guarding his flocks at Mitchelslacks was the artist and surveyor John Morrison. Morrison was a local man, born in 1782 at Terreagles in Nithsdale and brought up in Kirkcudbright. As a boy he became a protégé of the Earl of Selkirk, who taught him geometry, lent him books, and paid for this training as a land surveyor and for extra lessons in drawing. Morrison had studied painting in Edinburgh with the veteran artist Alexander Nasmyth and been employed by the celebrated engineer Thomas Telford. He had made Scott's acquaintance in 1803 over a correction to the *Minstrelsy of the Scottish Border*, and in 1806 found himself surveying the line of a road to Edinburgh in Closeburn parish, passing quite near to Mitchelslacks. When he enquired of Hogg at a plaided shepherd on his way to the hill the shepherd replied 'I am that individual'. The two sat down by a well to chat and swig brandy from a flask Morrison had with him. Subsequently Morrison called on Scott in Edinburgh along with Hogg and John Grieve, and the three visitors listened to and discussed Scott's description of the landscape surrounding St Mary's Loch in Selkirkshire read aloud from his manuscript of *Marmion*. Each of them then recited one of his own poems in turn, Hogg's choice being 'The Moon was a waning'.[56]

It was Morrison who introduced Hogg to Alexander Dirom, who was pleased with Hogg's society and invited them both to dinner in Edinburgh. Brigadier-General Dirom was a career soldier who had played an active part in the siege of Seringapatam in 1792 and subsequently published an account of his campaign experiences in India. His marriage to a Dumfriesshire heiress in 1793 had led to his settling on their combined estate of Mount Annan, where he was an improving landlord and an enthusiast for Telford's plan to open a route from Carlisle to Ireland via Portpatrick.[57] At this point Hogg's work on *The Mountain Bard* was virtually completed, since the volume was published in February. To add to his funds for leasing and stocking a farm of his own Hogg now projected a second volume publication, *The Shepherd's Guide*, announced in March 1807 in the *Scots Magazine* as follows:

> Mr Hogg, well known for his poetical talents, has in the press a work on the management of Sheep. Mr Hogg, from his professional employments, was led to pay particular attention to this subject, and has travelled over most part of Scotland, with the view of examining it more accurately.

Dirom had been a member of the Highland Society of Scotland since 1796, and was well-known as an improving landlord. He gave Hogg an essay for the work that had been addressed to him in 1792 by a Mr Malcolm, tenant of Burnfoot, that included tables showing wool prices between 1750 and 1795. Dirom may also have helped Hogg with the final part of the book, where Hogg's personal observations and reflections on sheep diseases are followed by several 'cases and observations, which are all quoted, or translated, from scarce and valuable books, or manuscripts'. Hogg included his own supplementary essay 'On the Utility of Encouraging the System of Sheep-Farming in Some Districts of the Highlands, and Population in Others', originally intended for the previously projected volume publication of his 1802–04 Highland Journeys. No doubt *The Shepherd's Guide* also included revised versions of the two essays on the diseases of sheep for which Hogg had been awarded premiums by the Highland Society several years previously at Ettrickhouse. Hogg dedicated his shepherd's manual to Dirom as 'a small testimony of esteem for a gentleman who has the welfare and improvement of his country so much at heart', and it was published in June, a few months after *The Mountain Bard.* Hogg received £86 from Constable for it.[58]

The Shepherd's Guide became a classic work for shepherds, store-farmers, and agricultural improvers. A similar work published a year or two later by Sir George Steuart Mackenzie, the Convenor of the Prize Committee of the Highland Society of Scotland, makes frequent reference to it. In *A Treatise on the Diseases and Management of Sheep* (1809) Mackenzie agrees or disagrees with Hogg's opinion of various issues, but always treats it as important. On the question of protecting sheep from snow-drifts, for example, Mackenzie states, 'There cannot be a better method of enabling sheep to escape from drifting snow than such inclosures as are mentioned by Mr. Hogg'.[59]

During the autumn of 1806 Hogg had taken steps towards becoming a Dumfriesshire farmer when his second year of shepherding at Mitchelslacks finished at Whitsunday 1807. His eye had been caught by an advertisement in the *Dumfries Weekly Journal* for a meeting at Penpunt on 19 September to let the farm of Corfardine in Tynron parish on an eighteen-year lease. The farm consisted of about 300 acres: 100 of them were arable and the 'pasture ground is reckoned amongst the best in the country'. The farm was described as suitable for a family because of its 'excellent steading of new houses'. Hogg, no doubt attracted by the fine new house, must have outbid the previous tenant Thomas Hunter and any other rivals, and perhaps he offered more than the farm was worth from the tone of his announcement to Scott on 23 October:

> I have agreed for a 12 years lease of a beautifull farm and residence in Nithsdale. It is indeed very dear but if a better should cast up I am offered a good sum on the head of it, and if no better cast up I must try myself with it, and have no doubts of doing well providing I once get a sufficient stock upon it.

The first year's rent (the amount of which is unknown) would not need to be paid until the end of the first year of the lease, but Hogg would have to purchase a flock of sheep and the necessary farming equipment on first taking possession. His impatience for a home of his own, he perhaps realised, had led him into once again involving himself in a venture beyond what his capital could support. Subsequently he estimated that he had agreed to pay 'exactly one half more than it was worth'.[60] He certainly bit off more than he could chew when, only a few weeks later, he agreed to lease another Dumfriesshire farm, Locherben.

This was the 'very extensive' farm adjoining Mitchelslacks and the existing tenant, William Harkness, was almost certainly a close relation of Hogg's master, since Locherben farm had been associated with the family for generations back. It was let by auction at the King's Arms in Dumfries on the morning of Thursday, 4 December. Hogg then took a seven years' lease of Locherben at an annual rent of £430, and considered that no such bargain had been got in the district for many years, the farm being worth a hundred pounds more. In securing his bargain Hogg had, however, broken the tacit prohibition against outbidding a sitting tenant whose family had occupied the land for generations back. William Harkness and his wife, Janet Walker, also had five young children, ranging from nine-year old Thomas Harkness to Mary, who had been born in April 1805. The agent was a Writer to the Signet named William Laidlaw, brother to

Scott's neighbour at Ashiestiel, 'Laird Nippy'.[61] Whether Laidlaw was dubious that a man currently working as a hired shepherd had the necessary financial backing for such a large undertaking, or whether he shared the local assumption that Harkness was entitled to retain the family farm, he opposed Hogg's tenancy.

Initially Hogg seems to have taken Corfardine for himself and Locherben on behalf of his friend Adam Bryden of Aberlosk, but he told Bryden, 'as I am loth to give you the best and keep the worst I have a thought of keeping a share of each'. On the same day that he bid successfully for Locherben Hogg requested Bryden to 'write instantly to Mr. William Laidlaw writer in Dumfreis that you will see a sufficient stock and crop put upon the ground'. Further pressure was soon brought to bear on Hogg to relinquish his agreement. The outgoing tenant, Hogg wrote, 'persecuted me every day to have it again but finding I was too far engaged to yeild he applied to Mr. Laidlaw and the other curators who as warmly seconded his suit'. Questions were raised about Bryden's solvency.[62] Things were no doubt difficult in the farmhouse kitchen at Mitchelslacks as well, but Hogg refused to give way.

It was not a promising start to settling permanently in Closeburn parish, and in fact Hogg seems to have decided to live on the smaller farm in Tynron parish instead. Locherben would then be without a resident master, since the birth of successive children to Adam Bryden and his wife in Eskdalemuir parish suggests that his family continued to live at their old home of Aberlosk. A farm where the managing partners were not only absentees but also resented in the parish as interlopers was hardly likely to flourish. Hogg himself had undertaken to pay some share of a rent of £430 a year and the rent of Corfardine too, with almost no cash in hand, since *The Mountain Bard* would not be published until February 1807 and *The Shepherd's Guide* until June.

As Hogg waited for the Whitsunday term and his removal to Corfardine more trouble was brewing. Sometime around the previous Hallowe'en he had become the lover of one Catherine Henderson, and at the start of February she must have told him that she was pregnant. Was Hogg undecided as to whether to marry her or not? His younger brother, Robert, had decided very recently in similar circumstances to marry his lover, Elizabeth Oliver, and Hogg's subsequent behaviour suggests strongly that he was genuinely attached to Catherine and concerned for her. Catherine's family seem to have applied only the gentlest pressure to secure a marriage:

The aunt [...] ventured in full assembly of friends to propose marriage to me with her lovely niece. I said I was sure she advised me well but really I could not get time. She said I had had plenty of time since Candlesmass. "O yes said I that's very true but then the weather was so wet I could not get through the water" at which they all burst out a laughing, the girl herself among the rest and there was no more of the matter nor was there ever a frown on either side.[63]

Despite the calvinist thunders of the church against fornication it is possible to sense, here and elsewhere, the survival of an older and more relaxed approach to sexuality. The birth of a child out of wedlock, while not good news, need not end a girl's prospects in life providing she did not have a reputation for promiscuity and her family was willing to stand by her. Common sense declared that while in some cases an unexpected pregnancy would simply hasten a marriage that was likely to take place anyway, it would be unkind to the girl herself to pressurise a reluctant or unsuitable man into turning bridegroom. Hogg was not a very good proposition as a husband. He was an attractive, clever, energetic man from a decent family, but at thirty-six dissatisfied with his profession as a shepherd and rather an unsettled sort of being. He had recently leased a couple of farms on the doubtful prospect of making a profit from a book of poetry, for instance. (In fact Catherine married Hogg's much more stable cousin, David Laidlaw, in 1812.)

By the time Catherine Henderson appeared before the kirk session of Closeburn on 7 June 1807 to confess to her 'uncleanness' with 'Ja[s] Hogg lately servant at Mitchelslacks' Hogg was living at Corfardine, since Dr Yorstoun had to obtain a statement from him through the minister of Tynron parish. Hogg responded by writing two letters, one to the Rev. Yorstoun himself and the other to Catherine Henderson's brother Thomas 'in which he confesses himself the Father of her Child and Promises to take care of her and it'. Little Catherine was probably born around the end of July or early August 1807, and was baptised Catherine Hogg on 13 December 1807. Whether Hogg offered any financial support to her mother is unknown, but he certainly saw his child from time to time as she was growing up and kept in touch with her progress.[64]

Very little is known of Hogg's life during the next two and a half years. His 'Memoir' is characteristically reticent about a time he clearly wished to forget, stating that he went 'perfectly mad' but was also cheated into undertaking Corfardine 'by a great rascal, who meant to rob me of all I had'. There is more than a hint of paranoia here, but Hogg's assessment of the hopelessness of trying to run the two farms is probably accurate enough. By his own account he 'got every day out of one strait and confusion into a worse', and 'blundered and stuggled on for three years between these two places, giving up all thoughts of poetry or literature of any kind'. Perhaps Hogg's behaviour approached the recklessness of the farmer in the fourth number of his subsequent essay-periodical *The Spy*, which some of his contemporaries said was autobiographical. This farmer keeps open house for his neighbours, plying them with brandy and amusing them by playing his fiddle:

> It had no end. I was sick of them, yet I drank on; sung, and played upon the fiddle with increasing rapidity—the servants joined in the same laxity and mirth; left the door half open, and danced to my music in the kitchen. I saw my folly as usual, but could not remedy it.

Scott heard (probably from John Morrison who visited Hogg at Corfardine), that Hogg had 'neglected his sheep & forgot his sheephook a little too literally', which Hogg partly admitted, though arguing that success at Corfardine was impossible anyway. 'The truth is that your information respecting my carelessness during the time I was in Corfardan though visibly augmented and delivered in malice is not without foundation *entirely* but it proceeded wholly from being engaged wholly in a hopeless job for in any other thing that ever I took in hand you know well enough that I was diligent and faithfull to my trust'. During the early spring of 1808, disaster struck Hogg's farming operations at Corfardine when all his sheep perished in a snow-storm. His stock being 'dead out' and his financial position 'a good many pounds worse than nothing' Hogg was obliged to relinquish the farm, and he then went to live with James M'Turk, the farmer of Stenhouse in the same parish, for three months, while he considered what to do next.[65] Clearly not all Hogg's neighbours were fair-weather friends.

James M'Turk was about fifteen years Hogg's senior, with a brood of seven children, ranging from fourteen-year-old Robert down to three-year-old Jean, and a notable agricultural improver in the parish, making improvements in fences, planting, and breaking up waste lands. Like Hogg himself he seems to have been fond of sporting activities, for he gave a silver medal as the prize in an annual parish curling contest, and he was long remembered in Dumfriesshire as a person of remarkable shrewdness and unbounded generosity.[66] Hogg was grateful for this kindness, and years afterwards when he was a successful poet wrote to him as follows:

But it pleased God to take away by death all my ewes and
my lambs, and my long-horned cow, and my spotted bull, for
if they had lived, and if I had kept the farm of Corfardin, I
had been a lost man to the world, and mankind should never
have known the half that was in me. Indeed, I can never see
the design of Providence in taking me to your district at all, if
it was not to breed my acquaintance with you and yours,
which I hope will be one source of happiness to me as long
as I live. Perhaps the very circumstance of being initiated
into the mysteries of your character, is of itself sufficient compensation for all that I suffered in your country.

In after years M'Turk was an important subscriber to *The Queen's
Wake*, Hogg inviting his eldest son, Robert, to the dinner John Grieve
held to mark the poem's publication at the end of January 1813. He
is also perhaps alluded to in the poem itself: M'Turk in 'Dumlanrig'
comes to the assistance of Douglas 'with troops from Shinnel glens
and Scaur' and standing 'deep in Southron gore, | [...] legions down
before him bore'.[67]

At the beginning of May 1808, Hogg was in Edinburgh for a fortnight to seek help from his friends. He called at Constable's shop in
the High Street, but was told that no more money was due to him
from his recent publications. Scott and General Dirom were both
out of town, but Scott, with the example of Burns in mind, wondered
if Hogg might be given an appointment in the Excise. Hogg wrote to
Dirom to say that he had decided to relinquish farming after his
losses and hoped that Dirom might procure him 'an appointment as
principal shepherd to some gentleman of your acquaintance [...] or
else an Ensigncy in some regiment of foot'. Hogg's Edinburgh trip
did no good from a practical viewpoint, but he did manage to read
Scott's new poem of *Marmion* on successive visits to Constable's shop,
and on one morning alone saw two hundred and forty copies sold.
He wrote to Scott to express his particular enjoyment of the verse
epistles prefacing each canto, and to pass on rumours of a forthcoming notice by Francis Jeffrey in the *Edinburgh Review* that was reputed
to be 'bitter to the last degree' and of a parody that was going to be
published shortly. He was also obliged to ask Scott to forward money
to settle the bill for his Edinburgh lodgings before he could return to
Dumfriesshire.[68]

At some point between this visit and the end of the year, Hogg
experienced 'a long and severe illness'. He was now in his late thirties, much the same age that Robert Burns had been at his death on
21 July 1796. 'I had learned to identify myself so much with my

predecessor', he recalled in 1834, 'that I expected to die at the same age and on the very same day of the month. So when the 21st of August began to approach I grew very ill—terribly ill and told the people who were waiting on me that I feared I was going to die. They said "they hopet no" But before midnight I was so ill and so frightened that I was skirling and haudding by the blankets but after the 21st was fairly over I grew better'.[69]

While the Corfardine flock had been Hogg's own, he seems to have been using the pasture of Locherben to graze sheep for other farmers. On 18 July 1807, for example, Hogg had made an agreement to fatten and smear 139 lambs for Walter Cunningham of Catslackburn in Yarrow. He could continue with this for a while until he found a more settled occupation. He was now seriously depressed, writing to Scott, 'you must not forsake me else I'm perfectly useless I will do or be any thing you like only let me retain a place in your affections and regard'. The death of a favourite dog seemed like a bad omen:

> As to prospects, excepting those from our hills on a clear day, I have none that can be depended upon, or at least none very flattering. My poor old Hector who has twice seen me turned out of house and hold and who was grown quite gray and blind in my service, was the other day run down by a horse and got his thigh broke, and his body much crushed; although his death would be an act of mercy I cannot consent to it. God grant that the afternoon of his unfortunate masters day may s[TEAR] more serene than his [...]

Hogg's hopes of becoming a prosperous farmer had vanished. 'I have been so peculiarly unfortunate in all my endeavours to succeed in that sphere' he wrote to a friend, 'that it seems to me as if providence had some other thing to do with me, or that my directing angel were wishing to divert my thoughts into some other scene of action'.[70] His literary ambition, however, now revived.

Hogg remained at Locherben until at least the end of July 1809, but he seems to have made frequent visits to Edinburgh and to have formed a number of significant new friendships there. Travelling by stage-coach between Edinburgh and Dumfries Hogg met with James Gray, formerly a teacher in Dumfries Academy and now classics master at the Edinburgh High School. While he had been living in Dumfries, Gray had married Mary Phillips, the daughter of a local farmer, and though she had died in November 1806 after giving birth to an eighth child, Gray was still on excellent terms with her family.

The two men enjoyed discussing Border scenery and Border lore, and on parting Hogg gave his new friend a copy of *The Mountain Bard* and received an invitation to visit him at home in Buccleuch Place in Edinburgh. Gray passed his copy of Hogg's poems on to his father-in-law, and it seems more than likely that his young sister-in-law, Margaret Phillips, also read them. A little later Hogg was to meet her at Gray's house, and in 1820 she became his wife.[71]

Hogg had also formed a friendship with Eliza Izett, the wife of the senior partner of his friend John Grieve. In Edinburgh the Izetts lived at 3 St John's Street in the Canongate district, and they also had a country house and estate at Kinnaird near Dunkeld in Perthshire, where Chalmers Izett offered to let Hogg have a farm. Hogg travelled to Perthshire to inspect it, but declined the proffered kindness because he had no capital to purchase farm stock and Izett did not propose to stock the farm himself. As he explained to Eliza Izett, 'a man who has not stock sufficient to make the most of a farm, and to enable him to carry his views into execution is only an encumbrance on his Landlord which I would certainly be on Mr. Izet'. Hogg's letters to Eliza Izett were both flirtatious and friendly—he joked about determining not to be in love with her and flattered her outrageously, but confided in her sincerely. Besides enjoying Eliza Izett's company Hogg was also impressed with the musical talents of her husband's niece, Chalmers Forest. Miss Forest was an accomplished amateur musician, and not only performed his songs but set some of them to music, including 'The Flower' and 'The Moon was a-Waning'.[72]

Despite making some disparaging remarks about bluestockings, Hogg was clearly on good terms with a number of Edinburgh's literary ladies. Mary Brunton, the future novelist, was Eliza Izett's bosom friend and neighbour in St John's Street. Mary Peacock had known Hogg's idol Burns, and on 25 October 1808 married Hogg's friend James Gray. Hogg was also very taken with Janet Stuart, the 'Adeline' whose poetry he had admired in the now-defunct *Edinburgh Magazine*. The morning after their first meeting he had run about the Edinburgh booksellers' shops trying to purchase a copy of her anonymous poem, *Ode to Dr Thomas Percy* (1804), and when he got back to Locherben he wrote her a flirtatious letter signed 'your sincere friend and passionate admirer' that included a verse reworked from his song of 'The Bonny Lass of Deloraine':

> If on a shepherd she would smile
>   And tend the ewes and lambs with me
> This world would then be worth my while
>   Its charms I never yet could see

Then all her joys should cheer my heart
And all her griefs make me repine
And never from my soul should part
My dear my lovely Adeline[73]

In his 'Memoir' Hogg stated that during the time he was farming at Corfardine and Locherben he had struggled on, 'giving up all thoughts of poetry or literature of any kind', and the list of his published work during that time is certainly not a long one.[74] His increasing involvement in Edinburgh literary circles, however, was now inspiring him to write. On 11 December 1808, for instance, Hogg promised to bring some song lyrics for Miss Forest with him on his next visit to Edinburgh, 'verses […] to the tunes of Lord Eglintons auld man and the other gaelic air', at least one of which was subsequently published in *The Forest Minstrel*. He also refers to 'a dialogue betwixt the poet and the Tay', which was probably written to please Eliza Izett, since her country home at Kinnaird was set in beautiful countryside overlooking the River Tay. While staying in Edinburgh he had been working on a critical poetry anthology with two other men, entitled *Beauties of the Scottish Poets of the Present Day*, and the last of his surviving letters from Locherben, addressed to Scott on 28 July 1809, reveals that he was also attempting to write longer poems for a future volume publication:

> My occupation is so laborious here that I have no time at all to finish any large work; several smaller pieces I am frequently producing. I projected and went a good length with a large poem entitled *The Sutors of Selkirk* but from being perswaded by friends of the incongruity of the title with the matter I sticked it. The principal one on the carpet at present is one on *love* which is already advanced considerably above an hundred single stanzas it is in English and much more refined and fewer fallings off in it than any of my former ones and must propably [*sic*] make the first in my next collection but hard work precludes the probability of its speedy conclusion and arrangement.[75]

Hogg's renewed literary activity rather contradicts John Morrison's reports of constant riotous living at Locherben. Calling at Locherben in June, when the annual sheep-shearing had just finished, Morrison found both masters and men were sitting drinking whisky for most of the night while he, working on his surveying papers, heard 'the distant sound of revelling'.[76] The end of shearing was a traditional time for festivity and drinking and revelling then does not necessarily mean that nights at Locherben were always like that.

More seriously, when Morrison called with some money and a parcel from Scott he was hospitably entertained by a pretty house-keeper who, he implies, was Hogg's mistress. She said that she had left her father's house 'in a *pet*, and was a servant for the first time', her work was easy enough but she had reason to regret that she ever left home, and although she had two masters she acknowledged only 'Jamie'. According to a letter written to Scott immediately after the visit, Hogg perhaps suspected that Morrison had been too well re-ceived by her. She now wore a pretty new brooch, and Hogg sup-posed that Morrison 'found things, I suppose, pretty comfortable; for he drank tea and toddy, and passed the evening, if not the night, very agreeably; and has left a dashing character behind him'. It may be that the housekeeper's father had been unwilling for her to go to Locherben because Hogg had already got another girl pregnant in the parish, and that such fears were justified. In the partly autobio-graphical fourth number of *The Spy* mentioned previously, the narra-tor is seduced by his housekeeper, who sits up to wait for his return one winter evening after the other members of the household have gone to bed, dressed only in 'a white wrapper and single petticoat'. He is drunk and his persuading her 'to take a share of my bed until it was day, *much against her inclination*' proves to be the start of a rather unenthusiastic love-affair. Eventually, the housekeeper grows 'nearly double her natural thickness about the waist', and the narrator runs away from her and his farming difficulties together.[77]

Hogg found himself 'run aground' in Dumfriesshire. 'I gave my creditors all that I had, or rather suffered them to take it,' he wrote, 'and came off and left them', without making any proper settlement. He may have had another reason, for during the following spring, on 15 April 1810, Margaret Beattie appeared before the Closeburn kirk session to confess that she 'had brought a child in uncleanness', naming Hogg as the father. She gave the occasion of the sin as 'some time after Whitsunday last' (i.e. May 1809), corresponding with the baby's birth on 13 March 1810. Her little girl was baptised Elizabeth Hogg the following June. Hogg kept in touch with Betsy, as she was known, in later years but he seems to have been unsure of his pater-nity. Whether or not Margaret Beattie was the Locherben house-keeper, her pregnancy surely gave Hogg another reason for leaving Dumfriesshire in a hurry. He retreated to his native district, but met with a cold reception:

> On returning again to Ettrick Forest, I found the countenances
> of all my friends altered; and even those whom I had loved,

and trusted most, disowned me, and told me so to my face
[...]. Having appeared as a poet, and a speculative farmer
besides, no one would now employ me as a shepherd. I even
applied to some of my old masters, but they refused me, and
for a whole winter I found myself without employment, and
without money, in my native country [...][78]

The term 'friends' then implied blood relatives, and whatever tidings had come of his doings in Dumfriesshire Hogg expected his own family to support him. His old masters too had personal experience of his care and probity as a shepherd. Hogg was bitterly hurt. Years later he told Henry Scott Riddell in confidence 'that nothing of all his misfortunes and vexatious difficulties ever half hurt his heart so much, and rendered him so long secretly sad, as when he found *that he had no home in the Forest of Ettrick*'. He soon decided to seek a home in Edinburgh instead.

[...] in February 1810, in utter desperation, I took my plaid
about my shoulders, and marched away to Edinburgh, determined, since no better could be, to push my fortune as a literary man. It is true, I had estimated my poetical talent high
enough, but I had resolved to use it only as a staff, never as a
crutch; and would have kept that resolve, had I not been
driven to the reverse.[79]

CHAPTER THREE

The Cause of Liberty

Although Hogg described his removal to Edinburgh in February 1810 as a dramatic caesura, something that cut him off sharply from his roots in the farming community of Ettrick and threw him suddenly into the literary life of Edinburgh, the practical shift was perhaps less abrupt than it seemed. He did not abandon rural occupations entirely, since he was occasionally employed for several years to come as a valuer of pasture land. Hogg accompanied one gentleman to the Highlands to estimate a sheep-farm for him only weeks after settling in Edinburgh, and his letters refer to similar jobs on the eastern Border, in the Breadalbane district of Perthshire, and at Langholm. Hogg also acted as factor to a 'good old English lady', whose property he visited from time to time, engaging and supervising workmen there on her behalf, and he tried to obtain valuation work on the Buccleuch estates as well.[1] He also replied as an expert to Sir George Mackenzie's book on sheep with a series of three papers in Constable's *Farmer's Magazine* during 1812.[2] Moreover, Hogg had been making lengthy stays in Edinburgh ever since his failure at Corfardine, forming new friendships and establishing connections that would help him to become an Edinburgh literary man. The emphasis now fell differently, however. Hogg was no longer a Borders shepherd and farmer who also wrote poetry but a would-be metropolitan writer.

Only a few years previously, Hogg had written, 'Not being acquainted with the cross lanes, I take a weary time to traverse Edinburgh; before I can find a place that I want, I generally walk thrice as much as I need'. Like the young Thomas Gilliespie Hogg had found Edinburgh confusing:

> The continued succession of passengers along the streets–the richness and splendour of the shops,–the variety and oddity of the signs,–the rattling and justling of carriages–the elegance and magnificence of dwelling houses, and public buildings,–and above all the sublime grandeur of the Castle;–all these and many other objects overpower and bewilder a stranger.[3]

During his regular visits from Dumfriesshire, Hogg had begun to place himself. His centre was the thriving commercial street of the

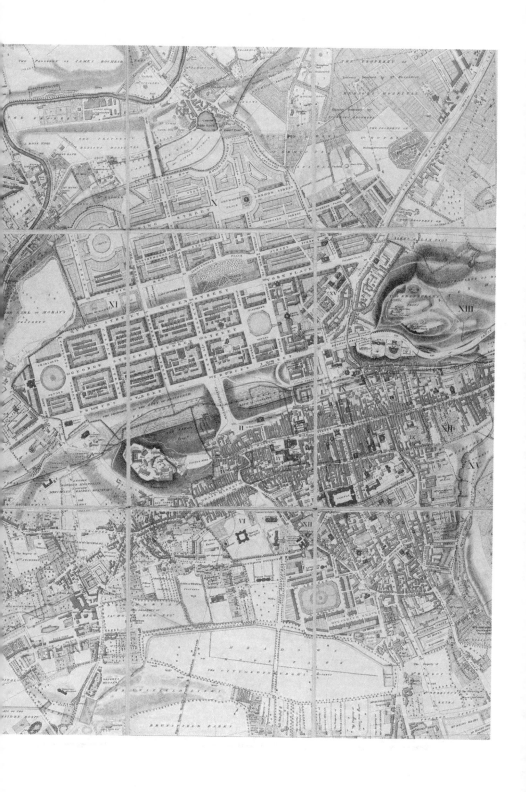

North Bridge, the main route between the Old Town and the New Town, where John Grieve's hatter's business stood. Hogg described Grieve as a true and liberal friend: 'He is some way or another convinced of my superior merit as a *poet* and nothing else influences him in the least: he has supplied me constantly with newspapers clothes, shoes, hats and pocket money whenever he knew I wanted it'. Hogg lived with Grieve and at his expense for at least the first six months of his residence in Edinburgh, and always acknowledged that he could not have survived them otherwise.[4]

To the south of the Bridge was the medieval Old Town, where myriad closes ran between the high buildings that lined the High Street, running downwards both north and south, to the North Loch and Edinburgh's Fish and Flesh markets or to the parallel commercial street of the Cowgate. The city's booksellers were still concentrated there and Edinburgh's dominant legal profession, focused around the old Scottish Parliament buildings. Further south still was the university district, and the elegant garden and mansions of George Square. To the north of the Bridge was the fashionable Georgian New Town, where Scott lived at 39 Castle Street. From the summit of Queen Street there were fine views towards the land across the firth of Forth, and the first of the New Town's long straight streets, Princes Street, was an important promenade. Hogg soon adopted the fashion of walking along it arm-in-arm with a companion for exercise, to observe the passers-by, and to hear the news of the day. The open space of Arthur's Seat in Holyrood Park and the neighbouring Salisbury Crags allowed for more energetic and solitary rambles.

Edinburgh, a true northern city, was most attractive in winter, and certainly at its busiest then. Edinburgh's leading lawyers came and went in accordance with the terms of the Court of Session, from November to March (with a three-week break for the festive season), and from May to July. Students also attended their university classes over the winter, for about six months of the year from November. During term-time Hogg now came to breakfast quite regularly with Scott in his Castle Street home in the New Town, sometimes even two or three times a week: he could be reasonably sure of enjoying an hour's conversation before Scott made his way to the Court of Session. Out of term, lawyers scattered to the country, the fashionable beauties disappeared from the public streets, and the places of public entertainment were comparatively deserted. It was during the hot, dusty summers that Hogg most regretted having no country home. Edinburgh was then an insanitary place, suffering from recurrent water shortages as well as the inevitable smells and dirt of a crowded city in hot weather.[5] A trip south to the Borders or north into the Highlands would provide a welcome respite.

Walking the city streets was educational. Hogg would grasp its contrasts, from Scott's elegantly-furnished house in Castle Street to the Old Town garrets of the poorest inhabitants, five stories perhaps above street level where 'there was no carpet, no chair, and indeed no article of furniture whatever, save two stools, two or three vessels of earthen ware [...] and a few cups and saucers'. The booksellers' shops were customary lounges, each with its distinctive character and slightly different clientele. A bookseller's shop, one Edinburgh writer remarked, 'is in a city what the barber's shop is in a village—the centre and focus of all information concerning the affairs of men—the arena for all disputation—the stage for all display'. Archibald Constable was Hogg's publisher, and his shop on the High Street was a thriving literary exchange, despite its plain appearance, 'a low dusky chamber, inhabited by a few clerks, and lined with an assortment of unbound books and stationery', without the sofas and prints of a fashionable London bookseller.[6] Hogg called there frequently, almost daily, to hear the gossip, observe what books were sold, and to read in instalments the latest volumes of poetry or issues of the *Edinburgh Review*. He was able to bring his knowledge of Scottish poetry up to date without buying copies of recently-published poems that might sell in handsome quartos for as much as a guinea. This allowed him to immerse himself in the work of his contemporaries. The Edinburgh newspapers too were on display for the convenience of callers.

Hogg also attended Edinburgh's Theatre Royal. Opened at the end of 1769, it was situated advantageously in Shakespeare Square not far from the eastern end of Princes Street at the junction of the Old Town and New Town, a plain building with a columned portico but marked out by the statues of Shakespeare and the Muses of Tragedy and Comedy surmounting it. Its auditorium was rather smaller than those of the London theatres, but the accoustics were good and it was handsomely decorated. In contrast to a modern theatre, where the spectators sit in twilight, the whole theatre was brilliantly lit and not just the stage. The Regency audience was itself part of the spectacle and felt at liberty to comment freely and audibly on the play, the actors, and the performance. Prominent figures in Edinburgh society would sit in the boxes, and their servants up in the gods, while the pit was dominated by staid citizens and young connoisseurs, lawyers and apprentices, who were less on show and less elaborately dressed. A place in the pit cost three shillings but Hogg soon became a familiar figure there, since through the kindness of the manager, Henry Siddons, son of the famous tragic actress, he had free admission. Hogg probably saw Mrs Siddons during the spring of 1810 as Lady Macbeth or as Belvidera in *Venice Preserved*.[7] A performance of Joanna Baillie's play *A Family Legend* that season encouraged Hogg's preference for distinctively Scottish tunes: it was heartening to witness the audience's enthusiasm for the native airs played by the theatre orchestra to accompany this tale of clan rivalries, in place of the staple music of 'Italian tirlie-whirlies'. Hogg may have got to know the theatre musicians, for the violinist James Dewar (who eventually became leader of the orchestra) subsequently set the songs of Hogg's *The Border Garland* to music. Hogg was particularly interested by the Scottish drama at the Theatre Royal, from the melodrama of Scott's *The Lady of the Lake* premiered on 15 January 1811 to the five-night run from 23 December that year of *Caledonia, or The Thistle and the Rose*, a three-act historical play with Scottish music.[8]

By 1813 there are signs that he was virtually a member of a theatrical claque. Anticipating the first performance on 24 March 1813 of a national tragedy entitled *The Heiress of Strathearn*, written by the antiquary John Pinkerton, for instance, Hogg reported to his friend Eliza Izett, 'We expect to have a glorious night of *sport* with Pinkerton's new tragedy to morrow evening'. He was active too in determining the failure of Sir George Mackenzie's play, *Helga the Maid of Iceland* on 22 January 1812. This was quite well received until an egotistical speech by the hero towards the end of the third act when 'from that moment every thing, however grave in itself, was transmuted into the ludicrous, and this temper of mind was improved to the prejudice of the performance, by several persons conveniently dispersed in different parts. There was, in particular, one determined enemy, with a catcall, who shewed, by the skillful management of this instrument of his spleen, that he was well versed in theatrical warfare'. Hogg admitted that Helga had 'died of a quincey the first night' and that he was one of the people who had 'helped the poor girl away'.[9] The subtitle of the despised drama, incidentally, was 'The Rival Minstrels': in a bardic contest at the court of the King of Sweden the hero, Edgar, defeats his rival Haco. Hogg also seems to have attended another kind of musical contest at the theatre, the Highland Society's annual competition of pipers. Hogg's familiarity with the Edinburgh theatre may have indirectly influenced the contest between minstrels which forms the narrative framework of his most famous poem, *The Queen's Wake.*

Besides the licensed Theatre Royal there were a number of other public entertainments on offer in Edinburgh. The professional strongman Belzoni, for example, demonstrated not only feats of strength but also tricks illustrating the principles of hydrostatics and hydraulics. A panorama of the scenery described in Scott's *The Lady of the Lake* was exhibited on the Mound, and there were annual exhibitions of Scottish painting under the aegis of Alexander Nasmyth and his friends in York Place.[10] Hogg, with his 'quick eye in observing the operations of nature', was greatly attracted to the visual arts, and it may have been at this time that he was initiated into the basement mysteries of the clothiers' shop of David Bridges and Son in the Lawnmarket. The shop was a meeting place for writers, artists, and theatrical people of every description, and the son was known to have forwarded the interests of more than one aspiring painter. Underneath the business premises was a room containing his 'bits', pictures and sketches given or loaned to him by various artists. A table contained books of engravings and other art-books, and plaster casts of famous statuary decorated the cellar.[11] Various reading-rooms offered an alternative meeting-place to the fashionable coffee-rooms. Hogg could find a comfortable fireside by which to read the newspapers and other recent periodicals, buy stationery for the writing of letters, and tickets to public entertainments and for the lottery.

Always a sociable, convivial man, Hogg now got to know his fellow-poets in person as well as print. A letter from the weaver-poet Robert Tannahill to his friend James King of 1 April 1810 records Hogg's expanding literary acquaintance in Edinburgh as well as on a recent visit to Paisley:

> Let me know if you be acquainted with the poems of Jas Hogg, the Ettricke Shepherd. He has written a number of excellent Ballads founded on Traditionary stories of the Border. He called on me last week […]. He is a clever intelligent fellow about our own age We had a good deal of conversation over the poets of the day—he tells me he has been in company with Walter Scott H M'Neil, and T. Campbell and other of our *Scotch Worthies*

A company of six or seven men, including the musician R. A. Smith, spent a jovial time together in the club-room of the Sun Inn, where Hogg, 'lively, healthy, and *off-hand*', formed a noticeable contrast to the 'quiet, delicate, and unassuming' Tannahill.[12] Tannahill drowned himself on 17 May, an event which in Hogg's subsequent recollections merged with their Paisley meeting, seeming as if he had scarcely reached Edinburgh before hearing of Tannahill's sad end. Hogg lamented him as 'the best imitator of Burns who hath yet appeared', suggesting that for all their apparent dissimilarity he nevertheless identified himself with Tannahill.[13]

His own prospects in Edinburgh were by no means encouraging. He was effectively living on the charity of his boyhood friend, John Grieve, and having decided to become a professional writer, he found that no-one wanted to employ him as such.

> On going to Edinburgh, I found that my poetical talents were rated nearly as low there as my shepherd qualities were in Ettrick. It was in vain that I applied to newsmongers, booksellers, editors of magazines, &c. for employment. Any of these were willing enough to accept of my lucubrations, and give them publicity, but then there was no money going–not a farthing; and this suited me very ill.

Perhaps the amateur poetry of the Edinburgh periodicals might be profitable to an author such as Hogg, however, when republished in volume form. By April 1810 a forthcoming volume of songs by Hogg and a number of his fellow-contributors to the *Scots Magazine* was advertised:

> [...] The Minstrel of the Forest; a selection of *new* Scottish songs, adapted to the most favourite national airs, and divided into the following classes: *pathetic, love, national,* and *comic* songs; furnished by the celebrated *Ettrick Shepherd,* and a few others whose manner and diction seemed most contrasted. This, we would conclude, cannot fail of being an acquisition to the lovers of Scottish song[14]

Hogg must have applied to Archibald Constable, the publisher of *The Mountain Bard,* to publish his song-book *The Forest Minstrel* within weeks of his arrival in Edinburgh, perhaps with the financial backing of his friend John Grieve since the title-page wording 'Printed for the Editor' suggests some form of authorial subsidy. Although Constable was 'rather averse' to the project, he agreed to print a thousand copies costing five shillings each and to give Hogg half the profits. It might, Hogg hoped, be only the first of an annual series of such volumes, since the lovers of Scottish song would surely be pleased 'if a small collection of new songs were mutually furnished once a-year by the authors of the present day'.[15]

The Forest Minstrel was eventually published in August, and combines Hogg's earliest songs written in Ettrick with others arising from an Edinburgh context. Hogg's title-page with its motto from the closing lines of Scott's *The Lay of the Last Minstrel* associates the collection with the Buccleuch family in Ettrick Forest as well as with the shepherds and lasses of Hogg's songs of rural courtship. Scott's minstrel sang to a past Duchess of Buccleuch and Hogg's collection was dedicated to her modern equivalent, the young Countess of Dalkeith, 'the Stay of Genius and the Shield of Merit'. *The Forest Minstrel* also contained a number of songs celebrating the role of the heads of the Scott family as beneficent landlords in the Scottish Borders, marking birthday celebrations for Henry, 3rd Duke of Buccleuch or his heir, the Earl of Dalkeith. National bonds were celebrated by the patriotic 'Donald Macdonald', 'Scotia's Glen's, and 'The British Tar', while the human costs of the national struggle with Napoleonic France were signalled in 'The Soldier's Widow', 'The Beggar', or 'Cauld is the Blast'. Hogg's collection also associates itself with Edinburgh music-making—with the theatre and with the North Bridge music-publisher John Hamilton, to whom readers were invited to communicate suggestions for Scottish tunes for Hogg's lyrics. *The Forest Minstrel* is meant for the young lady at her piano, reflecting the evenings spent by Hogg in the Izett drawing-room where he had probably first heard one of his songs with a piano accompaniment by Miss Forest. Eliza Izett's departure from Edinburgh for her Perthshire country house of Kinnaird is memorialised in 'The Bogles' with 'My bonny Eliza is fled frae the town, | An' left her poor Jamie her loss to bemoan'. 'The British Tar' seems designed for the theatre, the singing verses of one generic British sailor being interrupted by the comical comments of another 'Jack Tar' asserting British naval supremacy: 'The rest of the sailors of Europe, Jack, d'ye see, may lie on deck and fish eels and flounders, for d—n their hulks if we'll let them do any thing else'. Hogg's five contributors, T. M. Cunningham, William Laidlaw, John Grieve, James Gray and John Ballantyne, also represent both his Ettrick and his Edinburgh life as well as the collection's origins in the pages of the *Scots Magazine*.[16]

As the first major work of a professional literary man, *The Forest Minstrel* was a disaster, resulting in very little public attention and no payment from sales, though it is possible that the Countess of Dalkeith subsequently sent Hogg the handsome sum of a hundred guineas in acknowledgement of his dedication. During Hogg's early months in Edinburgh he must have formed and abandoned a number of other literary designs. One appears to have been preparing the work of the recently-deceased William Isaac Roberts (1786–1806) of Bristol for the press. The *Scots Magazine* for October 1810 noted:

> Mr Hogg has lately edited the posthumous works of Mr Roberts, a young man who evinced, it is said, great genius. These poems will be sold for the benefit of his family, who reside in Bristol, and are accompanied with a very interesting account of his life. He died at the age of 25, of a consumption.[17]

Hogg's hand cannot be traced, however, in *Poems and Letters* by Roberts of 1811.

The thought of the early deaths of Roberts and Tannahill was no doubt rendered even more depressing by the spectacle of some of Scott's literary protégés, such as William Scott Irving. Irving lived with his wife and family in Edinburgh in great poverty, writing screeds of poems in imitation of Scott and later Byron, and ignoring all the attempts of Scott and his other friends to provide regular employment as a teacher of writing, arithmetic, geometry, and book-keeping. R. P. Gillies remarked that 'his poetical propensity was a monomania that came betwixt him and every rational pursuit' and in 1818 he finally committed suicide. Hogg wanted recognition as a true poet, the successor to Robert Burns, rather than to be placed in the Irving category. When he told the Rev. James Nicol, however, that he felt he would 'yet live to be compared with Burns' Nicol told the story as 'a bitter jest' against him.[18]

During his residence in Edinburgh Hogg continued to seek out traces of his hero. Hogg's friend James Gray had included the poet's sons among his pupils when he had taught in Dumfries Academy between 1794 and 1801, and his second wife Mary Peacock had also met and corresponded with Burns briefly. Gray warmly defended Burns against the detractors who had labelled him as vicious, declaring that 'gigantic genius is his great crime; his unbending integrity is a satire on men of feeble and selfish minds'. He described the experience of those who, like himself, had known the poet in Dumfries:

> They not unfrequently enjoyed with him the morning walk, saw him clear and unclouded [...]. In the bosom of his own family, he was seen superintending the education of a son worthy of his culture; explaining to a boy of nine years of age, the beauties of Gray's Progress of Poesy, or pouring on his soul a love of the great and sublime in character, as they live in the immortal portraits of Gibbon, Hume, or Robertson[19]

Gray was on excellent terms with the surviving members of Robert
Burns's family. The poet's widow paid a visit to Edinburgh at about
this time and at Gray's house at 4 Buccleuch Place Hogg became
intimately acquainted with the woman he had once glanced at curiously during church services in Dumfries. He 'scarcely ever met a
woman, either high or low, who improved as much on acquaintance.
She had a great deal of good sense and good nature'. Mrs Burns
praised her husband's tenderness towards his family and uniform
good temper: 'Na, na, poor fellow; his complaints were a' of himsel!
He never complained either of the bairns or me. He never said a
misbehadden word to me a' the days o' his life'. Hogg also sought
out Burns's Chloris, the 'ruin of a fine woman', who kept a lock of
his hair in a box, and Hogg 'heard by her voice that she had once
sung well'. A more respectable friend of the poet was Robert Ainslie,
and Hogg was greatly amused by the contrast between what he termed
the 'hipperty-skipperty' style of Burns's epistle to Ainslie and the
rather stolid humdrum Edinburgh citizen he had become, 'a down-
right honest, sleepy-headed, kind-hearted gentleman, and his good
humour never failing him, not even in his sleep, with which he generally favours the company once or twice in an evening'.[20]

Gilbert Burns, the poet's brother, became a friend. On one occasion Hogg was sent for by James Gray to join a party in his house,
including Gilbert Burns and Ainslie, who were plotting to obtain a
sight of a portrait of Burns jealously guarded by the widow of Peter
Taylor, the artist who had painted it. Several of the party had known
Burns and were qualified to judge of the likeness, while Hogg had
previously met the lady's companion, a Miss Dudgeon, in company
with Eliza Izett and her friend Mary Brunton. Gray, Ainslie, and
Gilbert Burns all praised the likeness while Mrs Taylor related how
the poet had taken a liking to her late husband at an evening party
and sat to him on three successive mornings afterwards.[21]

James Gray shared Burns's radicalism, being 'a violent democrate'
who flew into a rage at the recollection of the Board of Excise haul-
ing Burns over the coals for his political principles. He could write of
Mary Wollstonecraft with sympathy, and abhorred the slave trade
and every manifestation of the use of unscrupulous power over the
weak. When the daughter of Francis Place, the celebrated Radical
Tailor of Westminster, became a governess in Edinburgh the Grays
were kind to the homesick girl. Her father wrote to Edward
Wakefield, a mutual friend who shared Gray's enthusiasm for the
Lancastrian educational system:

My daughter writes me the most satisfactory accounts of M^r and Mrs Gray she is quite happy with them, and too independent and too wise to be unhappy with the proud mean people with whom she resides—she will leave them in the Autumn—they do all they can to prevent her seeing or visiting any one and wonder she can think of keeping such people (as the Gray's) company—and they think that as she was paid to come and teach their children she has no business to do any thing else[22]

The Grays seem to have been at the centre of a literary culture for those with more intelligence and talent than money and social position, but one which has been less written about than that of the elite circle of Jeffrey, Cockburn, and Scott. Gray and his friends, for instance, had founded a Literary Association in 1807, the members of which met weekly at each others' houses, and which continued intermittently up to 1821. The titles of some of his own papers have survived. On 22 January 1808, for example, he spoke 'On the character of the tragic poet Aeschylus', and on 1 June 1810 'On the history of the poetry of the North'. James Ballantyne, Scott's printer, was a member and in later years treated the company to selections from the Waverley Novels as they passed through the press.[23]

One evening at Buccleuch Place in 1810 Hogg met a 'black-eyed Nithsdale lassie' named Margaret Phillips, who was on a visit to her brother-in-law accompanied by a cousin. Susan Phillips was not only good-looking but had the prospect of inheriting a fortune. After dinner when the ladies had retired Hogg was asked what he thought of Miss Susan Phillips and replied unhesitatingly, 'Margaret's the lass for me'. On subsequent visits he would look up at the window as he approached the Grays' house in Buccleuch Place to catch a glimpse of her sitting there reading. He teased her about her little tricks of speech such as the exclamation "'Pon my word', and probably flirted outrageously with her.[24] She was in a theatre party with him on 17 November 1810, and Hogg composed several songs about her in which her 'glossy een, sae dark an' wily' featured and she was described as 'Sae sweet, sae artless, an' sae bonny'. When she returned to Dumfriesshire he wrote her a tender, humorous song, beginning, 'Ah Peggy! since thou'rt gane away | An' left me here to languish'. An extract from his 'Love Pastoral' was also addressed to her, though not the whole poem, which contained passages of frank eroticism better suited to the gentlemanly readership of the *Scots Magazine*. After admiring his beloved's complexion, for instance, the poet moves on to fantasise about her concealed breasts:

Her bonny breast, sae fair and dink,
  Nae man may safely ponder on;
But ye may sigh, an' ye may think
  Of rosebud on an ivory cone;

Or cream-curd frae the silver cup,
  Sae gelid an' sae round to see,
An' plantit on its yielding top
  A ripe red little strawberry.[25]

They corresponded, a mildly improper proceeding on the part of a marriageable young lady. Margaret Phillips's early letters to Hogg have not survived but his are admiring and playful, affectionate and teasing rather than passionate—he must have been well aware that he was not in a position to marry a girl from a well-to-do farming background. He told her that he loved her and then qualified the declaration with a humorous 'do not be angry with me my dear Margaret—I am not courting you—nay I do not believe I would take you in a present (though it might make me cry to refuse you)'.[26]

Besides mingling with James Gray's intellectual, radical milieu, Hogg tried to make a mark in Edinburgh by celebrating local personalities, places, and events in the public prints, perhaps with the example of Robert Ferguson in mind. In 'The Dawn of July', published in the *Edinburgh Evening Courant* of 2 July 1810, Hogg celebrates the warmth and beauty of a summer morning, the rosy blush of 'sweet summer's queen' being a pleasurable response to the sight of 'EDINA, set mid hills of dew, | And spires that bore the welkin blue'. A contrasting poem memorialises the unofficial political ruler of Scotland, Henry Dundas, first Viscount Melville. He had come to Edinburgh to attend the funeral of an old friend, was taken suddenly ill on arrival, and died on the day of the funeral he had planned to attend. Edina on this occasion was told to veil her haughty brow, since her prop and shield had gone. The oak, rather than a lowly flower, should wave above the grave of this potentate. Hogg's 'Lament for Lord Melville' was published in the *Edinburgh Star* of 31 May 1811, a welcome poem on a topical news item.[27] A series of 'Epitaphs on Living Characters' was begun in the pages of the *Scots Magazine* in June 1810, with snapshots of Francis Jeffrey, the most important critic of Scotland, and Walter Scott, her foremost poet. As the influential editor of the *Edinburgh Review* Jeffrey is styled 'Bonaparte the second', since 'The one kept the monarchs of Europe in awe; | But this to the genius of Europe gave law'. The epitaph for Scott, though overall a tender lament for him as a Borders poet mourned by the country

maidens, also mocks Scott's energy and and parodies his early poetry like 'William and Helen' in asserting, 'No hand could stay his
rapid haste; | Thro' fire and flood he furious flew'. The other Edin-
burgh notables and eccentrics of the projected series of 'Epitaphs on
Living Characters' ranged from a radical banker from India, Dr John
Borthwick Gilchrist, through the Shakespeare Square brothel-keeper
Mrs Quin ('all her pre-eminence, all her demerit, | Was dealing so
fair in the flesh and the spirit!'), to Archibald Constable's tactless
and offensive business partner, Alexander Gibson Hunter, whose
soul Hogg predicted was destined for hell and his body to 'scream
like a goat at the grand resurrection'.[28] These ephemeral poems have
a Regency energy and roughness that are still appealing, even though
most of Hogg's targets are now forgotten.

Publicity was desirable, of course, but Hogg also required an income. With his characteristic mixture of rashness and obstinacy, he
decided that if periodicals really only produced an income for their
owners, then he must become a periodical owner as well as a contributor. On 1 September 1810 the first issue of his second Edinburgh literary venture, a weekly paper entitled *The Spy: A Periodical
Paper of Literary Amusement and Instruction* was published. This was a
bold venture, and begun without assurance of literary support. James
Gray and his circle and Hogg's fellow-contributors to the poetry
section of the old *Edinburgh Magazine* and the *Scots Magazine* did write
for *The Spy*, but in his 'Memoir' Hogg stated that they rallied round
only once the paper was already underway. Potentially, Hogg's most
significant supporter was Walter Scott, but although he became
Hogg's first subscriber he refused to contribute. The essay periodical, Scott reminded him, was a form particularly associated with
politeness, with manners and moral instruction, and readerly expectations were governed by the standard works of Joseph Addison
(*The Spectator*), Samuel Johnson (*The Rambler*) and Henry Mackenzie
(*The Mirror* and *The Lounger*). Did Hogg not think he was venturing
on 'dangerous ground'? Hogg replied, characteristically, 'Naething
venture naething won'.[29]

Finding a publisher (or at least a printer) for the work was no
easier, and Hogg tried all his acquaintances in the trade in turn:

> I tried Walker and Greig, and several printers, offering them
> security to print it for me.–No; not one of them would print
> it without a bookseller's name to it as publisher. 'D–n them,'
> said I to myself, as I was running from one to another, 'the
> folks here are all combined in a body'. Mr Constable laughed
> at me exceedingly, and finally told me he wished me too well

> to encourage such a thing. Mr. Ballantyne was rather more
> civil, and got off by subscribing for so many copies, and giv-
> ing me credit for ten pounds worth of paper. David Brown
> would have nothing to do with it, unless some gentleman,
> whom he named, should contribute. At length, I found an
> honest man, James Robertson, a bookseller in Nicolson Street,
> whom I had never before seen or heard of, who undertook it
> at once on my own terms [...]

Robertson's chief stock-in-trade was the chapbook, and the physical
appearance of the eight-page fourpenny weekly paper was not pre-
possessing. The editorial persona of the Spy himself also marked
Hogg's venture off from elite literary culture. The Spy presents himself as an alienated figure by comparison with his predecessors in
the essay-periodical tradition. His reader is told that 'though I am
bound to tell the truth, I am not bound to tell the whole truth; and
the omissions which I chuse to make have very little chance of being
discovered'. Unlike Addison's Mr Spectator he has no club, and, far
from passing unnoticed as a member of the society he observes, has
an uncanny ability to take on the thoughts and features of others that
renders him conspicuous and leads him into difficulties. He fails as
a preacher through taking on the feelings of a member of his congregation, and nearly drowns by trying to empathise with a party of
young girls while out walking. When he frequents the booksellers'
shops the clerks complain that 'they are eternally plagued with that
long, lean, hungry looking d–l'.[30] Hogg himself acted the part of Mr
Spy in Robertson's print-shop:

> [...] his first printer and publisher did not even know who
> the editor was, but took him always for one who transacted
> business between them, in order to keep the real one con-
> cealed. The inquiries concerning the author, and the obser-
> vations on the work which he witnessed in that shop, were
> certainly the most amusing scenes that can well be conceived.

The production of the work conducted Hogg into the subterranean
world of the Cowgate, where in company with James Robertson
and his workmen he indulged in heavy drinking that his 'respectable acquaintances' knew nothing about. Robertson sent for him at
lunchtime to consult about the weekly number of *The Spy*, Hogg recollected, 'and then we uniformly went down to a dark house in the
Cowgate, where we drank whisky and ate rolls with a number of
printers, the dirtiest and leanest-looking men I had ever seen. My
youthful habits having been so regular, I could not stand this; and

though I took care, as I thought, to drink very little, yet, when I went out, I was at times so dizzy, I could scarcely walk; and the worst thing of all was, I felt that I was beginning to relish it'.[31] Corrections were then made in the course of the print-run, whereas a more professional printer would probably have made corrections at the proof stage before any of the copies were produced.

Despite these disadvantages the early numbers of *The Spy* were well received, a number of the literary men who were sent the first issue as a sample choosing to subscribe. Although Hogg began his paper with Scott as his sole subscriber, he had 'upwards of 100 esq's exclusive of others' on his subscription list by the time the second issue was distributed, and was actively seeking for socially prestigious names to add to his list. Even though seventy-three people cancelled their subscriptions on the appearance of a story in the fourth number in which a Berwickshire farmer is seduced by his housekeeper and deserts her in her pregnancy, Hogg could still thank his subscribers, 'those highly respectable individuals', for their support, and boast of his contributors as 'some of the greatest geniuses of the age'. The appearance in the ninth issue of a letter from Scott, introducing two poems by John Leyden, argues that after he had seen some of the early issues Scott thought better of the work than he had expected.

Having a keen eye to the printing and production of his work, Hogg used his subscription list to secure the services of a better printer and publisher. His appeal to Archibald Constable to 'save The poor Spy from public execution for a year or two' fell on deaf ears, but with the backing of John Grieve he was able to transfer *The Spy* to Andrew and James Aikman after the first quarter-year. The Aikmans printed the *Edinburgh Star* newspaper, and produced a more professional-looking journal, with a clearer type-face and fewer errors. They too must have been impressed by the work, for they were willing to go to the trouble and expense of advertising it in other Edinburgh newspapers than their own.[32] Relations between Hogg and the Aikman firm were clearly more distant than his relations with James Robertson, and it seems likely that his new printer was sometimes inclined to censor the work. Andrew Aikman later gave a sour and embittered account of Hogg's relations with the firm, claiming that Hogg's list of subscribers was misrepresentative and that he had anticipated profits that never became due in retaining money paid to him for some of the weekly issues. However, the very fact that Aikmans produced thirty-nine issues of *The Spy* to complete a full year suggests that at the time they augured well enough of it. It would have been a simple matter to conclude the paper, for instance, after they had produced thirteen issues. Although subsequent volume sales were vital to the success of an essay-periodical, a volume of the half-year's issues was produced and advertised and the periodical could conveniently have been concluded at that point.[33]

Scott was unusual among Hogg's contributors in that he was already in 1810 an internationally-acclaimed poet and a household name, an unquestioned member of the literary elite. Hogg also secured a poem from Robert Southey, somehow. His other contributors, however, represented another social stratum: teachers, Presbyterian ministers, women, printers, and journalists. As *The Spy* became established it attracted the amateur writers whose work had previously found an outlet in the *Edinburgh Magazine* and *Scots Magazine*. Some of them, such as James Gray and the members of his radical circle, were personal friends. Others, such as the prosperous lawyer, Robert Sym, Hogg only became acquainted with subsequently. Welcome though this support for his paper was, however, Hogg aimed to take rank not with Edinburgh's secondary literati but as a national poet whose work would endure far beyond the ephemeral weekly issues of *The Spy*.[34]

Hogg was quite serious in comparing his own periodical essays with those of Johnson and Addison, and he wanted others to compare them seriously and impartially. In the final issue of *The Spy* Hogg revealed that he had presented papers by Samuel Johnson to his literary advisors as his own compositions, and his own compositions as 'the productions of such and such gentlemen, famous for their literary abilities'. The papers were, alas, assessed according to the names attached to them, and Hogg appealed for a more accurate assessment to 'the awards of posterity'. The Edinburgh literary world, he felt, was engaged in a conspiracy against him. In this paper the Spy is not simply an alienated observer but a condemned criminal ripe for execution, comparing himself to 'the culprit who has always persisted in maintaining an untruth, until his last moments, when he is obliged to speak, or for evermore be silent;—then it is that almighty truth prevails: of course, the last speech and confession of every person is sealed with a stamp so sacred, that the surmises of doubt are hushed to silence. This, then, is the last speech and testimony of the Spy [...]'. He has been persecuted not only by enemies 'swelling with the most rancorous spite' but also by pretended friends who 'took every method in their power to lessen the work in the esteem of others, by branding its author with designs the most subversive of all civility and decorum, and which, of all others, were the most

distant from his heart'. Besides expressing his mild paranoia, however, Hogg also showed his courage and his intention to test his
literary fate again, in thanking his true friends for their support and
assuring them that 'in whatever vocation he next appears, their favours will be doubly dear to him'.[35]

Besides rivalling the great British essayists in *The Spy*, Hogg also
tried to claim rank among contemporary Scottish poets. In one three-
part dream-vision, a Mr Giles Shuffleton puts on something like a
magic lantern show for the Spy and his friend. Each Scottish poet's
work is embodied in the form of his attendant muse, and judged
according to her performance during the exhibition. Besides James
Hogg, the poets represented are Walter Scott, Thomas Campbell,
John Leyden, James Grahame, Hector Macneill, James Nicol, William
Gillespie, James Montgomery, Thomas and Allan Cunningham, and
James Kennedy. There is also a separate category of poetesses, comprising Joanne Baillie, Anne Bannerman, Janet Stuart, and Anne
Grant. Although Mr Shuffleton denies any hierarchical significance
in the order in which the muses appear, claiming that he has given
no precedence to merit but 'placed those next to each other, who
were similar in appearance or whose manners formed the most striking contrast', it is noticeable that the most celebrated poets in the
male list, Scott and Campbell, do appear first. The most distinguished
woman poet, Joanna Baillie, also precedes all others of her sex. Hogg
thus attempts to conceal the significance of his own place in this
order, which is immediately after Scott and Campbell. Hogg's muse,
a country girl, the 'minstreless of the mountains', it is implied, would
receive even more attention were it not for the spectators 'having
been so dazzled with the splendour of the two last ladies' and for the
fact that snobbery leads them to conceal their interest in 'a girl so
low bred'. Despite the failure of *The Forest Minstrel*, Hogg claims third
place in the league-table of Scotland's national poets, though his standing is not generally acknowledged or recognised.

In the last of the three Shuffleton papers a court of Reason is held
to rank the poets according to the judgment of posterity, but it is
disabled by the literary world of Edinburgh. Scott and Campbell
each have their party who agitate for them to be proclaimed the first
of the Scottish poets, and Scott is given that distinction simply because his own party is the most numerous and the most strident and
can temporarily dethrone Reason. Scott's poem *The Lady of the Lake*
is acknowledged by Reason to deserve poetic immortality, but once
this is acknowledged the original purpose of the court, to judge of
the permanent merits of all the poets whose muses had previously

appeared, is abandoned. The court of Reason is replaced by 'a new judgment hall for poor authors, over which they made him [i.e. Scott] president'.[36]

In retrospect *The Spy* seems more important for Hogg's development as a prose writer than as a poet, exercising and developing the talent he had shown in the entertaining and often substantial notes to *The Mountain Bard* of 1807. By the end of the year's weekly issues of *The Spy* he had demonstrated his ability to detail the customs of the Scottish Borders (no. 12), to tell ghost stories and tales of Providential justice (nos. 13, 18), to write exercises in the picaresque (nos. 3–4) and the satirical (no. 48), and to explore gentle comedy (no. 16) and tales of country life and missing heirs (nos. 24–26 and 49 with 51). *The Spy* contains early versions of some of his best-known, best-loved tales such as 'The History of Duncan Campbell', 'The Adventures of Basil Lee', and 'Love Adventures of Mr George Cochrane'. The core of his wonderful *Winter Evening Tales* of 1820 is *The Spy* of 1810–11. Hogg may have been disappointed that his ambitions as a poet had not yet been realised, but by the end of August 1811 he had undoubtedly taken the first steps towards a future career as a writer of prose fiction.

At this point Hogg's chances of establishing himself in Edinburgh as a professional literary man did not look promising. After eighteen months of subsisting largely on the charity of his friend, John Grieve, Hogg seemed no nearer to earning an income than he had been on his arrival in Edinburgh in February 1810. In the estimation of his fellow-citizens he had produced only 'fourpenny papers an' daft shilly-shally sangs'. Far from being rated below the rank to which his genius led him to aspire it was considered that his talents for self-publicity were somewhat in advance of his claims to fame, that 'his celebrity was more than equal to the merit of any thing he had produced'. At the start of his year's work on *The Spy* Hogg must have been hopeful, for he apparently took independent lodgings in Edinburgh. After it was finished, he moved again, this time to a large flat he had taken at an annual rent of £36 on the High Street, above the shop of the bookseller Peter Hill. By taking fellow-lodgers Hogg could divide the rent and live in the centre of Edinburgh at modest cost. When his brother William asked if Hogg would lodge his eldest son, Robert, if he came to town to attend the Edinburgh High School, Hogg replied that he had reserved only a part of the flat for himself— 'If Robert comes here I must have a room for him too'.[37]

Hogg continued his education as a writer through physical closeness to Edinburgh's culture, gaining access to the latest publications through visits to bookseller's shops and reading-rooms, by attending the theatre and other public exhibitions. Perhaps he also considered a more formal course of study through the Edinburgh Institution, which held classes on Tuesday and Friday evenings in St Andrews Chapel in Carruber's Close off the High Street. The Edinburgh Institution, which depended solely on the contributions of its members for support, existed 'to afford Lectures on scientific and literary subjects, to those who are prevented by their professional duties from attending academical prelections', and during the winter of 1810–11 offered lectures on Astronomy, Belles Lettres, Elocution, and Chemistry and during the winter of 1811–12 on Natural Philosophy, Meteorology, Electricity and Galvanism, the Philosophy of History, and Oratory. Each member paid a guinea a session for this substitute for university lectures, and was entitled to a ladies ticket for the session as well as to twenty 'strangers tickets', each presumably admitting a guest on a single occasion.[38] Although there is no evidence of Hogg's having attended any of these lectures, there were firm links between the Edinburgh Institution and a debating society named the Forum, in which he certainly did participate and which he viewed as an important part of his literary training. He wrote, 'I never was so much advantaged by any thing as by that society; for it let me feel, as it were, the pulse of the public, and precisely what they would swallow, and what they would not'. The meetings of both societies were held in the same building, and one at least of the lecturers at the Edinburgh Institution, John Christison, subsequently served as Treasurer to the Forum.[39]

The first public meeting of the Forum was held in the evening of Thursday, 4 April 1811, admission by free ticket obtainable from any of the members, and the subject of the debate, designed to attract able speakers, was 'Which is the best field for the display of eloquence, the Pulpit, the Senate, or the Bar?'. Admission to subsequent debates was by sixpenny ticket, and any profits after the expenses had been covered was donated to a variety of charitable causes. During the first season from 11 April to 13 June 1811 £92-10 was disbursed from the takings of £115-17-6, and divided between charities such as the Edinburgh and Canongate Charity Workhouses, the Royal Infirmary and public dispensary, and the Gratis Sabbath School Society. One week's profits were allocated to 'Private objects of charity under the sanction of Dr. Sanders', and another two to help British prisoners of war and the Portugese people suffering during the Peninsular campaign against Napoleon.[40]

As a founder-member of the Forum Hogg rediscovered the pleasures of the debating society in which he had participated as a shepherd at Blackhouse in the 1790s. The society's objectives were thoroughly congenial to him: to 'engage the inhabitants of Edinburgh in frequent deliberations on literary subjects—to present instruction in an attractive dress—to combine utility with amusement—to exercise and invigorate the powers of reasoning and judging'. At first, though, his respectable Edinburgh friends advised him not to participate in the Forum debates, which may have been feared as potential hotbeds of political radicalism.

> All my friends were averse to my coming forward in the Forum as a public speaker, and tried to reason me out of it, by representing my incapacity to harangue a thousand people in a speech of half an hour. I had, however, given my word to my associates, and my confidence in myself being unbounded, I began, and came off with flying colours. We met once a week. I spoke every night, and sometimes twice the same night; and, though I sometimes incurred pointed disapprobation, was in general a prodigious favourite.

At the end of the first season Hogg gave a mocking parody of the debates in which he had participated. Malise, a name taken from Scott's *The Lady of the Lake*, visits the Trossachs in no. 44 of *The Spy*, published on 29 June 1811. Sitting on the top of the mountain of Ben-More, Malise reflects that his station in life is literally higher than that of King George III himself, 'a specimen of Forum reasoning'.

> I believe it is generally allowed, Sir, that the depression, or elevation of a man's mind, is in a great measure conformable to the disposition of his bodily frame; if this holds good in all cases, it is evident that nothing can contribute so much to the elevation of his sentiments, as placing him on the top of a very high hill. I think this might be demonstratively proved Sir; for, consider, that the body is the seat, or throne of the mind; that while in this state of existence they cannot subsist asunder; of course, where the body is, there must the mind be also; will any man then venture to deny that mind to be elevated, which is 4000 feet above the level of the sea?[41]

Hogg also composed a musical farce entitled 'The Forum, a Tragedy for Cold Weather', mimicking the formality of some of the society's presidents and the ludicrous manner and speeches of some of the members, himself included. All the same, he prepared carefully for the weekly debates, writing out his speeches beforehand. On one occasion when the question was 'Is Marriage or Celibacy the happier State?' Hogg was the first speaker on the side of celibacy, and after the president had proposed the question and the opening speech for marriage had been made, rose to reply. After a promising beginning, when 'he dwelt amongst "squalling weans and scolding Kates"' with great energy, carrying the audience along with him, he paused, lost the thread of his argument, and had to consult the written notes in his pocket.[42]

During the first season the biggest audience, judging by the takings, was something around five hundred people, and after February 1812 in the second winter season the meetings were transferred to the Freemason's Hall in Niddry Street to accommodate even larger numbers. This too was overcrowded at times. One debate at least had to be postponed 'on account of the great crowd at the House' and careful instructions were issued to those arriving in carriages so that traffic jams would be avoided. At the end of the second season in June 1812 the Forum was dissolved after a spate of General Meetings, and reformed as two separate societies, each considering itself the successor of the original Forum and entitled the 'Forum' and 'Edinburgh Forum' respectively. The party comprising the Edinburgh Forum, to which Hogg adhered, wished for 'new regulations, more fitted to give efficiency to its purposes, and better calculated to prevent improper individuals from acquiring the character and privileges of Members'.[43]

The Edinburgh Forum began its winter season in November 1812 by announcing its principles to be the same as those of its predecessor, 'all Subjects of a Political and Religious nature being excluded from discussion, and the free proceeds of admission devoted to charitable and benevolent purposes'. There was to be a Board of Charity to select proper objects for donations, 'consisting of five Gentlemen of the City, who are to be elected annually by the Society', and these initially comprised a Baillie, two clergymen, and two physicians. Four Presidents of the Society, a Treasurer, and a Secretary were appointed. The Presidents clearly took turns to chair the weekly debates and are listed as John Geddes, John Smith, M. D., John McDiarmid, and George B. Brand, while the Treasurer was named as John Christison. James Hogg was to be Secretary, his duties being to answer any correspondence and to advertise the debates and their outcomes in the Edinburgh newspapers. Letters were to be addressed to him at a public reading-room on the North Bridge. This must have been the most time-consuming office, as Hogg alone was paid a salary for his labours, amounting to £21 for the year. It was probably at this point that Hogg became acquainted with a bookseller named George Goldie, then only twenty-three years old, who told tickets for the weekly debates of the Edinburgh Forum from his shop on Princes Street.[44]

Some of the questions debated at the Edinburgh Forum seem so germane to the concerns of Hogg's own writing that they may well have originated with him. 'Are there any reasonable grounds for the prevailing belief in the existence of Apparitions?' and 'Whether is Campbell or Scott the greater Poet?', for example, had already been the subject of tales and essays in *The Spy*. The Edinburgh Forum maintained its popular appeal for this season at least, although attendance seems to have fallen away during the following one. The meeting of 18 March 1814 appears to have been the last one advertised and George Goldie stated that the session, normally continued into May or early June, was not completed. Hogg was not paid his full salary for the year 'because the Forum was in debt, and broke up before it was due, when the members were severally called upon to contribute their quota, about L.4 or L.5, in paying off all claims [...]'.[45] By the time of its dissolution the Forum had probably outlived its purpose in Hogg's life, however: he had achieved his ambition of being recognised as one of Scotland's major poets.

While he was still living in his flat above Peter Hill's bookseller's shop on the High Street Hogg had begun to formulate plans for another volume publication of his poetry. On 14 November 1811 he wrote to request a private consultation with Scott, to show him 'some *poetical tales* which I trust will draw your consent to my publishing of them'. Scott, he hoped, would read them over and give his opinion as to 'the general structure of the tales'. John Grieve had admired some of Hogg's poetry in *The Spy* and was encouraging him 'to take the field once more as a poet, and try my fate with others'.[46] Scott's reaction is not known, but it cannot have been long after their meeting that Hogg moved out of the centre of Edinburgh's Old Town to Deanhaugh in Stockbridge. In 1812 the painter Henry Raeburn began to develop this quiet village as a suburb of Edinburgh, although his scheme was overtaken by a new plan shortly before his death. The old-fashioned house with a garden in which Hogg lodged was part of the old Deanhaugh, 'a weather-beaten, rather ghostly, solitary looking domicile, like an old farm-house in the country'. There Hogg could have the freedom from interruption that was conducive to writing, and yet remain within a walk of Edinburgh's printers and publishers and his own literary friends, though the silence of the

place was in fact intermittent. Among Hogg's fellow-lodgers were a
pair of married ex-servants from England. The man was a violent
husband to a decent wife, whom he beat regularly, and Hogg with
his curiosity about abnormal states of mind observed the family closely,
noting the effect of the husband's aggression on the children. 'The
children did not cry, nor run out of the house, nor even cease their
play. It appeared to them as a matter of course–a sort of disagreeable duty which required to be performed'.[47] It was at Deanhaugh
that he wrote, 'within an incredibly short time', his narrative poem,
The Queen's Wake. By his own account he already had 'some ballads
or metrical tales' by him, some of which he had probably shown to
Scott in November 1811, and which were then woven into the framing narrative of a poetic contest before Mary, Queen of Scots. Work
was probably underway by March 1812 when the *Edinburgh Quarterly Review* announced that 'Mr HOGG, the "Etterick Shepherd," is
preparing for publication, a legendary Tale called the "Queen's Wake,"
in ten cantos, 1 vol. 8vo'.[48] The description is puzzling, though, since
the poem as published consists of twelve ballads, within a narrative
divided into an Introduction, three Nights, and a Conclusion. It is
hard to see how it could have been divided into ten parts in anything
like the form in which it was subsequently published. Two of the
ballads had previously appeared in numbers 20 and 40 of *The Spy*,
'King Edward's Dream' (the Fifteenth Bard's song) and 'Macgregor–
A Highland Tale' (the Eleventh Bard's song). Surviving manuscripts
in Hogg's hand of 'Earl Walter' and 'Glen-Avin' also suggest that
these were other independent ballads later incorporated into the
overarching structure of *The Queen's Wake*, while Hogg's letter to Eliza
Izett of 15 October 1811 referred to finishing 'a highland tale lately'.[49]

The fashionable persona of the minstrel, deriving most recently
from Beattie's eponymous poem and from Scott's *Minstrelsy of the Scottish
Border* and *The Lay of the Last Minstrel*, had already been employed by
Hogg in his two previous poetry titles, *The Mountain Bard* and *The
Forest Minstrel*. Various other influences determined the bardic contest between rival minstrels at the court of Mary, Queen of Scots
that made up *The Queen's Wake*. Douglas Mack has outlined the recovery of a lost national musical tradition, comprising both the courtly
and the demotic, in the publication under the auspices of the Highland Society of Scotland of John Gunn's *An Historical Enquiry Respecting the Performance on the Harp in the Highlands of Scotland* (1807). This
described two ancient harps from Lude in Perthshire, the Caledonian Harp supposedly owned by 'a succession of Highland Bards',
and Queen Mary's Harp, a royal gift to Beatrix Gardyn, the daugh-

ter of Gardyn of Banchory, which was despoiled after 1745 of its precious stones, the queen's portrait, and the arms of Scotland.[50] There are obvious precedents for Hogg's contest in the *Rejected Addresses* of James and Horace Smith, a volume of parodies published in 1812 which affects to represent rival entries by the most notable poets of the day for a competition for an address to mark the reopening of London's Drury Lane Theatre. Closer to home there was Hogg's attendance at the Edinburgh Theatre for the annual piping competition or the play entitled *Helga the Maid of Iceland, or The Rival Minstrels*.

In more personal terms the bardic contest is another attempt by Hogg to explore his standing as a poet. In the Shuffleton papers of *The Spy* he had created a hierarchical list of contemporary Scottish poets, placing himself after Scott and Campbell in real terms and denouncing the neglect he had nevertheless experienced in contemporary Edinburgh because of his poverty and low social status. The Ettrick Bard of *The Queen's Wake* is similarly poor and despised, an apparent oddity at Queen Mary's court at Holyrood. Even his name (Hogg, presumably) is ridiculous, and the courtiers are amused by his ragged and dejected appearance in a 'forest doublet darned and torn' and a 'rent and worn' shepherd's plaid:

> A clown he was, bred in the wild,
> And late from native moors exiled,
> In hopes his mellow mountain strain
> High favour from the great would gain.
> Poor wight! he never weened how hard
> For poverty to earn regard!

The Ettrick Bard, however, is thoroughly in earnest. Hogg's unworldly pursuit of his art was noted by contemporaries such as Francis Jeffrey, and at the end of the poem the Ettrick Bard, grieving for his failure to secure the prize of the courtly harp, is offered a future of material prosperity by Queen Mary, in the form of 'Precious remains of minstrel lore' and a 'cottage, by a silver rill'. The bard declines the role of antiquarian collector (an allusion perhaps to Scott's *Minstrelsy of the Scottish Border*) and a cottage like the one presented to the Last Minstrel by the Duchess of Monmouth and Buccleuch, and insists that only a harp will content him. He is then rewarded with the Caledonian Harp, the harp of the Border bards, a less costly instrument than the prize harp, but perhaps a better musical instrument. In possession of this harp, 'Never was hero of renown, | Or monarch prouder of his crown'.[51]

Besides appearing as the Ettrick Bard in *The Queen's Wake*, Hogg also features as the poem's narrator, defying the winter storms of adversity despite his 'wareless heart, and houseless head' and disregarding his poor fortune in the joy of rediscovering his 'Mountain Lyre'. His poetic gift is what remains to him, 'When pleasure, love, and mirth were past'. In the opening section of the poem accounting for the contest, Hogg as narrator is an outwardly mournful yet inwardly joyous figure who alternately presents and dissolves the richness of Scotland's past, 'When Royal MARY, blithe of mood, | Kept holiday at Holyrood'. Mary's beauty amid the tumultuous crowd scenes in Edinburgh alternates with the lonely figure of the bard, who fondly strikes 'beside the pen, | The harp of Yarrow's braken glen'. The reader is reminded at intervals that 'those lays of fire once more | Are wrecked 'mid heaps of mouldering lore', and that only the poet can render them present, living realities rather than antiquities. Hogg himself reappears in the conclusion to the narrative, separating himself from the 'minstrels long in dust' as the 'fond and ventrous swain | Who dared to wake their notes again' and assuming the role of guide to the reader through this forgotten world. In the poet's life spring will not follow winter, nothing can 'Renew the age of love and glee! | Can ever second spring restore | To my old mountain harp and me'. But of course his art has just achieved this very miracle, the revival through imagination of a golden age of Scotland and the unblighted youthful promise of Queen Mary. Interestingly, there are traces in the first edition that the poem, set at Christmastime, was originally intended to have an Easter setting, when the spring coincides with man's hope of spiritual renewal through Christ's death and resurrection.[52]

By doubling the figure of the poor aged rustic bard Hogg makes him more enduring than the glories of the Scottish court. While Queen Mary will be exiled, disowned, and executed and her court fade away, the figure of the Ettrick Bard lives on in the form of the narrator. Unlike Scott's Minstrel, he is no mere survival or relic of past ages. Although Scott is alluded to in several places in the mythology of *The Queen's Wake*, it seems significant that he is not one of the bards at the Scottish court. Neither are most of the Scottish poets of the day with whom Hogg had compared himself in the Shuffleton papers of *The Spy*. In *The Queen's Wake* Hogg presents an emotionally-charged personal and poetic history rather than ranking himself in literary Edinburgh. The entries for the poetic contest are all either his own work, or the Border ballads that were a major influence on his poetic development, and the poem contains several portraits of his personal friends, not all of whom are poets. John Morrison who reported critically and perhaps maliciously to Scott on Hogg's farming activities in Dumfriesshire and may have been a sexual rival too, is the Fifth Bard, a character of whom no-one can tell 'If *knave* or *genius* writ was there' and who sings the traditional ballad of 'Fair Margaret', a tale of sexual betrayal. Hogg's friend and host in Tynron parish, James M'Turk, who took Hogg into his family after he lost the farm of Corfardine, appears as a stalwart Scottish champion who helps to revenge the slaughter of Morrison of Locherben (the other farm Hogg rented in Dumfriesshire) in 'Dumlanrig'. That poem, with a Dumfriesshire setting, is sung by a bard based on Allan Cunningham, the young enthusiast who visited Hogg on the hillside at Mitchelslacks and honoured him as a poet at a low point in his life. Hogg's old Ettrick friend and present Edinburgh patron, John Grieve, appears as the nameless youth who sings 'Mary Scott' and who has abandoned the poetical ambitions of his youth without losing his engagement with and enthusiasm for poetry. Without Grieve's support Hogg knew that he could not have maintained himself in Edinburgh during the writing of *The Queen's Wake*, and it is a nice touch that he is the first to arrive at the scene of the poetic contest that comprises the poem itself. Hogg was probably also thinking of Grieve's part in *The Forest Minstrel* when he described him as singing the ballad of 'Mary Scott', 'Not for himself, but friends he loved'. Another significant figure in Hogg's Edinburgh life was James Gray, represented as the bard who sings 'King Edward's Dream'. Gray's career as a schoolmaster and love of the classics are alluded to. His almost obsessive and selfless devotion to poets and poetry are simultaneously mocked and honoured, and his function as the focus of various Edinburgh literary interests touched upon:

> When first of royal wake he heard,
> Forthwith it chained his sole regard:
> It was his thought, his hourly theme,
> His morning prayer, his midnight dream,
> Knights, dames, and squires of each degree,
> He deemed as fond of songs as he,
> And talked of them continually [...]
> About Dunedin streets he ran,
> Each knight he met, each maid, each man,
> In field, in alley, tower, or hall,
> The wake was first, the wake was all.

Gray's 'ardent mind' renders him selfless, but too emotional to perform well himself and he breaks down at the end of his song. But in a court riven by rivalries between the Highlands and the South of Scotland, he honourably cares only for poetic merit, 'Alike to him the south or north'.[53]

The poem's narrator and the Ettrick Bard are linked by their possession of a harp and Hogg accounts for its transmission from the one to the other through a series of local Borders poets. After being owned by the Ettrick Bard and then lost for a while the Caledonian harp is attempted by William Hamilton of Bangour (1704–54), Allan Ramsay (1686–1758), Langhorne (1735–89), John Logan (1748–88), and John Leyden (1775–1811). Walter Scott plays it in inspired fashion, but of 'change enamoured' moves from the Borders to other concerns and kingdoms, having tried unsuccessfully to wile the harp away from Hogg himself. Hogg warns, 'That harp he never more shall see, | Unless 'mong Scotland's hills with me'.

The Ettrick Bard's harp summarised a potent personal myth of original and national genius, of the natural and the native:

> Instead of arms or golden crest,
> His harp with mimic flowers was drest:
> Around, in graceful streamers, fell
> The briar-rose and the heather bell;
> And there his learning deep to prove,
> *Naturae Donum* graved above.
> When o'er her mellow notes he ran,
> And his wild mountain chaunt began;
> Then first was noted in his eye,
> A gleam of native energy.[54]

Hogg subsequently put this device on a number of his personal possessions, using it on his seal and having it printed on his book-labels. It was also a remembrance of Burns, who had signalled his possession of a heaven-bestowed poetic gift by employing Milton's phrase of 'Wood-notes wild' on his own seal.

Once Hogg had lighted upon his structure of the poetic contest, *The Queen's Wake* took shape rapidly and was completed within a few months, probably between March and September 1812. As he argued, the structure of *The Queen's Wake* had a double interest for the reader, 'both in the incidents of each tale, and in the success of the singer in the contest for the prize harp'. The legendary Queen Mary was a Romantic symbol of unrealised (and perhaps unrealisable) hopes, a Virgin Mary, 'the fairest of the fair', readerly knowledge of her later history lending pathos to Hogg's vision of her youthful arrival in Scotland.[55] Like King Arthur she attempts to combine nobility of birth with noble national enterprise, and her attempt contains the seeds of its own destruction. Rizzio's song in the poetic contest brings him to the attention of Queen Mary for the first time and prefigures a crisis in her unhappy marriage to Darnley, just as Arthur's Round Table lends Lancelot the glamour to supplant him in the affections of Queen Guinevere.

Hopeful that he had at last produced the major work he needed to justify his pursuit of a literary career, Hogg was eager to read it to his most supportive Edinburgh friends. John Grieve assured him it would do, but James Gray and his wife revealed a lack of discrimination that both amused and angered Hogg. On his first attempt to read *The Queen's Wake* to them at his Deanhaugh lodgings, Hogg was stopped by an argument between Mary Gray and John Grieve about Hogg's use of one particular word, and on the second attempt at the Gray home in Buccleuch Place the couple abandoned Hogg's reading to hear the recital of an itinerant bard in the lobby, 'a poor crazy beggar repeating such miserable stuff as I had never heard before'.[56] Hogg was obviously proud of his achievement, since he decided to dedicate it to the young Princess Charlotte, the daughter and heir of the Prince Regent.

When Hogg's poem was complete he offered it to Archibald Constable, informing him at the same time that the young bookseller George Goldie, whom he had met through the Forum, was already interested. His letter to Constable of 24 September 1812 asked £150 for every thousand copies printed, promising to obtain subscribers so that the cost of producing the work would be covered. He was not, however, prepared to hand over his manuscript before an agreement had been reached, and when he called on Constable

> [...] he said he would do nothing until he had seen the MS. I refused to give it, saying, 'What skill have you about the merits of a book?'–'It may be so, Hogg,' said he; 'but I know as well how to sell a book as any man, which should be some concern of yours; and I know how to buy one, too, by G–!'
>
> Finally, he told me, that if I would procure him two hundred subscribers, to insure him from loss, he would give me £100 for liberty to print one thousand copies; and more than that he would not give. I felt I should be obliged to comply; and, with great reluctance, got a few subscription-papers thrown off privately, and gave them to friends, who soon procured me the requisite number.[57]

Although Hogg was offered only two-thirds of the price he had requested, George Goldie agreed to add the profits of the subscription copies to the hundred pounds and he became the publisher of *The Queen's Wake*. By November 1812 the poem was being printed by Andrew Balfour and Hogg was able to make a series of puns about his Queen's forthcoming public appearance, reporting to Margaret Phillips, 'she is in bed, that is, she is in sheets, but not got into stays as yet: perhaps she will get them on about the end of the year'. The *Edinburgh Star* of 15 December reported the work to be 'in the Press, and nearly ready'.[58]

Hogg waited for the day of publication in a state of mounting tension. Scott's *Rokeby* was published on 11 January 1813 and a christening party hosted by his friend and printer James Ballantyne the following day. John Grieve would hold a similar dinner to mark the publication of *The Queen's Wake* on Saturday, 30 January.[59] A large-scale Forum debate held at the George Street Asssembly Rooms on the preceding evening was, no doubt, a welcome distraction. This was a charitable concern connected with Napoleon's retreat from Moscow in September 1812, disastrous for him but a great cause of rejoicing in Britain. The Directors of the Assembly Rooms had offered the use of the large room rent-free so that as much as possible was made 'for Relief of the Russian Sufferers in the war with France'. The question for debate, 'Are late or early Marriages more productive of Happiness?', was carefully chosen—everyone might be expected to hold an opinion on such a topic, and the debate would therefore attract a good number of speakers. Grieve's dinner no doubt passed off pleasantly enough, and on the next working day after *The Queen's Wake* was published Hogg walked in to Edinburgh from Deanhaugh to gauge the public reaction to it. For his title-page he had chosen a motto from William Collins's 'Ode to Fear', and now felt 'like a man between death and life, waiting for the sentence of the jury'.[60] Was the public execution of the Spy to be repeated, or was it not?

CHAPTER FOUR

Of Minstrel Honours

Hogg's anxiety was unnecessary, for *The Queen's Wake* was a triumph. As he paced the Edinburgh streets he was hailed by an old friend, William Dunlop, and forthrightly asked why he had bothered the reading public with 'fourpenny papers an' daft shilly-shally sangs' when he was capable of 'a thing like this!' The *Scottish Review* concurred, declaring that no-one who had formed an opinion of the Ettrick Shepherd from *The Mountain Bard* could imagine the treasures of *The Queen's Wake*, where an imagination once 'shackled down by local habits' soared 'into the furthest regions of human thought' and the reader encountered 'a great, original, and truly poetic mind'. The inset song 'O Lady Dear' was set to music and sold by an enterprising Edinburgh music-seller, while passages also appeared in various anthologies. As Douglas Mack has expressed it, Hogg had arrived.[1]

Immediately after the publication of *The Queen's Wake* Hogg left Edinburgh on a lengthy visit to his friends and family in Ettrick Forest, feeling himself to be no longer a ne'er-do-well but a successful poet who could now try again to obtain a home in his native district. Writing from 'Ettrick Banks' on 7 March 1813 Hogg addressed a letter to his patroness, Harriet, Duchess of Buccleuch, to ask for the small farm of Eltrieve Moss in Yarrow as a refuge for his aged parents. In *The Lay of the Last Minstrel* Scott had portrayed a former Buccleuch lady settling an aged minstrel in a home of modest comfort close by her own residence at Newark Tower, and Hogg now told the Duchess jocularly that he deemed the house of Buccleuch 'bound to cherish every plant that indicated any thing out of the common way on the braes of Ettrick and Yarrow'. He continued:

> There is a small farm on the head of a water called Yarrow posessed by a mean fellow named Wilson The yearly rent of it is only I believe £5. and now about a third of it is taken off and laid into another farm The remainder is as yet unapropriated. Now there is a certain poor bard who has two old parents each of them upwards of 84 years of age; and that bard has no house nor home to shelter those poor parents in, or cherish the evening of their lives. A single line from a certain very great, and very beautifull lady [...] would

PART OF THE OLD TOWN, FROM PRINCES STREET,
EDINBURGH.

Drawn by Tho. H. Shepherd.

Engraved by S. Lacey.

insure that small pendicle to the bard at once—but she will grant no such thing!—I appeal to your Grace if she is not a very bad lady that?

The tenant, Thomas Wilson, seems to have been the subject of a poem by Hogg in the same vein as his series of 'Epitaphs on Living Characters' published in 1810 in the *Scots Magazine* and *The Spy*. 'Tam Wilson' is a 'sauless, senseless, stupid creature', lost to everything but money-making and his own material comforts. Whatever Wilson's personal defects, however, Duchess Harriet did not feel able to dispossess him on Hogg's account. Hogg's hope of royal patronage also came to nothing: though he had sent a splendidly-bound copy of *The Queen's Wake* to the Bishop of Salisbury for his pupil the Princess Charlotte (to whom the poem was dedicated), Hogg never learned whether or not she had received it.[2]

Hogg's success brought him more tangible benefits in Edinburgh, where his society was now much courted. The elderly and eccentric Earl of Buchan, for example, wanted Hogg to attend the dedication ceremony for a huge statue of William Wallace that he was erecting at Dryburgh, and the Society of Antiquaries of Scotland at its meeting of 9 December 1814 added the name of 'Mr James Hogg, author of the Queen's Wake' to its list of members. A group of Anstruther friends sent him a membership certificate of their Musomanik Society.[3] The table in Hogg's lodgings was covered with notes of invitation, and he decided it would be better now to move from the semi-rural backwater of Deanhaugh into the centre of town. Hogg settled initially in lodgings in St Anne's Street, a steep unsightly little street in the hollow west of the North Bridge near the junction between the city's Old and New Town districts. His annual expenses in this street, designed by a speculative builder as cheap housing for tradesmen, were probably only about £35 a year. Soon afterwards he moved to nearby Gabriel's Road, an old lane that had originally linked northern hamlets such as Stockbridge with Edinburgh. Hogg rented the 'sky-parlour', or attic room, of the widow of a hackney coachman named Mrs Tunny.[4]

Among Hogg's new Edinburgh friends was Robert Pearse Gillies, the son of a Forfarshire landowner. Hogg's relations with the Scottish gentry and aristocracy were often more relaxed than with the less socially secure middle-classes, and there was a particular ease and mutual respect in this relationship. Though a reader of the classics, Gillies had found his own student experience at the university somewhat dispiriting, and his great interest was in the burgeoning Romantic literature of Germany, which he later translated and pro-

moted in various periodicals. He was therefore a sympathetic listener when Hogg defended the value of his own original work against
the antiquarian learning advocated by John Pinkerton:

> Every *sumph* that has been to schule and college, can read
> books; there's naething extraordinar' in that. But every sen-
> sible man has a book in his ain *heart and mind*, that's worth a'
> the leeberaries in the world, if he could but understand it,
> and make the best of it. Leeberaries ye can exhaust; that is,
> I'm thinking, if the corn was winnowed out o' the caff, there's
> no sae muckle in them as yin wad imagine; but the mind is
> like a magic well, that yields all things, if only ye hae discre-
> tion and patience, and work deep eneuch!

Hogg was a welcome guest in Edinburgh's drawing-rooms despite
his ignorance of social conventions and his roughness and bluntness
of expression. His blunders, like the shock of his first tasting of ice-
cream under the impression it was 'some fine, *het*, sweet *puddin''*
were amusing, and he was a sensible man without any false pretensions. Many of his fellow-guests at an evening party no doubt secretly shared his opinion of the cantankerous ancient gambler Mrs
Oliphant of Rossie, who attacked him for his carelessness as her
partner at whist, and who, he told Gillies, was 'a rudas carline' and
'downricht fearsome'. Hogg was also understandably taken aback
by the contemporary gourmet cult, and the emphasis even a 'rever-
end professor' laid on food, his 'very important discovery' concerning not science or metaphysics but that 'beet radish made a pickle
greatly superior to the radishes or cabbage of Savoy'.[5]

Some of Hogg's new friends made him completely at home in
their houses, so that he remarked in one case that he felt 'as if the
whole grand house, the books, the pictures, the wine-cellar, the *forte-
piano*, the organ, the fiddles, and a' the rest, were his ain', for he was
sure that he would have free use of them as long as he lived in
Edinburgh. Others, however, seemed to offer an intimacy that was
then unaccountably withdrawn, which Hogg found incomprehensi-
ble and wounding. Many years later he recalled his hurt astonishment when 'the very men with whom I had been so happy over night
[...] who had invited me to their houses, not on one day but every
day that suited my convenience, would the next day, when I addressed
them in the kindest and most affectionate way I was able, stare me in
the face, and shrink from the gloveless hand of the poor poet, without uttering a word!' Offering a gloveless hand was a mark of intimacy and sincerity as well as of low social status.[6] During these

Edinburgh years Hogg's general appearance was smart and even fashionable: he added some jewellery and also Regency top-boots to his good, well-made clothing. For a summer excursion to rural Lasswade, Hogg ('the gayest of the whole') wore 'a most picturesque fishing-jacket, of the very lightest mazarine blue, with huge mother-of-pearl buttons,—nankeen breeches, made tight to his nervous shapes,—and a broad-brimmed white chip hat, with a fine new ribbon to it, and a peacock's feather stuck in front'.[7]

It was while lodging in Gabriel's Road and beginning to mix more extensively in Edinburgh society that Hogg formed one of the key friendships of his professional life, with a young advocate named John Wilson. Hogg had been an enthusiastic reader of Wilson's *The Isle of Palms* (1812) and his curiosity about the author had been increased by hearing that he was 'a man from the mountains in Wales, or the west of England, with hair like eagles' feathers, and nails like birds' claws'. Unable to gain an introduction otherwise he wrote Wilson a note 'telling him that I wished much to see him, and if he wanted to see me, he might come and dine with me at my lodgings in the Road of Gabriel, at four'. Intrigued by this unconventional invitation, Wilson came to the usual Edinburgh lodging-house dinner of 'brandered skate and minced collops' and the two conversed in such an animated fashion that all too soon he realised it was eleven o'clock and that he must leave to attend a party in his own house. Hogg accompanied him, and played and sang to entertain the company until the early hours of the morning.[8] The two became fast friends, so that they were seldom twenty-four hours apart when both were in Edinburgh.

Wilson certainly cut an impressive figure, tall and athletic with blue eyes and fair hair and an eager manner, ready to talk, and amused rather than offended by any unconventionality. He was also, no doubt, flatteringly deferential to the author of *The Queen's Wake*, a far more successful poet than he was himself, and in many respects behaved as Hogg's protégé during the early stages of their relationship. As late as 1 September 1815, for example, he wrote to Hogg asking him to recommend another poem he was writing, *The City of the Plague*, to the London publisher, John Murray, adding 'I think that a bold eulogy from you (if administered immediately) would be of service to me'. Wilson was the eldest son of a wealthy Paisley gauze manufacturer, and had inherited a fortune of £50,000 at the age of eighteen. His mother's family set their social sights rather higher than trade, family members entering professions such as the law and the church, and claiming descent from the great Marquis of Montrose. He had

been educated at Glasgow then at Oxford, where he had written a
fan-letter to William Wordsworth, subsequently buying a cottage at
Elleray on Lake Windermere in 1805 to strengthen his intimacy
with the Lake poets.[9]

Hogg wanted a British as well as a Scottish reputation. Scott had
sent a copy of *The Queen's Wake* to Byron, who praised it highly in a
letter that the kindly recipient was pleased to show the author. Capel
Lofft, the busy patron of the shoemaker-poet Robert Bloomfield,
introduced Hogg's poem to his Suffolk neighbour Bernard Barton,
who wrote to enquire further details about this shepherd-poet from
his publisher. On hearing that Hogg was 'really and truly [...] a common shepherd, bred among the mountains of Ettrick Forest, who
went to service when only seven years of age; and since that period
has never received any education whatever', Barton wrote a celebra-
tory tribute which was published in the *Edinburgh Evening Courant* of
29 April 1813, and then revised as a Preface to the second edition of
The Queen's Wake, published on 14 June 1813, less than five months
after the first edition.[10] On 3 April 1813 Hogg wrote to Scott that his
poem had 'sold beyond all calculation in Edin. yet what is curious
the sale has almost been confined to that place as yet. I wish you
would review it in the Quarterly'. He also asked General Alexander
Dirom, then stationed in Liverpool, to draw it to the attention of his
influential friend, William Roscoe, and was disturbed when Roscoe
reported 'his never having been able to procure a copy of the Queen's
Wake neither from London nor Edin'.[11] George Goldie was young
and inexperienced, and Hogg may also have doubted whether his
London partner, Longmans, was pushing the work with sufficient
energy. At all events, when the time came he attempted to have a
third edition brought out by Edinburgh's leading publisher Archibald
Constable instead.

After *The Queen's Wake* Hogg felt that no literary object was beyond his reach: he was composing rapidly in several different gen-
res and projecting several new publications. One was a two-volume
publication of '*Scottish Rural tales* anonymous in prose I have one will
make about 200 pages alone some of the others you have seen in
the Spy', mentioned to Scott in April 1813 and offered to Constable
a few weeks later. Hogg also had serious ambitions as a dramatist.
He wrote two musical dramas as well as a historical play entitled
The Hunting of Badlewe, which carefully avoided 'national bravado'
and was intended for the London rather than the Edinburgh stage.
Hogg got his young publisher, George Goldie, to print off just half-a-
dozen copies that he could give to his literary advisers, hoping for

their help with revisions and improvements before offering it in London.[12]

While Hogg was waiting for these copies he was called unexpectedly back to Selkirkshire by the last illness of his mother, Margaret Laidlaw. Her death that summer at the age of eighty-four deprived Hogg of 'the warmest the sincerest and in a word the best friend that ever I had in this world'. The loss was a painful one, as Hogg told a friend that September: 'my attachment to her was no common one. [...] we knew we had to part—we talked of it [...] but yet a last adiew is painfull—it was very painfull to me and remembrance has a thousand little kind and tender offices treasured up in my heart which long will continue to melt it. The truth is that I feel a want of some one to be kind to a vacuity in my mind which is not soon likely to be made up—'. In his poem 'A Last Adieu' Hogg commemorated his mother as the teller of many legendary tales, the 'Minstreless' of the Border, whose kind heart had often grieved for his follies.[13] Hogg's long-delayed hope of being able to take care of her in her old age would now never be fulfilled, and his father, too, was a forlorn and solitary figure, deprived of his life's companion.

Back in Edinburgh again, Hogg dispatched copies of *The Hunting of Badlewe* to William Laidlaw and John Grieve as the friends of his youth, to his Edinburgh mentor Walter Scott, and to the English literary men Bernard Barton, Capel Lofft, and William Roscoe. A second edition of *The Queen's Wake* had been published in June, and Hogg decided it was time for a holiday, setting out on foot for Argyllshire in October, visiting his friends at Alloa along the way. It was rather late in the year for a walking tour of wild country and at the start, too, of an exceptionally hard winter when at times the frost was so severe that the sea itself began to freeze and it was only with great difficulty that ships could enter and leave Leith harbour. Whether from the chill weather or the stress of a recent bereavement Hogg caught an unpleasant cold and decided to stay for two or three weeks at Kinnaird House near Dunkeld in Perthshire with his friend Eliza Izett and enjoy the luxuries of her comfortable house with its beautiful wooded walks overlooking the Tay. His hostess gave him the use of a little study and urged him to write something in his morning or evening hours when he was not out fishing, suggesting the river itself as a suitable subject. Even though Hogg considered himself 'exquisite at descriptions of nature, and mountain-scenery in particular' he was concerned that a purely descriptive poem might be dull and grafted on to the nearby locality of Kincraigy farm a love-story concerning the wooing of a beautiful farmer's daughter by the disguised King of Scotland and her successful struggle towards worldly recognition as his true mate. It was written in the Spenserian stanza and Hogg made good progress both on the spot and during the following winter. By mid-November he had written '1100 lines and no appearance of any close', and on 11 February 1814 told Eliza Izett, 'I am positively within a few lines of the end now'. It was eventually published in 1816 under the intriguing title of *Mador of the Moor*.[14]

On his return from Perthshire Hogg stopped only a few weeks in Edinburgh and then passed to Selkirkshire to his lonely old father. During the next 'three months' he was 'enjoying the winter sports with […] avidity and relish'. Travelling to Edinburgh again on 21 January 1814 Hogg 'fought his way from Tweed thro' a terrible depth of snow and drift the wheeled carriages all being stopped' to pick up the threads of his literary life once more. His friends' opinions of *The Hunting of Badlewe* were not as favourable as he had hoped. Barton as a Quaker felt unqualified to pronounce on a stage-play and was guided by his friend Capel Lofft, who felt that Hogg's chances of its being produced in London were small when three tragedies of his own of 'transcendent merit, equal to Miss Baillie's' had been rejected. Walter Scott, though he had read it with pleasure and thought it might be staged if 'put into a completely corrected state', nevertheless pronounced that the plot was divided into too many characters and interests, and that 'the incidents of *the book*, and the discovery of King Robert […] might not be deemed altogether original', a good-humoured reminder of his own use of similar materials in *The Lay of the Last Minstrel* and *The Lady of the Lake*. William Roscoe was more overtly critical, both of its defects in plotting and for its lack of sympathetic characters. He considered one of the leading female roles 'too gross for the stage', while the heroine Annabel who is eventually married to the King of Scotland was morally weak and by her elopement with the villain 'forfeits all claim to our favour'. Reluctantly, Hogg decided to publish it separately in Edinburgh as a closet drama, and to save his public stage debut for a future play. He thought of himself as an apprentice to the stage, resolving to write a play every year and 'hoping to make myself perfect by degrees, as a man does in his calling'.[15]

Edinburgh was in daily expectation of news of a final victory over the French, and on Good Friday 1814 the London mail-coach arrived with colours flying and the words 'Surrender of Paris' painted on them. The Edinburgh castle guns were fired, the church bells rung, and commemorative songs and dances published. Hogg had his own celebratory poem to hand, rejoicing that 'the bastard eagle bears awa', | And ne'er will e'e thy shores again', which he sang at a party at Young's Tavern on the High Street that very evening and published in the following Monday's newspaper. It seemed to be the end of an era when a whole generation had grown up under the threat of potential French invasion. The relief was stupendous. The white cockade associated with Jacobitism was now worn in honour of the restoration of the Bourbon dynasty, a bonfire was lit on Arthur's Seat, and the city's artists and versifiers from Alexander Nasymth downwards were pressed into service for the illumination night when the city's houses and public buildings were brightly lit and decorated with emblematic pictures celebrating the recent national triumph.[16]

Meantime Hogg was occupied with yet another literary project, with the Shakespearean title of *Midsummer Night Dreams*. One of the best-loved ballads of *The Queen's Wake* was a tale of transportation to a fairy world, 'Kilmeny', and Hogg's new collection was an extended exploration of other worlds and altered states of consciousness. A series of Romantic poems would be hung on the thread of dreaming, from the comic grotesquerie of 'Connel of Dee' with its threats of castration, chases, and demon bride, to the bold cosmic adventuring of *The Pilgrims of the Sun*, Hogg declaring himself along with Wordsworth 'A Pupil in the many chambered school | Where Superstition weaves her airy dreams'. In *The Pilgrims of the Sun* Hogg explored a range of styles and metres, from the ballad to the fast-paced narrative of Walter Scott, from the Miltonic 'holy harp of Judah's land' to 'Dryden's twang, and Pope's malicious knell'. A beautiful and devout young lady has an out-of-body experience of touring the cosmos under the escort of a mysterious spirit guide named Cela. They visit the warriors of Mars and the lovers of Venus, and even stand upon the brink of heaven and hear the angels' song in honour of God, before returning to earth once again. Hogg's heroine, Mary Lee, reanimates her body and is restored to her mother, after which she marries a harper named Hugo of Norroway, who seems to be Cela in his human form. The poem came easily, Hogg recording that it was written 'in about three weeks'.[17]

Perhaps because of the similarity of *The Pilgrims of the Sun* to 'Kilmeny', Hogg's friend, James Park, on a visit to Edinburgh from Greenock praised the poem so extravagantly as to persuade Hogg to publish it before the previously-written *Mador of the Moor*, and on its own, without the context of the other *Midsummer Night Dreams* poems. The contrast between Hugo and the Bard of Ettrick of *The Queen's*

Wake as poetic alter egos shows how confident Hogg seemed in the spring and summer of 1814. Where the Ettrick Bard was a ragged figure, uncouth and mocked by the court despite his minstrel gifts, Hugo is:

> A courteous and a welcome guest
> In every lord and baron's tower;
> He struck his harp of wond'rous power;
> So high his art, that all who heard
> Seemed by some magic spell ensnared:
> For every heart, as he desired,
> Was thrilled with woe—with ardour fired;
> Roused to high deeds his might above,
> Or soothed to kindness and to love.

When he meets Mary Lee Hugo knew 'his bourn was gained at last, | And all his wanderings then were past'. On Mary's lands at Carelha' in Ettrick Forest the couple lead a natural peaceful life far from the theatre of war, combining minstrelsy and 'the shepherd's simple, romantic life'.[18] The end of the Napoleonic Wars and Hogg's success as a poet coming together seemed to promise him prosperity and peace. His next poetry publication would, he hoped, equal the success of *The Queen's Wake* and raise his literary reputation even higher.

Hogg's new-found standing as a national poet allowed him to exercise his natural generosity and help several other aspiring poets to achieve volume publication. In his prefatory advertisement to *Tales in Verse, and Miscellaneous Poems*, published in April 1814, the Galloway pedlar-poet William Nicholson expressed his gratitude to 'the celebrated Mr Hogg, for his generous and unwearied attention, since the Author came to Edinburgh, where he was almost friendless and unknown'. Nicholson's title-page quoted 'plain his garb and plain his lay' from the description of the Bard of Clyde in *The Queen's Wake*. Hogg also acted as a literary agent for his old friend James Gray's poem *Cona or the Vale of Clwyd*. Longmans addressed their acceptance of the work dated 19 January 1814 to Hogg, adding that the Edinburgh printer, James Ballantyne 'shall be requested to communicate with you as to the correction of the proofs'. (This volume too included a title-page quotation from *The Queen's Wake*.)[19] Subsequently Hogg seems to have been involved in the publication of his friend R. P. Gillies's *Illustrations of a Poetical Character* of 1816, which was not only dedicated to him but also contains an early version of his own poem 'Halbert of Lyne' under the title of 'Introductory Tale: John of

Manor'. He may also have been signed up by the Edinburgh publishers Fairbairn and Anderson to edit a volume in their 'Cabinet Edition of The Poets of Scotland'.[20]

Hogg's financial position was hardly affected by his improved literary standing however. He now had cause to regret that he had ignored Scott's advice to him to make a formal composition with his creditors from four years ago in Dumfriesshire, for after the success of *The Queen's Wake* he found the 'little old debts and claims which one would have judged quite forgot are pouring in upon me without any limit or mitigation'. Furthermore, by the middle of 1814 his young publisher, George Goldie, was on the verge of bankruptcy. During the autumn of 1813 Hogg had regarded Goldie as the publisher of his future work, reading *Mador of the Moor* aloud to him as well as to Grieve as the poem progressed.[21] Yet on 1 February 1814 Hogg offered *Mador of the Moor* to Archibald Constable instead. He also made arrangements for Constable to publish a third edition of *The Queen's Wake* itself, and only reluctantly agreed (under pressure and after the printing had begun) to give this to Goldie as the original publisher of the work.[22] Goldie's insistence is understandable, for not only had he taken the initial risk with *The Queen's Wake* but he had also shown his willingness to invest in Hogg as a potential dramatist by printing the six copies of *The Hunting of Badlewe* that Hogg had distributed to his literary confidants. He was fighting for survival and could not afford to lose one of the chief attractions of his author's list. For Hogg, on the other hand, the regular and reliable payments that Goldie could no longer provide were crucial.

During the summer of 1814 Hogg tried to secure both Edinburgh's Archibald Constable and London's John Murray for *The Pilgrims of the Sun*. Scott had praised *The Queen's Wake* to the star of Murray's author list, Lord Byron, and in an intial letter to Byron of 3 June 1814 Hogg dropped a hint that he too would like his work to be brought out from Murray's Albemarle Street premises: 'I get but shabby conditions from my booksellers here and these not very punctually fulfilled, what prodigous advantages your lordship has over me in publishing'. A few weeks later on 25 July he wrote to Constable to say that instead of publishing *Mador of the Moor* he was 'resolved first to publish one not half so long [...] *The Pilgrims of the Sun* A poem in four parts', which he wished to go to press 'in a few days'. On 30 July Hogg followed up his previous hint to Byron:

> I have a poem of 2000 lines *The Pilgrims Of The Sun* which I
> want to publish instantly in one volume price 7/6. I have an
> abominable shabby Book seller here who never keeps his

word with me nor even lifts his bills when they become due they come back on me and distress me more than I had never seen them. G—d d—m him and them both I wish you could procure me some feasible conditions with yours […]

Shortly afterwards Hogg made a definite arrangement for publication of *The Pilgrims of the Sun* in Edinburgh, though with the firm of Manners and Miller rather than with Archibald Constable. Robert Miller was suggested by Constable himself, who promised that if Miller were to publish Hogg's poem he would promote it just as if it were one of his own publications. Without waiting to hear the outcome of his approach to John Murray through Byron, Hogg accepted Miller's terms of £86 for a first edition of a thousand copies, and gave him Wilson's Elleray home as a forwarding address for the dispatch of author's proofs.[23]

Hogg was about to leave Edinburgh for the Lake District. When he had visited the lakes of Westmorland and Cumberland in the summer of 1804 Hogg had been an obscure man, but as the author of *The Queen's Wake* he would now become personally acquainted with the district's celebrated literary men. Hogg always enjoyed the idea of joining a literary fellowship or brotherhood, but he had another objective. In May 1813 he had been invited through Dr Robert Anderson of Edinburgh to contribute to R. A. Davenport's *Poetical Register*, an annual miscellany of poems by leading contemporary authors. He now planned to begin an Edinburgh-based rival, and this had been the main subject of his approach to Byron at the beginning of June 1814. Hogg's Edinburgh 'poetical repository' was to appear half-yearly, 'part of it to consist of original poetry and the remainder to be filled up with short reviews or characters of every poetical work published in the interim […]'. Byron and Scott were the two leading poets of the age and a contribution from one or both for the first issue of the work was essential, but Hogg also wanted to secure Wordsworth, Southey, and, if possible, Coleridge as contributors. In John Wilson he had an ally in their neighbourhood. R. P. Gillies was also a Wordsworth correspondent, and he and Wilson were to co-edit the publication with Hogg.[24]

On 18 July 1814, with publication of *The Excursion* imminent, Wordsworth, with his wife and sister-in-law Sara Hutchinson, set out on a tour of Scotland. The party arrived in Edinburgh on 25 August and were invited to dine at once with John Wilson's mother. Hogg received an invitation from Wilson's younger brother, James, who, as Hogg later recalled,

[...] asked me to come to his mother's house in Queen Street to dinner, and meet Mr. Wordsworth and his lady. I said I should be glad to meet any friend of his kind and venerated mother's at any time, and should certainly come. But not having the least conception that the great poet of the Lakes was in Edinburgh, and James having called him *Mr.* Wordsworth, I took it for the celebrated horse-dealer of the same name

Although Hogg listened to Wordsworth talk with the respect and admiration due to 'a superior being, far exalted above the common walks of life', his appearance was somewhat rustic and even eccentric. The poet 'was clothed in a grey russet jacket and pantaloons, [...] and wore a broad-brimmed beaver hat'. Hogg made the most of his company during the five days that Wordsworth was in Edinburgh. The Wordsworths walked on the Calton Hill and on Arthur's Seat, visited Rosslyn Chapel, and saw some of the city's public institutions such as the Bridewell and Heriot's Hospital. How many of these excursions Hogg participated in is unknown, but he was surely a fellow-guest when Gillies had the Wordsworths to dinner on Monday, 29 August.[25]

It was during Wordsworth's visit to Edinburgh that Hogg must have heard of the death of his kind patroness, Harriet, Duchess of Buccleuch on 24 August. According to Walter Scott, who also admired her greatly, she had been very fond of Hogg's society and well disposed towards him. Years afterwards Scott recalled to a London visitor to Abbotsford how Hogg would be sent for from his brother's cottage 'on a summons to play at cards with the late Duchess of Buccleugh who was very partial to him', and she seems to have responded generously to the dedication of *The Forest Minstrel*. Hogg's lament for her was published in the *Edinburgh Evening Courant* on 3 September 1814 while he was on his way to Windermere. To Hogg she was the 'fairest flower | That graced old Scotland's topmost tree', and one whose death he could not regret more had she been 'sister, lover, child' to him. He never forgot her, naming one of his children after her many years later.[26]

Hogg decided to make his own journey to the Lakes coincide with the Wordsworths' return home, and met them again at Traquair Manse, where they were the guests of another Scottish poet, the Rev. James Nicol. Dr Robert Anderson and his daughter were also staying there and walked with them 'to the Bush aboon Traquhair which is no bush at all'. On 1 September Hogg led the Wordsworths and Dr Anderson through Yarrow valley and they called in for refreshment at Hogg's father's cottage at Craig Douglas, Sara Hutchinson describing him as 'An old man upwards of 88–a fine old Creature'. The party then separated, agreeing to meet again at Rydal Mount. Scott was from home, but the Wordsworths breakfasted with his wife and daughter at Abbotsford and lunched with the eccentric Earl of Buchan at Dryburgh, before collecting the young John Wordsworth from Burnfoot in Eskdale where they had left him at the start of their Scottish excursion.[27]

Hogg's exact itinerary is unknown, but he certainly proceeded to Keswick, where he put up at the Queen's Head Hotel and being wearied from his long journey sent a note round to Greta Hall on the edge of the little town to notify Robert Southey of his arrival. Southey kindly came up to the inn on receipt of Hogg's note, although he refused to share in the rum punch which Hogg was enjoying. Accustomed to the free-and-easy tavern convivialities of Edinburgh, Hogg was taken aback at this refusal, doubting, he claimed, that 'perfect sobriety and transcendent poetical genius can exist together'. Hogg came to breakfast at Greta Hall on the following morning, and spent the next two days with Southey, mostly out of doors, 'rambling on the hills and sailing on the lake', accompanied by young Hartley Coleridge, Southey's nephew. Southey at once offered Hogg 'a poem and ballad' for the poetical repository, much to his satisfaction. Hogg came to venerate Southey in his own home, as the protector of not only his own wife and children but also of Coleridge's, and of another sister-in-law, the widowed Mary Lovell, and her child. The kind and affectionate manner in which he treated them all, Hogg felt, had 'something in it superior to any thing I ever saw of human nature before'. On 8 September he arrived at Rydal before the Wordsworths, but passed the time pleasantly with his host's sister, Dorothy, who was looking after her ten-year-old namesake and four-year-old William Wordsworth during the absence of their parents. Hogg liked children and their aunt's conversation was 'a true mental treat'.[28]

Shortly after the travellers' arrival Hogg moved on to Elleray on Lake Windermere, where the greater part of his holiday was passed as the guest of his Edinburgh friend John Wilson. From there parties of literary men were made up to see 'the various lakes Skiddaw and Helvellyn', and Hogg dined with De Quincey at Grasmere as well as with the Wordsworths at Rydal Mount. The party often included Charles Lloyd too, the poet, novelist, and translator of Alfieri, who lived at Low Brathay House near Ambleside. At some point during his visit, Wordsworth gave Hogg a copy of 'Yarrow Visited' for the 'Edinburgh Poetical Repository', a souvenir of the day they had spent there recently. Wilson and Hogg were both enthusiastic fishermen and sailors, and many years later Hogg remembered his stay at Elleray fondly, declaring, 'What with sailing, climbing the mountains, driving with Bob to all the fine scenery, dining with po- ets and great men, jymnastics [...] and going to tell our friends that we were *not* coming to dine with them—these were halcyon days, which we shall never see again!' Though much disposed to admire Southey and Wordsworth, Hogg was also aware of participating in a more confined social circle than the one he was used to in Edin- burgh. Writing to Byron on 13 September, Hogg agreed with his remarks about 'the poets here commending and flattering one an- other', and he was amused by their bardic recitation of their own compositions, 'singing out their poetry in a loud sonorous key, which was very impressive, but perfectly ludicrous'.[29]

Hogg was probably more inclined to belittle the vanity of the Lake poets because of a recent wound to his own pride. On Sunday, 11 September an unusual celestial phenomenon was visible in the north- west of England between about a quarter to and half past eight o'clock in the evening—a beautiful streamer of light shaped rather like a rain- bow stretching from east to west across a sky that was calm, clear, and studded with stars. Whether Hogg and Wilson had been dining at Rydal Mount that evening, or whether they simply called on their way to or from De Quincey's at Grasmere is unclear.[30] But at Rydal Mount the party went out to the little terrace walk immediately be- hind the house to look at the night sky and were walking up and down expressing their admiration to one another. Comets were tra- ditionally held as presages of misfortune and when Dorothy Wordsworth, walking arm-in-arm with Hogg, expressed some fears 'that the splendid stranger might prove ominous' he retorted, 'Hout, me'm! it is neither mair nor less than joost a treeumphal airch, raised in honour of the meeting of the poets'. De Quincey, who was prom- enading with Wordsworth himself, later reported that on overhear- ing this Wordsworth had drawn him aside and said disdainfully, 'Poets? Poets?—What does the fellow mean?—Where are they?'[31] No doubt the episode had its effect in shaping Hogg's literary output during his visit to the Lakes.

In wet weather Hogg and Wilson reverted to their pens at Elleray, engaged like the minstrels of *The Queen's Wake* in daily bardic con- tests, retiring to separate rooms after breakfast and meeting at din- ner to read out their rival productions. Hogg heard Wilson bellow- ing his lines through the wall from time to time and by that was able to judge of his progress, since when 'he came upon any grand idea, he opened upon it full swell, with all the energy of a fine fox-hound on a hot trail'. On days when he felt he had been less inspired Wilson would appear at dinner with a sulky look, to be coaxed back into good humour again by his wife and his guest. Among the poems composed by Hogg during this holiday was 'Superstition', continuing the unearthly theme of the *Midsummer Night Dreams* collection he had been working on in Edinburgh, and subsequently published as a tail-piece to *The Pilgrims of the Sun*. A deeply-felt analysis of his own regard for the superstitions of his native district, this poem is a fine critique of Enlightenment scepticism, which Hogg argues often accompanies loss of religious devotion, since 'No holy awe the cynic's bosom thrills'. Hogg's creed as a Romantic poet was embodied in the successive statements, 'Be mine to sing of visions that have been', 'Be mine the faith that spurns the bourn of time', and 'Be mine the faith diverging to extremes!'[32] Hogg's finest work does indeed present extremes and opposites without resolution, faithfully reflecting the inconsistencies of the human mind and condition.

Hogg had seen *The Excursion* on the booksellers' counters before leaving Edinburgh but at two guineas could not afford to buy it. He now read it with Wilson, who listened sympathetically to Hogg's critique of the Lake Poets, and even declared himself convinced by it, at least for the moment. As Hogg wrote to Byron:

> [...] after a serious perusal of *Wordsworth's Excursion* together and no little laughter and some parodying he has with your assistance fairly confessed to me yesterday that he now holds the *school* in utter contempt Wordsworth is really a fine intelligent man and one that must ever be respected but I fear the *Kraken* has peppered him for this world—with its proportion of beauties (by the by they are but thin sown) it is the most heavy and the most absurd work that I ever perused without all exception—

Parody is after all the most sociable of poetic forms. Hogg subsequently declared that 'though it is generally accounted of the lowest order, yet there is no sort that affords greater amusement'. Hogg wrote both 'The Stranger' (parodying *The Excursion*) and 'Isabelle' (parodying Coleridge's 'Christabel') at Elleray, noting, 'I know some of the poems that Mr Wilson wrote against these too, if I were at liberty to tell'.[33]

Hogg's visit to the Lakes lasted a month, and when he returned to Edinburgh on 8 October things looked well for the forthcoming 'Edinburgh Poetical Repository', contributions having been obtained from both Southey and Wordsworth. No proofs of *The Pilgrims of the Sun* had been received at Elleray, however, and it was time for Hogg to check on Robert Miller's progress. Furthermore, during his absence George Goldie had become bankrupt as expected, leaving Hogg with something like £200 owing to him and most of the copies of the third edition of *The Queen's Wake* impounded for the benefit of Goldie's creditors. Hogg was expecting a lengthy and very favourable review of *The Queen's Wake* by the exacting and influential critic Francis Jeffrey to appear in the next issue of the *Edinburgh Review*—indeed he had been aware of its existence since at least February, and had heard it read aloud some months ago.[34] But what was the use of that if no copies were on sale?

The Queen's Wake was liberated more easily than Hogg expected, through the good offices of a young but enterprising bookseller with a shop in the University district of Edinburgh on the South Bridge—his name was William Blackwood, and he was to become the founder of a thriving publishing house and of one of the best-known and most influential of all nineteenth-century periodicals, *Blackwood's Edinburgh Magazine*. Hogg wrote to him on 28 October as to one of the trustees of George Goldie's estate, explaining that as one of Goldie's creditors he was suffering 'a double injury by having my principal work thus locked up from the public', and arguing that half the copies belonged to him rather than to Goldie—probably best interpreted as a statement that the edition had been published on the half-profits system. Blackwood seems to have intervened very effectively with Samuel Aitken the principal trustee, who readily agreed to let Hogg have the remaining copies for the cost of printing them, and Blackwood subsequently sold them on commission. Since Blackwood was currently the Edinburgh agent of John Murray the remaining copies of the third edition of *The Queen's Wake* were issued with a new title-page as the fourth edition published by Blackwood in Edinburgh and John Murray in London. Copies were available again by the time the November issue of the *Edinburgh Review* appeared on 22 December 1814.[35]

Hogg's negotiations over *The Pilgrims of the Sun* were more complicated. He must have been chagrined when, almost as soon as the bargain with Manners and Miller had been struck in August, he found that John Murray had been genuinely interested in it. The Manners and Miller bookselling shop was a scene of 'elegant trifling', where young ladies and gentlemen flirted over a little light literature in 'the perfumed atmosphere of the place' watched from a corner by the odd Edinburgh bluestocking. By the time of Hogg's return to Edinburgh in October his poem ought to have been almost ready for publication, but instead was 'taken out of the press and passing thro' all the notable *blues*'. Within days Hogg had reclaimed his manuscript, a move which was probably as much of a relief to his dilatory and reluctant publisher as to himself.[36] Hogg could now attempt to re-ignite the interest of the prestigious London publisher John Murray in the work.

Hogg had learned, probably from the helpful William Blackwood, that Murray was expected to arrive any day with his Edinburgh wife, combining business with family visits. His letter to Byron of 14 October states somewhat nervously 'if Murray and I do not agree I am in a fine scrape'. All was however well. Blackwood introduced Hogg to the London publisher and one evening he read the first part of his new poem aloud to them both. The opening section of the poem is the one that most closely resembles the acclaimed 'Kilmeny', and the publishers had no idea at this time that the poem subsequently switched to a Miltonic description of Heaven. Murray liked what he heard, and much to Hogg's astonishment offered him £500 for the copyright. Hogg's confidence in his poem was such that he preferred to take £80 for a first edition of a thousand copies instead, with the privilege of receiving copies at prime cost for him to dispose of personally. Blackwood was content to take a quarter-share of this edition, even though he later blamed Murray for rashness in making a bargain with Hogg without insisting that the whole manuscript should be submitted to him first. 'Your quickness & rapidity', he wrote, 'which have enabled you to do so much and so well on many other occasions misled you here'. By 18 October Hogg was able to inform Byron, 'I have had a very pleasant crack with Mr. Murray and we have sorted very well I hope we shall long do so'. The production was undertaken in Edinburgh by the printers of the *Caledonian Mercury* newspaper, and proceeded rapidly. Little more than a week after reaching his agreement with Murray Hogg expected the work to be published in three weeks' time.[37]

While his manuscript was in his own hands, Hogg must have changed the ending of *The Pilgrims of the Sun* to reflect the death of Harriet, Duchess of Buccleuch. The bodily and spiritual fulfilment of the marriage of Mary Lee and Hugo the Harper, is followed by a succession of absences and deaths. Mary dies in old age, while Hugo simply vanishes, though his harp sometimes sounds in the vicinity of a fairy ring in the woods. Hogg writes that Duchess Harriet when alive and wandering near Bowhill was sometimes mistaken for Mary Lee herself, as the beneficent 'genius of the wild' bringing blessings on her people. She too has now gone, however, and he concludes his poem mournfully:

> I little weened when I struck the string,
> In fancy's wildest mood to sing,
> That sad and low the strain should close,
> 'Mid real instead of fancied woes.[38]

He also added 'Superstition', the poem he had written at Elleray.

Murray had presented Hogg with an engraved portrait of Byron, and Hogg hoped to bring him into a community of Scottish poets. The dedication of *The Pilgrims of the Sun* to Lord Byron urged, 'Then Oh round shepherd's head thy charmed mantle fling'. Hogg's shepherd's plaid was one poetic garment, and the cloak Byron wore in his portrait was another, that also, perhaps, evoked that Wizard of the North, Walter Scott.[39] At much the same time that these lines were written, however, Hogg quarrelled with his long-standing literary mentor.

In retrospect Hogg remembered two indications of being undervalued by Scott in 1814, something he could never bear. Scott had criticised Hogg's dramatic compositions harshly, but more significantly he had declined to contribute, as Hogg had assumed he would do, to the projected 'Edinburgh Poetical Repository'. In a sudden access of rage, Hogg wrote him an angry and reproachful letter stating 'that I had never been obliged to him (it was a great lie) and never would be obliged to him for any thing; and I fear I expressed the utmost contempt for both himself and his poetry!' Feeling himself lowered in Scott's esteem unfortunately also lowered Hogg in his own: he felt, he said, degraded by Scott's refusal of a poem for his work, he could not endure to see Scott even 'at a distance' and was 'more disgusted with all mankind than I had ever been before, or have ever been since'. Moodily, he told Margaret Phillips that he had never loved her, calling her a 'cold insensate girl'. She would in the end 'be courted married and bedded with as little tremor passion or palpitation as you would go to a supper party or the theatre Royal of Edinburgh'. While blaming his neglect on her coldness, however, Hogg had to admit that he had 'acted rather ungenerously' towards her. The reception of Hogg's second major poem was crucial to his future standing as a poet, and he confessed to Eliza Izett, 'though I have no serious doubts about the success of the Pilgrims yet I feel a certain anxiety which prevents me from composing to any sense—my mind always reverting to that'.[40]

When *The Pilgrims of the Sun* was published in Edinburgh on 12

December sales were buoyant to begin with. On the very day of publication Hogg was obliged to request twenty more copies from William Blackwood to meet the demand on him personally from various friends and admirers. Ten days afterwards Jeffrey's laudatory review of *The Queen's Wake* finally appeared in the *Edinburgh Review*. Hogg busied himself in planning a commemorative dinner in Edinburgh for Robert Burns, at which he was to appear as the inheritor of Burns's mantle. A number of Burns's personal acquaintances such as James Gray, George Thomson, and Robert Ainslie would attend, and professional musicians would bolster the usual after-dinner songs and toasts.[41]

Anxiety about the fate of his poem and the breach with Scott seem to have propelled Hogg somewhat manically into Edinburgh's drinking culture at the end of the year. He was a founder and a leading light of an eccentric social club called the Right and Wrong Club, whose members met nightly for heavy drinking. As R. P. Gillies subsequently recalled, the club originated in a tavern party hosted by a newly-qualified young advocate and a return dinner hosted by Hogg the next day, a party so uproarious that 'a mob gradually collected on the street, who listened to the songs, and echoed our shouts'. The same party met in different locations every day of the week for the next three months, 'Sundays not excepted', at five o'clock and continued its carousals until the early hours of the following morning, its chief principle being that 'whatever any of its members should assert, the whole were bound to support the same, whether *right or wrong*'. Hogg's constitution, though notably robust, gave out under the strain and before the end of the year he was seriously ill and confined to his bed.[42]

Members of the club made him drunken visits in the early hours of the morning, after which, Hogg later recollected, he had to purchase new bell-pulls and door-knockers for the inhabitants of flats in the same building. R. P. Gillies recollected that on one such occasion he and some fellow-members commanded Hogg to come with them to rouse another member from his bed and climb Arthur's Seat at dawn. After a great deal of half-humorous grumbling Hogg nevertheless managed to stick to his bed, and to give them a piece of advice into the bargain:

> But since ye're grown quieter, stay a bit, till ye get a screed o' my mind. Our club, na doobt, is vera poetical; I'll no deny that. But I'll tell ye *yae* thing that micht be started as an improvement; for example, if we had amang us twa three grains o' common sense! That's a commodity in quhilk we seem to

be terribly deficient, and its of great use now and then till a poet. Now tak' an auld shepherd's advice; gang hame, and think nae mair about Portobello, or the moonlight, or sunrising.

Fortunately some of Hogg's other visitors did possess common sense. His friend John Wilson's sister, Jane, sent medicine and his land-lady, Mrs Tunny, seems to have kept an eye on her sick lodger and provided some basic nursing, presumably under the direction of Hogg's doctor, James Saunders. Some of the Edinburgh publishers among Hogg's acquaintance called on him, and friends brought pe-riodicals and took his letters to the post. Although at times Hogg was too ill to sit up and had therefore to write in pencil, he managed to read the *Quarterly Review* and Scott's new poem, *The Lord of the Isles* and to delegate arrangements for the forthcoming Burns dinner on 25 January.[43]

An illness can sometimes provide a respite from care, but Hogg's was accompanied by mounting anxiety about the London publica-tion of his new poem. Day after day he checked the London newspa-pers for the advertisement that would reveal the publication of *The Pilgrims of the Sun* by John Murray, and checked them in vain. Almost a month elapsed between the Edinburgh and London publications, and when Hogg finally saw the expected advertisement it was in anger and dismay rather than with relief that he read it. When he had received his printed copies and read the entire poem Murray realised how unrepresentative the part he had heard in Edinburgh was of the whole. He effectively withdrew his name as publisher, replacing the Edinburgh title-page with one in which he featured simply as the seller of a book brought out by William Blackwood. Hogg wrote to Murray from his sick-bed on 21 January, stoutly main-taining the poem's worth, his own literary friends considering it 'as far superior to any thing in the *Wake* as Milton is above Mr. Crabbe'.[44]

Hogg's recovery seems to have been remarkably rapid, for only four days later he was the life and soul of the Burns dinner at Oman's Tavern, filling and refilling Burns's marble bowl with whisky punch until the approach of morning and singing a commemorative song beginning, 'O wha is it says that a bard is neglected, | When the cup of high honour o'erflows to his fame?'[45] He seems to have resumed his usual sporting activities at much this time, curling in a gold medal competition, probably that of the Duddingston Curling Society. He also agreed to sit to William Nicholson for his portrait.

Nicholson had been a pupil of the engraver William Bewick of Newcastle, but had then moved to Edinburgh and painted a series of portraits of Edinburgh's notable literati, subsequently engraved by himself for a projected series of *Twelve Portraits of Distinguished Living Characters of Scotland*, each of them accompanied by a short biographical note. Nicholson's portraits of Hogg are the earliest known likenesses of him, the two surviving oil portraits being similar in showing the poet's plaid-draped upper body and head. Under the badge of his calling as a shepherd Hogg wears a fashionable muslin cravat and high double-breasted waistcoat under a good broadcloth coat, his hair neatly cut but with the waywardness of natural curls and his eyes shining almost tearfully with innocence and naivete. (It is startling to recollect that this is the portrait of a middle-aged man rather than of an ingenuous youth, such as James Beattie's Edwin of *The Minstrel*.) Nicholson showed Hogg portraits in Edinburgh exhibitions both in 1815 and 1816, one of which, now lost, was clearly a full-length portrait of Hogg accompanied by his working colley-dog—one critic considered the dog the best-drawn figure in the composition, the likeness to Hogg not being particularly strong besides his being shown in 'too theatrical' an attitude.[46]

Most welcome of all these tokens of his poetical standing, however, was the news of a permanent home for Hogg in his native district. Towards the end of January 1815 Hogg received a call from the Duke of Buccleuch's factor, who delivered a letter granting Hogg a small farm of about forty acres near the river Yarrow known as Eltrieve Moss, the same one that he had requested almost two years previously.[47] The previous tenant, Thomas Wilson, had died on 1 July 1814, and the Duke remembered his late Duchess's wish to assist Hogg. The farm would be free at the Whitsunday term, and Hogg's rent was to be 'nominal'. Although his middle-class friend John Wilson considered the existing house 'not habitable', Hogg and his aged father moved in even though all the plaids had to be hung up at the door as a protection from the cold outside. Hogg's good fortune was a hot topic of conversation in Edinburgh, Blackwood reporting that the farm was valued at about £70 of annual rent, 'but it is of course worth more'.[48] Inbetween the Duke's announcement of his gift in January and 15 May when he took possession of the farm, however, Hogg must find the money to stock it and employ a housekeeper to take care of old Robert Hogg. In the longer term he would also need to build a more comfortable and convenient house. His pen had brought him a country home, and his pen ought now to enable him to live there in comfort.

Perhaps this very solid recognition by the head of the Scott clan restored Hogg's emotional balance where another Scott was con-

cerned. A month later Hogg made up his quarrel with Walter Scott on hearing from his friend John Grieve that Scott had enquired daily after him during his recent illness and had proffered to pay for the necessary medical attendance. Instead of averting his gaze from the figure of his old friend on the Edinburgh streets, Hogg now wrote to tell him, 'I find there are many things which I yearn to communicate to you and the tears always rush to my eyes when I consider that I may not'. Touched by this frank appeal, Scott replied with an invitation to Hogg to come to breakfast and simply resumed their friendly relations of the past, without any discussion of the grounds of the quarrel.[49]

His mind more at ease than it had been for months, Hogg began to urge the 'Edinburgh Poetical Repository' once more upon John Murray under the new title of '*The Thistle and the Rose*', a compendium showcasing the talents of both Scottish and English poets. He also told Murray that he felt there should be a new edition of *The Queen's Wake* 'before May-day' and tried to interest him in his other long poem, *Mador of the Moor*. At the end of March Hogg also invited Murray to consider embarking on a collected edition of his poetry, mentioning that in Edinburgh he had received 'a very pressing proposal for publishing all my poetical works in two neat post octavo vol's.' [50]

Though Murray was inclined to encourage Hogg, he was determined not to publish anything more for him without examining the manuscript beforehand and Hogg's objections to sending his contributors' manuscripts for 'The Thistle and the Rose' to London fell upon deaf ears. Scott was about to come to London himself, and Murray urged Hogg to accompany him and witness his meeting at Albemarle street with Lord Byron, 'a commemorative event in Literary History' as he considered it. Hogg might also secure Byron's support for 'The Thistle and the Rose' by addressing a poem of congratulation on her marriage to Lady Byron and asking her to use her influence with her new husband. Hogg excused himself from coming to London on the ground that he needed time to prepare for taking possession of his new farm in Yarrow, but seems to have stayed on in Edinburgh for most of April, carousing with John Wilson and Thomas Campbell and attempting to persuade them to make a run by steam-boat to attend the annual dinner of the Shakespeare Club of Alloa, of which Hogg's friend Alexander Bald was a leading light. The celebration of the poet's birthday on 23 April was the club's main festival, when Shakespeare's bust was garlanded with flowers in their hall: Hogg wrote his 'Ode to the Genius of Shakespeare' for the 1815 dinner. On 7 May Hogg thanked John Murray for the £30 balance of his author's profits for the first edition of *The Pilgrims of the Sun*, and a few days afterwards left town for Selkirkshire.[51]

Hogg wrote to Blackwood in August from his new farm (which he renamed Altrive or Altrive Lake) that he was leading a life of dull contentment in the 'plain rustic state in which I spent my early years' and that his thoughts were 'as vacant as the wilderness around me'. Hogg stated that 'the most graceful way' of relinquishing the contest for literary fame was to 'retire indignant into my native glens and consort with the rustic friends of my early youth'. He nevertheless demanded new books, ordered the *Quarterly Review* to be sent to him regularly, and was enjoying Byron's *Hebrew Melodies* though considering him inferior to the Irish poet Thomas Moore as a song-writer. Hogg's mind had been steeped in the language of the Old Testament from early childhood, and Byron's reconfiguration of this inheritance for a contemporary audience was instructive. A couple of years later, in the intervals of 'fishing sailing in St. Mary's Lake working at Hay &c.' at Altrive, Hogg responded by composing his own Hebrew melodies.[52]

That autumn Hogg received a request from George Thomson for songs for his ongoing publication, *A Select Collection of Original Scottish Airs*. Burns had been a key contributor at an earlier stage of the project, and Hogg wished to be regarded as Burns's successor. Song-writing came easily to him, and this might also provide an opportunity for him to publish his personal collection of traditional tunes. Thomson's 'unwearied exertions in rescuing our national airs and songs', Hogg told him, entitled him to 'the support of every Scottish bard'. His collection of 'about 20 ancient Border airs' was at Thomson's service, since he had long wanted to place them in the hands of some gentleman 'who would make something of them'. Thomson was pleased to receive Hogg's lively and charming lyric 'Could this ill warld hae been contrived | To stand without mischievous woman,' which he had previously heard him sing in Edinburgh, but he was less enthusiastic about the proffered music.[53]

Thomson's working method was to get a Scottish tune set by a notable composer and then ask a writer to provide lyrics for it. He had sent Hogg a Beethoven setting of a suitable tune for 'Mischievous Woman', despite the fact that Hogg sung it to 'Delvin-side'. Nevertheless the two men evolved a method of working together amicably: Thomson would send a musical setting with a request that Hogg should provide suitable words, then on receiving Hogg's manuscript returned him a corrected transcript, which Hogg would

revise again before Thomson accepted it for publication. Hogg probably enjoyed this paper dialogue for he seems to have borne
Thomson's suggestions and corrections remarkably cheerfully and
was philosophically resigned to Thomson's editorial interventions.
When Thomson erased his comic stage representations of the English spoken by a native Gaelic speaker in his version of 'Highland
Laddie', Hogg simply told him that his friend John Grieve 'assured
me you would alter the broken highland Scotch I thought so too but
what I had written I had written'. Thomson (probably with contemporary attacks on him for parsimony over previous dealings with
Robert Burns in mind) showed his appreciation with a series of handsome gifts. He gave Hogg the quarto edition of Samuel Johnson's
Dictionary, a fine table-cloth for his wife, and even offered to send a
new violin.[54]

During this and the following summers he spent in the country
Hogg's thoughts were much occupied with music and song-writing.
He was not only a proficient fiddler, but was also capable of anno-
tating a simple tune though always eager to have his transcriptions
checked and corrected by a trained musician. The melodies of *A
Border Garland*, published around 1819, were partly composed and
collected by Hogg himself who then sent his musical transcriptions
to be set by the London-based composer W. E. Heather. At least one
of these tunes, Hogg later recalled, he composed 'whilst sailing one
lovely day on St Mary's Loch'.[55]

Having failed to interest George Thomson in his collection of
traditional tunes, Hogg tried in the spring of 1816 to persuade the
Cambridge musician John Clarke Whitfeld to take them:

> I have for several years been engaged in picking up old
> border airs and chaunts that are just hanging on the verges of
> oblivion and have not I believe been heard for centuries save
> at the shepherds' *ingle nook* Though most of them consist only
> of one part they are so simply beautiful that even the cel-
> ebrated *Broom of Cowdenknows* lags behind some of them. What
> a treasure they would be for a musical miscellany such as
> yours and if you will swear to me by all the holy trinity to
> preserve the unaffected simplicity of the melody you shall
> have a part of them for I have been distressed for a scientific
> man into whose hands to put them that they might not be
> ever lost. In that case how happy would I be to write appro-
> priate stanzas for them all.

Whitfeld was not interested either, but Hogg was more successful

with the Edinburgh church musician Alexander Campbell. Supported
by the Highland Society of Scotland in his object of preserving a
peculiarly national music, Campbell made a series of rural collecting expeditions for the publication of his *Albyn's Anthology; or a Select
Collection of the Melodies and Vocal Poetry, peculiar to Scotland and the Isles*,
published in two volumes in 1816 and 1818 respectively. Campbell
called on Hogg in Yarrow and enlisted his help, rather as Scott had
done previously for his *Minstrelsy of the Scottish Border*. Campbell's 'Notes
of My third Journey in the Border' recounts his meeting with William
Laidlaw at Traquair, and his subsequent arrival at Altrive, on Saturday, 12 October 1816. In the course of the next five days Hogg took
Campbell over to Ettrick and introduced him to various singers, including his cousins Thomas and Frank Hogg, from whose singing
Campbell took down 'a few good melodies very old & entirely new
to me', one of them subsequently published by him as 'Lady Linley'.
Hogg also gave Campbell his own tune collection.[56]

On 18 June 1815 the battle of Waterloo was fought, and Scott
hurried overseas to Belgium and France to report on the aftermath.
Unlike the celebrations of the preceding Easter this was a permanent end to the French Wars, and one in which Scottish troops had
played a particularly prominent and heroic part. On 23 October
Scott published his commemorative poem, *The Field of Waterloo*, dedi-
cating the profits of the publication to the widows and children of
the British soldiers who had fallen in the conflict. Typically, it was
one of the first of a stream of such commemorative publications.
Hogg, preoccupied with his new farm, at first alluded to the battle
only distantly and in jest, remarking at the start of the shooting season on 12 August that it sounded 'to a peaceful listener at a distance
like me as if the French were arrived in the forest'.[57] At Altrive, however, Hogg was a neighbour of both Scott at Abbotsford and of his
patron and landlord Charles, Duke of Buccleuch at Bowhill. Scott
was proud of his close friendship with the Duke as head of the Scott
clan, and drew Hogg into this orbit. Writing as the Duke's guest at
Bowhill in the middle of November, Hogg was now inspired by Scott's
enthusiasm for 'the great events of late taken place in the world and
[...] our honour and glory as a nation lately won'. He had also begun
a poem on Waterloo, 'a small tribute to our heros which I think not
unbecomes every British Bard', and dedicated it to Scott.[58] But where
Scott's poem emphasises the location and course of the battle, apos-
trophising the defeated Napoleon, and is very much the outcome of
his visiting the scene of action, Hogg's is essentially visionary. Hogg
relates a dialogue between soldiers of Scottish, Russian, and Prus-

sian nationality in the immediate aftermath of the battle, arguing that while the Europeans fought for self-preservation the Scot fought simply for God and the right. The Scottish soldier's death-bed prayer is followed by the haunting of his native scenes and family in Scotland by his watchful and protective spirit.

'The Field of Waterloo' was not the only poem to result from Hogg's visits to 'his Grace and friends' at Bowhill in 1815. Under Scott's auspices an inter-parish football match between the Selkirk and Yarrow men was organised at Carterhaugh to symbolise the parallel between the national leadership of Wellington and the local leadership of the Buccleuch family. Writing to Scott from Bowhill Hogg announced that the match was to take place on 4 December and that the Earl of Home was 'to head the Yarrow shepherds against you and the *other* Souters of Selkirk'. An ancient banner of the Scotts of Buccleuch was to float over the proceedings, and Scott invited Hogg to write a celebratory poem to accompany one by himself. These were published in pamphlet form with an engraving of the banner itself as *The Ettricke Garland,* and the event was widely reported in the London as well as the Edinburgh newspapers.[59] Hogg's poem celebrates 'the olden day | The iron age of hardihood', and glances at the 'havoc and dismay' of the recent war, which nonetheless has purchased 'peace and happiness', concluding with his wish that the Buccleuch banner may in future 'never wave | O'er sterner field than Carterhaugh!'

Hogg was about to receive a sharp reminder of the need to have an eye to his literary interests in Edinburgh. On receiving 'The Field of Waterloo' for publication, Blackwood decided it was 'bitter bad' and tried to get Scott to persuade Hogg to withdraw it. When Scott declined any interference Blackwood got it 'knock'd on the head' with the help of John Wilson and another of Hogg's friends. Hogg was outraged at the presumption of the younger poet who had been to some extent his own protégé, asking him rhetorically, 'Who gave an ideot and a driveller like you a right to counterwork their designs to pick up manuscripts clandestinely and blab over them in taverns to your scum of acquaintance?' Hogg's anger was short-lived and he forgave Wilson when he responded to Hogg's outburst with amusement rather than indignation, but the incident reminded Hogg of the need to be watchful.[60] Over the next few years Hogg spent a considerable amount of time in Edinburgh, particularly in winter. His friend R. P. Gillies had feared once Hogg got possession of Altrive his Edinburgh friends would lose his company, but in the event they saw him more frequently, if anything, than before. In Yarrow, Gillies argued, Hogg's hospitality was so much abused by chance tourists and visitors that paradoxically he found Edinburgh a place of retirement and a refuge.[61] At John Grieve's house in Teviot Row Hogg would be alone every weekday during his host's business hours to write or read in peace, and in Edinburgh he could also keep a close eye on his publishers.

During the spring of 1816 Hogg failed to persuade John Murray that the time was ripe for a collected edition of his poetry, but he did get *Mador of the Moor* published separately in Edinburgh. It was at the press in mid-March and a month later the printing was almost complete, for Hogg was asking William Blackwood's advice about a suitable motto for the title-page and had decided against providing notes to the poem. Blackwood published *Mador* towards the end of April, with John Murray taking a share of it as his London partner. Initially the poem seems to have sold slowly, Blackwood reporting to Murray a week after publication that it 'is not doing much, but there are a number of beautiful passages which will make it sell'. Murray's subsequent report of the sales in London, however, was more positive. Reviewers commented very favourably on Hogg's descriptions of natural scenery even though they considered it 'a kind of second-hand "Lady of the Lake" in its construction', and its subject-matter of the elevation to almost Queenly rank of a farmer's daughter with a child born out of wedlock must have been thought unsuitable for family reading by some prospective purchasers.[62]

As the days lengthened Hogg set out on a little holiday jaunt into Argyllshire, visiting his friends in Alloa by the way. At the beginning of June he was staying at Meggernie Castle in Glen-Lyon in Perthshire, admiring the beauty and musical talents of his hostess, the oddly-named Ronald Stewart, wife to young Stuart Menzies of Culdares. The 'greatest beauty about the castle is its lady', Hogg wrote, subsequently terming her 'one of the sweetest singers and most accomplished and angelic beings of the human race'. From there he wrote to Mrs Bald, 'I have besides since I saw you taken very near 100-dozen of trouts and at a moderate calculation have waded I think at least 100 miles'. The weather was freakishly severe for the time of year and crossing the mountains between Glenorchy and Appin Hogg had fallen into a snow-filled ravine, and extricated himself only with difficulty. Many lambs had been abandoned by their mothers. On one day spent in the Braes of Glenorchy Hogg counted 'upwards of an hundred lambs by the way, that seemed all newly dead, and nearly as many more that had lain quietly down to perish, without further exertion'. In the evenings Hogg's spirits were recruited by whisky.

He confessed, 'I have drunk so much highland whisky that I actually dreamed one night that I was turned into a cask of that liquor that the gaugers took me into custody and fairly proved me to be a legal seizure about which I was greatly concerned'.[63]

Hogg owned copies of *Fingal* and *Temora* and had referred to the heroes of Ossian in his own early work.[64] In the glens of Lorn, Appin, and Morven he was now in Ossian's own country and finding inspiration for his next narrative poem in the localities around Ardmucknish Bay, Ossian's Selma. According to historians such as Hector Boece, Raphael Holinshed, and George Buchanan, as well as local tradition, this was once the location of Beregonium the splendid ancient capital city of the Pictish Kings of Scotland. Hogg's ambitious narrative poem *Queen Hynde*, though not published until December 1824, originates in this journey. (*Queen Hynde* has, indeed, been described as '*Fingal* with jokes'.)[65] He inhabited a dream country, the setting for a powerful fantasy of national origins and national pride and a landscape by which his imagination was possessed for a time. On 1 June 1816 Hogg confided, 'I have fixed all the scenery of my next and greatest poetical work; with the country which I have just left I must as a poet live or die for ever and you will not think it any thing strange that I have lingered so long in a country where I must so often wander in imagination while my sheepish and indolent frame is far distant from it in reallity'.[66]

As Hogg turned southwards at the end of his excursion, however, the present day forced itself on his attention again. Passing through Edinburgh on his way to Altrive later in June he was obliged to solicit from William Blackwood, the publisher of *Mador of the Moor*, an advance of £20 or £30 of the expected profits to help him to carry on his farming to the end of the year. His newly-conceived epic poem would take some time to write and finish, and once again Hogg needed money immediately. It may have been at this point that Hogg finally concluded that his poetical repository would have to be abandoned. Scott had refused to contribute, Byron had fled to the continent from the scandal surrounding the break-up of his marriage the previous spring, and other contributors had withdrawn their contributions for speedier publication elsewhere. Hogg's triumphant gathering of materials during his visit to the Lake District the previous autumn had apparently been in vain. But he still had the parodies of Wordsworth and Coleridge that he had composed on rainy days at Elleray. Soon after his return from the Highlands he decided to substitute these for genuine contributions by Wordsworth and Coleridge, and to write others for a collection of parodies in the style of James and Horace Smith's *Rejected Addresses* (1812). He executed his new idea with remarkable dispatch, his 'off-hand production' being written in three weeks, and published anonymously three months later in October 1816. The Edinburgh publisher of *The Poetic Mirror* was the volatile John Ballantyne, younger brother of Scott's printer James Ballantyne and a fellow member of the old Right and Wrong Club. Ballantyne entered heartily into the joke, and either he or his elder brother read 'The Guerilla', a parody of Byron's early Eastern tales, aloud to a large party. Hogg recalled that everyone present was deceived, 'except Mr. Ballantyne, who was not to be imposed on in that way; but he kept the secret until we got to the Bridge, and then he told me his mind'. Writing to Hogg on 10 October, John Ballantyne announced, 'Your volume is out, & the truth denied strictly by James & I, when questioned regarding the Author'. James ('who is of the most fastidious') considered it admirable and rather to his surprise John had advance orders for as many as a hundred copies.[67]

The original edition of *The Poetic Mirror* sold out within six weeks of publication, and a new one went on sale before the end of the year. Ballantyne thought that this success would bring Murray and Blackwood to Hogg's feet and enable him to bargain for his subsequent poems without 'being qualified by their opinion, or views of individual profit'. The collection was even reviewed in that prestigious London periodical, the *Quarterly Review*.[68] Hogg's popularity as a poet, which had languished a little since the success of *The Queen's Wake* more than three years earlier, had received a sudden boost.

At the time of publication of *The Poetic Mirror* Hogg reached an agreement with John Ballantyne to publish another anonymous work for him. Undeterred by the poor response of both his own literary advisors and the general public to *The Hunting of Badlewe*, Hogg produced a collection of 'Dramatic Tales, by the Author of the Poetic Mirror'. The talent for capturing other voices for which he had been praised as a parodist would be triumphantly maintained in the characters he created for the stage. Ballantyne had previously helped Hogg to submit one of his dramas, 'Sir Anthony Moore', to the Edinburgh actors for their consideration, though it was never staged.[69] With this play, a revised version of *The Hunting of Badlewe* under the more exciting title of 'The Profligate Princes', and a pastoral tragedy entitled 'All-Hallow Eve', Hogg had enough material in hand to make up two volumes.

The publication of Hogg's *Dramatic Tales* was quite unexpected, William Blackwood, for example, declaring that Hogg had said not one word to him on the subject until he saw it advertised in the *Edinburgh Evening Courant* of 17 February 1817 as 'in the press, and speedily will be published'. It did not in fact come out until late in May, perhaps because copy fell short for the second volume and Hogg had to compose a fragment of a new play about fairies entitled 'The Haunted Glen', 'offhand, to make the second volume of an equal extent with the first'. *Dramatic Tales* was poorly received, with only a solitary notice of it appearing in the *Monthly Review*, which considered it notably inferior to the same author's *The Poetic Mirror*, 'one of the happiest *jeux d'esprit* of the age in which we live'. The collection was pronounced 'a poor school-boy's performance,—a coarse and unenlightened *commixture* of Allan Ramsay, Robert Burns, and Walter Scott, into an irregular fairy tale, dramatized and *colloquized* for the occasion'. The language was 'a compound of the style of all writers and all ages', and although there were 'clever parts and passages' in the individual plays the overall effect was 'to obscure the well-earned credit, and damp the well-founded expectations, which his first happy composition had very generally excited'.

Hogg may have planned originally to reveal that the anonymous author of *Dramatic Tales* was also the author of *The Queen's Wake*, thus establishing himself as a leading dramatist as well as a poet. He was bitterly disappointed. According to his 'Memoir' the failure of *Dramatic Tales* led him to abandon not only his play-writing but the composition of substantial poetic narratives as well.[70] His half-written Ossianic epic *Queen Hynde* was laid aside. Hogg's minstrel honours were over.

CHAPTER FIVE

Ingenious Lies

Edinburgh and its literary culture were changing rapidly around 1817. The old City Guard was disbanded, the Tolbooth prison demolished, Hogg's old lodgings went when St Anne's street was swept away to improve the North Bridge area, and gas-lighting crept along the North Bridge and slowly across the New Town district. The publication of *Waverley* by Walter Scott in 1814 had marked a turn from narrative poetry to prose fiction in popular taste, so that Hogg felt he too was obliged to turn to tales and novels.[1] New kinds of periodical began to appear in the bookseller's shops. From London came the weekly *Literary Gazette*, a successful fusion of a literary magazine and a newspaper that reviewed new books on, or even before, the date of publication. *The Scotsman*, a Scottish weekly liberal newspaper, also began publication in 1817. William Blackwood had deserted the academic South Bridge district the previous year, and moved his business to elegant premises at 17 Princes Street in the New Town. He intended to become one of the city's leading publishers, a Tory rival to the Whig Archibald Constable, and decided to begin a new monthly magazine, the *Edinburgh Monthly Magazine*, to set against Constable's *Scots Magazine*.

Hogg had been discussing the establishment of a new magazine with his friends ever since the collapse of *The Spy* in 1811. One of them, Thomas Pringle, was a copying-clerk at Register House, whom Hogg had perhaps met through the Edinburgh Institution and whose poem 'Epistle to Mr R. S****' Hogg had included as a Scott parody in *The Poetic Mirror*.[2] The two men successfully submittted a plan and list of contributors to William Blackwood, and Pringle resigned his post to become the new magazine's editor. Pringle's friend James Cleghorn, an actuary and agricultural expert, became his co-editor. Probably a conventional eighteenth-century-style periodical along the lines of the *Scots Magazine* or *Gentleman's Magazine* was all that was originally intended when these two minor literary men were appointed as editors, and when (as the agreement between them and Blackwood demonstrates) only ten pounds was allowed for copy for each monthly issue. Blackwood calculated that a modest sale of two thousand copies would allow him to pay his editors about fifty pounds monthly.[3]

Hogg evidently did not consider the new magazine important

enough to demand fresh and specially composed work, but thought that the gift of 'any old thing worth publishing' and the name of '*the redoubted Ettrick Shepherd*' were sufficient to ensure the publisher's gratitude. The '*great guns*' who contributed to the prestigious *Edinburgh Review* might fire off a shot, he thought, but would naturally 'disdain to continue writing for a two shilling Magazine', so that Blackwood's venture might come to rival Constable's *Scots Magazine*. Blackwood, however, wanted a periodical of the calibre of the *Edinburgh Review*, while his arrangements relied, like those of other monthly magazines, on low-paid journalists and a substantial number of amateur and unpaid contributors. The magazine 'never reached the paying point', and Blackwood found himself appealing to the most successful authors on his publishing list for magazine articles he could not pay them for. His unreasonable expectations led to a series of quarrels with his editors, during which Blackwood 'domineered over and *brusqued*' Pringle and the quarrelsome Cleghorn '*brusqued* every body', Hogg being involved as a reluctant arbitrator.[4] Eventually Pringle and Cleghorn agreed to edit a new series of the *Scots Magazine* for Archibald Constable while Blackwood took his new magazine under his own direction.

This time Blackwood ensured a regular receipt of spirited articles by paying his contributors, a repeat of the revolution achieved by the *Edinburgh Review* in 1802. This was a crucial development for Hogg, since it opened up the prospect of regular payment for his poems, songs, and short stories apart from the larger but irregular sums gained by his volume publications. It is only in the light of this periodical revolution that the failure of the *Edinburgh Monthly Magazine* appears so dismal. Although by the terms of Blackwood's agreement with Pringle and Cleghorn neither party could now use the title *Edinburgh Monthly Magazine*, both Blackwood and Constable clearly wished their rival magazines to be regarded as continuations of it at the time. Constable's *Scots Magazine* became the *Edinburgh Magazine* and its rival was now *Blackwood's Edinburgh Magazine*, and both claimed in advertisements to have the support of the previous magazine's contributors. Hogg advised Blackwood to impress upon potential purchasers 'by the continuation of *subjects* and *signatures*' that 'it is a continuation of the former work *in reallity* though you are not at liberty to avow it'.[5]

Hogg was a valued and trusted adviser at first, urging Blackwood, for example, to retain the services of John Wilson, since 'a little custom would make him the best periodical writer of the age'. His idea of an account of the Blackwood-Constable magazine rivalry in biblical language, the 'Translation of an Ancient Chaldee Manuscript' kick-started the new magazine. Hogg described Blackwood's arrangements to begin the magazine with Pringle and Cleghorn, their subsequent defection to Constable, and gave a rollcall of Blackwood's supporters, who included Hogg himself as 'the great wild boar from the forest of Lebanon' and John Wilson as 'the beautiful leopard from the valley of the palm trees'.[6] John Gibson Lockhart does not appear to be included in the list, and yet he and Wilson together were to be the presiding spirits of the new *Blackwood's Edinburgh Magazine*, while Hogg found himself increasingly marginalised.

It was at much this time that Hogg really became acquainted with Lockhart, a handsome if seemingly rather haughty dark-haired youngster who after a notable academic career in Glasgow and Oxford had settled in Edinburgh as an advocate and was preparing a translation of Schlegel's lectures on literature for publication by William Blackwood, following his travels on the Continent and a meeting with Goethe. At this stage in his career Hogg judged him 'a mischievous Oxford puppy, for whom I was terrified, dancing after the young ladies, and drawing caricatures of every one who came in contact with him'. He was nervous of Lockhart's satirical powers, and saw little of him before the establishment of *Blackwood's Edinburgh Magazine*. Nor had Lockhart yet met Scott, his future father-in-law.[7]

On receiving Hogg's 'Chaldee Manuscript' Blackwood showed it to Lockhart, who recalled that 'Wilson and I liked the idea of introducing the whole panorama of the town in that sort of dialect. We drank punch one night from eight till eight in the morning, Blackwood being by with anecdotes, and the result is before you'. The extended version they created added a list of Constable's adherents and was much more aggressively polemical. After its appearance *Blackwood's Edinburgh Magazine* 'became at once the prevalent subject for gossip, both at Edinburgh and through the whole country'. Private copies with manuscript keys identifying the people alluded to were circulated, lawsuits were threatened, and the success and future tone of the relaunched magazine was at once ensured. Scandal, personal attack, and what were termed 'personalities' continued over the next few years, with attacks on prominent Edinburgh whigs and on the so-called 'Cockney' writers, Hazlitt, Keats, and Hunt, and with the creation of magazine characters such as 'the Odontist' (a portly Glasgow dentist named James Scott) and 'the Shepherd' (James Hogg).[8]

Hogg certainly relished the liberation from the staid constraints of an old-fashioned monthly magazine, the 'intermixing all things through other' that he compared to the heterogenous stew called an olio, so that when 'a man has done with a very interesting article he should just pop his nose upon another quite distinct but as good of its kind'. The reader's only guide was the table of contents at the start of each issue, and Hogg thought this far preferable to the old sections of '*Analytical notices* and *Antiquarian repertory*'. He was perhaps slower to relish the full implications of what was soon termed the Mohock magazine, which was no longer interested in agricultural articles like the essays on sheep that Hogg and his brother William intended to offer as contributions. Gradually Wilson at least adopted a rather supercilious tone in referring to Hogg's traditional tales too, reportedly saying of one of the best of them, 'The Old Soldier's Tale', that it would do perhaps for an old-fashioned periodical such as the *Mentor*.[9] Hogg was increasingly uncomfortable with the widening division of literary Edinburgh along political and partisan lines. His friends included the radical James Gray and Constable's editor, Thomas Pringle, as well as Wilson and Lockhart. When writing his own 'Chaldee Manuscript' Hogg had expected good-humoured 're-taliation of the same nature and to acknowledge it [...] and crack over it', as Perry and Stewart, rival London newspaper editors, regularly took their wine together in the evenings and concerted their morning attacks on one another.[10]

Two episodes in 1818 reveal his discomfort at being reputed a Tory firebrand. Hogg's friend James Gray had been planning an account of the Ettrick Shepherd's life and literary progress for several years, writing to William Hogg for information in 1813 and presenting a paper on the subject in 1818 at a meeting of the Literary Association. Part of this 'Life and Writings of James Hogg' was published in three instalments in Constable's *Edinburgh Magazine* in January, February and March 1818, when Constable himself apparently ordered it to be discontinued on the grounds that Hogg was a supporter of the rival magazine. It had also been the subject of mockery in *Blackwood's* itself in two letters by the supposititious Timothy Tickler in the February and March issues. Extremely angry, both at Constable's partisanship and at the way in which *Blackwood's* had turned 'the laugh both against my biographer and myself' Hogg was ready to call down a plague on both these Edinburgh houses.[11]

He also reaped more of the disadvantages than benefits of identification with *Blackwood's Edinburgh Magazine* when John Douglas, editor of the *Glasgow Chronicle*, smarting at his treatment in the magazine came over to Edinburgh by coach on 11 May to horsewhip its publisher, William Blackwood. Blackwood decided to retaliate in kind and, accompanied by Hogg as his backer, laid into Douglas with a stick as he was about to return from Princes Street to Glasgow again. Douglas's report of the incident in his own newspaper, describing Blackwood as 'apparently somewhat intoxicated' and his companion as 'a man having the appearance of a shop porter' was smartly countered by a Blackwood pamphlet containing his own and Hogg's account of the incident. The Ettrick Shepherd firmly asserted his right to be considered as a gentleman, alluding to his visits to Bowhill and Abbotsford in explaining that he was 'a welcome guest in companies where [Douglas] would not be admitted as a waiter'. Two men subsequently came over to Edinburgh from Glasgow to challenge Hogg to fight a duel with Douglas, and were too many for Hogg who, after locking them up and giving them in charge to the police, saw them discharged since their words could not be proved to refer to a challenge at all, and 'might as well imply an invitation to a dinner as to a battle'. Afraid of being further involved in such bellicose doings, Hogg promptly retreated to Yarrow and stayed there for some weeks.[12]

Oscillating between residence at Altrive and long stays in Edinburgh, Hogg seems to have been afflicted alternately by acute irritation at the political disputes of Edinburgh and by mild boredom in the country. When he heard on 12 October 1818 that Wilson and Lockhart were in Ettrick Forest intending to call at Altrive he remarked that there were 'few things in the world that could be so grateful as such a visit here at this gloomy season but though I am fidging fain to see them yet I intend to quarrel with them both and to tell them that I think it extremely hard to be set to the wall by men whom I consider and can prove to be inferior to myself at least in discerning what can amuse the generality of the public'. On the eruption of another quarrel arising from *Blackwood's*, this time an attack on Playfair, and the subsequent publication of a pamphlet aggressively entitled *Hypocrisy Unveiled, and Calumny Detected*, Hogg simultaneously congratulated himself on being out of the row and proffered his advice on the best way to settle the dispute to the advantage of Lockhart and Wilson.[13] Hogg's affection for Wilson and Lockhart was real, but he often wished that they promoted his work as often as they ridiculed his person.

The new-look magazine was gossipy and liked to react instantly to political developments and new publications as they occurred, and it would now be a disadvantage to be always in the country, as William Laidlaw found. Blackwood had ensured Scott's support for the magazine by providing Laidlaw with a regular engagement to write the 'Chronicle' section of the magazine, but this needed to be

longer or shorter depending on the other articles in a particular issue and Laidlaw living in Roxburghshire could not make last minute adjustments to the 'Chronicle' to suit. Hogg was Blackwood's negotiator when he tried to persuade Laidlaw to relinquish the position without giving offence to Scott, bearing a letter from Blackwood to Laidlaw to Abbotsford and speaking separately on the matter to both Laidlaw and Scott.[14]

Nevertheless, Hogg's own ties to the city were gradually loosening. His old friend John Grieve had provided him with an Edinburgh base for many years, but Grieve was now in poor health, unable to walk far due to a disease of the spine. Although he retained his interest in the hatters' firm on the North Bridge for the rest of his life, he retired from its active management around 1818 and then divided his time between suburban Newington, where his sister kept house for him, and his parents' home of Cacrabank in Ettrick.[15] The attractions of Abbotsford increased after Hogg's old friend William Laidlaw took up the post of factor to Scott in 1817, also undertaking what literary work Scott threw in his way. Scott, Hogg, and Laidlaw were at Abbotsford together at the beginning of January 1818, 'as merry as larks' within doors though bad weather prevented sporting activities, and shortly afterwards Scott's light-hearted 'Alarming Increase of Depravity among Animals' (published in the October 1817 issue of *Blackwood's*) was followed up by Laidlaw's 'Sagacity of a Shepherd's Dog' in January 1818 and Hogg's own 'Further Anecdotes of the Shepherd's Dog' in the March issue.[16]

William John Napier settled on his family's Ettrick property not long after his marriage in 1816 and brought the same determined energy that he had shown as a naval captain during the Napoleonic Wars to bear on the improvement of the district. He planted trees, improved roadways, built new cottages for labourers, and established a Pastoral Society of Selkirkshire drawing the leading Yarrow farmers into his orbit and holding annual sheep markets on his property at Thirlestane. Hogg was attracted by his energy and public spirit, terming him a 'real good fellow'. The Duke of Buccleuch too, treated Hogg kindly as a country neighbour as well as a tenant, franking letters and parcels for him and sending him newspapers regularly after they had been read at Bowhill.[17] During 1818 Hogg finally built himself a permanent home at Altrive, replacing the old cottage with its clay walls and thatched roof by a modern and convenient stone house. At the beginning of July he announced to John Murray that he was 'building a castle this year', by the end of the month the mason's work had been completed, the roof was finished by mid-August, and Hogg was finally able to move in by the end of the year, the old drafty building now serving as a stable.[18]

Hogg was now occupied with a project of national significance, looking beyond the limits of Edinburgh polemics. His earlier summer trips into the Highlands of Scotland had qualified the prejudices resulting from an upbringing in a district where highlanders were feared as savage enemies of Presbyterianism and despised as ignorant and bloodthirsty savages. The noble Ossianic Highlands underpinned *Queen Hynde*, while the tales Hogg had heard of bitter oppression in the wake of the 1745 defeat of the Jacobite cause moved him to sympathy. The first time Hogg was in the Aird district, for example, he had been told of a party of English officers arriving there after the battle of Culloden who had raped seven sisters of the name of Fraser and burnt them, their mother, and their home to ashes.[19]

Following the outstanding bravery and service to the British state of the Highland regiments in the recently-ended Napoleonic conflict, there was a general feeling that the wounds inflicted upon Highland culture in the past should now be staunched if not healed. The former savages and barbarians were now the survivors of an ancient and inherently noble way of life that ought to be recorded for posterity. The Highlander (like the Borders peasant) signified an *echt* Scottish culture that was rapidly being eroded by British modernity. Highland Societies and Celtic Societies were formed and in the autumn of 1817 David Stewart of Garth acting on behalf of the Highland Society of London tried to enlist the song-collector George Thomson to form and prepare for publication a collection of Jacobite songs. Thomson passed the commission on to his friend and contributor James Hogg.[20]

Hogg had an early familiarity with Jacobite songs and legends, from the singing of his mother and that of eccentrics like Betty Cameron. He had also been collecting Jacobite songs in a desultory way for some time from acquaintances such as David Constable, the eldest son of the publisher Archibald Constable. In making a definitive collection of Jacobite songs, he would surpass Scott on his own ground ('for Scott could not have collected the music'). As the creator of a definitive record of historic Scotland, Hogg reflected confidently, 'it is a serious thing to think that the last chance of preserving a Jacobite Relic is going out of one's power and lost for ever for a farther collection of them will never be attempted nor does any one need'.[21]

In both his verse Dedication to *The Jacobite Relics of Scotland* and in his 'Memoir' Hogg represents his work ('These strains, which a Shepherd has travailled to save') as the result of recent encounters between two primitives, Shepherd and Highlander:

> The jealousy of the Highlanders was amusing beyond conception. I shall never forget with what sly and disdainful looks Donald would eye me, when I told him I was gathering up old songs. And then he would say, "Ohon, man, you surely haif had very less to do at home; and so you want to get some of the songs of the poor repellioners from me; and then you will give me up to King Shorge to be hanged? Hoo, no!–Cot tamn!–that will never do.[22]

Hogg's Aberdeenshire correspondents, Peter Buchan and John Wallace, certainly undertook such field trips, Hogg telling Peter Buchan in June 1818, for instance, that he had been 'highly amused by the descriptions of your several rural excursions and have accompanied you in imagination every foot of the way, and in your humourous adventure with the old Jacobite have in idea made one of the number'. But there is no record of Hogg making similar collecting trips between the end of 1817 (when he received his commission) and February 1821 (when the second and final volume was published). He collected material from 'the old Jacobite families of Angus and Mearns settled in Edinburgh', attending their supper parties, listening to the songs and anecdotes of these Episcopalians, particularly of old men such as 'a Mr Hutchard, about a hundred years of age, who would never drink King George's health, either by one denomination or another, asserting that he was of the race of an usurper, and had no right to be there'. Hogg also laid his like-minded friends of all social classes under contribution: old Yarrow cottagers like Lizzie Lamb, north of England antiquaries such as Robert Surtees, the Tweedsmuir schoolmaster, young John Steuart of Dalguise, and David Laing the Edinburgh bookseller. Indirectly, Hogg also promoted his work through newspapers, the *Dumfries and Galloway Courier* of 1 December 1818, for instance, quoting at length from Hogg's appeal for further materials in his introduction to the forthcoming first volume.[23]

Walter Scott was of course particularly helpful, both as contributor and adviser. Hogg called on him at Abbotsford with 'a whole armfull of jacobite ballads' in December 1818. Although amused by Hogg's ignorance of Scottish historical detail, as when he mistook the Major General Canon who had distinguished himself at the battle of Killiecrankie for some 'Great dignified Clergyman', Scott was obliged to own 'Hogs Jacobite Songs is a curious book and he has grubd up a great deal of old poetry of one sort or other'. And as a keen amateur fiddler and occasional composer of melodies, Hogg took great care over collecting the music as well as the words to the songs.[24]

Hogg's reward was poorer than expected. The Highland Society of London paid only £50 where Stewart had promised £100, and any binding commitment on behalf of the Society was denied.[25] Blackwood, as the publisher of the work, offered Hogg £150 for each volume, but this was partly dependent on sales. In 1829 *Jacobite Relics* was plundered by the Glasgow publisher Richard Griffen for his *Jacobite Minstrelsy*, and no doubt for many subsequent collections, yet the core position of Hogg's collection has seldom been openly acknowledged. Murray Pittock has argued that it was not sufficiently 'selected, manipulated and controlled to present an image of Scotland which was both sanitized and unrepresentative'. While satisfying primitivist expectations Hogg alluded to the contemporary Highland Clearances and denied a wish for uncomplicated closure of the past and noble ahistorical sentiment. In *The Private Memoirs and Confessions of a Justified Sinner* Lockhart is made to comment on Hogg's imposition of 'ingenious lies on the public', but his fault here was fidelity to an authentic voice of the people.[26]

Hogg had, however, gained one important asset through his work on *Jacobite Relics* in the form of a new companionship and working relationship with his nephew, Robert Hogg. Born in 1802, the eldest son and second child of Hogg's eldest and closest brother William, Robert had been educated at Peebles Grammar School and Edinburgh University in preparation for a career in the ministry of the Church of Scotland. He had done well at university with some financial support from his parents and some from tutoring High School pupils, winning two prizes for Latin poetry. Hogg undoubtedly encouraged his literary ambitions at this time. Robert's methodical mind was of great assistance in classifying and arranging the multifarious materials Hogg sporadically assembled in making his collection of Jacobite song and he also shaped the system of appendices for the second volume.[27] Perhaps Robert's association with his famous uncle influenced his decision in 1820 not to proceed from the general university course to study theology and divinity but to try to find employment as a teacher or in connection with literary production instead.

More tangible assets were, however, required, not least to pay for the new house at Altrive. Hogg had been pressing for the publication of a collection of Scottish rural tales since 1813, before Scott's ground-breaking success with *Waverley*, a project which at the start of 1817 was described as a collection of 'Cottage Winter Nights', consisting of 'The

Rural and Traditionary Tales of Scotland', and by the end of the year as in four volumes. Blackwood seems to have been persuaded to publish two volumes only to begin with, though another two might follow if the first instalment sold adequately. On 13 January 1818 Hogg suggested the following copy for an advertisement for his forthcoming selection of the kind of tales told in remote cottages in Scotland during the long dark winter evenings when farm work was impossible:

> In the press and speedily will be published Vol's 1 and 2 of Mr Hogg's COTTAGE TALES containing THE BROWNIE OF BODSBECK and THE WOOL-GATHERER These tales have been selected by him among the Shepherds and peasantry of Scotland and are arranged so as to delineate the manners and superstitions of that class in ancient and modern times &c &c

The ethnological tone here is a reminder of Hogg's parallel activities at the time, collecting and recording Jacobite song. It offers a national history experienced by the people rather than as determined and interpreted by a political and social elite. The lead tale of the forthcoming Blackwood publication, *The Brownie of Bodsbeck*, fights for possession of the ground covered by an earlier Blackwood publication, *The Tale of Old Mortality* by Walter Scott—the significance of the Covenanting past. Hogg himself was emphatic about the priority of his own account, writing to the editor of *The Scotsman* shortly after publication in May 1818, for example, 'The Brownie was written long before Old Mortality but I could not get the Booksellers to publish it Scott knows this well enough'. Nevertheless it was judged by the standard of *Old Mortality* and not in tandem with the other tales in the collection, 'The Hunt of Eildon' and 'The Wool-Gatherer', one medieval and legendary, the other an archetypal finding of a lost heir. Scott himself, interestingly, had a half-recollection of hearing part of the former as an infant in his cradle. Hogg was bringing the pre-literary into literature, something wilder and more extravagant. In this respect his work was both a challenge and a tribute to Walter Scott, whom Hogg sincerely admired and even loved. Leaving a Castle Street dinner in March 1817 at which Scott had collapsed in excruciating pain from gallstones, Hogg had threatened to fling John Ballantyne on the pavement for daring to say that Scott's illness was serious.[28]

If Scott objected to Hogg's portrait of the Covenanters, others were appalled by its departures from literary politeness and formality. In the course of typesetting the printer, Ballantyne, flagged up a passage to William Blackwood for censorship where the heroine's would-be rapist is castrated by the eponymous Brownie, a 'most irregular abberation'. The work's London publisher John Murray when he saw an advance copy of the work threatened to repeat the action he had taken a few years previously with regard to *The Pilgrims of the Sun*, and remove his prestigious name from the title-page. Blackwood certainly heard rumours that Murray 'had refused to publish the Brownie', and Walter Scott wrote to Murray directly, admitting that Hogg, though 'sadly deficient not only in correct taste but in common tact', nevertheless possessed 'a very considerable portion of original genius' and that to cancel the title-page 'would be doing the poor fellow an irretrievable injury'. In the event Murray did not withdraw and he and Blackwood each advanced Hogg £50 from his author's profits on the publication, with the promise of a further payment to come as and when sales justified it. Unfortunately, after a promising start, sales flagged (compromised perhaps in London by John Murray's reluctance to push the work and the contemporaneous breakdown of the Murray-Blackwood publishing partnership), and about two hundred of Murray's copies were auctioned off to the remainder trade as late as 1822.[29]

Disappointment over *The Brownie of Bodsbeck; And Other Tales* may have motivated Hogg's decision to try to publish a second instalment of Scottish rural tales anonymously. His plan was to get a number of tales that had previously appeared in *The Spy* and other priodicals collected and arranged by his nephew Robert, under the title of *Winter Evening Tales*. Blackwood, to whom he offered the work, suggested the firm of Oliver & Boyd as publishers instead. This firm was printing the first series of *Jacobite Relics* and Hogg was impressed by the quality and comparative cheapness of what he described as 'a beautiful book I think I never saw the like of it'. By August 1819 he had a signed agreement with the firm, who were to pay him £100 for an edition of 1500 copies of two volumes of tales, each consisting of not less than 350 pages, and the work was advertised as 'forthcoming' before the end of that same month. In the event publication was unexpectedly delayed until the spring of 1820, Margaret Phillips writing to Hogg on 7 February 'Are your Winter's Evening tales come out yet, they are not in Dumfries'. In fact, they were not advertised as 'this day published' until 19 April 1820. It seems probable that, because the typeface of the volumes was so cramped, Hogg had been obliged to supply almost double the copy he expected, and his old tales from *The Spy* were not simply gathered together but radically rewritten and expanded in a number of instances. Hogg's collection, as Ian Duncan remarks, represents a sharp departure from the national fictions of Walter Scott or Maria Edgeworth, 'an alternative, non-novelistic genre of national fiction, close to its roots in popular print media (miscellanies, chapbooks) as well as in oral storytelling'.[30] There are ghost stories, picaresque adventures, satire, tales of war and murder, and love adventures, all told from the perspective of the Borders fireside during the long winter evenings.

With the necessary provision of funds for making Hogg comfortable at Altrive very much in mind, Murray and Blackwood planned to embark on a projected de luxe subscription edition of Hogg's best-known work to date, The Queen's Wake. Publication by subscription was characteristic of peasant poets, displaying the author as a suppliant of the well-to-do rather than as a professional writer. Scott's prospectus of May 1817, subsequently revised by Blackwood, accordingly invited Hogg's friends to 'add solid emolument to his barren laurels' by supporting a two-guinea quarto volume 'ornamented with engravings from designs by Scottish artists'. Hogg was clearly attracted by the promised illustrations, for when the number was reduced to one to form a guinea volume instead, he set about providing two further plates on his own responsibility. He arranged with Archibald Constable and Charles Kirkpatrick Sharpe respectively to present his publishers with a fait accompli, the inclusion of a portrait of Queen Mary and a picture of the bardic harp in the volume as well as the double-page illustration by Sharpe to 'The Witch of Fife'. But he also wanted his work to be available to purchasers of more modest means, and eventually a nine-shilling octavo edition set from the same type and without illustrations was also published in the summer of 1819.[31]

As the Regency decade drew to an end, Scots were preoccupied with the exhumation and use of the past as history, offering a continuum and parallel with contemporary events. After the Napoleonic Wars when Britain was fighting for survival in a Europe overrun by Napoleon's armies, the achievements of the heros of the early fourteenth-century Scottish Wars of Independence were newly celebrated. The body of Robert I, the Bruce, was exhumed at Dunfermline and a cast taken of the hero's skull, and citizens of Edinburgh, Glasgow, and Stirling all proposed to erect a Wallace monument. A member of the Highland Society of Scotland, returning to his native country after a working life spent in India, offered fifty pounds in prize-money for a poetic competition 'on the subject of WALLACE's inviting BRUCE to the Scottish throne [...] so expressed as not to give offence to our brethren south of the Tweed', emphasising the propriety of a Wallace monument in Edinburgh for which he proposed to leave a thousand pound legacy. Of the fifty-seven entrants Felicia Hemans was the winner, with a poem carefully tailored to the competition require-

ments. Hogg, on the contrary, drew Wallace as a giant of myth en-
shrined in the hearts and on the lips of the common people as a
figure of Scottish rather than North British independence, the symbol for Scotland of 'What once she was, and now is not'. When king
and nobles failed Scotland, her people kept the idea of independent
nationhood alive and Wallace led them to fulfil it.[32]

The body of Robert Burns too had recently been raised from the
earth before being deposited in an elaborate memorial in the churchyard in Dumfries. Hogg actively commemorated Burns as his predecessor during these years, and graced numerous dinners on 25 January to honour Burns in that role. The Edinburgh Burns dinner Hogg
had promoted in 1815 was succeeded by another two years later at
Hogg's favourite haunt Young's Tavern on the High Street, publicised in the *Edinburgh Evening Courant* by Hogg himself in all prob-
ability, since the anonymous writer described the profusion of dinner as 'much like that provided for "Wat o' the Cleuch" in Jedburgh
Abbey', a reference to one of the parodies of *The Poetic Mirror*. Although in later years Hogg was to feature at Burns dinners in the
Burns heartland of Dumfries (1822), as well as in London (1832),
the most spectacular and best-recorded occasion was probably the
triennial Burns dinner held on 22 February 1819 at the Assembly
Rooms on Edinburgh's George Street. Some three hundred and
twenty gentlemen attended, prominent whigs such as Francis Jeffrey
and Henry Cockburn among them as well as Hogg's Blackwoodian
cronies Lockhart and Wilson, and surviving friends of Burns. Gow's
band performed, as well as a number of professional singers, Lees,
Templeton, and Swift. Lockhart's account of the occasion in his *Peter's Letters to his Kinsfolk* is of 'a national assembly' meeting to 'do
honour to a national poet', yet he describes Whig participation as
unconvincing. Where the Tories of Blackwood's are enthusiastic, it
is recalled that Jeffrey, for example, has attacked both Burns and
Wordsworth in print. Hogg acted as one of the stewards, and his
health was proposed in an exemplary speech by John Wilson who
emphasised 'the high and holy connection [...] between the dead and
the living peasant', while Dr Morris is reminded by his appearance
of Wordsworth's Pedlar.[33] Hogg, like Burns, is shifted from national
poet to Tory icon of an appropriately naïve if gifted peasantry that is
maligned and misunderstood by Enlightenment whiggery.

Hogg's celebrity was marked by less partisan demonstrations of
respect. Shortly after the Burns dinner he visited John Aitken at
Dunbar and was awarded the freedom of the town on 9 April. Aitken,
a bank clerk with literary ambitions, had probably made Hogg's ac-

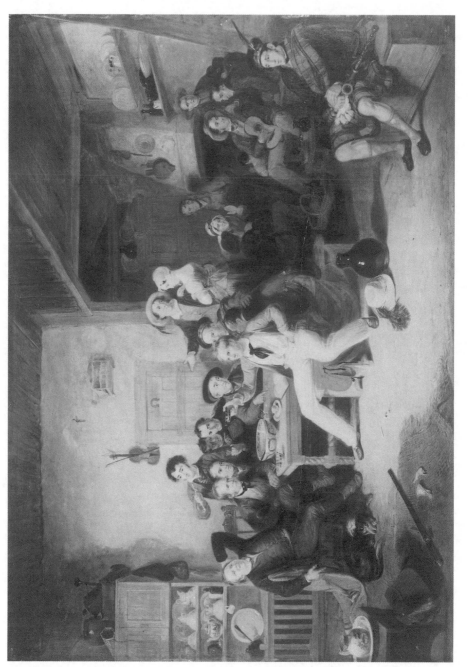

The Celebration of the Birthday of James Hogg by Sir William Allen. © Scottish National Portrait Gallery

quaintance when he was employed in Selkirk and enjoyed Hogg's confidence in respect of both literary secrets such as the authorship of the 'Chaldee MS' and personal matters such as the existence of Hogg's illegitimate daughters. At Aitken's house Hogg wrote 'The Mermaid's Song', a lament by a supernatural creature over the grave of her mortal lover. Hogg subsequently described Aitken as the only person alive who could ever collect his scattered songs from a multitude of newspaper and periodical printings over a thirty-year period. Hogg's Dunbar visit had been marked by more than one jolly evening, Aitken sleeping so late on one subsequent morning that wishing to send a parcel to the young bookseller and antiquary David Laing he was forced to write the accompanying letter in 'about fifteen minutes' before the coach departed 'and that too *sans* breeches'.[34]

Hogg was also an honoured member of the Dilettanti Society, a convivial association of Edinburgh artists and literary men that had been founded on the wreck of the old Right and Wrong Club. William Allan's painting, 'The Ettrick Shepherd's House-Heating or the Celebration of his Birthday' has a caricatured Hogg laughing at a toast proposed to him by Wilson among a party of members that included Scott, Ballantyne, Alexander Nasmyth, and the Society's secretary, David Bridges. The Society held fortnightly hot suppers at Young's Tavern on the High Street, that 'great resort [...] of a number of men of genius here in their hours of relaxation and hilarity'. In a large room with a 'sky-blue ceiling, pink cornices, and transparent linen blinds' Bridges' bowls of punch rivalled 'Jamie Hogg's pitchers of toddy'.[35]

With Edinburgh society increasingly divided along party lines, however, Hogg seems to have favoured the idea of a permanent settlement in his new house at Altrive, and perhaps also marriage. When Hogg had first been granted the farm in 1815 he had asked John Murray, jocularly, to look out for a suitable bride: 'I wish you or Mrs. Murray would speer me out a good wife with a few thousands I daresay there is many a romantic girl about London who would think it a fine ploy to become a Yarrow Shepherdess'. He had also jested with Lord Byron about marrying a '*fair West Indian*' heiress. Perhaps by 1818 he was taking the idea of a prudent marriage seriously? A gap in his correspondence with Margaret Phillips coincides with Scott's playfully telling the Duke of Buccleuch that Hogg 'intends to propose [...] for one of the *rich* Miss Scotts–first however he is to try one of the *rich* Miss Brodies of Inverleithen'. Margaret Phillips may have felt hurt, since she told Hogg that he could get no other body for a wife but her. Hogg was in fact reluctant to make that commitment to any woman. In his younger days his acquaintances would say that he 'would do any thing for the women but marry them'.[36]

Margaret Phillips was in Edinburgh again in May 1819, and Hogg seems to have alternately avoided and sought her company. For a man so obviously at ease with women and so openly flirtatious, Hogg appeared to need a great deal of encouragement to marry, and told her that he was only 'earning [...] grief and dissapointment' in his pursuit of her. Before she left Edinburgh for her Dumfriesshire home on 16 July, however, he did pluck up the courage to make her a serious proposal of marriage which she accepted on condition that her parents approved. The couple seem to have agreed that she would sound out her father on the matter when she reached Mouswald again, rather than Hogg making the conventional application to old Peter Phillips for his daughter's hand, and that if the news was well received Hogg was to make a visit to the family in form later in the year.[37]

Hogg's diffidence is surprising. Although Peter Phillips had farmed in Dumfriesshire for more than thirty years and was apparently prosperous, he had, after all, been content to marry his eldest daughter to James Gray, who as the son of a shoemaker had no income beyond his schoolmaster's salary and Margaret's chances of marriage at the age of thirty were diminishing. Hogg was a celebrated man, even though forty-nine years old and (apart from having Altrive) dependent for his living on his pen. Margaret Phillips took her time to mention her agreement with Hogg to her parents. Initially she confided privately in her brother, Walter, with whom she had lived as housekeeper before his marriage. His advice was 'not to be in a hurry' and to say nothing to their father 'until we see what time brings about', a course of action more suitable to a very young lover than to a middle-aged one. Hogg was anxious and annoyed, telling her, 'Whenever you feel disposed to be cordial and affectionate and steady to what was fairly understood between us I will meet you with open arms but think not that I am coming either to plead with them or to brag of my riches and run the risk of biding jibes on my poverty. It is yourself that I want. I would do a good deal to court you but I cannot court any other body'. His heart recoiled, he told her, from this 'mentioning of matters and making of treaties' more than from anything he had ever set about. Nevertheless, the visit was paid in September 1819, and a few weeks afterwards Margaret seems to have had a heart-to-heart with her father who gave them his blessing. Hogg on his side made what he felt to be a necessary confession to his intended bride of his having fathered two illegitimate daughters some years previously.[38] The way appeared to be clear for the wedding.

Hogg was then attacked by renewed doubts. He had received an anonymous letter advising him not to marry and been troubled by an ominous dream about Margaret's family, which 'terminated at an old church with gothic windows among graves and gravestones and strangers'. He could not bear to lose Margaret but, he told her, had 'for the present taken such an aversion to the married state that in the same mood of mind in which I am just now I dare hardly trust myself to venture into it'. Sensibly, Margaret Phillips assured Hogg of her affection for him and told him to take time to consider the matter deliberately. He continued to hesitate, making resolutions of 'prudence and caution' while knowing that if Margaret were living in the immediate vicinity he would marry her next week. Hogg could not expect much in the way of fortune with his bride, or at least not immediately. Old Peter Phillips in making his will in 1812 had devised legacies of a thousand pounds to his unmarried daughters, but Margaret advised Hogg on 24 November 1819, 'we must not expect much from him just now though he said he was willing to do all he could for us and should you require his assistance you should have it [...] perhaps any thing which might be for us would be as acceptable afterwards'. No specific dowry was mentioned in the eventual marriage settlement.[39]

By September 1819 Hogg's Edinburgh friend John Wilson had heard rumours of his forthcoming marriage:

> The world assert that the Shepherd is about to take unto himself a wife, in which case, he will no doubt have a patriarchal Family. All his Friends wish him well—and if a Wife is to encrease his happiness, may the nuptial knot be speedily tied. Yet I confess that to him the Bachelor's life would seem to be best fitted. But probably our excellent Friend has no thoughts of changing his condition.

An article on curling in the issue of *Blackwood's* for February 1820 spread such rumours. As Hogg and the narrator travel through Leadhills on their way to Closeburn, Hogg, who is is surmised to have 'a matrimonial arrangement on hand' looks on Nithsdale 'perfectly stiff and motionless, as a pointer dog at a dead *set*'. It was the middle of March before Hogg finally made up his mind, and sent what reads curiously like an ultimatum to Margaret Phillips. Sending a document for her to sign and hand in at Mouswald church for the proclamation of banns, and requesting her signature to a similar one for Yarrow, he demanded to know 'once for all [...] if you are willing that we should be proclaimed in the two churches on the 16th and 23[d] of April and married the week following?'[40]

Thereafter Hogg concerned himself with practical arrangements. Margaret Phillips was taken aback at this unexpected decisiveness, protesting 'you have given me little time to prepare for this very important event', particularly as her mother had been ill. Hogg urged her not to send any new furniture to Altrive apart from a chest of drawers for her clothes and perhaps a mirror to stand upon it, and to ask her niece Janet Gray to accompany her as her bridesmaid. Hogg's final letters to her before the marriage were gently reassuring. There was no need to be flurried since she would be very happy and 'very much made of'. His own agitations and doubts now apparently forgotten, he wrote tenderly, 'Farewell my dearest Maggy till I see you Keep a good heart the braes of Yarrow will soon be very wildly bonny and every one here is wearying to see you but scarcely one yet believes you are coming'.[41]

The distance between their homes made it impossible for the Rev. Robert Russell to marry the couple in Yarrow, and the ceremony was performed instead by the Mouswald minister in the drawing-room of Margaret Phillips's home of Mouswald Mains. Accompanied by his best man, James Ballantyne of Whitehope, and a black servant, Hogg set out for Dumfriesshire on Monday, 24 April, sleeping a night at Corhead en route and staying on arrival with Margaret's brother Walter at Longbridgemoor in Ruthwell parish. Her other brother, Peter, could not be present since one of his children had recently died, and it seems likely that the wedding was a very quiet one. A marriage contract was signed in Dumfries on 27 April, witnessed for Hogg by his old friend John McDiarmid, now editor of the *Dumfries and Galloway Courier*. The couple were married on Friday, 28 April, and passed the wedding night at Moffat, perhaps at the Black Bull Inn there, where they were met by a party of Hogg's friends from Yarrow who accompanied them back to Altrive the following day.[42]

Hogg's marriage immediately became the subject of public remark, *Blackwood's* giving a highly charged and comical account of the event and a reviewer of his *Winter Evening Tales* in *The Scotsman* advising Hogg to read the whole work to his wife before the publication of a second edition, 'and strike out every paragraph which, either as to thought or expression, offends her delicacy'. The *Caledonian* reviewer hoped that now he was married Hogg would 'eschew the wicked wits of Prince's Street, and set up his staff permanently in the country'. Hogg's Edinburgh cronies do indeed seem to have missed him from among them at this time, John Aitken grumbling to David Laing that 'the worthy Bard has banished himself from civilized society and I may wait till doomsday ere he be in Edin'. Blackwood invited Hogg to bring his new-made wife to call upon himself and Mrs Blackwood at Newington, and gave the latest information on John Wilson's campaign for election by the Edinburgh town council to the vacant chair of Moral Philosophy at Edinburgh University as an incentive for a visit that did not materialise.[43]

Wilson's raffish reputation (though oddly enough not his total ignorance of the subject he proposed to teach) clearly stood in his way. It was alleged, for instance, that among other blasphemies he had at an evening party parodied a psalm and the ceremony of baptism. Scott and other Tory friends defended him vigorously from such allegations and canvassed on his behalf for what was essentially a political appointment. Hogg also expressed anxiety for Wilson's success, as 'a desiderratum in his literary life', but stayed at home in Altrive, Blackwood writing him a triumphant report on 21 July of Wilson's election to the post by 21 votes to 9. Hogg's old friend James Gray was also electioneering with the Edinburgh town council, for the post of Rector of the Edinburgh High School. An admired and effective teacher of many years' standing and already senior master at the school, Gray was to be disappointed. Although a firm friend to both men, Hogg must surely have wondered that only Wilson, so much the less deserving, was successful. His inaugural lecture would take place in mid-November. Hogg planned to be there in support 'with a dozen men and plaids about them and great staves in their hands' but in the event remained at Altrive.[44]

Hogg's new wife soon set her mark on his modest establishment. She was reputedly shocked, for example, that horn rather than silver spoons were in common use, and promply sent off to Edinburgh for more genteel replacements. Messages of goodwill came in from everyone, from James Cunningham the Dalswinton mason to Walter Scott of Abbotsford, and Hogg rested from his literary labours for a while to enjoy a few honeymoon excursions in the Borders and to introduce his bride to his friends, relations, and local patrons. At the beginning of August he gave a brief itinerary:

> We spent three days visiting in Etterick and among other places were a night with the Hon. captain Napier and his lady in Thirlstane castle with whose attentions Margaret was much pleased We have likewise been at Selkirk Newark &c. and also at Traquair and purpose in a few days to be at

Abbotsford, Melrose, Dryburgh, &c.

After his doubts about being welcomed into Margaret's prosperous farming family, it must have been a great satisfaction to Hogg to show her how well-respected he was by the local aristocracy and gentry. Walter Scott the famous poet and novelist led Hogg's bride into the dining-room at Abbotsford, placed her by his side, and took pains to become acquainted with her. When the ladies left the room after dinner, Scott humorously wondered how Hogg had chosen so sensibly to which he responded, 'I dinna thank ye ata' for the compliment'. It is not clear whether the couple met the eccentric Earl of Buchan himself at Dryburgh Abbey, but Hogg would certainly show his bride the huge sandstone statue of Sir William Wallace there and the earl's Temple of the Muses, a vault containing plaster-cast portrait masks of the luminaries of the age, including one of the Ettrick Shepherd, exhibiting, Lockhart wrote, 'abundant marks of the agony with which that excellent but unsophisticated person must, no doubt, have submitted to the clammy application of the Savoyard castmaker'. Etiquette demanded a similar series of wedding visits to Margaret Hogg's 'innumerable relations' and a trip to Dumfries and Galloway was planned for September.[45] Naturally enough, Hogg's literary work was being somewhat neglected.

During 1819 Hogg had begun a Border Romance about Sir Michael Scott the legendary Wizard of Aikwood and the conflict between the English and the Scots for the possession of Roxburgh Castle, taking advice from the Durham antiquary Robert Surtees about localities when they met in Edinburgh that summer and discussing it with Scott on a visit to Floors Castle and Abbotsford in November. By 16 November he had one volume of 'The Perilous Castles' written, and hoped to publish it the following spring. As Hogg's work was 'a Romance or Tale of Chivalry [...] descriptive of the Scots and English Borderers in former times' he inevitably feared it was to be pre-empted by the publication of Scott's own *Ivanhoe* in December 1819. When his fears proved to be unfounded and his attention was engaged by preparations for his wedding and his marriage visits, Hogg seems to have allowed his manuscript to gather dust. On 20 August 1820 he told Blackwood that he had made no progress with it for the past three months and was now aiming to publish it in the spring of 1821 instead.[46] Could Blackwood act as his agent to secure anonymous publication in London, preferably with the Longmans firm?

Hogg also had a new and much-revised edition of *The Mountain Bard* on hand, originally offered to Oliver & Boyd as part of a multi-volume edition of his collected poems. On 21 June 1820 Hogg sent

D.O.Hill S.A   W.Richardson

Aikwood

THE RESIDENCE OF MICHAEL SCOTT

the first half of his copy for the volume off to Edinburgh, hoping for a November publication. On leaving for Dumfriesshire on 13 September he wrote a hasty note to the publishers asking them to go on with the printing during his absence from home and correct the proofs themselves 'all the way till you come to the incomparable Laird of Kirkmabreeke which I must look over for fear of mistakes in the obsolete language'. This was the only new addition in Hogg's pseudo-medieval 'ancient style', a comic tale in which a laird fond of beating women is duped by all and then hanged for the murder of his elderly wife. Others included 'The Wife of Crowle' from *The Spy* and 'Robin and Nanny', the oldest of his surviving literary manuscripts. He also thought of adding 'Glendonnen's Raid, An Ancient Scottish Ballad', published anonymously in three parts in the old *Scots Magazine* in 1807 and 1808, but did not as it was still incomplete.[47] The volume would also introduce the poetry of his nephew, Robert Hogg, who had written a fine imitation of the Border riding ballad entitled 'The Tweeddale Raide'.

Hogg was absent in Dumfriesshire about a month, spending part at least of that time staying at Ruthwell Manse as the guest of the Rev. Henry Duncan, now famous as the founder of savings banks, whose sister Christian had married Margaret Hogg's brother Walter Phillips some years previously. On his return to Altrive he found that his old father, Robert Hogg, was seriously ill. Given that he was over ninety years old he was not expected to recover, but lingered on for most of October receiving farewell visits from his friends and relations until his death on 22 October 1820. Writing to John Aitken the day after Robert Hogg's funeral, Hogg reflected that this deprivation was one 'that by the regular course of nature I had reason to expect'. He was now aware that his wife was pregnant. She had been 'a new motive for desiring to stay at home and truly a very delightful one and I hope soon to have more'.[48]

Recent Edinburgh vexations included the suppression by George Boyd of Hogg's dedication of *Winter Evening Tales* to Dr Peter Morris, the fictional narrator of Lockhart's *Peter's Letters to his Kinsfolk* (1819) and a public Whig and Tory dispute about the first volume of his *Jacobite Relics of Scotland*. A disapproving notice in the prestigious *Edinburgh Review* was succeeded by a defensive letter in *Blackwood's* signed with his own name but which he knew nothing about until publication. Besides taking Hogg's name in vain, William Blackwood had also been huffy that the forthcoming edition of *The Mountain Bard* had not been offered to him rather than to Oliver & Boyd. Hogg was about to add to his Edinburgh discomforts with the publication of an updated version of the 'Memoir of the Life of James Hogg' for the new edition of *The Mountain Bard*. So that no one should censor it Hogg demanded before sending his manuscript, 'that no one out of the office sees any part of this life till published, for without that promise I will not send you the M. S. at all'.[49]

Serious trouble was also brewing in Selkirkshire as Hogg's marriage into a well-to-do Dumfriesshire farming family led him to extend his own farming operations. Writing on 30 April 1820 to congratulate Hogg on his marriage, Scott also reported on his success in requesting the lease of a larger farm for Hogg from the managers of the Buccleuch estates. Hogg's kindly patron Duke Charles, who had granted him Altrive, had died on 20 April 1819 and the new Duke was a boy in the early teens being educated at Eton. Scott was willing to approach his guardians on Hogg's behalf, but at the same time felt constrained to issue a well-meant warning:

> Lord Montagu made me no promise but I sincerely believe he has a wish to serve you and I trust you will be accommodated next year with a Yarrow grazing In the mean while follow Iago's rule "put money in thy purse" A farm without a reasonable capital is a horse without a bridle on the which a man is more likely to break his neck than to make his fortune[50]

As Hogg was well aware, farming was in a precarious state following the artificial stimulus temporarily given to prices during the Napoleonic Wars. In his article 'On the Present State of Sheep-Farming in Scotland' published in the May 1817 issue of Constable's *Farmer's Magazine* Hogg had predicted that 'things are fast approaching to a crisis with the sheep-farmers of Scotland'. The market prices of sheep were not '*one half* of that they were wont to bring to the seller' and the farmer 'owes the last year's rent to his laird, or has paid it from some other fund than the profits of his farm'. Since Hogg believed that 'the present fall in the prices of wool and live-stock, is no temporary one' it is hard to understand why he should have been so eager four years later to take on an extensive Selkirkshire store-farm, particularly as he had no reserve of capital himself and would need his father-in-law's assistance to stock it. In August 1820 Hogg had told Peter Phillips, 'I have had some correspondence of late with the Chamberlain of Buccleuch. It is likely that I am to get the offer of one of the best and the very cheapest farm [*sic*] on the estate only I fear it is too large. It keeps at the fewest 65 scores of Cheviot sheep'. Hogg needed around £1700 for stock to be able to secure 'certain independance'. The farm was probably the neighbouring Mount

Benger, the annual rent of which was £370 and which, far from being cheap, was probably worth only £300. Ominously, it had already 'ruined two well qualified farmers in the preceding six years'.[51] Against his better knowledge, however, Hogg signed a nine-year lease of Mount Benger to begin at Whitsunday 1821.

Winter Evening Tales had sold so well that Hogg now considered Oliver & Boyd his chief publishers. They were already negotiating terms for a second edition in November and the new edition of *The Mountain Bard* was well underway. The firm was also printing the second series of *Jacobite Relics* for William Blackwood. Hogg also invited Oliver & Boyd to reissue the unsold copies of his *Dramatic Tales* and the second edition of *The Poetic Mirror*, acquired in settling accounts with Longmans. In offering the Edinburgh firm a poetical anthology too he told them that he wished 'the public to see that you are not only my publishers but my principal ones'.[52]

The expected birth of a legitimate child in the spring of 1821 was another hopeful event. Normally the neighbouring farmers' wives would give birth at home, with the assistance of the local midwife and perhaps a doctor, but Hogg took the unusual step of hiring lodgings for his wife at Park Street in Edinburgh and placing her under the supervision of Dr John Thatcher, a noted teacher of midwifery. His present anxiety may perhaps have been prompted by previous feelings of guilt. In his tale of 'Cousin Mattie', Sandy, the childish playmate and subsequent lover of Mattie, is termed her murderer because she dies in giving birth to a baby of which he is the father. This may reflect a hidden episode in Hogg's own early life, for Wilson described his usual dress as including 'a brooch in his unfrilled shirt, adorned with the hair of a Tenant Lass in Ettrick Forest who died in a certain condition in the 89'. On the present occasion, however, all was well and Hogg triumphantly announced the birth on 18 March of his 'nice young poet' to various friends and acquaintances. After Margaret Hogg had completed the customary month of lying-in after a birth, Hogg fetched her home to Altrive on 21 April, at the same time purchasing a number of items of kitchen equipment, perhaps with the new house of Mount Benger, to be taken over the following month, in mind. Margaret Hogg's niece, Janet Gray, probably accompanied them to assist in running the household for a little while and stayed until at least mid-June. The baby was baptized James Robert Hogg in Yarrow on Hogg's first wedding anniversary.[53]

Although 'the callant' was 'thriving like a mushroom', Margaret Hogg's health after the birth was not good. Besides the bustle of taking over the new Mount Benger farm, she had been shaken by the

death of her only surving sister, Jessie Phillips, on 14 June. At the
end of August, following news that her mother was ill, Margaret
Hogg left for Dumfriesshire to pay her elderly parents a visit of more
than a month and show them her baby. She was probably in need of
a rest, for the next day after arriving at her parents' house she engaged a maidservant to take care of the baby, while her mother subsequently had little James sleeping with her at night.[54]

From the outset there were problems with Mount Benger. Although the first year's rent would not fall due for a year to come, in
order to make the farm pay Hogg must buy livestock and farming
utensils. It also 'needed many improvements, such as building, fenc-
ing, and draining'. At the start of his lease Hogg was only able to
purchase half the necessary stock, and was seeking loans from friends
and profits from further volume publications to obtain the remainder. At least one old creditor from his farming failure in Dumfriesshire more than ten years previously had not been paid, for Walter
Cunningham of Catslackburn successfully claimed £31-17-10 from
Hogg through the Selkirk Sheriff Court on 30 May 1821.[55] Hogg
thus entered a period when he was writing in desperation and inclined also to count as certainties payments that were only conditional and probable. Unfortunately, about three months after taking
possession of Mount Benger, his promising connection with the firm
of Oliver & Boyd collapsed and at the same time a serious breach
with William Blackwood ensued.

The publication of the new edition of *The Mountain Bard* on 19
February 1821 was followed by an outcry over the prefatory 'Memoir'.
Wilson was offended by Hogg's imaginary impression of himself
before their meeting as 'a man [...] with hair like eagles' feathers, and
nails like birds' claws; a red beard, and an uncommon degree of
wildness in his looks'. More seriously, Hogg had accused George
Goldie, the first publisher of *The Queen's Wake*, of commercial mal-
practice in disposing of copies of the third edition when on the eve
of bankruptcy. Even a close friend like John Grieve felt that Hogg
was wrong, while Laidlaw was inclined to blame George Boyd for
agreeing to publish the 'Memoir' knowing that Hogg was 'purposely
concealing it from his friends'. David Laing in a review of *The Mountain Bard* agreed that had Hogg consulted his friends about his
'Memoir' they would have voted for its suppression. Even Scott judged
that 'Goldie's publication might with some people have a bad effect
because he had certainly reason to complain'.[56] Goldie read the
'Memoir' about a month after publication while staying at Blackburn
in Lancashire and immediately wrote both to Hogg and his pub-

lisher demanding the suppression of the passages relating to himself. When this was not done he published a spirited if over-angry pamphlet rebuttal, *A Letter to a Friend in London*, dated 23 May 1821, denying the charges and attacking Hogg in his turn. Hogg pretended to be less irritated by 'Goldie's farrago of impotent rage' than he clearly was—to Hogg, with his memories of being cast adrift in childhood and his consequent lifelong sympathy with the dispossessed, the implicit accusation that he was ' a low swindler that would even have defrauded the poor and distressed out of the proceeds of the forum' was unbearable. He even considered prosecuting his former publisher for libel. When George Boyd requested that Hogg should revise the 'Memoir' to omit the passages relating to his dealings with George Goldie, he lost his temper completely, retorting, 'I'll see the firm of Oliver & Boyd and the dog Goldie d—d to hell before I suffer a syllable of aught I have ever published to be altered'. It was at this point that Hogg gave up keeping the journal on which his 'Memoir' had been based.[57]

Unfortunately, at just this time George Boyd was considering the manuscript of Hogg's Border Romance for publication. Hogg had sent the first two of its three volumes to Boyd on 5 May, and clearly had no doubt that Oliver & Boyd would publish it, declaring, 'I ask no conditions at present for this my new work, nor will I have any till it is printed and subscribed, that we see how it looks, and how the public relishes it, *and then* if we cannot agree about what my share is to be, I take my chance of half profits'. He was also proposing that Blackwood, George Boyd, and John Grieve should sign a guarantee, effectively allowing him to borrow the necessary cash to stock Mount Benger adequately, being obstinately determined not to relinquish his lease. 'I dont care' he told Boyd, 'I have resolved on it and I'll be independant if I live and that I will let them see though I should pay the first year's rent out of my *own head* and let the land lie waste'.[58]

Hogg was concurrently pressing the Highland Society of London for a second £50 payment to make up the fee David Stewart of Garth had promised for *The Jacobite Relics of Scotland*, and pushing John Murray to make an outstanding payment for the sixth edition of *The Queen's Wake* (1819) and to join with Blackwood in making a final settlement of the author's profits from *The Brownie of Bodsbeck; and Other Tales*. It is a mark of Hogg's desperation that he was prepared to draw a bill for £50 on John Murray without direct permission, simply trusting to his good nature that it would be honoured. (In the end, Blackwood turned up an account which demonstrated that Murray had paid him the balance of the author's profit for this edition of *The Queen's Wake* and he had failed to credit Hogg's account accordingly.) The two or three hundred pounds he wanted, Hogg declared, was partly his own 'which even if it were not I could soon redeem'.[59]

Hogg's publishers merit sympathy as well as himself, pressed by him to make cash payments promptly, asked to sign bonds of credit, and offered a series of further works of varying saleability to publish one after another. At the same time that Oliver & Boyd, for instance, were offered the splendid Border Romance later entitled *The Three Perils of Man* they were also asked to take the doubtful anthology, *The Beauties of Living Poets*, a venture Boyd had refused once already in February on the grounds that the notes to the selections were plagiarised from various magazines and that the asking price was too high.[60]

Having sent in the manuscript parcel of his Border Romance to Boyd on 5 May, Hogg had still had no response from his publisher by 18 June and this made him uneasy given Boyd's 'accustomed punctuality'. Could he have been influenced against Hogg by 'Goldie's farrago of impotent rage' or Murray's 'airs'? Boyd's response arrived at Altrive on 26 June like a bombshell exploding. He refused the work on the grounds that 'it is of that cast that must draw down comparisons with the romances of the author of Waverly and manifestly to its disadvantage'. In desperation Hogg appealed to Scott, explaining that his father-in-law had recently suffered losses of about £7,500 himself and could no longer give the assistance he had promised with the farm. Could Scott lend him money, or could he get a London firm such as Longmans or John Murray, or perhaps Archibald Constable of Edinburgh, to publish Hogg's Border Romance by agreeing to revise it in proof himself?[61]

Scott did make Hogg a loan and also had a money-making literary scheme in mind for him. George III having died on 29 January 1820, the erstwhile Prince Regent was to be crowned as George IV on 19 July 1821. Hogg could accompany Scott to London and write a popular account of the coronation for publication in Scotland. As Scott explained to Lord Montagu

> I have been instigating the great Caledonian Boar James Hogg to undertake a similar trip—with the view of turning an honest penny to help out his stocking by writing some sort of Shepherds Letters or something to put the honest Scots bodies up to this whole affair. I am trying with Lord Sidmouth to get him a place among the Newspaper gentry to see the whole

ceremony. It is seriously worth while to get such a popular
view of the whole as he will probably hit off.

In the event, however, it was John Galt who produced this 'popular
view' in one of his papers for *Blackwood's Edinburgh Magazine* called
'The Steam-Boat', the London adventures of a Glasgow cloth-mer-
chant. Hogg reluctantly decided at the last minute that attending that
'great day at London' must be abandoned because it was the day
after St Boswell's Fair when he had to look after the purchasing of his
remaining farm stock for Mount Benger. Hogg's promise to Scott to
write something celebrating the coronation at home was duly fulfilled by the publication of an anonymous article in *Blackwood's*, a
coronation dinner held by the Dilettanti Society as described by a
visiting commercial traveller or 'Bagman' from Glasgow. Scott had,
however, a secondary purpose in wanting to take Hogg with him to
London, to put him forward as a worthy recipient of one of the royal
pensions of £100 per annum allocated by the newly-formed Royal
Society of Literature. This would be a delicate matter, since Scott
himself had little sympathy with a body he termed 'the Gaffers or
Gammers of literature' and had refused to be associated with it himself. Loyally he gave his opinion that 'nobody has a better or an
equal claim to poor Hogg [...] I know not where they could find half
a dozen with such pretensions as the Shepherd'.[62] No pension, however, resulted.

The breakdown of Hogg's relations with Oliver & Boyd was shortly
afterwards followed by a breach with his other Edinburgh publisher,
William Blackwood, who was similarly harassed by Hogg's financial demands. Hogg was no longer quite so prominent an author on
Blackwood's list as he had been when their connection was formed
in 1814. Blackwood's business was expanding and Hogg was now
only one acceptable star in the growing constellation of Blackwoodian
authors. Wilson and Lockhart were now the leading lights and main
contributors of *Blackwood's Edinburgh Magazine*, and Hogg's Scottish
fiction was soon to be overshadowed by that of others. John Galt
published *Annals of the Parish* with him, which was praised by Scott
and Henry Mackenzie among 'fifty others' and of which Blackwood
remarked 'I have seldom published a more popular & saleable book'.[63]
Blackwood also published Lockhart's *Valerius* and John Wilson's
mawkish but popular *Lights and Shadows of Scottish Life*.

In early August 1821 there was a sharp and increasingly acrimo-
nious correspondence between Hogg and Blackwood about a bill,
backed by Blackwood for Hogg's benefit, and cashed by him with
George Craig the Galashiels banker. Blackwood had apparently

required in granting Hogg a loan of £50 a guarantee that the eventual repayment was to come out of a bill for £150 paid to Hogg by Oliver & Boyd, and had failed to receive Craig's assurance that this would be so. He at one time threatened to 'apply to the directors of the Leith Bank, and lay the correspondence before them' but in the end gave way and allowed Hogg the credit without insisting on this security. Hogg was affronted, as he told Blackwood, 'at the fright and jealousy you have expressed to the only man I do business with, which must do me more harm in all my future transactions than I can name'.[64]

On 2 December 1820 Blackwood had promised Hogg that 'there shall nothing appear in the Magazine of or concerning you, but what you yourself shall previously see', and he now accordingly showed Hogg a vicious attack on his 'Memoir' that, Hogg imagined, could only have been written by the aggrieved George Goldie.[64] Blackwood denied this. 'If you refer to the article of which I shewed you a part in slips, and suppose this to be written by Goldie, I have only to tell you that you never were more absurdly mistaken in your life. It is from a very different pen indeed, else you may rest assured I never would have had any part of it in types. In its original state it certainly was objectionable, and such as would never have appeared in my Magazine'. It was so offensive, indeed, that James Ballantyne had threatened in the event of its publication to withdraw as the printer of *Blackwood's Edinburgh Magazine*. Publication of 'that most clever but most indecently scurrilous attack' he argued was 'absolutely unwarrantable, and *in your Magazine* peculiarly and shockingly offensive'. The article was in fact by John Wilson, who had written in the surviving portion of his manuscript, 'Mr Hogg has favoured the public occasionally with descriptions of the personal appearance of some of his Friends. Why has he not given a slight sketch of his own?' The inevitable pig puns are followed up by detailed description of Hogg's animal and repulsive person. Hogg's fingers, for instance, are 'brown & dumpy, and matted with reddish hair. In hot summer weather this gives them a sultry look–and when suddenly protruded to grasp his toddy, his "bunch of fives" at first sight is not a little startling'. The article was grossly offensive even after being toned down for publication in the August 1821 issue of *Blackwood's* (published on 30 August), but Blackwood justified its inclusion to Hogg on the pretext that the freedoms Hogg had taken with other people in his 'Memoir' justified any liberties taken with him.[65]

When Hogg received the relevant issue early in September he exploded with rage. 'Well sir,' he told Blackwood, 'you have now put the crown on all the injurious abuse that I have suffered from you for these three years and a half, and that in despite of your word of honour which no miserable pretext can justify'. Blackwood refused to divulge the writer's identity as requested and Hogg felt that he had done with 'Blackwood and his set [...] for ever'. Hogg was stunned when he realised that the author was Wilson, having regarded him hitherto as 'rash and thoughtless' but as one in 'whose heart I never before at least believed that any malice or evil intent dwelt; but highly as I before esteemed him I never will forgive him, especially for not at once acknowledging it to me'.[66]

Alone at Altrive and brooding over his wrongs while his wife and son were in Dumfriesshire, Hogg contracted measles, a disease that was then widespread and dreaded as potentially fatal or disabling, particularly to young children. The high fever associated with the disease could cause secondary infections leading to bronchitis or pneumonia and even inflammation of the brain. There seems to have been an epidemic in Yarrow that summer, and it may be that Margaret Hogg's visit to her parents had been timed in part to remove her baby from the danger zone. Writing to John Aitken on 27 September 1821, Hogg described his cottage as 'a perfect hospital with the meazles three of my servants are lying extremely sick and I am obliged to write you these few lines under the influence of the disease myself'. At his age, Hogg thought, the disease was 'quite ridiculous'.[67]

The same keen sense of the ludicrous that made his own sickness seem amusing also influenced his request to Scott for advice regarding his quarrel with Blackwood. He asked, 'Shall I answer him in print? pursue him at law to which it will soon come if I answer him? or knock out his brains?' No doubt entertained by this blunt way of putting it, Scott responded, 'As to knocking out of brains that is talking *no how*—if you could knock any brains into a bookseller you should have my consent but not to knock out any part of the portion with which heaven has endowd them'. More seriously, he advised Hogg to take no notice of the attack at all as the course most favourable to 'your peace of mind your private fortune and the safety of your person'. Such a thing did not affect Hogg's reputation, after all, unless 'it arms on your favour those generous feelings which revolt at seeing your parts and talents made the subject of ill-natured ridicule'.[68]

Except for one or two formal exchanges of letters regarding payments for his past literary work, the publication of Wilson's article in *Blackwood's* made a complete breach between Hogg and William Blackwood. He was now at odds with both of his current Edinburgh publishers as well as in desperate need of money for Mount Benger. It was probably at this time, too, that a serious quarrel with his friend John Grieve occurred, partly from Hogg's pressing him for financial assistance with his farming and perhaps too from Grieve's evident feeling that George Goldie had indeed been injured by Hogg's 'Memoir'. But as Hogg put it 'there is ane old door re-opened for me should another shut', in that negotiations were underway with Robert Cadell, Archibald Constable's partner, for Hogg to contribute to the firm's *Edinburgh Magazine*. Cadell's letter of 27 September, thanking Hogg for a magazine contribution sent to him, promised, 'You shall have as high remuneration as E. M. can afford to give you—It is almost unnecessary I think to express my abhorrence of the treatment you have met with in a certain quarter—& this opinion is that of all whom I heard mention the subject'.[69]

Over the next few months a succession of articles did appear in the revamped *Scots Magazine*, but this was not a periodical that stimulated Hogg to produce his best work even though he was now being paid adequately. His contributions included old papers from *The Spy* and the mawkish 'Old Isaac', which hesitates between a spoof and a genuine attempt to imitate Wilson's sentimental and pietistic deathbed scenes. The best of Hogg's work for the *Edinburgh Magazine* was the brilliant comic mock-medieval 'The Powris of Moseke, Ane Rychte Plesant Ballaunt'. An old blind musician attracts by his playing a bull who thinks the music is the call of a love-sick cow, while misled by his own egotism and the impishness of his attendant boy, the minstrel thinks that his music has called up the devil in person. An article on Jacobite Relics not published in Hogg's collection is similarly playful and would not have been out of place among the Blackwoodian games with authorship and anonymity but looks distinctly odd in its more sober rival. Robert Cadell, too, could be a difficult person to deal with. Hogg knew him reasonably well since both men were members of the Dilettanti Society, where Cadell was reckoned 'a perfect Nabal; and in all our social parties we were wont to gibe him about his niggardly hardness, which he never took the least amiss'. Typically, when Hogg again became a Constable author, Cadell examined old accounts and drew up a long list of outstanding debts owed to the firm by Hogg, going all the way back to 1807 and including the cost of copies of Hogg's own *Shepherd's Guide* and *Forest Minstrel* and three shillings and threepence for writing paper obtained by Hogg in 1810.[70]

During the final months of 1821 Hogg gradually pulled himself up from the pit into which he had so abruptly fallen in August and

September. For one thing in a letter of 18 October the London firm of Longmans, who had been his first choice back in 1819, accepted Hogg's Border Romance for publication. The edition of a thousand copies was to be printed in Edinburgh by Hogg's chosen printer, John Moir, so that he could conveniently deal with proofs himself. By November he was starting to receive them, but also having second thoughts about naming his rough-spoken Borders chieftain Sir Walter Scott of Buccleuch, and managed through Laidlaw to get Scott's opinion. In the end the matter was resolved with only a slight delay by renaming him Sir Ringan Redhough, but keeping the correct territorial designations for all the subordinate Scott lairds. He was also able to take Scott's opinion about the title, and finally abandoned his earlier 'The Perilous Castles' in favour of *The Three Perils of Man*.[71]

At much this time Hogg was also manoeuvering to get the Constable firm to publish the longed-for multi-volume collected edition of his poetry. By deferring to Scott's opinion about his forthcoming Border Romance he was able to involve him in negotiations for this other work. Having spoken to Cadell himself, probably during his visit to Edinburgh for All-Hallow Fair in the first half of November, Hogg then wrote to Scott on 10 December, 'I wish you would settle with Mr. Caddell about them He will grant you much better conditions than me [...] I intend writing to him this day or to morrow and think I must refer him to you'. Cadell wrote to Hogg on 2 February 1822 'I have had a conversation with Sir Walter Scott on the subject of an edition of your prominent poetical productions—I think we can manage with the addition of the original poems alluded to in your letter of 15 Decr to make 4 vols foolscap size'. He offered £150 for an edition of a thousand copies, since 'the advertising will be considerable in order to start you as a collected author'. Hogg managed later in the month to increase his payment to £200, and the printing was then begun by the firm of Walker & Greig who had formerly produced *The Forest Minstrel* for Constable.[72] Hogg's admirable resourcefulness had enabled him, despite his quarrels with both George Boyd and William Blackwood, to get *The Poetical Works of James Hogg* published in June and *The Three Perils of Man* in July 1822.

This was just as well, for the first year's rent of Mount Benger was due at Whitsunday 1822 and Hogg's financial situation critical. He visited Edinburgh only a few days beforehand to try to obtain advance payments for his forthcoming publications and to negotiate a fifty pound bill due for payment at one of the Edinburgh banks on 9 May. Longmans declined to pay anything until they had received the printed copies of *The Three Perils of Man* in London, but Hogg may have been more successful with the Constable firm. He stayed with James Gray and his family, where he was met by grim news of the heavy financial losses recently incurred by his father-in-law Peter Phillips through backing his son Walter's farming ventures. Walter's stock at Locharwoods was in danger of being seized by his creditors, his partner and maternal relation John Carruthers had escaped to America, and bankruptcy was imminent. Another Phillips brother, Peter, the farmer of the Carse near Kirkcudbright, was to die in June.[73]

It is not clear how well *The Poetical Works of James Hogg* sold, but probably not as well as Hogg had hoped. As it was essentially a repackaging of previously-published work, it appears to have received little attention, and significantly no new collected edition of Hogg's poetry was published during his lifetime. (By contrast, the collected poetical works of Scott of 1820 was updated and republished several times before Scott's death in 1832.)[74] Hogg's *Poetical Works* is a valuable and interesting representation of how he viewed his career as a poet from the perspective of 1822, therefore, rather than a comprehensive collection of his poems.

The Three Perils of Man may have fared rather better. It was extensively reviewed, and while Scott was not alone in condemning it for its 'extravagance in demonology' its energy and brilliance clearly made an impact even on those who were inclined to mock. It was reported in *Blackwood's* that the work had been turned into a play in America, and Lockhart paid a jesting compliment to Hogg's vivid characterisation when he told him that the cross-grained mule belonging to the Gospel Friar was 'the hero of the romance'. He also apparently suggested that Hogg write a companion work to be entitled *The Three Perils of Woman*.[75] Sales must have been satisfactory for Longmans to publish this second work only a year later.

Despite his success in publishing these volumes with Constables of Edinburgh and Longmans of London, however, Hogg plainly missed the regular contact with William Blackwood and the coterie of *Blackwood's Edinburgh Magazine*, and in the spring of 1822 he managed to mend his quarrel with the Edinburgh publisher. When Robert Cadell refused his 'Hints to Reviewers' for the rival *Edinburgh Magazine* Hogg sent it to William Blackwood on 11 April 1822 with a kindly note declaring 'should I never see your face again I shall always wish you well'. Blackwood had been in London chasing bad debts caused by bankruptcies there, but eventually responded on 24 May, 'On coming home a few days ago I was glad to see your letter and article', and as a goodwill gesture sent Hogg several copies of works he had recently published. Hogg responded gratefully, and in particular strategically praised *Lights and Shadows of Scottish Life*, written by the magazine's mainstay John Wilson, as possessing 'a great deal of very powerful effect purity of sentiment and fine writing'. If he felt obliged to add that it was remote from 'real nature as it exists in the walks of Scottish life' he did this tactfully and under an overall assessment of it as 'a fine and beautiful work'. The gratified William Blackwood responded on 18 June 1822, 'I would be happy if you found it agreeable to give your aid to Maga, as I am sure it would be both pleasant and advantageous to you'.[76] The way was once more open for Hogg's shorter tales and poems to be published in *Blackwood's Edinburgh Magazine*.

During Hogg's temporary defection to Archibald Constable a new series of papers had commenced in *Blackwood's* that was to have a lasting effect on his reputation. 'Noctes Ambrosianae. No. I' in the March 1822 issue was a dialogue between the fictional Editor of *Blackwood's* and the blarneying Irish contributor Morgan Odoherty in the parlour of William Ambrose's tavern in Gabriel's Road in Edinburgh. Seventy-one numbers were to be published in a series continuing to 1835, with a semi-fictional Hogg or The Shepherd coming to be the heart of this symposium of tavern sages. A fast-paced and often outrageous glancing treatment of the passing issues of the day in literature, politics, and art, it was hugely influential in the first half of the nineteenth century and spawned a host of imitators. The early numbers, roughly to 1825, were multi-authored. Lockhart or Wilson, the Irishman William Maginn or Blackwood himself, assembled disparate materials sent in by a variety of hands. London literary gossip, for example, appears to have been supplied in letters from Alaric A. Watts. The later numbers were largely the creation of John Wilson and increasingly featured the Shepherd as the focus of set-pieces, sentimentalised, mocked, and given bravura passages of Scots. Ian Alexander has described the Shepherd as 'only superficially a "boozing buffoon", a complex embodiment of profoundly intuitive responses to experience, standing in a teasing and stimulating relationship with his original'.[77] The circulation of *Blackwood's Edinburgh Magazine* grew during the 1820s and it was well-distributed in British colonies such as India as well as in England and Scotland, so that the Noctean Shepherd became rather better known than his prototype James Hogg.

Opinions have varied as to how far the magazine articles represented actual tavern parties, how far the Shepherd represents James Hogg, and how much of a problem this characterisation caused him. William Blackwood appears to have used the term 'Noctes' loosely, sometimes referring to the magazine articles and sometimes to a social evening with his family and chief contributors that was never intended for transmission into print. Writing to his son William in India, for example, on 27 April 1827 he described such a dinner at Ambrose's as a 'Noctes':

> Hogg was in town, and we had a capital Noctes at Ambrose's on Tuesday. The Professor was in the chair, and I was croupier. Captn. Hamilton, Robert and Jas. Wilson, Delta, your uncle Thos., &c., fourteen in all of us, sat down to dinner, and kept it up till nearly 12 o'clock.

On the other hand some of the published *Noctes* include songs and speeches by the Shepherd at a time when Hogg himself was in Yarrow and could not have taken part in an Edinburgh dinner, as for example with 'Noctes Ambrosianae. No. XLII' published in the magazine for April 1829. In other cases, elements of an actual tavern dinner were selectively transposed into a magazine article, so that contemporaries such as R. P. Gillies were inclined retrospectively to state that it was 'nothing more than a faithful sketch from real life'. He instances a meeting of 1824 or 1825 in which the party at Ambrose's had consisted of Hogg, himself, William Blackwood, 'Timothy Tickler' (Robert Sym), two young Americans, a lawyer, and two Leith merchants, while Lockhart and Galt joined the party after attending the theatre in nearby Shakespeare Square:

> Blackwood, who for the last hour had been fast asleep, tried to awake on the entrance of supper, and flopping of champagne corks; and opening half of one eye, helped himself to an *entire* Finnan haddock. The conversation, the songs, the practical jokes of that night, were all so extravagant and ridiculous, that it would have been impossible for any sober man to have *invented* the like. Within two days thereafter, the proceedings were fairly written out by L[ockhart], and printed by James Ballantyne.

Hogg appears to refer to the same evening in his *Songs by the Ettrick Shepherd*, as the occasion for which he composed his 'Noctes Sang', when 'a number of foreign literary gentlemen were to be of the party. I did not sing it till late at night, when we were all beginning to get merry [...] Mr Gillies ruffed and screamed out so loud in approbation, that he fell from his chair, and brought an American gentleman down with him'. From this it would appear that the published record of this evening must be 'Noctes Ambrosianae. No. XIX' in *Blackwood's*

Edinburgh Magazine for March 1825, in which Hogg's song was published.[78] There is, however, no mention in this of the American gentlemen or the Leith merchants and Edinburgh lawyer, these visitors presumably ranking among the company as spectators rather than participants in the symposium, and nor is there any mention of Gillies himself, who does feature in other *Noctes* as the Germanist Kempferhausen. The dialogue is a three-hander between Tickler, the Shepherd, and Christopher North, the fictional editor of *Blackwood's Edinburgh Magazine*. The magazine article is clearly a highly selective version of the actual evening at Ambrose's, though both Hogg and Gillies on reading it recognised elements of a party at Ambrose's at which they had both been present along with some American gentlemen.

The relationship of the Shepherd to James Hogg appears to be similar—some grains of fact in an elaborately-constructed invention. Precise details of James Hogg's life and writings were continually mapped upon the Shepherd. During an Edinburgh visit of May 1823, for instance, Hogg put up at Mackay's hotel on Princes Street and the Noctean Shepherd remarks 'I put up at Mackay's noo, when I'm in town [...] Ballantyne's deevils [engaged in the printing of *The Three Perils of Woman*] they can come jinking back and forrit in no time by the playhouse stairs [...]'. Obviously the fictional Shepherd must have resembled Hogg in many ways to have been a recognisable likeness to contemporaries, while being unrepresentative enough to cause Hogg real embarrassment. In November 1830 when Scott's health was failing Hogg would not have described his anecdotes as 'nine out o' ten meanin' naethin', and the tenth itsell as auld as the Eildon hills', but readers of the *Noctes* might believe he had.[79] The *Noctes Ambrosianae* have often acted as a light that led astray both for Hogg's contemporaries and for subsequent readers, simply because they are so entertaining, absurd, and eminently quotable. In fact, the Shepherd's opinions can only be taken as those of James Hogg when they coincide with those expressed by Hogg in his letters or published writings or as reported by reliable contemporaries.

Although from time to time Hogg did object to the Shepherd, he generally acquiesced or even enjoyed his *alter ego* of the *Noctes Ambrosianae*. He sent songs of his own in to Blackwood for the Shepherd to sing, continued to attend parties at Ambrose's, and prefaced many of the songs in his 1831 collection by snatches of the dialogue that surrounded their first appearance in the magazine. The series was undoubtedly good publicity for his work throughout the British empire, although it probably had a negative effect on the nature of his fame. Year after year, the *Noctes Ambrosianae* repeatedly boosted 'Kilmeny' in *The Queen's Wake* as the finest thing he had written, and ignored or denigrated his prose fiction.

The great public event of 1822 for Edinburgh was the visit of George IV from 15 to 29 August, ably choreographed by Scott as a Highland affair, with Jacobite descendants reclaimed as loyal adherents of the House of Hanover. The issue of *Blackwood's Edinburgh Magazine* for September 1822 was entirely given over to commemoration of the visit, the Noctean group (though excluding Hogg) going to visit the Royal Yacht and joining in the jollifications of a farmer's household in the vicinity of Hopetoun House. Hogg himself almost certainly heard that the King was coming to Scotland directly or indirectly through Scott, who had been anticipating the event ever since the royal visit to Ireland during the preceding year. Lockhart had then written confidingly to Hogg at Scott's request 'what is not known generally but is now quite certain that the King *is* to be here in a few weeks time on his way back from Ireland. There must be a Kings Wake for certain & you must clear forthwith your brawest pipes for the nonce'. Scott seems to have heard in mid-July 1822 that after all his hesitations George IV would be in Scotland that summer, and that his arrival was expected on 12 August, his sixtieth birthday. Hogg, clearing his pipes as expected, wrote a Highland Song for his Majesty's birthday to the Jacobite tune of 'When the King comes o'er the Water'. He also wrote a commemorative version of the old Jacobite song 'Carle an' the King Come', and hastily sent it by post to the young composer and music-publisher Niel Gow on 27 July with instructions to publish it 'with the music and accompaniments without any delay for my sake'. He asked Gow to get it introduced on the stage if possible, adding as 'I will be in town I can easily effect that'. (No record of its publication or performance has survived, and it was possibly made redundant by Walter Scott's own version of the same song for the same occasion.)[80]

Hogg did come to Edinburgh for the King's Jaunt as he intended, but his role was that of a spectator rather than a participant. A *Blackwood's* writer claimed to have spotted him among the crowd assembled on 15 August when the newly-arrived King came in full procession from Leith to Holyrood:

> When he first caught a sight of the King, we verily thought he would have leapt off the platform, over the heads of five hundred people, into the King's coach. We stood prepared to intercept him in his flight; but turning our head towards our gracious and beloved monarch, when we looked again

for the Shepherd, he was gone.

Gillies subsequently recalled meeting Hogg on the lawn in front of Melville Castle on 27 August while the king was breakfasting there with Lord Melville. He was 'accompanied by the Rev. Dr. Croly, to whom he had been introduced at Blackwood's', and both men dined with Gillies that evening at his cottage at nearby Lasswade.[81] Although Hogg was probably in town for most of the King's Jaunt, the details of his visit are disappointingly sparse.

Hogg's personal commemoration took the form of a half-crown pamphlet publication of a Scottish masque entitled *The Royal Jubilee*, wrapping a number of his songs into a dialogue between spirits representing different geographical districts and historical parties of Scotland meeting to discuss the Royal Visit in Holyrood Park. As Valentina Bold has indicated, the tensions between factions, represented by such as the 'Genius of the Gael, with Highland Spirits' and the 'Genius of the West, with Spirits of Covenanters', are represented forcefully within the masque and only superficially resolved. The work was reviewed enthusiastically in *Blackwood's*, but Hogg's hopes of a popular success were almost certainly disappointed for surviving copies are extremely rare. Royal patronage also passed him by, Hogg receiving only a second-hand acknowledgement from Robert Peel, transmitted through Scott.[82]

Hogg may have been partially consoled, however, to learn that his writing was now becoming known in Germany. Gillies, recently returned from several months' residence there, brought Hogg back a translation of some of his tales, and reported to Lockhart on how Hogg was presented to the German reader as a companion author to Sir Walter Scott:

> Hogg you know has been knighted at Berlin. I have the works of *Sir* James Hogg translated by Sophia May and others. His work on Sheep is also translated; and in "Abend Zeitung" he is called The "Hippocrates of Sheep".

Gillies's return to Edinburgh was, however, soon counterbalanced by the departure of James Gray in December 1822. After failing to become Rector of Edinburgh's High School he had accepted the post of Rector of the Belfast Academy. On his departure the members of his first Edinburgh class presented him with a silver cup and his current pupils with a complete set of Bell's British Poets in a hundred and nine volumes. Gray was a much-loved teacher who some years earlier had taken the unusual decision to abolish corporal punishment in all his classes. Most of his large family accompanied him

to Belfast and the Gray house at St Leonard's was advertised as to
let or for sale. Whatever the popular impression in Berlin, Hogg was
not a Sir Walter Scott with an Edinburgh house of his own as well as
a country home in the Scottish Borders, and he was now obliged to
look for another base in Edinburgh, where he could stay periodically to supervise the printing of his publications. Visiting Edinburgh
in May 1823, Hogg reported to his wife that he was staying in one of
the city's leading hotels, Mackay's on Princes Street, since neither
Gillies nor Lockhart offered him a bed and he did not like to force
himself on either of them.[83] Hogg's Edinburgh visits would be far
less frequent when he must pay for his accommodation.

In compensation Altrive was far from being short of company at
this time, Hogg noting to William Blackwood how the number of his
literary visitors had increased after George IV's Edinburgh visit, his
house being so crowded at times that he found it hard to make time
and space in which to write. The Danish author Andreas Andersen
Feldborg (1782–1838) was among his visitors, as was the Cornish
traveller in the Middle East, John Carne (1789–1844). One day when
Hogg hoped to get across to Abbotsford to visit Lockhart he was
prevented by the arrival of a chaiseful of visitors from Edinburgh.[84]

Write Hogg must, however, no matter what the distractions were,
because of his increasing financial problems. In October 1822, at
Lockhart's suggestion, he began his double narrative of *The Three
Perils of Woman* and published it the following August.[85] Intended perhaps to follow up the recent success of John Wilson's *Lights and Shadows of Scottish Life* it was subtitled 'A Series of Domestic Scottish Tales',
but is a far more radical and unsettling work. In the first narrative,
centred upon the family of homely Borders farmer Daniel Bell, social climbing spirals out of control into madness and death. Hogg's
hysteric heroine Gatty is morally responsible for the early death of
her innocent country cousin, Cherry, and must pass through the
purgatory of an insane asylum, before reaping the rewards of her
ambitious marriage to a Highland chieftain. In the second narrative,
the pain and destruction following the Jacobite defeat at Culloden in
1746, so skilfully sidestepped by Scott in *Waverley* and during the
recent Royal visit, is hauntingly and graphically described. The death
and sufferings of Hogg's second heroine, Sally Niven, conclude the
work most uncomfortably for the modern as well as the contemporary reader.

Besides the obvious pain and suffering of his characters, Hogg in
The Three Perils of Woman expresses some personal discomfort of his
own. As tenant of Mount Benger his finances were already spiral-

ling out of control and making him unduly dependent on his publishers. In January 1823 he had been obliged to call on William Blackwood while in Edinburgh with a drove of sheep to solicit a loan of fifty pounds for which, as his note of acknowledgement admits, Blackwood had received no value and which was granted solely to accommodate him in a financial strait. That he could not pay his rent of £370 comfortably even after a year when he had published a novel, a collected edition of his poetry, and a number of magazine articles is an indication of how disastrous the new farm had proved to be as a source of income. Hogg clearly valued the status of Borders store-farmer, but his descriptions of farming in *The Three Perils of Woman* are hardly inviting. Good-natured and prosperous Daniel Bell is obsessed with his sheep in a way that James Hogg clearly intended his reader to find comical, and he has very little interest in anything else. 'There is no life so easy as that of a sheep farmer', Hogg's narrator declares, 'but there is none so monotonous. No stirring, no animation; but the same routine from day to day, and from year to year; looking at tups; taking a glass of toddy; talking of rents, dogs, and shepherds; buttoning and unbuttoning; lying down in bed, and rising up again, from generation to generation'. There can be little doubt that Hogg found the conversation of his worthy fellow-farmers in Yarrow very limited. 'Converse with our hinds and shepherds', he declared, 'you will find men willing to communicate, and anxious to learn; but with the store-farmers, it is *tups*, lambs, crock-ewes, and prices, without end, and without mitigation. I would rather sit in a cottage, with an old wife smoking tobacco, and listen to Ralph Erskine's Gospel Sonnets'.[86] Hogg would not be the last labouring-class writer to be bored by the conventional money-getting culture of the middle classes. Perhaps even the feverishness of Hogg's own financial juggling could be a relief at times, since it at least kept him alert and awake and he needed excitement.

Hogg's marriage to a girl from exactly this background may also have seemed a little dull at times. Margaret Hogg was a handsome woman of the physical type Hogg most admired, with black eyes and hair and a well-developed figure. She was a good manager, and a sweet-tempered affectionate wife and mother, with a sterling sense of humour and a kindly welcome for his many visitors, literary tourists as well as genuine friends. A daughter was born to the couple on 23 April 1823 and named Janet Phillips Hogg, after Margaret's much-loved invalid sister who had died almost two years previously. Describing his very happy domestic life to Southey in July 1824 Hogg wrote, 'I am now myself a husband to a wife whom I love from my soul, and father to a little son and daughter both healthy and promising chubs'. A second daughter, Margaret Laidlaw Hogg after Hogg's own mother, was born in January 1825, and when Margaret Hogg was suddenly taken ill after the birth Hogg was extremely anxious for his 'beloved' wife. The marriage was undoubtedly a happy and successful one. On the other hand, despite his pejorative comments about blue-stockings Hogg tended to prefer the company of intelligent and unconventional women, the natural result perhaps of his having had a clever, individualistic mother. In the autobiographical 'Love Adventures of Mr George Cochrane' the narrator grows bored with the faithful devotion of the girl he intended to marry and his attention is held by the one who plays tricks on him.[87] Hogg's hesitation in 1819 and 1820 about making the commitment of marriage indicates that he took his marriage vows very seriously, but nevertheless rumours circulated from time to time that he had broken them.

Such rumours may have been based on nothing more than a general awareness of the existence of Hogg's illegitimate daughter Katie and his enjoyment of banter with a lively woman, but Lockhart reported gossip in the summer of 1824, for instance, that Hogg had fathered a child on one of the Altrive maidservants. Writing to John Wilson's married sister, Elizabeth MacNeill, he mentioned a recent meeting with their mutual acquaintance Hogg at St Boswell's Fair and then added jokingly: 'Jamie is in bad odour hereabouts at present in consequence of a discovery that took place about two months ago when Mrs Hogg was about to lie in—viz that there was another female of the household in a similar situation'. The Shepherd's literary friends, he informed her, intended to combine forces and produce a volume 'for the Education of the worthy so unwelcome to Mrs and indeed also to Mr Hogg'. Lockhart's jesting apart, there is little evidence that Hogg was anything but a faithful husband. But despite his happy family life he did once privately acknowledge a degree of boredom to William Laidlaw, his oldest and probably his closest friend. Laidlaw, who had called on him at Mount Benger, reported to Lockhart:

> I understand he is become more able to keep within bounds of the matrimonial contract. The Mistress has continued very handsome for some time which may be one reason—But the fellow now seems inclined to be now intellectually unfaithfull "She is a verry bonnie woman Margaret" he says, "but" rubbing his mouth "—I would have liked a cleverer woman—!"

Hogg's temperamental restlessness prevented his being entirely satisfied with a quiet domestic life all the time. His periodic letters
home from his trips to Edinburgh are inevitably affectionate and
reassuring—he tells his wife that he misses her and the children, and
promises to return as soon as possible—but his enjoyment of a wider
society and a busier scene are also perfectly evident. Entering Edinburgh he always found himself involved in bustle and hurry, supervising his publications, visiting various publishers, friends, and family connections, and taking part in the meetings of the clubs and
societies to which he belonged.[88]

Hogg's protective tenderness for his wife extended to caring for
her parents in their old age. At the time of Hogg's marriage Peter
Phillips had been an apparently prosperous man but he had since
sunk into real poverty. Of the Phillips's six children only two were
still alive by 1824, and their surviving son Walter was now in no
position to assist his father as he had been obliged to leave his farm
in Ruthwell parish and take up employment in Newcastle. Although
Hogg was also in financial difficulties he did have two houses, the
comfortable modern stone-built cottage of Altrive and an old-fashioned thatched farmhouse at Mount Benger. In June 1824 he moved
into Mount Benger and his aged parents-in-law moved themselves,
their maidservant, and their furniture from Dumfriesshire into the
cottage at Altrive. Peter Phillips, Hogg told a friend, was 'an excellent old man, reduced from great affluence to a total dependence on
me'.[89] Considerately, he always tended to underplay the loss of the
financial assistance Peter Phillips had promised him as a factor affecting his own farming difficulties.

Hogg describes himself during this time as 'all this while writing
as if in desperation' and his output between his marriage and the
start of 1825 is truly astonishing—a revised edition of *The Mountain
Bard*, the second series of *Jacobite Relics*, the four-volume *Poetical Works*,
his narrative poem *Queen Hynde*, *The Three Perils of Man* and *The Three
Perils of Woman*, and most recently what is now his best-known work,
The Private Memoirs and Confessions of a Justified Sinner. For all his uncertainties Hogg was at the centre of a solid and supportive family, and
in portraying his deepest fears and anxieties through the solitary
Robert Wringhim he was no doubt aware that he was offering his
reader what Peter Garside has termed 'a dark counter-version of his
own family practice'. Despite its narrative instabilities, its challeng-
ing and oppositional points of view, its inconsistencies and illusions,
the centre of *Confessions* is clearly a Christian ideal of fellow-feeling
and moral community. The Cameronian Samuel Scrape may not be

over-nice in the question of taking double payment for the same services, but he is adamant that the only test of conduct is the Golden
Rule, to do unto others as you would have them do unto you.
Blanchard's definition of true religion also emphasises community
of feeling and of interest, when he advises Robert that it is 'the bond
of society on earth, and the connector of humanity with the Divine
nature'. Robert's sins, on the other hand, isolate him one by one—on
his assurance of election he immediately envisages himself as 'an
eagle among the children of men, soaring on high, and looking down
with pity and contempt on the grovelling creatures below'. He has
no friends and before the close of the book no family either, and is
left a prey to every childhood terror. Hogg at the centre of his loved
and loving family could finally exorcise those demons of a solitary
child, the horses shifting below his bed in a darkened outhouse, the
indifferent masters, and the displacement of being sent out to earn
his bread among strangers almost in infancy. Significantly, the start-
ing-point of his narrative appears to have been the unearthing of an
outsider in Yarrow, the exhumation of a suicide, someone 'not a native of the place' who is generally reconstructed by Selkirkshire shepherds and Edinburgh literati alike as an object rather than as a person in 'utter despair'.[90]

No easy solutions are offered to the mysteries of the *Confessions*,
however, and Hogg's own sense of having almost exhausted his resources remains a strong driving force behind the narrative. The
historical suicide's 'utter despair' is put down to material poverty,
and Robert Wringhim ends up lame and despairing, also at the end
of his resources. Hogg's own phenomenal energy must have seemed
all too finite in the summer of 1824, for it was proving inadequate to
pay the Mount Benger rent and he was in any case losing faith in his
ability to keep on publishing a volume of prose fiction every year to
meet his financial exigencies. *Blackwood's Edinburgh Magazine* was the
closest indicator of reception to Hogg, both mentally and geographi-
cally, and Maga had, after all, found little to praise in Hogg's successive prose publications. Odoherty in the *Noctes* had pronounced *The
Three Perils of Man* 'a mixture of the admirable, the execrable, and the
tolerable', and when in a subsequent episode Hogg reproaches Tickler for his coarseness Tickler rejoins, 'In the meantime, James, read
that, and you will know what I say about yours', that being copy for
a patronising and offensive review of *The Three Perils of Woman* published in the same issue of Maga.[91]

Hogg's relatively stable relationship with the prestigious London
publisher of Longmans was beginning to falter. Hogg had been paid

his half-profits for the two *Three Perils* works, and the firm was content apparently to publish *Confessions* on similar terms, but reluctant to follow it up with a selection of his shorter tales. Longmans letter to Hogg of 11 August 1823, written as the firm was expecting delivery of the printed copies of *The Three Perils of Woman*, advises him to compress the tales as much as possible and to send them to London for inspection. The second edition of Hogg's *Winter Evening Tales* was now hanging on Oliver & Boyd's hands, and Longmans were plainly wary of infringing the rights of the Edinburgh firm. In the same letter of 25 October 1823 in which they accepted *Confessions* for publication they warned Hogg that it would be necessary to have the consent of Oliver & Boyd to publish the shorter tales and 'after all it may be doubtful whether a republication at this time would answer'. A subsequent letter of 12 December noted, 'We thank you for what you say respecting the Tales; but at present we would rather decline them'. (Longmans' lack of enthusiasm for Hogg's prose fiction can only have increased subsequently when *Confessions* sold so poorly, Hogg's author's profits more than two years after publication amounting to only two pounds.)[92]

In this situation Hogg, ever resourceful, looked out the long-abandoned and incomplete poem he had begun to write after his visit to the Ossianic country of Morvern and Appin in the summer of 1816, *Queen Hynde*. On 12 February 1824 Longmans accepted it for publication. The new narrative poem by the author of *The Queen's Wake* would be his first since *Mador of the Moor* in 1816, and was eagerly anticipated. In March 1824 John Wilson, as the fictional editor Christopher North, reported in the *Noctes* that Hogg was at work on his Epic poem, and that the exordium was splendid, and in the following month's symposium he referred dismissively to Hogg's 'brose tales' but pronounced firmly that 'Queen Hynde will do'. By returning to poetry Hogg had rekindled interest in his work and secured the publication of another much-needed volume. Hogg seems to have been fatigued after the rapid production of under-appreciated prose fiction works and in need of encouragement, referring to himself uncharacteristically in January 1824 as 'the most easily discouraged being alive'. By June further composition of *Queen Hynde* had slowed down to the point where the printers had caught up with the author in producing fresh text and the work was almost at a standstill. 'If you would read the proofs', he told Blackwood, 'it would be a great comfort to me'. The poem was at length finished on 10 July 1824 when Hogg noted triumphantly in a letter to Southey, 'I am just sending the last sheets of an *Epic Poem* to press!!'[93]

Blackwood was undoubtedly enthusiastic, writing to Hogg on 4 December 1824 when the printing was complete, 'I have read the whole of Queen Hynde, and I am quite sure it will make a sensation'. Although Adam Black was Longmans' current Edinburgh publishing partner, he took a quarter-share himself in October and by 20 December had effectively bought out Longmans interest in the whole work, promising Hogg advance payment of £150 for the edition, though the London firm retained the management of the work.[94]

The rollicking headlong pace of *Queen Hynde* provides no hint of Hogg's tiredness in 1824. Douglas Mack has characterised it as Hogg's greatest poem, likening it as a myth of Scottish national origins to Ossian. The young and beautiful Queen Hynde in the ancient city of Beregonium attempts to foil a threatened Viking invasion with the assistance of Saint Columba, and eventually locates and marries her cousin, Prince Eiden, the true lineal heir to the throne, brought up in Ireland by his maternal grandfather. Eiden wins his birthright against all odds, in disguise as the uncouth but vigorous peasant M'Houston. While the earlier section, written in the period following Hogg's triumph with *The Queen's Wake*, focuses on the young and beautiful Scottish Queen, in the later-written portion M'Houston is the primary character. His prowess and 'strength of mind, | In such low rank of human kind' lead King Eric of Norway to mistake him for the Norse god Loki in disguise and after fighting as the champion of Scotland Hynde chooses him as king because 'though humbly born' he is a 'hero at the heart'.[95] Hogg too could fight against odds to achieve his proper place in the world.

When the poem was published on 18 December 1824 Hogg was in Edinburgh waiting for early indications of its reception just as he had done more than ten years previously on the publication of *The Queen's Wake*. His high hopes, however, were immediately dashed:

> I was invited to a public dinner given by a great number of young friends, a sort of worshippers of mine (for I have a number of those in Scotland). It was to congratulate me on my new work, and drink success to it. The president made a speech, in which, after some laudatory remarks on the new poem, he boldly and broadly asserted that it was much inferior to their beloved "Queen's Wake." I was indignantly wroth, denying his assertion both in principle and position [...]

William Blackwood, anxious no doubt to protect his investment, did all that he could to boost *Queen Hynde* in the pages of *Blackwood's Edinburgh Magazine*. The issue for January 1825 contained a long comparative review of Hogg's new poem and one by Thomas Campbell in which the palm was definitely awarded to *Queen Hynde* rather than to *Theodric*. In the *Noctes Ambrosianae* in the same issue Hogg dozes while the other characters read aloud long extracts from his new poem. North urges Tickler to read it properly since 'you have seldom read anything more worthy of being treated with respect'. Although there are elements of mockery (as when Hogg is told that the water-pipes of Beregonium mentioned in his notes are in fact gas-pipes) the poem is declared better than the narrative parts of *The Queen's Wake*, and the final verdict delivered to a maudlin Shepherd is, 'Sir, there are passages in this volume, that will kindle the hearts of our children's children'.[96]

Unfortunately, Hogg himself was not to equal the triumphant comeback of his hero M'Houston with *Queen Hynde*. It was described as incongruous in tone and characterisation, and even impious and irreverent. Some six months after publication more than a thousand of the fifteen hundred copies printed remained unsold and most of the edition was eventually remaindered. Hogg was, and remained, incredulous at its failure. He expressed his surprise to William Blackwood in September 1825, and again two years later. 'I am grieved as well as dissapointed that Queen Hynde should stick still. I cannot believe that she does not deserve notice'. His disappointment was still vivid in 1832 when he revised his 'Memoir':

> It is said the multitude never are wrong, but, in this instance, I must take Mr. Wordsworth's plan, and maintain that they *were* wrong. I need not say how grievously I was disappointed, as what unsuccessful candidate for immortal fame is not? But it would have been well could I have refrained from exposing myself.[97]

The failure of *Queen Hynde* was a crushing blow. It marked the end of a period of tremendous literary productivity when Hogg had published a major new work each year: he had now apparently exhausted his resources both as a novelist and as a narrative poet. What should he turn to next?

CHAPTER SIX

The Hard-Earned Sma' Propine

Fortunately Hogg could now look for an income to the periodical market, which was flourishing and expanding in the later 1820s. William Blackwood had revolutionised it in October 1817 by paying a handsome ten guineas per sheet for contributions to *Blackwood's Edinburgh Magazine*, and both as the Shepherd of the *Noctes Ambrosianae* and as an author of magazine tales and poems, Hogg was now becoming well-known through Britain and the British Empire. The twelve-year old Charlotte Brontë, for example, in her father's remote Yorkshire parsonage, wrote enthusiastically in 1828 about 'James Hogg a man of most extraordinary genius a Scottish Sheppherd [*sic*]'. In January 1825 Hogg had remarked, 'I never had so many applications for communications in my life as this winter nor such liberal offers'. Two years later he acknowledged to William Blackwood a debt to the increasing fame of the convivial song-singing Shepherd of the *Noctes Ambrosianae*:

> I am perswaded that some things in Maga have operated singularly to my advantage for the applications for contributions from my *highly gifted pen* have of late increased to a most laughable and puzzling extent. Three came with your letter last night all from music publishers in London.

Subsequently he noted that 'the writing for these miscellaneous works is become a kind of business now and I find it one that suits me [...] very well'.[1] Temperamentally, Hogg had always perhaps inclined more to the ballad and the tale than the long narrative poem and the three-volume novel. *The Queen's Wake* embeds a series of shorter poems into a framing narrative of a contest of minstrels, and *The Three Perils of Woman* is aptly subtitled 'A Series of Domestic Scottish Tales'. Hogg now put most of his energies into this lucrative market for shorter pieces and 'continued for six years to write fairy tales, ghost stories, songs, and poems for periodicals of every description, sometimes receiving liberal payments, and sometimes none, just as the editor or proprietor felt disposed'. In fact, his income from periodical writing became a very comfortable one: in the final year of his life he estimated it as 'from one to two hundred pounds annually'.[2] Hogg was probably also happier to receive smaller cash payments month by month on publication of his work than unpredictable lump sums for occasional volumes, which were all too often paid by bills, or promissory notes.

After the failure of *Queen Hynde* Hogg projected a collection entitled, 'Lives of Eminent Men', consisting of stories whose length was somewhere between that of a magazine contribution and a novel. Two of these tales, 'Some Remarkable Passages in the Life of an Edinburgh Baillie' and 'The Adventures of Colonel Peter Aston', were composed at the end of 1825 and beginning of 1826, but Hogg could not persuade Longmans to take them. They were only finally published in rewritten versions in the final year of Hogg's life in his *Tales of the Wars of Montrose*. Another long poem called 'Love's Legacy' also proved unpublishable after his 'grievious dissapointment with Queen Hynde', and remained on Hogg's hands until 1834 when one section was abstracted and published as a separate poem, 'Mora Campbell', in *Blackwood's* and the rest published in three parts in successive issues of another magazine.[3]

Queen Hynde had left Hogg with an increasing debt to William Blackwood in the shape of a bill for £100. In December 1824 when Blackwood agreed to pay Hogg £150 for the poem he protected himself against loss by specifying in his agreement with Hogg how any money previously advanced by Longmans should be settled. If sales permitted this could be done when terms were arranged for a second edition of the poem or for a new edition of Hogg's tales, but in the meantime, he specified, 'should any sum be deducted by L. & Co I am to debit your account with it'. Since Hogg had already received £100 and it was clear that this would not be covered by profits from either *Queen Hynde* or *Confessions* Blackwood wanted to be repaid at once. Both men knew that Hogg was quite unable to raise the cash, so Hogg was persuaded to put his name to a bill for £100 in Blackwood's favour. At the end of the period specified on the bill for settlement, Hogg was obliged to renew it as he could still not pay the money and a sum for interest and a stamp fee was added to the previous total. By March 1826 Hogg's debt of £100 had increased to £103-15-0 and by January 1827 to £109-3-9.[4]

As Hogg's debt slowly mounted, however, Blackwood created the mechanism by which he could extinguish it. Hogg's magazine series 'The Shepherd's Calendar', begun in 1819 with descriptions of a snow-storm and a country wedding, had been revived in March 1823 with the tale of 'Rob Dodds'. In a letter of 23 March 1827 Blackwood explained:

> I rec^d your letter [...] with your capital portion of the Shep
> herd's Calendar. It is most interesting and will be liked by

every one. To show you how I value it I have credited your acc[t] with ten pounds for it, of which I enclose you a five pound note, and I hope in this way you will soon extinguish the bill. I am very anxious to receive your next N° on Dreams and Apparitions which I am sure will be excellent.[5]

This was a winning formula for the rapid creation and publication of a successful magazine series, for while Hogg received some much-needed cash in hand as a half-payment for his work he was gradually freeing himself from debt with the other half. He was also receiving steady encouragement in the form of reminders and praise from Blackwood.

More than his debt tied Hogg to Blackwood, however, during these years. Cash was always scarce in the Mount Benger household. Writing to Blackwood on 5 April 1827 Hogg looked back to the Yarrow Games on 17 March in reporting that before he received Blackwood's latest payment for a magazine article Margaret Hogg 'was just saying she had forgot the time she had money in her pocket and I replied that I had just one shilling in my possession which I had kept alone since the Border games and it had remained so long a solitary residenter that I thought it would be a lucky one'. This discouraged very frequent stays in Edinburgh, where Hogg would have to meet numerous small expenses, even if he put up at a modest hostelry such as the old-fashioned Harrow Inn on Candlemaker Row. At home in Yarrow Hogg could get by on a day-to-day basis with very little money, living on the produce of the Mount Benger farm and dairy, the fish he caught, and with small running accounts with local tradesmen. William Blackwood provided far more than a publishing service in Edinburgh for Hogg. Among other things he supplied Hogg with pens, ink, and writing-paper, received and forwarded parcels from London and elsewhere, cashed bills on Hogg's behalf, advertised his cottage to let, paid the occasional small debt in Edinburgh for him, and purchased the necessary annual licence so that Hogg could go out shooting game in August. He also strengthened their friendly relations by regular gifts of any books he published that he thought would be of particular interest to Hogg—particularly sermons, poems, and Scottish fiction. He sent the issues of *Blackwood's Edinburgh Magazine* every month as soon as they were printed, a real boon to Hogg who needed to pick up the mood and concerns of any periodical for which he wrote and who would be instantly informed thereby of the extent of his work that had been used and able to check that due payment had been made.[6] The practice also fostered Hogg's sense of being a member of the

Blackwoodian circle, and encouraged him to identify his work with the magazine.

Hogg's earnings of between one and two hundred pounds a year as a periodical writer would not, however, enable him to pay the Mount Benger rent of £370 and nor it seems did the farm itself. Besides being short of the necessary capital with which to stock it adequately, Hogg had little aptitude for or interest in farm management. Mount Benger employed a number of farm-workers who would need overseeing, but Hogg's authorship and his trusting good nature together meant that his servants were frequently left to their own devices rather more than was either customary or prudent. James Russell recollected that

> On a fine summer afternoon he would be sitting in the cool of the dining room, when he would take it into his head to see what his workers were doing. Getting hold of a spy glass, he would stand at the front door, looking through it, benevolence beaming on his jovial face, surveying the peaceful scene, with all the serenity attached to the lord of the Manor. This line of conduct [...] was neither energetic nor commendable, however satisfactory it might be for his servants.

The tenant of an extensive store-farm would only prosper by giving it his unremitting attention and Hogg's writing rendered this impossible. Scott indeed had thought when Hogg first took on the Mount Benger tenancy that he would do as well to take his more prosaic brother David into the concern as his manager. Hogg was also afflicted with a never-ending stream of visitors who occupied his attention and expected feeding and lodging. It was perhaps with these in mind that he had founded the modest Gordon Arms Inn on his property in 1821, vouching year by year to the authorities in Selkirk for the respectability of the landlord, John Gordon. He still kept open house himself, however, firstly at Altrive and later at Mount Benger. Unfortunately, the *Noctes Ambrosianae* of *Blackwood's Edinburgh Magazine* referred to the fictional editor Christopher North's visits there and misleadingly described Hogg as a prosperous man. Small wonder then that Hogg frequently reported an inundation of callers, and that on one such occasion his house was 'exactly like an overcrouded small inn'. After dealing with these callers Hogg, according to the former herd-boy at Mount Benger, generally did his writing 'at night, when the labours of the farm were over, and often sat up till two or three in the morning'. Writing to his wife during one of his later absences from home Hogg himself recalled 'my hours of study my nap and my glass with you late at night'.[7]

By July 1826 Hogg's position as tenant of Mount Benger farm was becoming desperate: he was 'very much embarrassed and threatened with arrestment'. He had signed a hypothec, effectively a preferential claim on his farm-stock, in favour of the Duke of Buccleuch as security for the rent that was then outstanding, but in January 1827 'recieved word from his Grace's curators either to pay up my arrears at Whitsunday or give up my farm'. Hogg then estimated that Mount Benger, far from producing an income, was costing him a hundred pounds a year, so the sensible course was undoubtedly to relinquish his lease and retreat to Altrive which cost him nothing and where he would be able to support his family by his literary earnings.[8] Perhaps Hogg hoped that when the young Duke of Buccleuch came of age in November 1827 and took control of his own property he would follow his parents' example of generosity towards the Ettrick Shepherd? Surprisingly, he retained Mount Benger.

The anxiety of the managers of the Buccleuch estates at this time reflected a national financial crisis. At the end of 1825 the house of cards of mutual promissory notes and bills of credit collapsed at a touch and one after another businesses fell, one bringing down another and that another in turn. Most famously Sir Walter Scott, Britain's best-known and most successful writer, was ruined. As an author and as a partner in the Ballantyne printing-house he had issued and guaranteed bills depending on other bills issued by his publisher Constable and that publisher's London connections in the trade, and in January 1826 found himself liable for debts totalling more than a hundred thousand pounds.[9] Declining to become a bankrupt, which as a gentleman he considered a mean evasion of his obligations and as a lawyer realised would probably threaten his son's future ownership of Abbotsford, Scott set his foot on the path of gradually redeeming his debt by the use of his pen, killing himself in the end by overwork and the adoption of such a massive responsibility. To Hogg's sorrow for his friend was added the knowledge that he could no longer rely on Scott's financial backing, and indeed that some of his existing debts in the form of bills from Scott or from the Constable firm might now be called in question.

Turning things over in his mind, Hogg recalled that Scott had mentioned a scheme of trying to get him established as one of the Royal Associates of the Royal Society of Literature, each with a lifetime pension of £100 given by George IV. Hogg's chances of success were poor. The number of royal pensioners was limited to ten so that one of the existing pensioners would have to die or retire from the list before another could be appointed and by April 1828 not a single vacancy had occurred in the body since the election of the original Associates. The original Regulations of the Society had also dictated that the Royal Associates should be 'persons of eminent learning' and that each would on admission 'be invited to communicate, from time to time, to the Council, some Essay or Disquisition, to be read at the Ordinary Meetings of the Society, and published in the Transactions'. In other words, a scholar rather than a labouring-class poet was the sort of person the institution wished to encourage. There was also some insecurity about the continuation of these pensions in future, since they were a personal gift from George IV and not made by the monarch *per se.* A new king might not wish to continue allocating a thousand pounds every year to the RSL. (And indeed when George IV's brother succeeded him as William IV this is exactly what happened and there was a scramble to find alternative pensions from the civil list for the existing Royal Associates.)[10]

Scott was as ever willing to use what influence he had with the RSL, however, and he was able to utilise the services of his son-in-law, John Gibson Lockhart, now resident in London and occupying the influential post of editor of John Murray's *Quarterly Review.* For all his haughtiness and distrust of overt displays of emotion Lockhart had a loyal and constant regard for his old friends in the circle surrounding Scott at Abbotsford. The early years of his marriage were the happiest of his life, and many years later he wrote to Hogg that in Ettrick Forest, 'I also have left all my *local* affections buried & lost'. Although he had never succeeded at the bar he left Scotland with great reluctance despite the glittering promise of future literary eminence in London, telling his friends at his farewell dinner in Edinburgh, 'you know as well as myself, that if I had ever been able to make a long speech, there would have been no occasion for our meeting to-night'. Lockhart's genuine affection for Hogg was undoubtedly reciprocated. Lockhart's marriage to Scott's daughter on the day after his own wedding, Hogg felt, had made them virtually members of the same family, 'I a step-son, and he a legitimate younger brother'. Lockhart's departure for London at the end of 1825 had been a double loss to Hogg, in that his own nephew and literary assistant Robert Hogg had accompanied him. Hogg's nephew, a corrector of the press at the Ballantyne firm, had been a useful and willing intermediary between his uncle in Yarrow and the Edinburgh book trade and was greatly missed. Grumpily Hogg wrote to a mutual friend, John Aitken, some months after his nephew's departure,

'Have you ever heard from Robert Hogg? I have not He certainly is the queerest callant ever was born'.[11] (However, Robert Hogg was back in Edinburgh at his old post little more than a year after his departure.)

Early in 1827 Hogg wrote to Lockhart in London explaining the dire financial straits he was in and requesting his influence with the RSL. Lockhart responded warmly, 'Robert will tell you that I have *not* lost sight of your project in regard to the Royal Society of Literature: nor shall I do so'. He recommended Hogg to approach William Jerdan, editor of the *Literary Gazette* and Secretary to the RSL, as 'he has kindly feelings towards you & being an active bustling sort of man has it in his power to serve you among the Dons of the Institution'. Jerdan replied that the Society was 'rather for the encouragement of learning than of that kind of Literature which may be sustained by making itself popular', but his sympathy was practically demonstrated when he approached the Royal Literary Fund on Hogg's behalf and obtained a grant of £50 to assist him in his present difficulties.[12]

As Hogg himself remarked, anyone reading an account of his financial situation might suppose that he lived 'a life of misery and wretchedness'. On the contrary, he declared,

> I never knew either man or woman who has been so uniformly happy as I have been; which has been partly owing to a good constitution, and partly from the conviction that a heavenly gift, conferring the powers of immortal song, was inherent in my soul. Indeed so uniformly smooth and happy has my married life been, that on a retrospect I cannot distinguish one part from another, save by some remarkably good days of fishing, shooting, and curling on the ice.

During these years, Hogg settled comfortably into the lifestyle of a local celebrity in Ettrick Forest. Less than gracious locals commented sourly that Hogg 'was hand and glove with great men in Edinburgh, Professor Wilson, and Scott, and the like; he was aye going to Abbotsford and Lord Napier's; and so he thought himself a very great man too, and Mrs. Hogg thought herself a great woman, and looked down on her neighbours'. William Laidlaw, however, reported to Scott that the poet's neighbours were all his friends, and he was certainly a kind man to the poor. Stories circulated of how he had given a boy a shilling on observing his kindness to his old blind father. A former servant recalled that once, when a local joiner had bought a cow from Hogg which shortly afterwards died, Hogg, knowing him to be a poor man, invited him to choose a free replacement from among the rest of his own farm-stock. Thanks to his literary celebrity Hogg was a prominent man among the Buccleuch tenants in Selkirkshire. They would meet annually at Mitchell's Inn in Selkirk on 25 November to celebrate their young landlord's birthday with a formal dinner. He wrote an account of the 1825 dinner for *Blackwood's Edinburgh Magazine*, when after-dinner speeches were interspersed with songs by Hogg himself and David Thomson, the weaver-poet of Galashiels. Some of Hogg's audience were so drunk and inattentive that when they encored him they failed to realise that the repeat performance was actually one of a different song altogether. Hogg's support for the Buccleuch family was an unspoken bargain made when he had accepted his little farm of Altrive rent-free, but it was also natural to him because of his affection for the memory of Duchess Harriet, his former patron and the mother of the present Duke. In a speech he made at an 1827 dinner in Selkirk marking Duke Walter's majority, Hogg described how in her death the poor folk of the Border dales had 'lost their most bountiful benefactor, one who watched over all their wants as with the eye of a parent'.[13]

Although Hogg had long since exchanged the outdoor life of a shepherd for the more sedentary one of a writer, still his active temperament and habits were not well suited to constant confinement at a desk. From 1822 onwards he held an annual shooting licence, to go out on the moors in pursuit of game-birds during the second half of August and early in September. His love of tramping the countryside comes over clearly in his description of the enjoyments to be found 'on the waste among the blooming heath, by the silver spring, or swathed in the delicious breeze of the wilderness'. This was very different from a Victorian country-house shooting-party, with half-tame pheasants shot by the cartload. Hogg's sport was an opportunity to explore the countryside and observe the birds and animals around him in relative solitude. He would walk and wade for miles, filling and carrrying a bag slung across his shoulder, sometimes alone and sometimes with a chosen friend or two. As a shepherd Hogg had tended his sheep but also slaughtered them when the time came, and he both loved and shot wild birds. In 1827 he wrote a touching lament for those trapped and killed in a late April snowstorm, many of them nesting birds at that season of the year. Hogg was by no means a crack shot, and humorously described his own ineptness when it came to shooting partridges. 'They give such a skirl when they rise that they not only make me start but they make my heart leap into my windpipe; and before the momentary agitation goes off I have fired both barrels in the air'.[14] At three-and-a-half guineas the licence was expensive, a gentleman's perquisite, but a game course was one of the distinguishing features of the gentry as opposed to the bourgeois dinner-table, and an Edinburgh friend with social aspirations like William Blackwood was happy to make Hogg an annual present of his licence and to receive regular presents of game sent in with the Yarrow carrier in return.

Hogg also became a noted angler during his Mount Benger years, his careful observation of weather and water enabling him to invent a new fishing-fly suited to local conditions, which was sold in the St Ronan's Fishing Tackle Warehouse of his Innerleithen friend, Robert Boyd. Most of his own tackle was of the homeliest description, and on one occasion the reel stuck when he had caught a twenty-pound salmon. It was landed only because the tackle was too strong to be broken, after performing 'a series of desperate evolutions, which ended in its throwing itself high and dry upon a bed of gravel close to the angler'. On another such occasion a party watching him from a distance immediately became convinced he had gone mad as he dashed to and fro by the side of the water.[15]

Hogg's other sporting and leisure activities were a mixture of the traditional sports he had enjoyed from his youth, and those resulting from his position as a leading man in the district. He had enjoyed curling for many years past, both locally and with the Duddingstone Curling Society in Edinburgh, and was a good and active player even in late middle-age. He also enjoyed hare-coursing with his greyhounds, humorously named Clavers and Burley after characters in Scott's novel *Old Mortality*. The Forest Club, meeting socially at Mitchell's Inn in Selkirk, held coursing competitions for a silver dog-collar and a silver cup. Hogg was also a member of the Crookwelcome Club, a society of farmers who met periodically for convivial evenings and agricultural discussions at the celebrated inn of that name near Tushilaw in the Ettrick valley. The club kept a record of sheep and wool prices, notable storms, and so on, but at one dinner held in February 1826 the twelve members present paid twenty-four shillings for their dinner (at two shillings a head), but a heftier guinea and a half for '7 Bottles of Whisky Made in Toddy at 4/6'.[16] Rather more soberly agricultural was the Pastoral Society of Selkirkshire, formed in 1819 at the instigation of Captain Napier of Thirlstane as a local agricultural improvement society for the county, and meeting annually sometimes at Tinnis in Yarrow, and sometimes at Thirlestane in Ettrick. Prizes were given for the best livestock shown and a members' dinner ended the day.

For years Hogg had kept the traditional Yarrow Games alive, an annual event taking place on 17 March, St Patrick's Day, when leaping, running, and wrestling contests were keenly-contested by local shepherds and young farmers. Hogg provided the modest prizes awarded, such as new blue bonnets, and he generally acted as judge too and threw the ball into the air to begin the inter-parish football match that followed, between the young men of Ettrick and of Yarrow parishes. This bore little resemblance to the modern game played on a marked pitch by eleven men on each side: everyone who wanted to join in seems to have done so, the game ranged over a wide extent of country, and it could last for several hours. At the Yarrow Games of 1828 the ball was thrown into the air to begin the game at 3.15 p.m. and, as the two parishes were evenly matched and the result indecisive, play continued until it was pitch-dark and the ball itself was lost.[17]

It was from a wish to keep these traditional sports alive that Hogg gradually became involved with the society of the rapidly expanding village of Innerleithen. Scott's novel *Saint Ronan's Well* (1824) put it on the map as a mineral spa, and the chief local landowner, the Earl of Traquair, enthusiastically capitalised on his property afterwards. In 1827 the Earl built a well-house, and he also encouraged the building of larger houses along the line of the turnpike road linking the village to Peebles and Selkirk. A handsome modern inn with a ballroom was built. The neighbourhood included some wealthy men. Hogg's friend, James Ballantyne, the farmer of Whitehope who had been best man at his wedding, had since inherited the estate of Holylee and built a handsome modern mansion there. Glenormiston, another estate in Innerleithen parish, had been bought by in 1824 by William Steuart, a prosperous Welshman, who built a fine house and doubled the value of the property by careful management and planting.[18] Robert Boyd of Marmion House had returned to the district after a successful mercantile career in Edinburgh, and opened a shop, which told tea, wines, and spirits, and acted as a small circulating library. Here too fishing-tackle was hired and sold. Innerleithen was a convenient weekend and holiday destination from Edinburgh, and Hogg's publisher William Blackwood, for example, rented rooms during several seasons from a Mrs Roughead for his family to have a holiday and would supervise his thriving business in Edinburgh during the week and run down to see them at the weekends. By the end of Hogg's lifetime Innerleithen even had a penny postal service, letters addressed to the Peebles office being forwarded to

Innerleithen for an extra penny and delivered to houses within the town limits.[19]

Hogg's contribution to the development of Innerleithen as a holiday and tourist resort was the formation in 1827 of the St Ronan's Border Club to support the traditional athletic sports of the Borders. Like much of his written work, the Club both celebrated tradition and adapted it to the requirements of a genteel and prosperous early nineteenth-century audience. This was the loyal and stalwart Borders peasantry as featured in Scott's novels and *Blackwood's Edinburgh Magazine*. The annual St Ronan's Games, indeed, prefigure the Highland Games so beloved of the Victorians and associated with royalty after Queen Victoria's attendance at the Braemar Gathering in 1848. Members of the Club wore a special uniform, the distinctive feature of which was a green coat trimmed with gold, which cost £4-10s from Archibald Donaldson, the Peebles tailor who supplied it. Shepherds and local farm-workers competed at wrestling, leaping, running, and throwing, in front of a large crowd of spectators (almost three thousand in 1828), some of whom arrived in carriages as well as on horseback or on foot. Hogg was one of the judges, 'full of bustle—for the conduct of the games devolved on him—his voice loud and cheerful, his eye glancing with the excitement'. Prizes of blue bonnets or commemorative silver medals donated by the likes of Edinburgh's Six Feet Club were awarded to the victors, and the day's events concluded with a formal dinner in one of the local inns. A second day's events catered much more specifically for the Club's membership of Edinburgh professional men and local gentry, with archery and rifle-shooting contests. Archery was not a popular local sport in the first half of the nineteenth century, but one which was associated with the Jacobite aristocracy of the Royal Company of Archers, then as now the monarch's official and ceremonial bodyguard in Scotland. Hogg had never had a bow in his hand in his youth, and adopted the sport late in life at the instigation of Colonel Ferguson of Huntly-Burn who had given him a bow and some arrows to practise with.[20]

As the St Ronan's Club became a focus for middle-class social activities during the Innerleithen season, roughly from May to October, an official piper was advertised for. In return for playing on both the Highland and Irish pipes during the summer months the successful candidate would receive a salary of five guineas and 'a handsome Dress of the Stewart Tartan', and could be sure of making a considerable sum besides from 'the increasing celebrity of the St Ronan's Mineral Waters, the numerous Nutting and Pic-Nic parties which generally take place'. The Club's own activities gradually expanded. A silver arrow was given to the St Ronan's Club by Sir William Patrick Hume Campbell of Marchmont, and first contested at the annual games of 1830. Another archery contest was held separately in October or November among a 'small but select' group of Club members termed the Bowmen of the Border, under the captaincy of William Steuart of Glenormiston, when a sweepstake was shot for after a contest for a prize bow, and a dinner at Riddell's Inn ended the proceedings of the day. There was also an annual angling contest held in May or June among the club members for a silver medal awarded to the angler who could kill with the rod the greatest weight of trout in a given time, and occasionally an informal salmon-fishing competition the day after the autumn archery contest as well.[21]

Such social and sporting events enlivened Hogg's life as a tenant-farmer, and his residence in the vicinity gradually became one of the inducements laid before holidaymakers to come to Innerleithen. Among the local attractions named in the *Edinburgh Evening Courant* were 'Melrose Abbey, Dryburgh, Abbotsford, the residence of the Ettrick Shepherd, the romantic scenery around St Mary's Loch, and the cataract of the Gray Mare's Tail, which issues out of Loch Skeen, and falls into Moffat water, the height of nearly three hundred feet'.[22]

Until the mid-1820s most of Hogg's periodical contributions had been directed towards Edinburgh, but around this time a new kind of London publication began to establish itself, a hybrid between a magazine and a book, the literary annual. These pretty anthologies combined a variety of shorter verse and prose pieces by different authors with high-quality steel engravings, and were published once a year in large print-runs prepared for the seasonal market for Christmas and New Year gifts. The shorter tales and poems of well-known professional writers were much in demand by annual editors, and there was plenty of time between one issue and the next for the transmission of manuscripts, proofs, and payments between Altrive and London. Hogg's first contribution to an annual was 'Invocation to the Queen of the Fairies' in the *Literary Souvenir* for 1825, a passage which appeared almost simultaneously as the opening lines of Book Sixth of his long poem *Queen Hynde*. Hogg's sense of a distinctive new market opening out is revealed in his letter to the annual's editor, A. A. Watts, about the overlap: 'I regretted' he wrote, 'that my work appeared so soon after yours; however it has rather had a good than bad effect, for the reviewers of The Souvenir quote it on the one hand, and the reviewers of Hynde on the other, and even the same reviewers quote it without at all seeming aware that it is in both works'. As the pioneers, the *Literary Souvenir* and the *Forget Me Not*, were joined by a host of rivals, demand for Hogg's work increased, and by 1830 he was contributing to half-a-dozen different ones. The annuals were keenly compared by reviewers as they appeared in the weeks leading up to Christmas, and Hogg's work in them was frequently singled out for praise in English as well as Scottish magazines and literary papers.[23] Other London periodicals were also increasingly prepared to solicit and pay for his shorter pieces.

Gradually Hogg was becoming a national as well as a local institution as the Ettrick Shepherd, regarded as second only to Scott for his depiction of an older and more traditional Scottish society. A generation was now reaching adulthood for which *The Queen's Wake* had been formative reading in boyhood, whose members looked affectionately on Hogg in the Edinburgh streets or in his native district, and who felt honoured to make his acquaintance. For them Hogg was a living link between the traditional rural Scotland of their childhood and the glittering new world of polite culture that they hoped to enter. A young poet such as John Goldie of Ayr 'respectfully dedicated' his *Poems and Songs* of 1822 to Hogg, as did James Telfer his *Border Ballads, and Other Miscellaneous Poems* of 1824. In 1828 Lockhart in London dedicated his *Life of Robert Burns* 'To James Hogg and Allan Cunningham [...] in Testimony of Admiration and Affection'. Hogg, he thus indicated, was Burns's worthy successor in his own time. Hogg was also beginning to feature in works of fiction. The narrator of *Marianne, The Widower's Daughter* of 1823, for example, introduces his daughter to Hogg, explaining that he admires both his character and writings. In spite of every disadvantage Hogg 'cultivated his powers, though unnnoticed and unknown, and now enjoys the reward of his labours in a very extensive fame'. More satirically the young heroine of *Scotch Novel Reading* (1824) 'saw, in imagination, the sunny ringlets floating over the rosy cheek of poor Hogg; and the plaid, in graceful drapery, thrown over his form: she declared she would walk leagues, barefoot [...] to get only one sight of him'. Blackwood reported the admiration of Mrs Mary Anne Hughes of London, wife of a canon of St Paul's cathedral, in rather similar terms. She would 'almost travel to Scotland on foot to hear you talk even half so well as you do in the Noctes', he told Hogg, and she intended to recommend warmly the two-volume republication of his magazine series 'The Shepherd's Calendar'. Scott and Lockhart also reported Mrs Hughes's enthusiastic praise of his work to Hogg. She sent him an appropriate gift of some Bramah's patent steel-nib pens from Edinburgh and when they finally met at Abbotsford in

August 1828 enthusiastically praised *The Private Memoirs and Confessions of a Justified Sinner* as 'positively the best story of that frightful kind that ever was written'. Indeed, Hogg was so encouraged by her obvious and sincere admiration that he suggested Blackwood might buy up the remaining printed copies and reissue them with a fresh title-page.[24]

A circle of young Scottish writers gradually formed around him. Hogg seems to have been particularly kind to Henry Scott Riddell, a shepherd with literary ambitions in whom he must have recognised a resemblance to his younger self. On receiving Riddell's poem 'Ode to the Harp of Zion' from Hogg, which appeared in *Blackwood's* for September 1829, Blackwood commented, 'Ridell's Ode I suspect has recd not a few of your touches if it be not your own altogether'. Robert Gilfillan of Leith was another of Hogg's young protégés. His 'Write, Write, Tourist and Traveller' (a parody of Scott's 'Blue Bonnets Over the Border') was sung by the Shepherd in the *Noctes Ambrosianae* for January 1828, who introduces it as 'by a fine fellow— a freen o' mine in Leith. I promised him that I wad sing it at a Noctes'. In sending Hogg a presentation copy of his volume of *Songs* in 1831 Gilfillan modestly jested that some of the critics had 'the impudence to say that in dashes of Scotch humour I almost approached the Ettrick Shepherd!! there was effrontery for you'. Robert Chambers, an old school-fellow of Hogg's nephew Robert, had presumably been introduced to Hogg in Edinburgh, and when he was on a walking tour of the Borders gathering materials for *The Picture of Scotland* Hogg not only recommended him to the good offices of Rev. Dr William Brown, the minister of Eskdalemuir and a noted local antiquary, but wrote an account of Ettrick Forest in his own hand to be incorporated into his young friend's work. He was now an authority on the Scottish Borders, and when David Low, who edited Blackwood's new *Quarterly Journal of Agriculture*, failed to secure Scott as the author of an article on the changes in the lifestyle of the Scottish Borders peasantry he was pleased to secure Hogg instead.[25] Despite financial hardships Hogg's status as respected elder of Scottish letters must have been gratifying.

Hogg's own family circle was reduced on 16 May 1827 by the death of his father-in-law, Peter Phillips. His financial affairs were confused, but it was rumoured at least that he had been a modest landowner at the time of his death, William Laidlaw reporting in February 1828 that Hogg '*is now a Laird*. I actually mean Hogg himself–His Father in law having left Mrs Hogg six & thirty acres of good land in Dumfriesshire'. Burnswarkpark, twenty-seven acres in

Tundergarth parish, had been bequeathed by Peter Phillips in his obsolete will of 1812 to his son Peter Phillips to provide for various legacies, including one of a thousand pounds to each of his unmarried daughters. On 19 August 1825 he had, however, signed a disposition at Annan effecting the sale of Burnswarkpark to a Peter Pattie of Lydiafield for an undisclosed sum.[26] It may be that Hogg, unaware of the sale, hoped that his wife would now inherit Burnswarkpark. On 29 May 1827, the following announcement, possibly drawn up by Hogg himself, appeared in the *Dumfries and Galloway Courier*, where the friends and relations of the Phillips family would be sure to see it:

> At Altrive Lake, on Yarrow, on the 16th curt. Mr Peter Phillips, aged 79. He was upwards of 40 years tenant of Longbridge Muir, and other lands in this country, and was highly respected for every moral and religious virtue. His numerous relations in Dumfries-shire and Galloway will please to accept this notification of his death.

It is possible that Peter Pattie then saw the announcement and asked for the signed agreement conveying Burnswarkpark to him to be formally registered in Dumfries to establish his ownership beyond question, since this was done on 28 April 1828. Hogg and his wife also received a summons of transference from the Court of Session in February 1828, as Peter Phillips's heirs, concerning the sale of some land known as Longdyke, but responded that they were 'entirely ignorant of the proceedings'.[27]

Peter Phillips's widow Janet Carruthers was left alone after a marriage of more than half a century. Hogg ventriloquised her distress in a little poem published in the *Dumfries and Galloway Courier* of 5 June that year and subsequently revised as 'An Aged Widow's Own Words' for the London annual *The Bijou*. The speaker, remembering the deaths of her 'braw and boardly' sons and 'daughters in their prime', complains how 'fearfu' thus to be | Left in a world alane'. It was decided that the feeble old lady would be better living at Mount Benger as a member of her surviving daughter's family than on her own at Altrive. Hogg reported to the young James Gray on 5 July, 'Grandmother is fully better than her ordinary', but she did not survive her husband many months.[28] She died on 4 March 1828 and was buried with him in Ettrick kirkyard.

Her removal from Altrive left the cottage vacant, and Hogg decided to keep the rooms and beds aired and add a little to his income by letting it during the summer months. He advertised it as 'the best angling station in the South of Scotland', to let weekly, monthly, or quarterly. In 1827 Henry Scott, Grieve's former partner in the North Bridge hatter's business in Edinburgh, displayed a notice in his shop, Blackwood put up one in his Princes Street premises, and it also seems to have appeared in the advertising leaves of the magazine. Altrive was to let again the following year at five guineas per month or £25 for the season, the resident housekeeper to be paid by the occupier, and advertised both in Blackwood's shop and in the *Edinburgh Weekly Journal*.[29] Possibly Hogg managed to find a tenant for the summer and autumn of 1829 without advertising.

More Phillips relations found a temporary home at Mount Benger at about this time. James Gray had fallen into financial difficulties in Belfast. In February 1826 he resigned from his post as Rector of Belfast Academy and, having taken orders as an anglican priest, accepted a post as chaplain to the East India Company. His daughters Mary and Janet did not accompany him to India since both were engaged to be married. When the engagements were broken they stayed with the Hoggs for a time and then visited their Edinburgh relations before sailing out to join their father in India. Always sympathetic to those in misfortune, Hogg was touched by the obvious grief of the younger of the two girls, Mary Gray, at being jilted, and wrote two poems about her, again for one of the London annuals, *Friendship's Offering*. In parting with her and wishing her renewed health and spirits in India, Hogg gently reminded her of his own love for her:

> And long as beats this kindred heart
>   My love shall be as it hath been—
> There shalt thou occupy thy part
>   Though half the world lie us between!

It took months for letters from India to reach Europe, since there was no general postal service in India at this time and letters were transmitted to the coast by runners maintained by the landholders of each district. The time of their arrival there was very uncertain, and after that they would have a long voyage by sailing-ship. The usual time for a letter posted in France to arrive in Upper India as late as 1830, for example, was eight months. When Hogg wrote to the younger James Gray on 5 July 1827 he reported that they were 'wearying grieveously to hear the first news from Cutch', where James Gray was due to settle as tutor to the young Rao.[30] He must have wondered how he could inform Gray of his daughters' planned arrival, or indeed of the death of his old mother-in-law.

Before her death old Mrs Phillips would have been cheered by
the birth of an additional grandchild, for Hogg's third daughter,
Harriet Sidney Hogg after the former Duchess of Buccleuch, was
born at Mount Benger on 18 December 1827. She quickly made a
very special place for herself in her father's heart, perhaps because
during the initial days and weeks of her life Hogg was tied to the
house himself and had more of her company. Days before her birth
he 'got a stroke from a horse in the dark', an episode which recalls
the night terrors of Robert Wringhim in *Confessions*. Hogg could not
walk for a while and was initially concerned that he might be 'rendered lame for life'. Confined to the house over the Christmas and
New Year holidays he wrote his 'Eastern Apologues' for the annual
Forget Me Not, in which the lame old bard Ismael, possessed of 'the
gift of song [...] an emanation from the Deity', feels himself to be
happier than Prince Sadac despite his crippled state and lowly fortunes. By 5 January Hogg was walking about again, though not yet
able to go fishing.[31] The threat of lameness seemed to have passed
over Hogg himself to light on his new daughter. The family had been
puzzled as to why the baby cried so constantly when she was lifted
or touched, but Hogg himself eventually realised that her ankle was
broken in two places. The maidservant who looked after her had
dropped her and then been afraid to confess for more than a month
what she had done. It looked as though poor Harriet might be lame
for life as a result of this neglect, and the couple decided to consult
an Edinburgh surgeon. Margaret Hogg took the eight-month old
Harriet to town in late July or August 1828, staying with Dr William
Crighton, a clever surgeon whose sister Euphemia was the widow of
her own older brother, John Phillips. Little Maggie, then aged three,
also went with her mother. The Gray girls were in Edinburgh too,
and Hogg hoped to join the party later to see the two girls safely on
board ship for India, either in London or Liverpool.[32]

Left alone with the older two children at Mount Benger that August Hogg fretted about his baby daughter's treatment in Edinburgh.
One night he dreamed that she had a fever and awoke saying 'dear,
dear, sweet Harriet'. Writing to his wife he enquired, 'How is my
poor Harriet and what are they doing with her I can hardly think of
my darling being put into steel boots like the ancient Covenanters'.
Hogg's imaginative transformation of a special boot to hold the twisted
foot straight into the tortures suffered by the likes of Macbriar in
Scott's *Old Mortality* is a measure of his special protectiveness towards
her. 'I am very glad that you have not as yet put my darling Harriet
to any unnecessary pain or trouble' he wrote subsequently, 'for my

own opinion always was that there was very little the matter with her'. Letters must have been received eventually from India and the Gray daughters sailed out to join their father, though Hogg was unable to get into Edinburgh to escort them to Liverpool.[33]

While his wife was in Edinburgh Hogg was busy harvesting at Mount Benger, and negotiating the sale of his wool to the Galashiels manufacturers. He also had his friend John Harper to stay for the shooting, and went over to Yair as the guest of Alexander Pringle, who was giving a dinner for the local gentry to mark the disbanding of the Selkirkshire Yeomanry. The guest of honour was the young Duke of Buccleuch, who had been educated in England, at Eton and then at Oxford, and was therefore not a familiar figure to his Selkirkshire neighbours and tenants. Hogg judged him a 'respectable' though not a fluent public speaker. Flatteringly, he seemed to take a liking to the Ettrick Shepherd. Hogg wrote to his wife, 'I got a good deal of chat with him in the drawing room for he conversed while there more with me than any other body and when taken away from me once to have some one introduced to him he immediately came back again'. On another day Hogg joined a picnic party of more than seventy people at St Mary's Loch, such a joyous day that John Wilson proposed that they should build a cairn to mark the spot and form a society to meet there annually, to be named the Brethren of the Braes.[34]

On 2 October Scott and Colonel James Ferguson dined with Hogg on their return from a public dinner in Dumfries, and took kindly notice of his only son, then seven years of age. Colonel Ferguson gave young James his own two-bladed pocket-knife, though the boy was much more taken with one owned by Scott that incorporated a saw. Hogg was vexed at James's inability to answer the questions Scott put to him and showed it, declaring that though a most amiable affectionate boy he would never be 'the Cooper of Fogo' (his father's better). Scott tactfully responded that he had never liked precocity of genius and that young James would yet turn out to be an honour to his father and all his kin. Hogg was always proud of Scott's visits to his house, arranging for a particularly lavish breakfast to be served and rushing out to welcome him before he could reach the door of the house.[35]

That autumn Hogg noticed in the newspapers the prospectus for a new Edinburgh weekly publication, the *Edinburgh Literary Journal*. It was to be printed by James Ballantyne and edited by the youthful Henry Glassford Bell on the model of London literary weeklies such as the *Literary Gazette* and *Athenaeum*. It intended to focus particularly on Scottish publications:

> [...] the Editor pledges himself to maintain, as far as possible, *a priority over the London press in his Reviews of all Works published in Scotland.* Nor is it his intention to limit himself in his notices of these works to a mere selection; but to express an opinion, however brief it may occasionally be, on *every* book that issues from the Scottish press.

A favourable opinion was rapidly expressed by Christopher North in the *Noctes Ambrosianae* for November 1828, and when the Shepherd responded that 'ane gets tired o' that eternal soun'–Blackwood's Magazine' North concluded, 'One does indeed'.[36] It seems doubtful whether William Blackwood agreed with him, facing the prospect of his prime contributors supporting another Edinburgh publication.

Hogg at least was becoming increasingly dissatisfied with his treatment at Blackwood's hands. A republication of his magazine series 'The Shepherd's Calendar' in volume form had been under discussion since at least September 1825, though Blackwood seemed to be more anxious to prevent it going to another publisher than to produce it himself. On 9 February 1829 Hogg's frustration found vent in the angry query, 'Is the Shepherd's Calander ever to see the light? or is it fairly to be strangled in the birth once more'. And while his songs for the *Noctes Ambrosianae* were always gratefully received, Blackwood was becoming more reluctant to publish his ballads and prose fiction in the magazine. 'You have an Egyptian story of mine' he had told Blackwood in July 1828, 'which you promised to publish at any rate do not lose it'. Hogg's wife also felt that at times Blackwood failed to treat her husband with the respect that was due to him, so his amusement was sadly misplaced when he said in front of her, 'O its delightful to see what a rage he's in when I send him back a cartfu' Manuscripts! It's quite grand!'[37]

'A Letter from Yarrow' in which Hogg announced his support for the new publication was published in the first number of the *Edinburgh Literary Journal* on 15 November 1828. Since it did not pay Hogg for his work it ought not to have been a rival Edinburgh outlet to *Blackwood's* for Hogg's work, but he became a regular contributor. Part of the attraction was undoubtedly the respect shown to him as a celebrated Scottish author. The 'To Our Correspondents' column for 18 April 1829, for example, contained the following paragraph:

> The Ettrick Shepherd requests us to mention on what subject we should like his next communication to be. All we can say is, that with the genius he brings to bear upon every sub-

ject, we do not think he can go wrong. Let it be grave or gay—
verse or prose—just as the mood is on him. The great rule we
should like him to attend to is, that the *sooner* he favours us
the better.

When A. A. Watts accused Hogg and Cunningham of mutually puff-
ing one another's publications, his 'dirty suspicions' were immediately denigrated in the *Journal*. The paper's enthusiastic reviewing
of every Hogg publication as it appeared (including his song collections for the London music publishers) also made a very pleasant
change. *Blackwood's*, as Hogg must have remembered, had in the past
not even reviewed those of his works published by William
Blackwood himself, such as *The Brownie of Bodsbeck*. Many of his Edinburgh literary acquaintances also contributed to the *Journal*, giving
Hogg the feeling once more of belonging to a brotherhood and enjoying a forum for debate. When William Tennant of Dollar Academy, the poet of *Anster Fair*, announced his plans to modernise the
psalmody of the Church of Scotland, Hogg asserted its special associations with the Covenanting past and humorously threatened to
make the new version 'an edition of dolour to somebody'.[38] Hogg
was well aware that the new periodical was a thorn in Blackwood's
side, and sometimes preferred to publish an article there rather than
in London where he would have been paid for it. Hogg's account of
a wild balloon ride, rejected by Blackwood on the grounds that John
Wilson intended at some point to write a *Noctes Ambrosianae* with a
similar setting, was 'transferred [...] to Mr Bell to be published next
week [...] it shall appear before any other aerial tour at any rate'.[39]
Mutual recriminations between Hogg and Blackwood increased
over the next couple of years as Hogg's financial situation worsened
and Blackwood seemed reluctant to publish Hogg's work in the magazine. Hogg's letter of 3 June 1829, for example, submits a poem with
the comment that it 'will only be the 13th article returned since the
beginning of this present year which is as good encouragement for
writing as can possibly be'. Hogg also implied that his daughter's
health was suffering as a consequence of Blackwood's neglect, stating, 'As soon as Margt and I get a little money in our purses we are
coming to town but a real scarcity of the needful has caused us to
neglect our little darling's foot much too long and about which I am
very much concerned'. Blackwood retorted that Hogg was 'the most
cross grained impenetrable mortal I daresay that ever existed' and
his statement simply one of his 'poetical imaginings'. He did send
Hogg five pounds and added more kindly, 'I am excessively vexed
to hear that your child's foot is not better. You should not lose a day

in coming to town, and if you want £5– more when you come it will be at your service'.[40]

Little Harriet was a general favourite. Sir Walter Scott, lame himself after infant poliomyelitis, always greeted the Hoggs with a genial query after the lame foot. Hogg, in enquiring whether it would be possible for her to be boarded in lodgings near a doctor in Hawick in the charge of a servant, ruefully added that 'I fear that would cause me to come every day myself'. In her high spirits and facility in observing and imitating what went on around her Harriet, of all Hogg's children, most closely resembled him. 'A Bard's Address to his Youngest Daughter' is Hogg's tender portrait of nursing this toddler on his knee and hearing her imitate her elder sister's tantrums and the noises made by various animals and birds around the farm. When she entertained herself out-of-doors in this way, he surely remembered a solitary herd-boy who had re-enacted leaping and running races to relieve his solitude out on the hills many years ago. Hogg was determined that his children's educational and social needs should be fully met. Yarrow was a rural parish and the school was near the church five miles away. When a side school was started in the vicinity of Mount Benger, Hogg boarded the teacher whose duties were 'somewhat miscellaneous' as one of them recalled, and involved being amanuensis to Hogg himself and reading up the many presentation copies of poems sent him so that he could comment on them to the the anxious authors.[41]

Hogg's own health during these years was good. He was vigorous enough to walk the forty miles from Edinburgh in a day and was seldom ill, apart from the odd dental abcess suffered by almost all middle-aged people then. With his good constitution, his active habits, and the fact that in his late fifties he had a young and increasing family growing up around him, Hogg's age was often underestimated. He competed in various sporting activities with friends whose fathers would probably be not many years older than himself.

The storm-clouds were, however, gathering throughout 1829 and 1830 as Hogg's nine-year lease of Mount Benger drew towards its close. Other tenant farmers besides Hogg were finding it hard to pay their rent, and landowners were often obliged to make a virtue of the necessity of giving annual discounts. The Duke of Buccleuch, for instance, gave a deduction of 30 per cent on pastoral and 20 per cent on arable farms in Selkirkshire on rents for 1827, due to 'the present depressed state of agriculture'. Having bought his farm-stock at the higher prices prevailing in 1821, Hogg now found its value greatly diminished. His herd-boy John Burnett recollected Hogg selling his lambs for only six shillings and sixpence a head, and Hogg himself estimated at the end of his lease that his ewes were sold at twelve shillings each less than he had bought them for, a loss on a thousand sheep of £600 on its own. In October 1829 he described the stock and wool markets as 'altogether ruinous'.[42] It was also rumoured Hogg's flocks were infected with the rot, a highly infectious disease. Hogg himself had urged that the first symptoms of this 'mortal ravager' of a flock 'should be guarded against with the utmost care and perseverance'. According to Henry Scott Riddell no-one would 'purchase sheep out of a stock which is even suspected of being tainted with it. Besides, a sort of disgrace attaches to it; so that master and man [...] feel degraded by and ashamed of having it in their flocks'. Though William Laidlaw hoped that the sickness in Hogg's flocks was only 'the *scab*', an ailment easily eliminated by an experienced shepherd, Hogg had probably been inattentive as well as unlucky.[43]

Those among Hogg's friends who understood his situation best, however, were not inclined to be hard on him, recognising that Mount Benger was over-rented and not in the most thriving condition at the beginning of his lease. His carelessness there, as at Corfardine many years previously, was partly the result of being engaged in 'a hopeless job'. He had to undertake many improvements, and it is not clear how much of his outlay was reimbursed by the Buccleuch estate. Although the cost of these was often met ultimately by the landlord and in a letter to the Duke of Buccleuch's Hawick factor of 17 March 1829 Hogg requested that his 'building receipts' should be put to his 'credit of rent', a subsequent letter refers to his being refused redress for 'the houses that I had built at my own expense'.[44]

The early death of the young Duke of Buccleuch's parents and his English education had necessarily distanced him from their friends and their pursuits. He built a kennels at St Boswell's Green and kept a pack of fox-hounds, for example, which met four times a week in the season. Reports of their runs were given in the newspapers, as was the young Duke's hunting accident in November 1831 when he was thrown from his horse and injured his face. Scott, while wishing to view him as a worthy successor to his much-loved parents, found him stiff and unaccommodating and was aware that in intervening in any ducal concern he risked being '*Chappit back*'. When he had attempted to put in a word for Hogg in 1828 the Duke simply replied that 'he had referrd the matter to Mr Riddell for some fuller information'.[45] Despite his annual losses Hogg hoped to remain at Mount Benger. He told William Laidlaw in 1829 that he had sent in a 'letter or memorial to the Duke' in which he 'left it to his Grace's goodness to lower the rent [...] to the average of the estate or to give him a *led-farm* equal to his means'. His own preference, he confided, was 'to *sit still*'.[46]

On 6 January 1830 Hogg was refused a renewal of his Mount Benger lease from Whitsunday, unsurprisingly in view of the size of his debt to the Buccleuch estate which amounted to £818-17-2 when finally settled on 8 January 1836. So far the young Duke had acted wisely both for himself and Hogg, who would otherwise only have sunk even deeper into debt, but the harsh manner of his Chamberlain was deeply felt. Hogg told Scott that 'Mr Riddell would not promise me *positively* Altrive Lake, the late Duke's present to me for life. What can be the meaning of all this? [...] I suspect some person must have poisoned my noble young master's ear with something prejudicial to me'.[47] In practice, however, Hogg's right to Altrive was never seriously questioned.

Hogg subsequently received a warning on 7 March 1830 that Major Riddell had given orders to the Duke's factor and a local lawyer to procure a warrant from the Sheriff of the county in order to roup his 'stock and all effects immediately for ready money'. As one of the wealthiest men in Scotland, the Duke could hardly be in urgent need of a few hundred pounds and he already had a preferential claim on Hogg's stock in the shape of the hypothec granted some years earlier. It was undoubtedly hard on Hogg to force a sale in advance of the termination of the Mount Benger lease at the Whitsun term-day. Sir Walter Scott, as Sheriff of Selkirkshire, was 'much concerned on finding myself obliged to subscribe a warrant of sale against poor James Hogg'.[48]

Hogg's creditors were now pressing him hard, and it seemed that the sale of his goods would include even his books and such tokens of admiration as the silver punch-bowl given to him by James Frank in February 1816 and the silver cup presented by the Shakespeare Club of Alloa at their 1816 annual meeting. Hogg was probably ignorant of precisely what he did owe. While he told William Blackwood on 6 April that the end of the Mount Benger lease would leave him 'without a farthing', in the event his debt was considerably in excess of the value of his possessions. Blackwood offered little more than sympathy, for though the long-expected publication of *The Shepherd's Calendar* in two neat volumes in March 1829 had been enthusiastically reviewed, sales had been disappointing. He made no payment since it had not 'nearly paid the expences'. In fact Hogg never received a payment for *The Shepherd's Calendar* any more than for *The Private Memoirs and Confessions of a Justified Sinner*.[49]

It was perhaps during these dark days that Hogg sat to John Watson Gordon for what was for many years his best-known likeness, since the engraving published in July 1830 for the *Edinburgh Literary Journal* appears to have been made almost as soon as the picture was painted for the publisher Robert Cadell. In this portrait Hogg, seated clasping a staff and draped in his trademark chequered plaid, looks towards the viewer with a furrowed brow and greying though still abundant and unruly hair, possessed of a quiet if rather melancholy dignity. Lockhart considered the likeness 'perfect', though it embodied a rather less ebullient Hogg than the one he chose to describe in his great Scott biography.[50]

With the sale of all his goods in the offing Hogg became depressed and unwell. He was prevented by illness from taking his usual place as master of ceremonies at the Yarrow Games of 17 March at Mount Benger in 1830, and unhappily wondered if he should relinquish all his own sporting activities. 'I am thinking' he told William Blackwood on 26 May, 'of giving up shooting and fishing and every thing of the sort as unsuitable to my years and circumstances although I do not expect that I can live long without them'. As he watched his own young children Hogg no doubt remembered the traumatic sale of his own father's goods more than half a century before, when his education had ended and his hard life as a farm-servant had begun. He felt that he was back where he had started. 'You need not be speaking of these hard circumstances to any body', he instructed Blackwood touchily, 'as it is rather hard to have to begin the world anew at 60 years of age'.[51] Could he manage (or indeed bear) to stay in the location of his disgrace? Fleetingly he wondered about moving his family to London and becoming a hack-writer for the newspapers and periodicals there.

The sale of Hogg's goods did not in fact take place before the expiry of the Mount Benger lease. It was advertised towards the end of April to take place at Mount Benger on 22 May 1830. Livestock consisting of fifty scores of sheep, thirty cows and young cattle, and six horses, together with farming equipment such as carts, ploughs, and so forth was specified, as well as personal effects such as 'household furniture' and everything was to be 'sold off without reserve'.[52]

When the long-dreaded time came there were some crumbs of comfort to be gathered. The young Duke of Buccleuch in the event 'sent orders to his factor to drop all claim whatever on the heavy arrears and not to suffer one thing of Hogg's to be rouped either out of doors or within doors *on his account*'. Hogg was also able to retain his furniture and presentation plate. They were valued by independent arbitrators at fifty pounds, and he was permitted to issue a promissory note to his creditors for that sum, to be paid on 5 April 1831. He also seems to have retained his personal library, for an advertisement appeared in the *Edinburgh Weekly Journal* of 16 June 1830 to say that the sale of Hogg's books was postponed indefinitely. Hogg issued another promissory note for £81 to cover the value of the final crop he had sown at Mount Benger, so that his creditors would be paid when it was harvested and sold. Although he was now 'several hundreds of pounds minus nothing' he was also freed of a crushing responsibility, and was able to delegate the final settlement of his affairs to a committee of his farming friends. Returned to his old cottage of Altrive, Hogg rallied his spirits and reported himself and family as 'in good health and as happy as want of room will let us be'.[53]

Hogg now began to record his earnings, noting 'a regular account of every man's pay$^{ts.}$' in a 'broad day-book'. Casting about for a lucrative new publication to support his family, he reflected on the *magnum opus* edition of the Waverley Novels. By securing the copyright to all Scott's novels in 1828, Robert Cadell found himself in a position to bring out a collected edition, including fresh editorial matter by Scott himself and high-quality engravings. The monthly volumes which had begun to appear in June 1829 were designed to appeal to a new middle-class market and sold for only five shillings each, the high costs of production being offset by huge sales in a relatively untapped market. Sales indeed rose as high as 30,000 copies and the *magnum opus* edition seemed likely to clear Scott's enormous debts. Perhaps the collected tales of the Ettrick Shepherd would clear his own more modest liabilities and enable him to provide for his wife and four young children? Four days after the Mount Benger roup, Hogg outlined his plan to William Blackwood:

> It is to publish all my tales in numbers like Sir W Scott's to re-write and sub divide them and they being all written off hand and published without either reading or correction I see I could improve them prodigiously. But as my good taste has been watched with a jealous eye by the literati I would have the work published under the sanction of Lockhart [...]
> If the tales included the lives of Col Aston Bailley Sydserf Col Cloud &c &c they would not amount to less than twelve numbers one for every month of the year of the same size of [*sic*] Sir Walter's.

Hogg was not the only person attracted by the possibilities of the

collected edition in five shilling monthly volumes. Several other publishers also aimed to produce drawing-room sets of volumes 'cheap
enough for the deal shelves of the mechanic, and handsome enough
for the boudoir of a lady'.[54] The first of a seventeen-volume Byron
edition was issued by John Murray in January 1832, and an eight-
een-volume monthly set of *Tales and Novels by Maria Edgeworth* began
in May 1832. Henry Colburn and Richard Bentley advertised a
monthly 'National Library–Series of Standard Novels. Uniform with
the Waverley Novels' early in 1831. Hogg was remarkably quick in
noting this new publishing opportunity as early as May 1830.

Although Blackwood's initial response was cautiously favourable,
Lockhart was probably unwilling to commit his time to the project
or to feature publicly as Hogg's editor. Hogg missed seeing him in
Edinburgh at the end of May when he arrived in Scotland for his
summer holiday, and a meeting at Chiefswood on the Abbotsford
estate on 3 July was fruitless. Hogg decided to let the matter rest for
a few months and to press Blackwood to publish a smaller work
meanwhile. On 20 October he wrote:

> I still hope that my 'Scottish Tales' published in 12 No's with
> a preface by Lockhart and some pains taken in the arrange-
> ment may be made available by and by but in the mean time
> I should have something going on to keep *the banes green*.

A single-volume selection of Hogg's best songs was prepared to test
the market. In *Songs by the Ettrick Shepherd* a series of headnotes introduced each song, providing biographical information or some anecdote about the song's composition, first publication, or reception.
The work also resembled one of Scott's *magnum opus* volumes in appearance and price, an atttractive pocket-sized volume in a red binding with gold lettering costing a modest seven shillings. Hogg himself suggested the popular one-volume editions of Thomas Moore's
Irish Melodies as another successful precedent.[55]

Over the summer and autumn Hogg gradually resumed his usual
course of life, contributing to *Blackwood's Edinburgh Magazine*, enjoying various sports, and taking an active part in various Borders social activities. His June visit to Edinburgh was a convivial one. He
stayed, along with his wife and little Harriet, with her family connection Dr William Crighton. A letter written on his return home to
Altrive thanks his host for his 'disinterested kindness and good hu-
moured forbearance with me when so often allured into late companies', and argues 'sociality is so completely interwoven in my nature
that I have no power to resist indulging in it'. One of the parties

Hogg attended during his stay was given by William Blackwood to mark the removal of his publishing business from 17 Princes Street to even grander New Town premises at 45 George Street. The back room was 'upwards of 26 feet square, and [...] lighted from the roof'. Hogg was gratifyingly astonished when he saw it, terming it 'ower grand'. Blackwood had never seen him 'in such force and spirits' and the party continued until nearly two o'clock in the morning. Blackwood's brothers, John and Thomas, simultaneously moved their flourishing drapery business next door. Business was evidently flourishing, for not long afterwards the Blackwood family left their villa at Newington to the south of Edinburgh for a fashionable house in Ainslie Place in the New Town, and Blackwood also set up his carriage.[56]

On 3 and 4 August 1830 Hogg was at the St Ronan's Border Games in Innerleithen as usual, taking part in the first archery contest for the Marchmont silver arrow. Peter Muir, the officer of the Royal Company of Archers, directed the proceedings and 'professed himself utterly astonished at the proficiency of so many archers for the first time'. Hogg took the chair at the dinner at Riddell's Inn following the contest and was appointed a captain of the club along with Horsburgh of Horsburgh. He was ready for the moors in mid-August, acknowledging the safe receipt of his licence from the Blackwood firm in 'great haste my shooting utensils all lying around me'.[57]

If Hogg had feared that he would lose his place in local society when he lost Mount Benger he must have been reassured that autumn. In October he won the archery sweepstakes held by the Bowmen of the Border after their annual contest for a prize bow, and acted as croupier at the dinner at Riddell's Inn that followed. On 25 November he took the chair at the annual dinner in Selkirk held by the Duke of Buccleuch's tenants to celebrate their young landlord's birthday.[58]

Hogg's high spirits were, however, only intermittent. What proved to be a final interview with Scott on the road by the Gordon Arms Inn on 28 September was particularly depressing. Now a broken man, Scott had 'grown peculiarly grave of late and completely wants that elasticity of spirits which he used to have'. Hogg reported that he seemed 'to feel very deeply for the bare state in which I am left with my family and says he is sure I have written plenty that might be made available with proper management'. Scott's lameness was now pronounced and he leaned on Hogg's shoulder while they walked up and down the road in conversation. His mind appeared as shaken as his body, 'both his memory and onward calculation' being much decayed. Scott warned him that the Duke of Buccleuch had been prejudiced against Hogg by one of the estate gamekeepers. Hogg retorted that 'the chap that tauld the Duke thae lees will gang to hell that's ay some comfort', wishing but failing to make Scott smile. When Lockhart made his farewell call at Altrive that October before returning to London he was shocked to find Hogg 'wet, weary, and melancholy'. Even in the reduced household of Altrive money was still extremely tight. On 8 October, with shearers at work harvesting his final crop at Mount Benger as well as the smaller one at Altrive, Hogg had not a pound in his pocket during the week before their wages were due to be paid and had to appeal to William Blackwood for a cash advance.[59]

Blackwood pushed on smartly with the execution of *Songs by the Ettrick Shepherd*, in marked contrast to his previous delaying tactics with *The Shepherd's Calendar*. Hogg's songs had been sung and appreciated throughout his writing career, and were constantly publicised by the Shepherd of the *Noctes Ambrosianae*. In the later 1820s there was a great demand for them from music publishers in both Edinburgh and London. Goulding & D'Almaine of Soho Square had published his *Select and Rare Scotish Melodies* to music by the fashionable theatre-composer Henry Rowley Bishop in 1829, and Robert Purdie of Edinburgh brought out an extended version of *The Border Garland* with music by James Dewar, a well-known Edinburgh instrumental teacher and leader of the Theatre Royal orchestra. A challenge to Purdie's right to the songs 'O Jeanie There's Naething to Fear Ye' and 'The Sky-Lark' by a London firm in the summer of 1830 shows that Hogg's songs were deemed a valuable commodity.[60] By 20 October Hogg had prepared twenty songs as a first instalment of copy for the volume, had promised Blackwood to 'send you twenty every week if you require them', and was giving instructions on the page layout for the volume. He was checking proofs by 10 November, and urging Blackwood to advertise the volume as to be published on New Year's Day 1831. When Hogg was ill and the supply of songs temporarily failing, Blackwood even sent a special messenger to Altrive for a few more to keep the press going. By 9 December Hogg was hunting down an elusive copy of *The Forest Minstrel* in Edinburgh in order to pick a few songs out of it for the new volume.[61]

Back in the city once again for Christmas, his spirits clearly boosted by the imminent publication of the volume, Hogg gave himself a little holiday from care, refurbishing his wardrobe at the Edinburgh clothiers' shops and curling with the Duddingston Curling Society.

Hogg's activity in the contest for the Society's gold medal on 30 December was particularly noted by the Edinburgh newspapers. He and one 'R. Welch, Esq. [...] lost only by one shot, and both of them hit oftener than the winner, though not with the same success'. Hogg reported that he lost the medal 'almost by a hairs breadth' and gained great honour as a player before being chosen to preside at the club dinner that followed at the Royal Exchange Coffee-house, where he proposed a great many toasts to the more distinguished members. It was undoubtedly a convivial evening, the *Edinburgh Weekly Chronicle* of 5 January noting, 'It is perfectly ascertained at what hour the society *met* and sat down to dinner, but not one of the members whom we saw yesterday could give us any account when they *parted*'. Margaret Hogg must have been anxious about her husband's late hours and possible heavy drinking in Edinburgh, since he wrote that he was quite well, adding 'although in one constant round of dissipation I have contrived to drink very moderately and have kept myself always sober'. Writing subsequently to wish his family a happy New Year, Hogg said, 'I hope you are all enoying yourselves as much as I am doing' and he was in no hurry to return to Altrive. Margaret Hogg, that sweet-natured wife, seems on this occasion to have lost her temper, writing on 12 January, 'What in the world has become of you, you promised to be home a week ago [...] all I shall say is if you are well it is too bad & beg you to come home'.[62]

Songs by the Ettrick Shepherd was advertised as 'just published' on 12 January, rather late for sale as a Christmas or New Year's gift. Blackwood was initially enthusiastic, writing to Hogg on 26 February, 'Your Songs are liked by every body, and the sale is going on well. Mrs Hughes wrote me the other day how much she was delighted with them'. On 12 March he offered Hogg £120 for the copyright, and when Hogg declined to part with it re-offered £70 for the current edition with another £50 when a thousand of the fifteen hundred copies printed had been sold.[63]

Hogg immediately tried to interest him in a companion volume of ballads and shorter narrative poems from *Blackwood's* and other periodicals and annuals. He probably discussed the volume with Blackwood during his Edinburgh visit, for the generally well-informed *Edinburgh Literary Journal* announced on 25 December 1830, 'There is preparing for publication, in Edinburgh, "Ane rychte queire and mervoullous buik, compilit be Maister Hougge"'. On 26 February 1831 Blackwood asked for a plan of the contents and requested some new poems to supplement the reprinted items. He explained that Shortreed would print the volume, and Hogg's nephew see it through the press. By mid-March all the preliminary arrangements appear to have been settled and Blackwood had promised to 'get on speedily' with the production of the volume.[64]

Production and publication of *A Queer* Book did not, however, go as smoothly as Hogg expected. As Peter Garside has demonstrated, the pseudo-medieval language of many of Hogg's *Blackwood's* poems was eliminated at the publisher's instigation, and although the printing seems to have been completed by early summer publication did not follow.[65] Blackwood printed 500 fewer copies of this volume than of *Songs by the Ettrick Shepherd*, which suggests that he thought it less marketable. Moreover, the sale of the *Songs* had itself slowed down after a promising beginning. On 13 February 1832, more than a year after publication, Blackwood reported that he had 'hardly sold 500 copies', not a good omen for the success of *A Queer Book*.[66] Blackwood's publishing business was in fact being seriously hampered by the agitation surrounding the passage of the parliamentary Reform Bill.

Ever since the ending of the Napoleonic Wars pressure had been growing to extend political power beyond an oligarchy consisting largely of the aristocracy and landed gentry. Members of parliament were elected by only a small fraction of the population, and while decaying boroughs in the south of England returned an M.P. to parliament many of the thriving industrial cities in the north of England, such as Manchester, Birmingham, and Leeds, did not. In Scotland county voters tended to return nominees of local landowners, influenced by hopes or promises of enjoying their patronage and influence, and even in cities the electorate was a small one. The M.P. representing Edinburgh's population of 162,000, for example, was chosen by the thirty-three members of the town council. If a British manufacturer wanted to exercise political power he had to join the existing elite by purchasing an estate, as Sir Robert Peel's father had done.[67] Waterloo was succeeded by Peterloo, when a peaceful and unarmed crowd gathered in Manchester's St Peter's Fields to listen to Henry 'Orator' Hunt had been fired upon by soldiers at the orders of the panicky local magistrates. Scotland had witnessed the so-called Radical War of 1820 when an abortive Glasgow rising had been brutally repressed and three of its leaders executed for treason. Fear of revolution now began to open up political power to the middle classes.

The myth of an unchangeable British Constitution based on the Revolution settlement of 1688 was shattered in 1829 by the passage of the Catholic Emancipation Act, a measure which split the domi-

nant Tory party and allowed a Whig revival to occur in the first half
of 1830. George IV died that summer and since the monarch's decease then necessitated a new parliament, elections were held in July
and August 1830 at which the Whigs made significant gains. At the
end of the year the highly aristocratic Whig government formed by
Earl Grey embraced moderate reform, introducing a parliamentary
bill in March 1831 designed to secure future support from the middle-classes by admitting them to political power. The rejection of the
bill by the House of Lords in October 1831 triggered a period of
general unrest throughout the country. From this point all parties
essentially regarded parliamentary reform, whether desirable or otherwise, as inevitably on the way.[68]

Although Hogg's support for the Buccleuch family and for
Blackwood's Edinburgh Magazine implied a basic acquiescence in the
status quo, his political position was complicated and contradictory,
as he was aware himself in writing how 'his Whiggish heart, with its
Covenant tie, | Was knit to the Highlands, he could not tell why'. A
strong feeling for outsiders deriving from his childhood experience
led him to sympathise both with the Covenanters of the 1680s and
the Jacobites after 1746. Temperamentally he was a natural conserva-
tive, valuing tradition and suspicious of innovation, but he disliked
Edinburgh social divisions along party lines intensely and had good
friends of every political complexion. An honest man, he wrote, was
not one who adhered to a political party but one who was 'faithful to
his friend, grateful to his benefactor, kind to his neighbour, compas-
sionate to the distressed, and indulgent in his family'. During the
1820s the little political comment there is in his letters voices an old-
fashioned Toryism. On one occasion he told William Blackwood,
for example, that his magazine was too hard on George Canning,
who as a good Tory had been obliged to fulfill 'his king's mandate'.
At the end of his life he wrote that he had been a Tory as long as he
could remember, 'but why or wherefore [...] is really more than I
can tell you. People's principles seem to be born with them, for, God
knows, I never had any interest in being a Tory'.[69]

Some of his work in *A Queer Book* and in *Blackwood's Edinburgh Magazine* does demonstrate anxiety over the Catholic Relief Act of 1829 as
a possible threat to British Protestantism. In 'Will and Sandy', Hogg
expresses, as so often in his work, the viewpoint of ordinary
countryfolk with little direct involvement in politics but who must
suffer the consequences of decisions taken by others. Of the two
shepherd protagonists Will trusts the judgement of his betters, argu-
ing that 'Ruin awaited the denial | 'Tis fair and just to make the trial'

of granting political rights to Catholics. If the measure is not successful then Parliament must repeal it. Sandy, on the contrary, feels that
the measure is a betrayal of their Covenanting ancestors, who suffered outlawry and death at the hands of 'popish tyrant's slaves' before the 1688 Revolution settlement. The two views are left unre-
solved at the poem's conclusion, for when a gigantic apparition appears on the Border hills before them Will interprets it as the joyful
guardian spirit of Ireland, a good omen, while Sandy sees it as the
wrathful angel of the Covenant, a portent of disaster.[70]

'The Last Stork' describes the death and dying words of a stork
killed in Scotland. The bird, an emblem of faithfulness to true religion, dwells firstly in Jerusalem before the destruction of the temple
by the Romans, and then in the cradle of the Reformation in Swit-
zerland ('Where Zurich meets with Appenzell'). Its subsequent residence in Scotland ends, it seems, with the Catholic Relief Act and its
death is that of 'the last guest of heaven'. As Blackwood told Hogg, it
is 'a beautiful & spirited Poem, though [...] it wants something to
make it more direct and applicable as a Satire on the late Papist
measure'.[71]

If 'The Last Stork' is somewhat imprecise, the drift of 'The Magic
Mirror' could hardly be plainer, mocking the personal peculiarities
of Tory as well as Whig politicians. The royal lion is defended from
attack by various beasts in a dream vision, and the reader is given
clues to their identity by means of the poem's rhyme scheme and a
set of asterisks. It recalls the 'Chaldee Manuscript' as well as the
Shuffleton papers in *The Spy*, for Hogg explains that he canot relate
the whole of the vision lest it might 'in Dunedin breed a squabble |
For Maga's jokes are actionable'. As it was, he almost offended a
local family who had been kind to him, in a passage implying that
Scott of Harden was effeminate. Blackwood excised it before publication at Lockhart's instigation and Hogg on this occasion was grateful for the intervention, remarking 'I am obliged to you for when I
get into a funny joke I write on without reflecting on any thing save
the joke itself'.[72] The poem concentrates on personalities and makes
little comment on the Reform agitation itself.

Hogg was mainly affected by the agitation for Parliamentary reform as it adversely affected the publication and reception of his
literary work. William Blackwood, whose commercial astuteness is
indisputable, thought that it was causing a general stagnation in the
publishing trade. On 24 October 1831 he wrote to his son William
in India of the 'dreadful stagnation in every kind of business' caused
by the 'cursed Reform Bill'. His explanation to Hogg of 25 June for

delaying the publication of *A Queer Book* is in much the same terms:

> Our trade never was in such a state as it is in just now.
> This cursed Reform agitation has completely put a stop to
> the sale of Books in London and every where else. It would
> be ruin therefore to attempt to publish your Ballads till busi-
> ness gets into a more healthy state. I was never so out of
> spirits in my life, for we have no orders almost at all, and
> Longman & C° and every publisher is in the same state. Maga
> is the only thing that keeps us alive

If *Blackwood's* was selling it was as an influential organ of Toryism,
increasingly dominated by long political articles that were excluding
poems and prose tales like Hogg's. During the last six months of
1831 only three Hogg articles (excluding poetry in the *Noctes
Ambrosianae*) were published in *Blackwood's*. As a leading Tory member of Edinburgh's town council, Blackwood himself was becoming
increasingly involved in politics and in May 1831 the windows of his
George Street premises were smashed by a mob demanding Reform.[73]

Hogg in the meantime was once more in urgent need of money.
The modest cottage at Altrive had been built in 1818 before his marriage and now had to contain his large and expanding family of a
wife, four children, their teacher, and various servants. He had compared their removal to Altrive at the end of the Mount Benger lease
as like 'a swarm of bees at the casting' for they could 'scarcely all get
within the door'. By November 1830 he also had a lodger, Mr Brooks,
a weak-minded Liverpool gentleman with literary aspirations whose
mother paid for his maintenance at Altrive. Then Margaret Hogg
became pregnant once again, so that Hogg's four children would
become five in August of the following year. Hogg decided to build
a large extension, in order to transform Altrive into a substantial
house of ten rooms with cellars and a dairy. The enlarged house
would include a small study in which Hogg could write in peace and
a library to contain his books. From the surviving plan drawn up at
about this time it is clear that the extension would be built as a separate cottage and a passageway then knocked through to unite the
two buildings into one. Hogg began to build without having the cash
in hand to pay for the work, depending on his literary earnings to
pay the workmen as they progressed just as he had done for the
original Altrive cottage in 1818. Estimates were obtained from the
Galashiels firm of Sanderson & Paterson, who had formerly been
employed at Abbotsford. The lower story of the extension had ap-

parently been built by July 1831, when Hogg also consulted with James Brown, an Innerleithen architect, about the wood to be used in the rest of the new structure. A postscript to his letter to Blackwood of 29 June 1831 casually remarks, 'I am building an addition but have thought it prudent to do it in your name all things considered'.[74]

Hogg's imprudence was exacerbated by the fact that his outstanding debts at the end of the Mount Benger lease had not yet been settled. His Selkirkshire creditors would naturally view the new building with extreme suspicion, as indicating a renewed prosperity from which they were not benefiting. The settlement had apparently been delayed because the Duke of Buccleuch had neither made a claim on Hogg's estate nor formally relinquished Hogg's debt to him. Hogg himself hoped that the situation might be tweaked to benefit his own family. If the Duke, he told Blackwood, '*is determined* as represented not to participate in the funds the best way of serving me is to make his claim to the full amount and settle the reversion on the Shepherd's only son or his darling daughter Harriet'. A subsequent letter re-emphasised Hogg's use of Blackwood's name to ease the situation locally: 'I must have all the receipts of the new house made out in your name as if you had built the house for me as there is no appearance of my getting any settlement'. On 1 October 1831 he stated, 'The Ballads [*A Queer Book*] must be published the beginning of next month come of the Reform what will as I must have the proceeds to pay for my new house'.[75]

Fortunately Hogg was not entirely dependent upon William Blackwood's payments, since his poems and tales were becoming increasingly marketable in London. His name was increasingly associated with a new London periodical, *Fraser's Magazine for Town and Country*, which began publication in February 1830. From the beginning *Fraser's* set out to rival *Blackwood's* and to have a Scottish flavour. The cover device, for example, was a spray of thistles crossed with one of strawberries, the first being an emblem of Scotland and the second a punning allusion (from *fraise*, a strawberry) to the clan Fraser whose armorial bearings include seven strawberry flowers. John Galt had written to Hogg on 6 February 1830, to invite him to become a *Fraser's* contributor:

> Their intentions are to do the handsome thing by their contributors, and any thing pretty and pathetical will be duly appreciated. I have promised an occasional article, and others of Ebonys friends have done the same. Do write me "and that early," anent this.

Fraser's partly aimed at a return to the early days of *Blackwood's* as its effective editor William Maginn (himself a former *Blackwood's* contributor) explained in an article of September 1832 comparing the two magazines. Admitting the resemblance, he continued, 'There was once a time, indeed, when our *northern model* [...] bore a nearer resemblance to ours than he does now: we allude to the high and palmy days, the days of *Ebony's* juvenescence'.[76] *Fraser's* was relatively free from the sexual prudery and Calvinist orthodoxy that occasionally prevented *Blackwood's* from printing Hogg's work, and several tales refused by William Blackwood subsequently appeared in the rival London magazine. 'On the Separate Existence of the Soul', for example, had been refused by Blackwood in September 1831 as doctrinally unorthodox, for 'it is directly in the teeth of revelation to permit the soul to exist separately for one moment without at once having it's eternal state fixed'. Blackwood had also rejected 'A Remarkable Egyptian Story', in which the beautiful Ada resists attempted rape and scorns bribes designed to secure her compliance with sexual demands. She retains her virginity and eventually becomes Queen of Egypt. *Fraser's* subsequently defended Hogg's plain-speaking at length, arguing that he 'was a moral man and a Christian; but his morality was no more affectation than his religion was cant'.[77]

By the end of 1831 a dozen Hogg contributions had appeared in *Fraser's Magazine*, and Hogg believed that Blackwood was showing some jealousy of the new periodical. Writing to James Fraser in June 1830, Hogg noted that it was in high repute among the Edinburgh literati for 'its dashing and fearless cleverness, but Mr Blackwood is very ill pleased about it'. When copies of *Fraser's* failed to reach Hogg promptly at Altrive, he was suspicious that Blackwood 'who does not take in the work himself' had 'unfairly detained' them in Edinburgh. On 30 September 1830 he accused him directly, 'You are surely keeping up Frazer's Mag. I have recieved none since No 7'. The obvious suitability of *Fraser's Magazine* as an alternative outlet for Hogg's periodical contributions, however, clearly overcame any such problems with transmission of copies and payments between London and Altrive. By June 1831 Hogg, while expressing continuing loyalty to Blackwood, was making it clear to him that he had other lucrative outlets for his magazine contributions:

> I fear it is needless for me to attempt any thing farther for Maga without giving up writing for the London Magazines which I would with great pleasure do could I please you but one does not like to lose his little lucubrations altogether. I

looked on Duncan M,Gaber as one of my very best. Send me them all back again and we'll see how the country in general judge of them.[78]

He was also writing for the *Royal Lady's Magazine*, edited in London by George Glenny. Half-a-dozen Hogg items appeared there that year, including one, 'Ballad of the Lord Maxwell', that Blackwood wanted for his own magazine. During a visit the Edinburgh publisher made to Innerleithen in late August or early September Hogg had read the poem aloud to him, a touching account of the exciting escape from prison of the Jacobite Earl of Nithsdale masterminded by his loyal wife. In his letter of 10 September Blackwood wrote, 'By the bye you should have sent me in the Ballad of Lord Nithsdale which you read us. Do so next week'. He found, however, that it was already spoken for, Hogg replying, 'I wrote "Lady Maxwell" for a lady's Magazine in London and had sent it off before your request for it arrived I never thought of it for Maga'.[79] Some of Hogg's best new work was now being composed specifically for the London magazines.

Murray's *Quarterly Review* had alerted its readership at the start of 1831 to the travesty of Hogg's character embodied in the Shepherd of the Blackwoodian *Noctes Ambrosianae*. In an article on 'Southey's Lives of Uneducated Poets' Lockhart described Hogg as a serious and unremitting student, well worthy of the patronage of the Royal Society of Literature, a 'distinguished poet, whom some of his waggish friends have taken up the absurd fancy of exhibiting in print as a sort of boozing buffoon'. Blackwood was extremely annoyed at this championship, as he told Hogg, who responded blandly that Sir Walter Scott and the Laidlaws considered it 'the best thing about me ever had yet been said for as much as had been' and that he personally thought there was no doubt that it was well meant on Lockhart's part. Wilson, he considered, was getting far too touchy and 'jealous of these trifles'.[80] This too may have turned Hogg's attention from Edinburgh to London as a favourable publishing centre for his work.

A new London publisher named James Cochrane was apparently interested in publishing something for Hogg, and might be induced to undertake the multi-volume edition of his collected prose fiction. Cochrane later declared that his name was drawn to Hogg's attention by the Edinburgh publisher, John Anderson junior, who had published works by several of Hogg's young friends and protégés, such as Henry Scott Riddell's *Stanzas on the Death of Lord Byron* (1825), and had briefly acted as the Edinburgh agent for *Fraser's Magazine*. Cochrane, however, seems to have made an initial approach to Hogg by letter, for on 29 June Hogg told Blackwood, 'I had a letter from apparently a new London firm the other day requesting to publish something for me'.[81]

Cochrane, now in his late thirties, had been employed by two London publishers, Sir Richard Phillips and Henry Colburn, before setting up his own business at 11 Waterloo Place, impressive premises in London's West End.[82] His name was featuring in the Edinburgh newspapers as the donator of books to institutions such as the Artizans' Reading Room, and Hogg would be familiar with it as that of the publisher of a fiction anthology to which he was contributing entitled *The Club-Book.* As Blackwood's reluctance to undertake Hogg's collected prose fiction series became increasingly obvious, Hogg looked more and more to London. 'Do you not think a London publisher would be best?' he asked Lockhart in mid-August, and on 2 November he told Blackwood, 'I shall have my tales commenced this winter by some publisher since you are so faint hearted about publishing. I never had so much need of making something'. Before the end of the year Hogg had come to an arrangement with James Cochrane to publish *Altrive Tales,* for the *Morning Chronicle* newspaper of 2 January 1832 reported, 'We understand that Mr. Hogg has arranged with his new publisher (Messrs. Cochrane and Co., of Waterloo-place) for the speedy appearance of a series of "Altrive Tales, by the Ettrick Shepherd," which are to be printed in London'.[83] Blackwood was losing his hold on Hogg.

Relations between the two men continued to be friendly during the early autumn, however. Hogg visited the Blackwood family during their Innerleithen holidays, and exchanged family news. He expressed concern about the ill-health of the eldest son, Alexander, and sent instructions on the best way to cook the game he sent the family. Hogg also reported the birth of the youngest Hogg daughter on 21 August and her baptism as Mary Gray Hogg on 8 September. Hogg knew he could appeal to Blackwood when unexpected demands were made upon his purse. Early in September, for example, he was in need of a new horse:

> I have a queer story to tell you. The other day I bought a capital mare from one of my neighbours. About 24 hours after I brought her home the mare vanished. I sought her through the whole district for two days and advertised her. On the third day I found her lying quietly and snugly drowned in Altrive Lake a small part of her broad side then appearing above. I was so chagrined at the loss of my mare that I half ran home seized my pen and resolved to make her price

before I slept and not last night but this have finished the accompanying essay. You are to send me the price of my mare for it for a horse I cannot want and I am quite out of money.

In this case Blackwood sent Hogg ten pounds, but refused the proffered magazine contribution, not altogether a satisfactory state of affairs to Hogg, particularly as there was still no date fixed for the publication of *A Queer Book*. On 24 October Hogg declared, 'Surely my new work should now be published'. On 2 November he re-urged, 'By all means let the Miscellanies be published. What signifies letting a thing lie over for a year after printing let it take its chance'.[84] A serious quarrel was in the offing with Hogg desperately in need of money, Blackwood increasingly reluctant to publish and pay for either his periodical contributions or his volume publications, and the literary market of London looking increasingly attractive. When the breakdown occurred, however, it was ostensibly about something else entirely.

In 1830 a young, London-based Scottish writer named Andrew Picken had the bright idea of producing an anthology of tales by well-known writers under the title of *The Club-Book*. The work was immediately perceived to be a novelty worth imitating, a 'Scottish Club-Book' being projected and an *Atlantic Club-Book* actually published in New York. Hogg had been an enthusiastic contributor ('Snap your thumbs and begin printing immediately'), sending Picken several of his own tales, including 'The Adventures of Colonel Peter Aston' which he had written in 1825. Picken rejected Hogg's story while admitting that he had reworked key incidents taken from it in one of his own contributions to the volume, 'The Deer-Stalkers of Glenskiach' and offering Hogg five pounds for the use of them. Although Hogg had given Picken permission (as he generally did to annual and periodical editors) to 'make what alterations you see meet' to his manuscript for publication, he could hardly have envisaged his work being used as raw materials for another man's work and was initially uneasy until reassured by Picken's statement that their mutual friends Galt and Cunningham agreed that this did not amount to plagiarism. Picken's tale was duly included in *The Club-Book* with a footnote stating, 'For several of the particulars on which this tale is founded the author is indebted to the talented Ettrick Shepherd'. When Hogg saw a copy of the printed work in the autumn of 1831, however, he was of the opinion that Picken's use of his work certainly did amount to plagiarism. On 1 October he requested Blackwood to print 'The Adventures of Colonel Peter Aston' in

Blackwood's Edinburgh Magazine, along with a note in which he invited the magazine's readers to judge for themselves if the story was 'really and truly the work of Mr Andrew Picken'. Hogg's demand was essentially a test of loyalty to him as one of the magazine's earliest and most faithful adherents. 'I therefore request of you to publish this tale', he wrote to Blackwood, 'as you value my friendship and corespondence for I cannot expose the mean and extraordinary transaction any where else than in the pages of the periodical which has always been my defender and chief support'.[85]

Blackwood's initial response was to play for time. He sent Hogg's manuscript to D. M. Moir, and received his confirmation that 'almost the whole merit of the invention and of the incidents belongs to the Shepherd, whose passages in the life of Col. Austen [*sic*] I distinctly remember reading, and writing you about I think in 1825'. On 15 October he replied to Hogg's letter with a request for further details of Hogg's dealings with Picken, though soothingly terming Picken a 'pirate'. Blackwood also regretted that he did not have room to include Hogg's tale in that month's issue of *Blackwood's Edinburgh Magazine*, and assured him it would appear in the next one. Hogg's explanation given in his reply of 24 October, however, did not settle the matter since Blackwood then asked to see the letters exchanged between Hogg and Picken, though once again stating, 'I am most anxious that you should have ample justice done you in Maga, and that the plundering pirate Picken should be fully exposed'. Hogg duly sent the letters, but when the December issue of *Blackwood's* also appeared without his tale, he exploded with fury in a letter which reveals all the reasons for the ending of their connection:

> [...] I asked a small favour of my friend Christopher [North] and begged him to comply with it *as he valued my friendship and correspondence*. He has now shown in the most supercilious [*sic*] and disgusting manner that he values neither [...] Therefore return every M. S. article of mine [...]. As to the trivial work which you have printed and dare not publish I will try to get some minor bookseller to pay you the expence and take it off your hand. [...] I am very glad your contempt has driven me to this as I found that every London publisher has this last year paid me triple what you have done

The following day Hogg wrote to his wife's nephew James Gray, 'I am thinking of going to London for a few months'.[86]

Energised by his anger, Hogg left home in a hurry and without much preparation, though he did write to Lockhart on 14 December to announce his imminent arrival in London and to ask his assistance in the publication of the envisaged series of prose fiction volumes, perhaps under the title of 'The Tales of Altrive'. He gave his wife no time to supply any deficiencies in the wardrobe he would need to take with him, and indeed left home before he received the balance of eleven guineas due to him from William Blackwood together with his unused manuscripts. Margaret Hogg was instructed to forward these to him in London once they did reach Altrive, and he told her that he would let her know his detailed travelling itinerary once he had reached Edinburgh. Her situation indeed was far from enviable, left to manage her household and the small farm at Altrive, with the house extension half-built and unpaid for, and with five children to care for including a four-month-old baby. To add to her vexations John Gordon, the landlord of the Gordon Arms Inn, had done a moonlight flitting owing Hogg £5-15s., a sum which before departing he had instructed the Selkirk lawyer Peter Rodger to recover on his behalf.[87]

On his arrival in Edinburgh Hogg booked his passage for Friday, 23 December sailing for London from Leith in the *Edinburgh Castle* steam-packet. He sent his wife notice the day before and urged her to keep 'a good heart, and everything as right as you can' in his absence. He also fired a parting shot at William Blackwood, assuring him that 'I never will submit to be treated with such absolute contempt again' and telling him roundly, 'You have starved me fairly out of my house and country'.[88]

CHAPTER SEVEN

The Glee of the City

When Hogg booked his passage to London for Friday, 23 December he was the only cabin passenger to date, though the *Edinburgh Castle* could make up a hundred beds. It was a handsome vessel with 'a deck as long as a frigates to walk upon and to sleep on also' if the cabins were crowded.[1] The journey down the east coast in winter weather lasted more than a week instead of the optimum sixty hours. The ship had to anchor at Lindisfarne (or Holy Island) in Northumberland for three days, and was again delayed in the Yarmouth Roads, as well as at the mouth of the Thames. Characteristically, Hogg settled down comfortably during this 'tedious but pleasant passage' and 'took his nap after dinner, and his toddy at night, the same as at home'. He practised on the flageolet he had acquired from the Edinburgh music-seller Robert Purdie about two months previously, played cards, and was well looked after by the steward, James Aitken, who had received orders from the ship's owners to attend particularly to his comfort. Aitken heaped 'luxuries of meat and drink' on the distinguished passenger for which he would take no payment, and Hogg probably found him a congenial companion since on arrival in London he wrote requesting William Blackwood to give Aitken a number of copies of his own works, including copies of *The Queen's Wake, Queen Hynde, Confessions of a Justified Sinner* 'and any other that is of little value to you'. Over the years Hogg had seen many friends on board at Leith, such as lively Jean Walker going to her Southwark wedding to Allan Cunningham in 1811, but it was the first time he had made the London voyage himself.[2]

He disembarked at Blackwall on the last day of the year, and went straight to the lodgings of his wife's nephews, Peter and Phillips Gray, who were about to take up posts in India. His family at Altrive must have been anxious by then for news of his safe arrival, and Hogg had to reassure his young son that he had been perfectly comfortable and 'ran no danger of being drowned'. He also let his wife know that he had begun to make arrangements for the London printing and publication of his collected prose fiction, reporting on the day after his arrival, 'I have seen Cochrane and Lockhart, and everything is likely to be amicably arranged'. By 7 January the weekly paper *The Athenaeum* was able to announce details of the forthcoming publication:

It seems, that the Ettrick Shepherd, obeying the call of these times for cheap reprints of works of genius, has arrived in London and made arrangements with Cochrane & Co. for the reproduction of his prose works in monthly volumes. They are to be called 'The Altrive Tales', and a memoir of the Poet's Life is to accompany them.

Hogg also made an early call on William Jerdan who edited the influential *Literary Gazette* and was therefore a friend who could be useful to him in promoting the new publication.[3]

His first day in London being a Sunday, Hogg duly attended the Rev. Edward Irving's Regent Square church. Irving's fashionable following had decreased somewhat since the days when he held the old Scottish chapel in Hatton Garden, partly perhaps because of the inordinate length of the services, which could include a three-hour sermon. By January 1832 Irving was not so much fashionable as scandalous, his services being interrupted by outbreaks of 'speaking in tongues', an ecstatic babbling with Pentecostal associations supposed to herald Christ's Second Coming. He had previously been prosecuted for heresy, and was to be removed from his pulpit in April by the trustees of his church. Hogg was an attentive listener to Irving's sermon, but considered it a 'strange exhibition!' To someone of his intellectually rigorous Calvinist upbringing 'the ravings of enthusiastic madness' had little attraction. Two days later he was equally unimpressed by the London production of *Rob Roy Macgregor* at the Theatre Royal, Drury Lane with Macready as Rob Roy, and Mrs Wood as Diana Vernon. He judged it inferior to the Edinburgh dramatisation of Scott's novel, first staged in the spring of 1819 and repeated for the visit of George IV in August 1822.[4]

Hogg set about a little sixteen-page pamphlet gift-book, partly intended as a keepsake for his children, *A Father's New Year's Gift*. On 10 January he wrote to Margaret Hogg that his 'manual of prayers and hymns' was in the press and that he hoped to send copies to Altrive that same week. Some of Hogg's prayers and hymns for children had previously appeared in children's annuals such as Mrs S. C. Hall's *Juvenile Forget Me Not* or Ackermann's *Juvenile Forget Me Not*, and these items could quickly be combined with new material to meet the market for seasonal gifts. Production of this 'sixpenny trifle' by James Cochrane and his printer, A & J Valpy of Red Lion Court off Fleet Street, would also allow Hogg to familiarise himself with the working methods and arrangements of his new publisher before embarking on the all-important *Altrive Tales* series. It was probably published nearer the end of the month, however, since *The Athenaeum*, generally quick to report on Hogg's London doings, only reviewed it on 4 February, and it was during the first week in February that copies arrived at Altrive.[5]

Early in January Hogg requested Cochrane to obtain copies of books he needed to prepare copy for the first volume of his *Altrive Tales*. This was to include the inset Laird of Peatstacknowe's tale from *The Three Perils of Man* (1822), retitled 'Marion's Jock', and also an updated version of Hogg's 'Memoir' from the 1821 edition of *The Mountain Bard*. The London firm of Longmans had published the first, while Whittakers had been Oliver & Boyd's London partner in the other. Hogg requested Cochrane to send a porter to fetch copies from the publishers, and concluded, 'Mr Lockhart will call on you to day or to morrow'. Just over a week after his arrival Hogg was actually lodging with his new publisher.[6] Peter Gray was due to sail to India on 6 February, and Cochrane's premises at 11 Waterloo Place were conveniently situated for Hogg, just off Pall Mall in the West End and within sight of the Athenaeum club. From there it was only a short walk to John Murray's premises in Albemarle Street. Hogg still no doubt hoped for Lockhart's advice and guidance for *Altrive Tales* and Lockhart, as a member of the Athenaeum and editor of Murray's prestigious *Quarterly Review*, would frequently pass by.

At first Hogg found London strange and bewildering. Ten days after his arrival he wrote to his wife, 'It is so boundless that I cannot for my life get out of it, nor can I find any one place that I want'. She replied that he would soon get used to London and its customs, adding 'few people like it at first but I believe you have but to stay a while & then get very fond of it, so I hope you will leave before you get too fond of it'. He did make his way to the Fishmarket, where he went more than once to examine the many different kinds of fish on sale, which were naturally of interest to him as a keen angler and occasional amateur naturalist. But it distressed him, as he told Henry Scott Riddell subsequently, 'to see the great cartloads o' dead laverocks that they bring into yon city'. When he had read in his young days, he recalled, 'in Bruce's Travels, that the larks sing the same notes in Abyssinia as they do here [...] I thought that it must be a tolerable country after a'. But I trust that our Scottish laverocks, at least, will never show themselves sic fools as to cross the border into England to be baken into pies and devoured yon gate'. For Hogg the skylark was 'like myself, an inmate of the wilds, and the companion of my boyhood'. His poem 'The Skylark' fuses the poet's inspiration with the soaring bird that he now saw as a multitude of corpses.[7]

Relief from the interminable streets and a glimpse of living birds was available in the neighbouring parks, and Hogg walked there on most days in company with one friend or another, often young John Murray III:

> From Waterloo place into St. James' Park was a step. A delightful walk along the banks of the lovely lake with its islands and variety of water-fowl. Then through the Green park which has nothing very remarkable and into Hyde park where all the nobility and gentry of the kingdom were chassing round and round in their carriages and on horseback if the afternoon was fine.

Young Murray's chief drawback as a companion was that he was short-sighted and therefore unable to identify the folk that Hogg enquired about in the course of these walks. During his London promenades Hogg wore his checked shepherd's plaid, partly no doubt as a form of self-advertisement but partly too from a wish to preserve his normal mode of life as far as possible in these alien surroundings. Allan Cunningham certainly thought so, defending Hogg in *The Athenaeum* from accusations of wearing it in town as a publicity device: 'Now, we have personally known the poet these eight-and-twenty years, and we know him to be incapable of any such conduct. He wears the shepherd plaid on Sunday, when he goes to church; for he never in his life went, on that day, without it, at least during the inclement period of the year—there is no other mystery in the shepherd's plaid'.[8] Gradually Hogg made himself comfortable and more at home in the Modern Babylon.

Living in Waterloo Place, Hogg soon became intimate with his publisher's wife and children. He was amused that when he appeared with them at church on 15 January a newspaper reporter mistook them for his own family, as he told his son.

> [...] it was only Mrs Cochrane and Miss Cochrane who is the age of Jessie and Alexr who is a year older than Maggy. Mrs Cochrane is a very beautiful lady with black hair and eyes very like your Mamma's but she is not half so bonny to me. But she is very kind to your Papa indeed so kind that she does not know what to do with me. I dream every night of your mamma and Harriet.

Cochrane's only daughter, Mary Anne, soon became a firm favourite with the visitor from Scotland. The eleven-year-old often got a sip of his nightcap of whisky toddy, a ritual that seems to have been

continued with her father after Hogg's return to Altrive. Hogg never
forgot her, and Cochrane in his letters to Hogg occasionally provided little indications that she remembered him in return. On 9
August 1833 for example he reported, 'Mary Anne, your favourite
[...] often asks me when Mr Hogg is coming to London'. In November 1832 Hogg had proposed that she should be educated with his
own eldest daughter Jessie, the two girls living in London and at
Altrive year about, and in 1834 he asked Cochrane if she might not
accompany him on a proposed visit to Scotland, adding, 'How I am
wearying to see and kiss that lovely girl! I know if you were to leave
her here I should like her too well better than any of my own'.[9] This
reads uncomfortably to a post-Freudian generation, but the very open-
ness of Hogg's captivation by the little girl seems a guarantee of its
entire innocence. Hogg's own bairns were often his companions,
and in London he was without the company of his own little Harriet.
Moreover both James Cochrane and Margaret Hogg clearly regarded
his affection for Mary Anne with sympathy and indulgence.

During his stay in London Hogg intended to gather up 'every scattered fragment' of his work from the various periodicals and volumes in which it had appeared and make a detailed plan of contents
for each volume of *Altrive Tales*. On 17 January, for instance, Hogg
wrote to John Aitken in Edinburgh to request copies of two articles
that had appeared during 1829 in the *Edinburgh Literary Journal*, that
he could revise and include in the section of reminiscences that would
conclude his 'Memoir'. To these papers, giving an account of his
first meetings with Scott and Allan Cunningham, Hogg could add
details of his encounters with the likes of Wordsworth, Southey,
Wilson's uncle Robert Sym, John Galt, and Allan Cunningham, a
suitable mixture of Scottish and English literati. Lockhart appears to
have assisted Hogg with this during February, persuading Hogg to
cancel a section concerning Francis Jeffrey, checking a detail of the
Scott section, and supplying recollections of his own first meeting
with Hogg.[10] These short, self-contained gossipy sections were, as
Hogg and Lockhart no doubt anticipated, easily excerpted as attractive column-fillers by the newspapers on publication. Once his materials had been ordered and assembled Hogg might then return to
Altrive, he told his wife, since Cunningham, Lockhart, and Pringle
had agreed to take the charge of the press off his hands. These pre-
liminaries were time-consuming, however, and Hogg reported that
his time was increasingly cut up by social engagements.

> I never get home before three in the morning, and have been
> very much in the same sort of society. I have been with

Lockhart, Jerdan, Captain Burns, Pringle, Cochrane, Murray,
and last night I was with Martin, the sublime painter, and the
list of the great literary names and those of artists would of
itself fill up this whole letter

Hogg must have been delighted to add John Martin to his acquaintance among London publishers and resident Scottish literary men.
The Northumbrian-born Martin was one of the most popular artists
of the day for his vast Romantic perspectives of Biblical and literary
subjects, and even more so for the prints based upon them. Hogg
himself owned two Martin prints, one of them being 'The Fall of
Nineveh'.[11]

James Cochrane was ambitious for *Altrive Tales*, which from the
prospectus was to consist of twelve volumes published one every
other month with illustrative engravings in a neat binding but costing only six shillings each. George Cruikshank was employed as an
illustrator, and Cochrane intended to print four thousand copies of
each volume instead of the thousand or fifteen hundred that was
more usual for Hogg's prose fictions, dividing these into two separate editions. He did not, however, seem to be pushing production
of the first volume along very vigorously. Hogg was warned by several friends that Cochrane was venturing far beyond his capital, and
realised himself that Cochrane's delay was partly due to the fact that
his end-of-year accounts with his printer had not been settled.[12] Hogg
seems to have been well aware that Cochrane's business was financially unstable and his credit 'already tottering', but wilfully shut his
eyes to the problem and hoped that he and his friends were mistaken and that all would turn out for the best.

Fears for Cochrane's financial stability prompted Hogg's literary
friends to celebrate the anniversary of Burns's birth on 25 January
in an impressive public manner. Hogg himself said, 'though the name
of Burns is necessarily coupled with mine, the dinner has been set
on foot solely to bring me forward and give me *eclat* in the eyes of
the public, thereby to inspire an extensive sale of my forthcoming
work. It was mooted by Lockhart, Murray, Jerdan and Galt, who
have managed the whole business'. Burns's eldest son, also Robert
Burns, had a minor government post in the Stamp Office in London,
and his brother Captain James Glencairn Burns was home on furlough from his service with the East India Company. Hogg met the
brothers frequently during this London visit, and they would naturally grace the Burns dinner advertised for Wednesday, 25 January
at the Freemasons' Taven. A glittering array of aristocrats, literary
men and artists were named as stewards, including, for example,

Macleod of Macleod and David Wilkie. The 'Scotch Dinner' was to be chaired by Sir John Malcolm, a native of Dumfriesshire who was now Tory M.P. for Launceton in Cornwall, having returned to England the previous year after a distinguished career as a diplomatist and administrator in India. Tickets cost twenty-five shillings and two or three hundred diners were expected.[13]

In the event between four and five hundred gentlemen attended, crowding the premises and causing some problems for the promoters and caterers, since insufficient food for the number had been provided. The start of the dinner was delayed for about an hour after the advertised time of six o'clock while the tables were extended, and many of the newspaper reports complained that gentlemen on the centre table got a scanty meal. Questions were subsequently asked in the press about the surplus cash arising from the sale of tickets where no meal was provided, one such letter being signed 'Minus a Dinner'. Convention dictated that respectable ladies did not participate in public dinners, but the galleries of the hall were crowded right up to the close of the meeting at half-past twelve with ladies eager to see Hogg and the rest of the company and to hear the songs and speeches. To Hogg it seemed curious that ladies should be admitted in hundreds 'merely to *smell* a good dinner, without being permitted either to eat or drink'.[14]

After the customary loyal toasts and one to the memory of Burns, which was replied to by his son, Malcolm proposed the health of that other light of Scotland, the Ettrick Shepherd. Hogg, sitting on his right hand as the guest of honour, received an ovation, and then rose to reply. As his face was obscured by a hanging lamp he had to stand on a chair to be seen, and some of the newspaper reporters at a distance thought that he had mounted the table, a detail which later startled Margaret Hogg when she read of it. Their lack of familiarity with Border Scots caused problems with reporting his speech, though even so *The Spectator* pronounced it the best of the evening. The *Atlas* gave a memorable sketch of Hogg's public manner:

> His action in speaking is semi-comic, and his intonation full of humour. He does not boggle at a 'thumper,' but does it with such an air of simplicity and rusticity that you believe him sincere in every thing, and are fain to think that he is only deceiving himself when he is in truth spiriting away your own judgment. The mixture of shrewdness and fun in his manner, his looks, and his words, must be seen to be understood.

Hogg's opening remark, as he looked down on the distinguished Chairman beside him, was that if it were said he was not to rise in the world it was wrongly said. He continued with an account of how 'on the evening of his birth, a man and horse were dispatched for the midwife, but the night being wild, and Ettrick deep in flood, the rider was lost; nevertheless, the familiar spirit called Brownie [...] supplied his place, and brought the marvelling midwife [...]'. This sounds like a test of the audience's sense of humour or its gullibility, or perhaps of both, and recalls his comment on his training as a public speaker in the Forum some twenty years previously that it let him feel 'the pulse of the public, and precisely what they would swallow, and what they would not'.[15] Its playful mixture of jest and earnest marches with the narrative instability of some of his more extravagant prose tales.

There were nine vocalists present, and Hogg particularly noticed one song performed by a Mr Broadhurst about his own domestic happiness with the refrain, 'For I loe my Maggie an' dear she loes me'. He had arranged that one of the 'professional gentleman' should give his protégé David Vedder's 'Song for the Anniversary of Burns' a London airing. The toastmaster caused some amusement by proclaiming silence for a song by 'Mr Shepherd'. Hogg's own song, specially composed for the occasion, was 'Robin's Awa' to the Jacobite tune 'There'll never be peace till Jamie comes hame'. A lass laments 'O there's nae bard o' nature sin' Robin's awa!' and reflects on the inadequacies of a number of contemporary Scottish song-writers, including Hogg himself. ('Poor Jamie he blunders an' sings as he can'.) Hogg was also kept busy brewing punch in Burns's own black marble punch-bowl, then owned by his friend Archibald Hastie of the London Burns Club. He was the hero of the evening, complimented in many speeches and flatteringly described by *The Times* as 'a bluff, hale, fresh-looking man, apparently not more than eight-and-forty'.[16]

Hogg was thenceforth regarded as 'the great object of attraction at all literary dinners, *conversaziones*, and *soirees* in the metropolis', a position which had its inconveniences in the way of casual callers and more invitations than he could cope with. Even with the help of a small notebook in which he recorded his engagements Hogg sometimes became confused, and did not manage to reply to all of the numerous invitations he received. Despairingly he told his wife 'If I had you to receive all these grand people and keep me right, I could live here, but as it is, it is impossible'. On 2 February, for example, the publisher John Murray called for Hogg in his carriage to take him to dine with the well-known host Sir George Warrender, M.P., complimented at the Burns Anniversary as the giver of the best dinners in London. Hogg told his wife that he felt himself as much at home as at the farmhouses of Sundhope or Whitehope in Yarrow, even though the company included 'two earls two lords and seven Scottish Baronets', and he went on to describe the grandeur of Sir George's establishment:

> The drawing-room chairs were all gilded and covered with blue satin and there were six mirrors that reached from the ceiling to the floor so that I felt in spite of all I could do as if I had been in a small drawing-room in the midst of a set of immense large drawing-rooms. The first glance I got into one of these large drawing-rooms I got a terrible start thinking I had seen my brother William whereas it was myself The dinner service was on silver and the desert on gold

Although Warrender's cellar was famous, Hogg persuaded several of his fellow-guests to desert the claret for his own brewing of whisky punch.[17] As the literary lion of the season he was repeatedly shown off to large parties, despite his accepting a dinner invitation only on condition that it was not to be followed by an evening party:

> Well I go at 7 o'clock no fashionable dinner before that! By the time we get a few glasses of wine drunk the rapping at the door begins and continues without intermission for an hour and a half. Then we go up stairs and find both drawing rooms crammed as full as ever you saw sheep in a fold and there I am brought in and shown like any other wild beast all the ladies courtesying and flattering and begging for one shake of my hand such flummery I never saw in this world and every night I am taken in that way the master and mistress of the house always pretending they cannot help it [...]

On one such occasion there were sixty guests even in the small house of Samuel and Anna Hall in Sloane Street, where Hogg met the poetess Miss Landon, known as L. E. L. Looking down kindly at the petite young woman, Hogg told her, 'I didna think ye'd been sae bonnie!' He was however rather taken aback by her fashionable evening dress, for she was 'quite naked all above the apron string'.[18]

Hogg's gallant, open, hearty manner was very much liked, even when his behaviour was somewhat over-familiar. Dining at John Martin's house with the Cunninghams, Godwin, Pringle, and James Glencairn Burns and his wife, Hogg greatly amused his fellow guest

Ralph Thomas by his performance of his song 'Paddy O'Rafferty'. As he sang he would 'slap the shoulder of Mrs. Burns, who sat beside him, hug and cuddle her with his right arm in so hearty a manner that, after the first shock, we were all much amused. Mrs. Burns, with the best possible good nature, laughed at it as much as any of us'. Dining with Macleod of Macleod one day he was informed after singing an anti-Whig song that the Duke of Argyll was at the table and quickly calling out, 'Oh, yer Grace, never mind noo, I will give you another', sang 'Donald Macgillavry' in a way which elicited shouts of laughter. In general, those whose mental picture of Hogg was drawn from the Shepherd of the *Noctes Ambrosianae* were surprised to find him 'so smooth, well-looking, and gentlemanly'. Hogg's company was in great request, and he dined with Scottish aristocrats, members of Parliament, and dignitaries of the church as well as with many artists and other Scottish writers. He even received an invitation from Andrew Picken, the erstwhile 'plundering pirate'. Despite this immersion in the social whirl, though, Hogg still found time to accompany Peter Gray to Gravesend on 6 February, and see him on board his ship for India—a private moment in a life spent very much in the public eye.[19]

Hogg seems to have particularly enjoyed the private clubs into which he was introduced. He was invited by Lord Saltoun to dine with the Society of Beef Steaks, for example, on 17 March. At their Saturday evening meetings at the Bedford Coffee-house near the Covent Garden theatre the food was simply beef-steaks rounded off with toasted cheese and accompanied by porter, punch, port, or whisky toddy, and no presents were to be made unless leave had been granted previously. When Hogg dined there Lord Saltoun was condemned to stand wrapped in a penitential white table-cloth and endure the recorder-general's rebuke for having sent in a dozen bottles of Highland whisky without permission. The newest member waited on the company, having also to fetch the wine from the cellar, decant it, and see things were in order, while the Tavern's waiters simply brought up the food and 'stood behind breaking their jokes with the members'. Hogg supposed that the club had originally been formed to teach the members good humour and forbearance, 'for there is no wicked insinuation that can be alledged against each other which they do not bring forward in the most extravagant and laughable terms'. The membership, however, was limited to twenty-four and very exclusive—rumour had it that George IV when Prince of Wales had to wait three years before being enrolled as a member.[20]

Hogg also dined with the Walton and Cotton Club, for lovers of angling, where there were twenty-four kinds of fish served at table, and was made an honorary member of the Club. Dinners were also given by the Canada Company, the Royal Literary Fund, and the Society of True Highlanders. The Highland Society of London, which had been so unreceptive to Hogg's ground-breaking collection of *Jacobite Relics* more than ten years earlier, now invited him to a public dinner at the Freemasons' Tavern on Saturday, 18 February. He was made an honorary member as an acknowledgement of his loyal and national songs and poetry, Sir George Murray hanging a splendid silver medal around Hogg's neck.[21]

Hogg was invited to a public ball by the Thistle Club, to the private view of the Society of British Artists annual exhibition in Suffolk Street, and received a splendidly ornate invitation card to Miss Smithson's Benefit performance at the Royal Coburg Theatre on Thursday, 8 March 'under the immediate patronage of His Grace the Duke of Devonshire'. The evening created one of the most curious conjunctions of Hogg's London visit. Among the distinguished audience the presence of two men was particularly noted, 'the French veteran, Talleyrand, and the Scotch Bard, James Hogg, the Ettrick Shepherd'.[22]

If Hogg's social life in London, with its constant succession of parties and public appearances, was an exciting one it was also extremely tiring. Writing to reassure his wife that he was not drinking too much, Hogg was obliged to admit that the late hours were a strain. 'I never spent a more sober winter season', he told her. 'The people here are all sober there being no deep drinking here as in Scotland'. But he admitted that he was growing gray for lack of sleep, to which she teasingly responded, 'As for your hair having got gray, I suspect it is only that you have a better opportunity of seeing yourself in your *grand mirrors*. You know I often told you how gray you had got; however, we shall be glad to have you back though your hair has changed its colour'. Deprived of his normal country exercise of fishing, shooting, curling, and archery, and ferried about in carriages to elaborate dinners, Hogg was also putting on a lot of weight. When he did get back to Altrive none of his clothes there would fit him except for one baggy old shooting-jacket, and he 'threeped on the Mrs she had been washing them and they were a' cruppen in'.[23]

Hogg's literary work was by no means forgotten, however. He tried to get *A Queer Book* published in London during the weeks succeeding the Burns dinner. John Murray sent Hogg a note on 30 January declaring that he had taken a fancy to the title of the new work and wanted to read it, so Hogg requested its reluctant Edinburgh publisher, William Blackwood, to forward one of the printed copies to London, informing him pointedly that Murray had made him a conditional offer for it, which 'suits my circumstances at present and varies considerably from your way of dealing'. James Cochrane wanted it too, but Hogg confessed himself 'unwilling to risk my fortune all in one bottom' and also feared that from Cochrane 'the cash would scarcely be forthcoming'. Blackwood replied stiffly on 13 February, 'The impression of your Ballads is 1000 copies and the expences of the paper & printing is £92-16—on payment of which the whole will be shipped to your order', information which Hogg relayed to John Murray on 17 February. Unfortunately, Murray did not receive the inspection copy he had asked for. When Hogg complained to Blackwood at the beginning of March that it had never been sent. Blackwood huffily retorted that it had been awaiting collection from the London firm of Cadell for many weeks so that if Hogg had not got it and made suitable arrangements for a London publication he had only himself to blame. When Hogg received this letter on 13 March he immediately sent to Thomas Cadell to request the book, but by that time Murray's initial enthusiasm had perhaps waned.[24] At all events Hogg left London without having made any arrangement with him.

At the suggestion of a number of Hogg's literary friends, another subscription edition of *The Queen's Wake* was set on foot. Cochrane's precarious solvency had clearly worried them and soon after the Burns dinner Thomas Pringle called on Hogg to ask if he had any objection to a group of friends joining to purchase a small annuity for Hogg's wife since the poet was 'wearing far up in years' and she might be left 'with a destitute family'. Hogg refused immediately, without even referring the matter to Margaret Hogg, replying, 'I did not come to London to beg but to try my fortune as an author'. She understood this professional pride and supported his decision unequivocally. She told him that she was pleased with Pringle's kindness, '& I am pleased too with your answer, with whom do you think had the plan originated it was exceedingly kind & considerate & we hae aye been provided for & (I hope) sae will we yet—but this is a piece of generosity & kindness which cannnot fail to make an impression on my mind'.[25] Publication by subscription was a more dignified way of appealing to the public. One subscription edition of *The Queen's Wake* had already been issued in 1819, and John Murray might now publish another, with Lockhart keeping the list of subscribers. John James Ruskin heard rumours of the project at an early date and on 9 February Hogg was surprised to receive £20 from him. Notifying Lockhart of this windfall Hogg described the proposed edition as an attractive illustrated gift-book, modelled on one of the fashionable literary annuals. 'It should be a work something like The Keepsake with fewer ornaments yet so as to make it a drawing-room book. If Martin would paint bonny Kilmeny first wakening in the land of thought or the sinking of the Abbot M,Kinnon's ship I know some others who would do one for me *con amore* But I leave the whole to your better judgement'. John Martin, though he did not paint either of the scenes suggested by Hogg, did in fact make a water-colour illustration of 'Kilmeny' which may have been originally intended for this second subscription edition of *The Queen's Wake*. At Hogg's suggestion Martin's daughter Isabella sat for the heroine, Kilmeny, depicted as a tiny figure looking through 'an endless whirl of glory and light' at an idealised Scottish landscape. It was exhibited in the annual show of the Society of British Artists in April 1833.[26]

A silhouette portrait of Hogg by Field of the Strand was shortly afterwards offered to John Murray to face the title-page of the proposed new subscription edition of *The Queen's Wake*. As the latest literary celebrity, Hogg was solicited by as many as ten or twelve artists to sit for his portrait in the days following the Burns Dinner. He sat to Charles Fox for the painting that was engraved as a frontispiece to the *Altrive Tales*, a likeness described on 11 February as bearing 'the true stamp and impress of the poet', and also to the young Irishman Daniel Maclise at the request of the publisher James Fraser, for a pen-and-ink drawing showing him at full length, wearing his shepherd's plaid. This was to be engraved for the 'Gallery of Literary Characters' series for *Fraser's Magazine* for February, and the original drawing was also made available for inspection at Fraser's business premises in Regent Street. Although he felt that the engraved version had been 'spoiled in the lithography' Hogg commented, 'I never in my life saw any thing so like as the drawing was'.[27]

Hogg's celebrity was undoubtedly helping to market *Altrive Tales*, but his social engagements in combination with his publisher's shaky finances meant that production of the first volume was taking longer than expected. An announcement of 'Works in Progress' in Cochrane's own magazine, *The Metropolitan* for February 1832 had announced that 'Vol. I. will be published on the First of March'. Hogg's letter to Lockhart of 24 February indicates, however, that at that point he was still preparing copy and checking proofs for the preparatory 'Reminiscences of Former Days'. His part of the work was then almost complete but Cochrane was slow to publish. 'My publication has not proceeded one step these two weeks' Hogg wrote

to his wife on 14 March. 'I cannot understand it'. The first volume was eventually advertised for 31 March.[28]

Hogg had also been marketing songs in London, calling on the well-known music-publisher and pianoforte dealer Samuel Chappell at his shop at 50 New Bond Street. Chappell described himself as music-seller to King William IV and Queen Adelaide, and his business, founded in 1811, had been commended in 1819 by Beethoven. After Samuel Chappell's death in 1834 at the age of fifty-two the firm, under the charge of his formidable widow and his sons, was to go on to publish Gilbert and Sullivan's operas. A beautifully-engraved two-shilling publication of Hogg's song 'The Stuarts of Appin' was brought out by Chappell during Hogg's London visit. The music was written by Hogg's Edinburgh friend Peter M'Leod in an arrangement by John Thomson, and it was dedicated to 'The Right Honble. The Ladies Anne, Margaret, & Harriet, of Buccleugh'. Hogg also tried unsuccessfully to persuade Chappell to take a collection of songs by some of his young Edinburgh friends set to M'Leod's music. Chappell was not interested in 'these unknown young men', though Thomson sung all the songs over to him. While he admired some of the melodies, he thought they would do better 'interspersed with other more fashionable airs by Bishop &c'.[29]

The fashionable composer Henry Rowley Bishop had set Hogg's collection of *Select and Rare Scotish Melodies* to music in 1829, as well as some Hogg contributions to the *Musical Bijou* annual. Chappell was perhaps willing to spent a considerable portion of his working day listening to the songs of 'these unknown young men' because he wanted to enlist Hogg for another Bishop project he had in hand. Not long after Hogg's arrival in London Chappell had published the first part of *Historical Ballads and Songs*, 'embracing the most striking Incidents in the Annals of the United Kingdom', for which the music was 'partly original, and partly selected from the National Airs of each Country'. For 'Part the First, from the History of England', the lyrics had been written by James Robinson Planché and the music by Bishop. It seems likely that Hogg was invited to supply verses for the subsequent part relating to Scotland, since on 24 March John Bond wrote to Hogg on Chappell's behalf:

> Mr. Chappell's compliments to Mr Hogg & begs to say that he would be very sorry to give him any unnecessary Trouble but could wish as many as possible of the Historical Facts to be introduced in the Poetry of the Ballads as the first Part is written on that plan [...] he presumes M^{r.} H would not object to write a part to National Airs of which he is in daily expect-

ance & which shall be (with his Permission) immediately forwarded

While the work was never published, several of Hogg's projected
lyrics for it can be identified. He published two 'Historical Ballads'
in the *Monthly Magazine* for January and February 1834, 'The Queen
of France and James IV', and 'The White Rose o' Scotland'. A footnote to the first says, 'The Musical Copyright of this Song is the
property of Mr. SAMUEL CHAPPELL, Bond Street'. At much the same
time Hogg also offered his American contact Simeon De Witt
Bloodgood 'two little historical ballads written I suppose long ago'
and asked him to preface them with extracts from Scott's *Tales of a
Grandfather*. A Hogg lyric entitled 'Bruce and the Spider', in an uni-
dentified newspaper cutting at the Beinecke Library at Yale, may
also have once been intended for Samuel Chappell's Scottish volume.[30]

Hogg made a new friend in Chappell's young and ambitious
shopman, John Macrone, who paid him 'the kindest attentions' during his London stay. When Hogg returned to Scotland he left
Macrone his shepherd's plaid as a memento, and later that year received a long visit from him at Altrive. Macrone, James Cochrane
subsequently recalled, 'was introduced to me by the Ettrick Shepherd, who had been accidentally acquainted with him, while Shopman
in Chappell's the music shop—in Bond Street. He represented to me
that he had some Capital & would be glad to join me in business'.[31]

Hogg had contributed to *Fraser's Magazine* and the *Royal Lady's Magazine* before coming to London, and his presence in town clearly fa-
cilitated his work for London-based periodicals. 'A Scottish Ballad',
revised from an unused annuals contribution, appeared in *The Athenaeum*, for example, only a week after Hogg's arrival in London, and
James Cochrane was naturally eager to benefit from his resident
celebrity author. At one point he proposed that Hogg should take
charge of a new magazine, a 'Shepherd's Journal', enlisting his literary acquaintances both in England and in Scotland as contributors.
Hogg also contributed several pieces to Cochrane's new monthly
magazine, *The Metropolitan*, even though he subsequently described
it as a 'hopeless and absurd thing'. 'A Good Story of a Glasgow Tailor' had previously been offered to *Blackwood's Edinburgh Magazine*
and reclaimed by the offended author just before sailing for London,
but two further items were probably written specifically for
Cochrane.[32]

A cholera epidemic swept through Britain from Europe that winter. As Joan McCausland has outlined, the first outbreak was in Sun-

derland on 23 October 1831, and from there it spread locally and to Haddington in Scotland. 'During the first few weeks of 1832 the epidemic spread rapidly westward, reaching Edinburgh at the end of January and Glasgow in mid-February. Cholera arrived in London on 9 February, probably on a coal-ship from Newcastle, but most of the large cities in England were not affected until much later in the year'. Hogg was anxious about the safety of his family in Yarrow. The Gordon Arms Inn at Altrive was vacant and occasionally used by tinkers, and Hogg thought that the Yarrow parish minister and elders might appoint guards along the roads to turn away the beggars and other vagrants who were spreading the disease. 'Some Terrible Letters from Scotland. Communicated by the Ettrick Shepherd' reflects this anxiety, while also providing a blackly humorous commentary on the contents of *The Metropolitan* itself. Towards the end of 1831 Cochrane had published James Kennedy's *The History of the Contagious Cholera* (1832), and a work curiously entitled *Chaunt of the Cholera. Songs for Ireland.* His magazine contained such articles as 'Is the Epidemic Cholera in London?' and 'Progress of Cholera'. Hogg's macabre contribution consists of three first-person accounts of personal experiences of the disease. In one a man supposedly dies, is coffined, and comes to life again; in the second a visiting ship brings the disease to the inhabitants of a remote fishing-village; while in the third the narrator's mother, who has recklessly infected her two daughters, is haunted by their ghosts.[33]

An advertisement for the issue of *The Metropolitan* published on 1 March lists 'Gilfillan's Scottish Songs, reviewed by the Ettrick Shepherd' among its contents. Like Peter M'Leod, Gilfillan was one of Hogg's friends, and it was natural that Hogg should promote his work in London. The unsigned review reflects Hogg's anxieties about pursuing his profession in a diverse metropolitan literary culture.

> Othello's occupation's gone; and the 1832 poets and poetesses of Great Britain and Ireland are ruined! for Mr. Theodore Hook has actually contrived and produced a small elegant steam-apparatus, by which he can manufacture capital poetry at a penny a page: and the most curious property of the machine is, that he has nothing to do but tear a leaf out of an Annual or a Magazine, which he puts into his machine as a sample: after which it will grind him off as much as he likes, exactly of the same description, and annex the signature of each writer, so that the inventor defies any one to distinguish the difference between the original composition and the imitation.

Admitting a general dislike of 'dismissing manual operators for steam-engines', the reviewer intends to retain a proportion of the 'manual operators' of literature in his pay, 'but only such as we believe it impossible for the new-invented machine to imitate', of whom Gilfillan is clearly one. After reprinting a few of Gilfillan's best songs the review ends, 'The Annuals will flourish, but woe to the operatives who had to earn their bread by weaving poetry at so much a yard!' Comparing poets to the handloom weavers who had suffered such hardships during Scotland's rapid industrialisation reveals some anxiety about his literary future. After the loss of his Mount Benger farm in May 1830 he had written to William Blackwood that if he could not replenish his purse by literary work in Edinburgh he 'must go straight to London and become what De-quinsey calls *a literary hack*'.[34] Perhaps he also had the fear of Grub Street before his eyes even as a London celebrity?

When the young Thomas Carlyle met Hogg at James Fraser's he was the centre of attention, seated in the easy chair of honour surrounded by his fellow contributors to *Fraser's Magazine*, chatting, joking, and singing his songs for the benefit of callers. To Carlyle he appeared 'in the mingled character of zany and raree show', everyone bantering him while he appeared 'as if unconscious, or almost flattered'. Even Carlyle's habitual sarcasm seems to have given way temporarily before Hogg's charm, though, for his final impression of the 'cheerful, mirthful, and musical' poet was 'that he *is* a real product of nature, and able to speak naturally, which not one in a thousand is', a man with an authentic talent whose significance, though not fully understood, was nevertheless considerable.[35]

Even in the year of the Reform Act London society seemed to be less overtly divided into political parties than that of Edinburgh, and Hogg admired the way in which adherents of each side 'intermixed all in the most perfect harmony' and political differences were only mentioned 'by way of joke'. One evening when he was dining at Sir George Warrender's there was an unexpected parliamentary division and Hogg noted how peremptory the Tory whip Billy Holmes was about getting the Tory M.P.s present off to the House by cab.[36]

At first sight it seems odd that Hogg had little to say about politics in his letters. After the rejection of one Reform Bill by the House of Lords the previous autumn, provoking serious riots in towns like Nottingham and Bristol, an amended Reform Bill had been introduced into the House of Commons on 12 December 1831. As it passed through its various stages during the early months of 1832 speculation was rife as to what would happen when it reached the

House of Lords. Would the Lords reject Reform again? If so would William IV be persuaded by Earl Grey to create a substantial number of new peers to secure its safe passage? The Bill finally passed its third and final reading in the Commons on 22 March, at the conclusion of Hogg's London visit, when the excitement was at its height. Hogg's chief correspondent, however, was his wife, who was more interested in his personal experience and well-being. In practice politics could hardly be avoided, and Hogg did go down to Westminster to hear some of the debates.

> [...] as for the parliament house if ever ye gang there dinna out o' pride use interest to get yoursel placed amang the members below the gallery as I did ae night. There was I placed sittin cockin up fornent the Speaker frae sax o'clock at night till sax o'clock i' the morning an' didna ken how to get out. It turned rather a serious business wi' me an' sickan a bore I never heard about some English burghs which I had never heard of afore. Na na! If ye ever gang in to either the house o' lords or Commons gang into the Reporters' Gallery look at the system and arrangement o' the house. Get a' the great members pointit out to you. The callants belanging to THE TIMES are very obliging that way at least they were always sae to me an' I popped aye in beside them.[37]

This was the old Westminster building destroyed by the fire of 1834. Among the reporters in the gallery was the young Charles Dickens, taking down shorthand notes of the debates for the *Mirror of Parliament*. No doubt someone would point the Ettrick Shepherd out to him in the reporter's gallery, and they may even have met.

Hogg admitted that 'there is a principle in my constitution that requires constant excitement' but he was wearing himself out in London, and by the end of February Margaret Hogg was beginning to wonder how much longer his visit would last. She reported that young James was surely 'sick for want of you. He won't try the fishing. [...] Now be sure to take care of yourself and write immediately, and do try to fix a time for coming home'. On 10 March Hogg told her that he would probably come home 'about the end of the month or the first week of the next'. He would like to see the King and Queen while he was in London. On 6 March Lord Montagu had promised to advise him when he came to town the following week, and added jocularly, 'Had you asked my opinion in 1822 I should have felt less difficulty in forming one. The tone of the present reign does not seem much in tune with the "Joyous Science" to say nothing of the danger you would run of being knighted'. Hogg's old friend David Brewster *had* just been knighted, and Hogg may seriously have wondered if this honour was in contemplation for him. He asked his wife if she would 'like to be Lady Hogg or remain the Ettrick Shepherdess'. She sensibly responded that the Queen 'must be entirely ignorant of your circumstances if the thing has *really* ever been thought of'. Hogg was delighted to tell her that he had received an invitation to dine with 'the Duke of Sussex, His Majesty's brother and the heir to the crown of Hanover'.[38]

Margaret Hogg decided to apply a little emotional pressure to secure a prompt return, for her letter to Hogg of 15 March lays more emphasis on the ill-health of the couple's son, a message reinforced by a postscript from young James himself, saying 'I have not been well since you left us but I think I shall get well when you come home now dear Pappa come this month'. Hogg's response was immediate and unequivocal—he went out and booked his passage home. His boy's health was dearer 'than either honour or riches of course I shall neither see the King nor queen'. His last important social engagement in London seems to have been on Thursday, 22 March, dining at the Freemasons' Tavern with the Highland Society of London, to celebrate the battle of Alexandria of 1801. This was 'a general court of this Corporation', at which members were requested to appear either in military uniform or Highland dress and a general invitation was extended to members of other Highland Societies.[39]

As Hogg's imminent departure became known it was regretted by many of his new friends, but he probably realised the wisdom of his wife's earlier advice to him to 'leave before you are threadbare [...] leave the Londoners something to guess at'. Arrangements were now well in hand for publication of the first volume of Hogg's *Altrive Tales* on 31 March. Hogg hoped to direct the production of the next few volumes from his Yarrow home with the support of London friends like Lockhart, Thomas Pringle, and Allan Cunningham. He left a list of contents for the first seven of the twelve projected volumes with Cochrane's pressmen, adding, 'The rest I will come and superintend'. He also made one or two parting gifts, including an autograph poem for his hostess, Mary Cochrane, and his shepherd's plaid for young John Macrone of Chappell's.[40]

Hogg probably left the fashionable centre of London in the evening of Saturday, 24 March to spend the night in the vicinity of Blackwall, since the *United Kingdom* steamship on which his passage was booked left from the Steam Navigation wharf there at nine o'clock on Sunday morning. By starting in the morning passengers could expect to be on board only two nights instead of the usual three. Hogg might hope to reach Leith late on Tuesday, 27 March.[41]

The *United Kingdom* seems to have been a day late, for on 2 April the *Edinburgh Evening Courant* reported, 'The Ettrick Shepherd arrived from London by one of the steamers on Wednesday afternoon. He left this city on Friday for his native hills, in excellent health and spirits'. Hogg devoted his single day in Edinburgh to business. He called on James Cochrane's Edinburgh agent, Samuel Aitken of the firm of Bell and Bradfute, to collect a promised letter from Cochrane together with a payment of £20 due to him on publication of the first volume of his *Altrive Tales*. He also followed up a rather stiff and formal letter sent to him by William Blackwood on 7 March requesting him to send details for the title-page of *A Queer Book* if he had not come to any arrangement with a London publisher, so that it could finally be published. Since friendly relations had not been resumed, instead of calling in person Hogg sent a note to young Alexander Blackwood to say, 'you may publish it along with a second edition of the songs of those that remain. The title page is decidedly "A Queer Book"'.[42] When he left Edinburgh on 30 March he must have been impatient to get home after an absence of more than three months.

CHAPTER EIGHT

Man of the Mountains

Hogg found all well at Altrive on his return. Though the building work for the new extension was exactly as he had left it the preceding December, his son James was in better health than he had feared and there was great joy in the family on his return. Hogg had brought various gifts from friends and admirers with him, among them a musical box given by Archibald Hastie. In high spirits, he used it to trick some of the locals into believing that Altrive was haunted by the fairies. 'What consternation' he reported to the donor: 'if the servant girls had not outed the secret some of them would never have entered the door again'. He had also brought back a special gift to Mungo Park's family, a book of Psalms belonging to Park's brother-in-law Henry Anderson, kept by an African chief as a fetish and retrieved by the Cornish explorer John Lander, one of the celebrated men Hogg had socialised with in London.[1] More at leisure than for months past, Hogg reflected on the contrast between 'the mighty goings on of nature' around him and 'the scenes of confusion and roving merriment' of the great Babylon, and between times wrote his thank-you letters to new and old London friends while waiting for news of his *Altrive Tales*.[2] So many of Hogg's London friends were M.P.'s or senior administrators with franking privileges that his correspondence would be easier than ever before.

As he resumed his country life and his favourite sporting activities Hogg gradually lost some of the weight he had gained and his clothes began to fit him once again. On 8 June he acted as a judge in the annual contest of the St Ronan's Angling Club and presided with 'urbanity and good humour' at the dinner that followed at Riddell's Inn in Innerleithen. He was also a judge at the annual St Ronan's Border Club Games on 1 August, and on the next day he competed for the Marchmont arrow at archery and in the rifle-shooting contest which followed. In the archery sweepstakes that followed the prize arrow competition Hogg was beaten by his mentor, Colonel Ferguson, by a single shot, and as Chairman at the convivial dinner held that evening sang 'with great applause several of his own beautiful songs'. After the archery contest held by the Bowmen of the Border at the end of October Hogg proudly reported '*the old Shepherd* won both the grand prize bow and the sweepstakes afterwards and likewise the Silver Cup from The Forest Club on the Tuesday following for the conquering Grayhound in the chase'.[3] He was still a strong man physically, ordering Peter Muir, bowyer to the Royal Company of Archers, to make his prize bow one that would draw at least fifty pounds weight. Visitors to Altrive were sometimes challenged to see if they could draw Hogg's bow but few were able to do so. The Highland Society of Scotland invited Hogg to act as a judge of Cheviot sheep at its livestock show held at Kelso in October.[4] All told, he had plenty of social engagements to relieve the quietness of home.

Dr William Gray, the son of Hogg's old friend James Gray and Margaret Hogg's nephew, was in Scotland on a two-year furlough from his post as surgeon at Bombay to the East India Company. He was now thirty-four years old and, Hogg considered, 'one of the finest and most intelligent fellows I ever met with'. He boarded at Altrive that summer and autumn, where he was frequently visited by his brother James from Edinburgh. The Gray brothers joined Hogg in practising archery, and it may well have been William Gray who presented Hogg with a curiously curved bow made of buffalo horn that had once been owned by an Indian prince.[5] At the start of the shooting season that August Hogg and William Gray walked up together to Birkhill for a few days, stopping at Loch Skene for a picnic lunch on their way. They lodged at modest cost with Walter Boa, the Birkhill shepherd, and his wife. Boa's father had been a herd at Hopehouse for more than twenty years and Hogg probably knew the family well.[6] William wanted to take a wife back to India with him, and during his stay in London Hogg had been very taken with William Jerdan's daughter, Mary, who was said to resemble some of the old portraits of her namesake, Mary, Queen of Scots. Towards the end of the year Jerdan was greatly amused to receive a letter from Hogg suggesting that perhaps she might visit her relations in Kelso to be 'wooed in due form' by his nephew, but no meeting resulted.[7]

There was a more satisfactory outcome to Hogg's intervention in the love affair between Christian Anderson of Crosscleugh farm and Thomas Richardson of the neighbouring Tibbie Shiels Inn. When Thomas had got Christian pregnant the previous year Hogg earnestly advised that he should acknowledge paternity of 'that fine girl's child'. On 4 May 1832 the couple married and Hogg was the chief fiddler to the wedding party, playing 'the reel-tunes o' auld Scotland' with such spirit that the dancers could barely keep time to 'the hurrying pace of the Shepherd's fiddle-stick'. It was on the morning following this unwonted exertion that Hogg, staying the night at the little inn on St Mary's Loch, drank the contents of the water-jug and then called to his old friend Tibbie Shiel to 'fetch in the Loch'.[8]

Hogg did not go far from his home and family that summer and autumn after his lengthy absence. 'A fonder or more affectionate husband and parent does not exist than your old hair-brained friend' he wrote to an old acquaintance, describing his bairns individually and with obvious pride:

> I have one only son James aged 11 a fine boy very amiable and with good capabilities but the idlest scholar ever was seen Then Jessie Phillips aged 9 a fine rosy soncy lass and beats her brother hollow even at the latin. Then Margt Laidlaw aged 7 pretty and clever but a terrible hempy having an overflow of spirits quite irrestrainable. Then Harriet Sidney 4½ years old her father's darling [...] she is a most interesting child very like Maggy in form feature and high spirits Then Mary Gray aged nine months this week a fair blue eyed little cherub the very picture of health and happiness as indeed the whole of them are

The Hogg family travelled locally in what was known as the 'caravan', an open cart with a moveable green-painted tin dome over it to protect the occupants from the weather, this elementary roof being fitted with curtains at either end. In London Hogg had met a much more sedate and delicately-nurtured child, the teenage John Ruskin, whose father was a friend of the publisher Alexander Elder. Hogg subsequently invited the lad for a holiday among his own carefree brood, who were 'noisy romping healthy brats but good learners'. The young Ruskin, however, wrote gratefully, 'I do not wish to leave my parents, and they are equally tenacious of me'.[9]

At the beginning of May Blackwood finally published *A Queer Book*, perhaps without Hogg even being aware of the fact since on 15 June he enquired if the printing had been completed and asked that it should be advertised for November. Hogg's preoccupation with the fate of his *Altrive Tales* as well as his quarrel with the firm must have been responsible for such uncharacteristic ignorance.[10]

Hogg's 'Memoir' proved as controversial in *Altrive Tales* as it had been eleven years previously. Firstly, it delayed the publication of the all-important first volume of the series since 'some requisite alterations' were required, in order to eliminate 'some inconsiderate expressions [...] respecting a worthy bookseller', apparently Owen Rees of the Longmans firm. Probably copies were not generally available until mid-April, an inauspicious delay for the first volume of a monthly reprint series since prospective purchasers would be unlikely to begin to acquire a series that did not promise to continue at regular intervals. When it did appear, George Goldie, seeing Hogg's account of their dealings over the third edition of *The Queen's Wake* revived, reprinted his 1821 pamphlet attacking Hogg, and another scarifying pamphlet was published in mid-May by Dr James Browne of Edinburgh, entitled *The Life of the Ettrick Shepherd Anatomized. By an Old Dissector*. William Blackwood, following Hogg's angry statements in the 'Memoir' about his witholding payment for various Hogg works, found himself termed one of the 'paltry pilferers of the profits of genius' by *Fraser's Magazine*.[11] The rift between Hogg and his Edinburgh publisher was undoubtedly widened.

Worse still, Hogg's hopes received a crushing blow when Sir Richard Phillips wrote on 27 April to tell him of the 'Executions, Seizures, Attachments, Arrests' that had taken place at Cochrane's Waterloo Place premises in the preceding few days:

> The day before yesterday he was not in his business the whole day, a man from the Sheriff being in possession, nothing being to be delivered on credit, & the man receiving all money. Another Execution, but a few days since nearly swept the premises [...]

Within a fortnight of the publication of the first volume of the all-important *Altrive Tales* series, its publisher had become bankrupt. A brisk sale should have followed Hogg's London visit and fifteen hundred copies were reputedly sold within twelve days after publication, but with Cochrane's bankruptcy the remaining copies were impounded for the benefit of his creditors. With the help of two London friends, John McDonald and Thomas Pringle, Hogg set about trying to retrieve them for sale by another publisher. He wrote a carefully-worded appeal to Cochrane himself, expressing his regret for the publisher's misfortunes and appealing for his co-operation:

> [...] I would rather that paper printing &c of the remaining copies were paid by some other house and the copies sold for me On Commission until we see if you get matters arranged again so as to go on. Now I beseech you my dear Cochrane as you hope to be respected to go hand in hand with my friend in securing the remaining copies for me and I shall stick by you in literature as long as I live.

Hogg's thoughts naturally turned to the retrieval of *The Queen's Wake* in 1814 and he hoped that 'as Goldie's turned out so good a concern for me ultimately so may this but the present time is the worst'. The publication of *Altrive Tales*, however, was not so easily continued. In London it was offered without success firstly to Richard Bentley and then to Smith and Elder, who agreed to publish it on Hogg's behalf only if he provided securities for two hundred pounds, a proposal which Hogg as an established author regarded as 'rather an insult'. In Scotland he sounded out both Oliver & Boyd and Archibald Fullarton of Glasgow with no better success.[12] By the autumn the momentum of *Altrive Tales* as a monthly reprint series had broken down entirely.

Fortunately, Hogg had received a lucrative literary commission just before hearing of Cochrane's bankruptcy. The Glasgow publisher Archibald Fullarton asked him to provide a memoir and notes for a new edition of the works of Robert Burns, a most congenial task, and promised a minimum payment of a hundred pounds. Hogg signed a letter of agreement on 23 April promising to complete his work by the start of 1833 and promptly appealed to friends for assistance, notably to Lockhart who had written a short biography of Burns in 1828. Lockhart and Murray also pushed the subscription list for the *de luxe* edition of *The Queen's Wake*, ably supported by William Jerdan of the *Literary Gazette* who urged 'the hundreds of high rank and great wealth, who enjoyed the Shepherd's original and entertaining society whilst in the metropolis, to help him in the hour when all his humour and hilarity must be turned to grief and bitterness'. One reader at least, a C. D. from Sheffield, transmitted a bank note for twenty pounds to the *Literary Gazette* offices for Hogg's benefit, which was duly forwarded and acknowledged in the issue of 15 December. The members of the Royal Literary Fund agreed to subscribe *en masse* for *The Queen's Wake*, and this added £40 to numerous other donations and subscriptions so that Murray's son was able to transmit £100 to Altrive in June.[13]

If Hogg was not able to make provision for the future of his family he was at least freed from present anxiety and presumably able to finish building the extension to his house. The cottage at Altrive was now a residence far beyond what any future tenant of around forty acres might expect. An American visitor who previously had the impression that Hogg lived 'in humble style' was surprised by its 'tolerably spacious dimensions'. The dark slate roof of the white-washed building dipped in the middle, giving it the appearance of two houses rather than one, built on a mound and surrounded by a pleasant flower garden enclosed with palisades. Hogg now had a little study in which to write, about ten feet by nine, with a fireplace and a window facing to the south-east, and a handsome library adja-

cent to it. This was painted blue and white with windows facing to
the east and south, and the whole of the unbroken north wall from
floor to ceiling was covered with books.[14]

That summer Sir Walter Scott began his sad return to Scotland
through Germany, desperate to reach his end in Abbotsford and
avoid laying his bones in foreign soil. By the time he reached London on 13 June he was generally known to be dying, and on his
return to Abbotsford on 11 July was seen by few people outside his
immediate family. Hogg went over to Abbotsford twice in order to
stand by his sick-bed, but was not permitted to see him. Hogg's distress was such that on one occasion, on 20 July, he was thrown from
his gig on the return journey and so badly bruised as to be confined
to the house for some days. 'The great and good Sir Walter' he wrote
to a London acquaintance, 'is lying in a state so utterly deplorable
and degraded that there is nothing in nature so painful to contem-
plate'. Less than a week later, presumably as soon as he had recov-
ered from his injuries, Hogg was at Huntly Burn on the Abbotsford
estate. From there he could hope to receive the latest news of Scott
from Lockhart or from William Laidlaw. Scott, he learned, 'was then
reduced to the very lowest state of degradation to which poor pros-
trate humanity could be subjected'. His motions and slurred speech
resembled those of a drunken man, and while in his lucid intervals
he could recognise old friends and pronounce a recognisable word
or two his efforts to speak at other times issued in sounds 'the most
revolting that can be concieved'.[15] The end came on 21 September
and Hogg, who had not seen Scott since October 1830, at least had
the satisfaction of attending his funeral and interment in Dryburgh
Abbey.

Scott's death was the end of an era for Hogg, and Abbotsford was
no longer a friend's house. Scott's elder son was in the army and, if
he retained the estate, could not afford to live there as his father had
done. Apart from his published work, Hogg argued, Abbotsford was
Scott's great monument, 'that will always be visited in after ages in
preference to any other'. People would be proud to possess a slip of
wood from one of the trees Scott had planted with his own hand.
Literary pilgrimages began that very autumn, Hogg's young London
friend John Macrone, for example, securing a note of introduction
from Hogg to William Laidlaw during his lengthy visit to Altrive,
who was requested to show him 'all that can be seen about
Abbotsford'. In the spring of 1834 the house was advertised as to let
for two or three years, while by the end of the year it was shut up and
'deserted except by one domestic'. Lockhart would no longer pass

his summer holidays there, while William Laidlaw, Scott's faithful steward, and Hogg's brother David, who had charge of the Abbotsford flocks, must look for posts elsewhere. Scott's loss was severely felt, Hogg writing sadly to Lockhart a few days after Scott's funeral, 'I cannot help writing to you thus early as I find that now having lost the best and most steady friend that I ever had in the world I have none now to depend on for advice or assistance but yourself. I never applied to any body for these but to him and they never were wanting'. The loss of Laidlaw's society he was to describe subsequently as 'a blank to me which cannot be filled up again'. In this melancholy mood Hogg had two snuff-boxes made, sending one to his 'dear brother' Allan Cunningham and requesting him to have 'James Hogg' engraved on the lid, while he marked the one he kept with Cunningham's name.[16]

At the conclusion of his reminiscences of Scott in *Altrive Tales* Hogg had promised 'if I outlive him [...] I shall draw a mental portrait of him, the likeness of which to the original shall not be disputed'. John Macrone's lengthy autumn visit was partly designed to gather materials for a Scott biography, to which he hoped Hogg would contribute his own recollections. He was also there to inform Hogg that if James Cochrane could get his discharge as a bankrupt the two intended to set up in partnership as London publishers, and hoped to retain Hogg as an author. In that case *Altrive Tales*, they hoped, would be continued by them. Hogg, however, was wary of entering into an agreement with a firm that had as yet no existence, and told Macrone that he had already authorised Lockhart to try to find another publisher. (It was not until 13 January 1833 that Cochrane was able to announce that the new partnership was a reality.) Macrone was a congenial companion, and during his visit Hogg gave him his own copy of the Edinburgh edition of the poems of Burns. Nevertheless, he almost outstayed his welcome. Hogg wrote a letter for him to deliver to Cochrane on 4 November, and added an impatient postscript ten days later. 'We have had an idle time of it' he wrote. 'Nothing but eating and drinking and rural sports. God forbid that every one of my acquaintance should pay me such a long visit for since John arrived I have not written one page for the press'.[17] Despite the distraction of London visitors Hogg did meet Fullarton's deadline for the supply of copy for the new Burns edition. By mid-September he had drafted the biographical part, was well on with the notes to Burns's works by mid-October, and a month later pronounced, 'I have inserted every thing to which my knowledge and capacity reaches'. When Fullarton made it plain that Hogg's copy was not quite what he expected, Hogg was prepared to be conciliatory. 'I am always open to conviction' he declared, 'especially with one who has a deep stake along with me. [...] I will always be glad to hear from you and shall attend as much to your insinuations as you can expect any original and jealous author to do'. While this difference of opinion may have delayed the publication of the work, Hogg was paid, in two bills of £50 each.[18]

In the longer term Hogg needed to make some provision for the future of his family and to settle his debts from the termination of the Mount Benger lease at Whitsunday 1830. He still wanted the Duke of Buccleuch to make his claim and settle the money on 'my little Harriet your mother's namesake and her father's darling', but was refused a personal interview whenever he called at Bowhill. On 7 December he wrote asking the Duke, who probably found the whole affair a nuisance, 'to attend to this request of *The clown*'. His letter was irritably addressed to 'His Grace The Duke of Buccleuch At Kennae-where By Selkirk', and he reminded his landlord of his political services to the family both at election time and in the form of newspaper journalism.[19]

The royal assent had been given to the Reform Act for Scotland on 17 July 1832 and a general election was in the offing, with reforms to widen access to local government almost inevitable afterwards. Lord John Scott, the twenty-three-year-old brother of the Duke of Buccleuch, seems originally to have intended to stand for Roxburghshire as a Tory candidate prepared to support a moderate and limited measure of reform. Hogg attended him some days that summer, describing him to the Duke as 'an uncommon callan' and reporting that at St Boswell's Fair on 18 July a club of his supporters were holding up their caps with shouts of 'Lord John Scott and Reform! Damn a' pensions an' sinecures!!' Grateful for Hogg's support, Lord John then promised that he would call on the poet sometime at Altrive. At the first elections for the reformed House of Commons in December the liberal party under Earl Grey was victorious, and Tory candidates were defeated by Reformers both in Selkirkshire and Roxburghshire, Robert Pringle of Clifton ousting the sitting member Alexander Pringle of Whytbank for Selkirkshire and Lord John Scott being defeated by Captain George Elliot. The widening of the county franchise gave great landowners such as the Duke of Buccleuch the opportunity to create new voters in their interest, since in the absence of a secret ballot tenants would be almost certain to vote as their landlord directed.[20] In September 1832 Major Charles Riddell consulted a lawyer and advised the Duke that if Hogg was given a

formal lease for the house and garden at Altrive he could be registered as a voter. William Laidlaw told his brother George on 22
September, 'Hogg has got a 99 years Lease […] at a Rent of 5/ a
year—but the Sherriff has found it was granted on purpose & he has
no vote this time'. A quarter-acre of land, together with the house,
was apparently specified in the lease, though a half-acre had been
suggested initially by Riddell. A surviving receipt for a pound paid
for four years' rent from Whitsunday 1829 to Whitsunday 1832 was
dated 17 July 1833 and presumably represents an attempt to get this
decision overturned subsequently, though there is no evidence that
Hogg ever did obtain a vote. An informal arrangement regarding
Altrive had now been turned into a legal contract, and since the lease
post-dated Hogg's marriage it implied that his widow could retain
the farm after his death or receive a payment in lieu of it. Hogg
reflected on the arrangement with great satisfaction for the remainder of his life—'as I have nothing as yet to leave my comely family
save this little farm' he wrote in 1835, 'there is not a day passes over
my head on which I do not feel grateful for it'.[21]

Although he had no vote, Hogg spoke on the Selkirk hustings in
favour of the defeated Tory candidate, Alexander Pringle. 'There is
such a revolutionary mania abroad', he reported subsequently, 'that
it is quite needless to speak to people even the eloquence of the
Shepherd failed in a place where he is perfectly understood and the
Tories lost by eight votes! Damn these whig bodies we are fairly
under their feet now'. Hogg's Toryism became more aggressive during the early 1830s. He told Allan Cunningham, for instance, that his
recently-published poem *The Maid of Elvar* 'never will be popular in
this damned reforming canvassing age'.[22]

The fortunes of the Phillips family appeared to be looking up
after the sharp decline of the previous decade. Margaret Hogg's only
surviving brother Walter had recently been able to return to Ruthwell
parish in Dumfriesshire as factor to Lord Mansfield. He was now
living at Comlongan Castle, a traditional Border tower with battle-
ments surrounded by fine old woods. 'How wonderful are the ways
of providence' Hogg wrote to him, 'which have brought you to be
the head and guide of that estate from which you were so unfairly
expelled'. Could Walter perhaps recommend Laidlaw for the situation he was leaving, as factor to a Mr Ord?[23]

That Christmas Hogg was 'waiting for the frost', so that he could
join the Duddingston Curling Society's games in Edinburgh. He was,
however, delayed by a cold and chest infection until the middle of
January, and impatiently set off almost as soon as he was able to

leave his bed, staying with William Gray in his winter lodgings in India Street in the northern New Town and socialising with Margaret Hogg's Crighton and Phillips relations. The competition for the Society's gold medal was held on 17 January, a 'damp and disagreeable' day when there were few spectators and the ice not in the best condition. The dinner at the York Hotel that followed was such a convivial one that some members failed to turn up on the ice the following morning because 'they were still sitting at the York Hotel, with a certain celebrated W. S. at their head'. A birthday dinner to Hogg (and Burns) on 25 January at the National Hotel on West Register Street was attended by sixty gentlemen, to whom Hogg 'gave an interesting account, with his usual *naivete*, of his early days', and sung a quota of Scots songs. He was also engaged to dine on 30 January with the Peebles Club at the York Hotel.[24]

The late hours of such convivialities were not the best aids to recovery from a cold and chest infection, and Hogg was unlucky enough to fall through the ice and into the freezing water one day when out curling. The resulting chill obviously turned to bronchitis if not pneumonia, and for once Hogg did not shake off an indisposition so easily. On 5 February he wrote to his wife, 'I have been confined to my bed nearly the half of the time I have been in Edin[r] merely I believe from a neglected cold but chiefly from a severe stitch in my side. I have been bled I have been blistered and dosed almost to death with drugs and am up in my night gown for the first time this eight days to write to you. [...] You will not know me when I come home to you I am so much altered for the worse'. Hogg's illegitimate daughter, Betsy, now twenty-two years old, paid a great deal of attention to him during this time, and Hogg afterwards wrote her some affectionate letters.[25] Eventually Margaret Hogg came into town from Altrive to take care of her husband.

During the whole of the following summer Hogg was ailing occasionally ('never well above three or four days at a time' he described himself that June), and often confined to bed a day or more each week with 'a sort of asthmatick cough' and sometimes 'rather unwell and nervish'. On 17 September he declared 'that for the last six months my constitution has undergone a great change for the worse', and told John Grieve, 'I feel that the best days of my writing are over'. Dr William Gray's diagnosis was that Hogg was suffering from water on the chest, and this was subsequently confirmed by an Edinburgh physician. Hogg tried to joke that this could not be since he never drank water, but was evidently much depressed.[26] He was obliged to recognise that his iron constitution was beginning to fail and he was now past his physical prime.

Anxiety about Hogg's health perhaps prompted the efforts made during his Edinburgh visit by John Wilson, John Grieve, and the Izetts to effect a reconciliation between him and William Blackwood. Wilson wanted to continue his characterisation of the Shepherd of the *Noctes Ambrosianae*, a series which had faltered and stopped during the period of Hogg's estrangement from *Blackwood's Edinburgh Magazine*. He now suggested that, if a reconciliation could be effected, Hogg should be paid an annual sum of a hundred pounds, to cover payments for the appearances of the Noctean Shepherd as well as for his own contributions to the magazine. Blackwood, however, insisted on receiving a written statement contradicting the aspersions cast upon his honesty in Hogg's 'Memoir'. He was, Hogg told Lockhart, 'such a mule and such a purse proud ideot that he would do nothing without an apology from me for something which I had published that was not true while I denied that I had published a word that was not true and refused any apology'.[27] The attempt at a reconciliation probably only deepened the quarrel.

This was the age of the cheap periodical, designed to educate the new post-1832 electorate. Robert Chambers had written to Hogg on 4 November 1832 inviting him to contribute to his cheap weekly paper, *Chambers's Edinburgh Journal*, promising two guineas at least for 'a rural tale or so, constructed as much as possible with a moral or useful object', and drawing Hogg's attention to favourable notice of his own poetical character in a series entitled 'Popular Information on Literature'. Hogg was held up to the working man as an example of the triumph of talent and perseverance over social disadvantage. Such periodicals, however, were relentlessly improving in tone, morally as well as educationally, and Hogg found writing for them restrictive. In accepting the humorous tale of 'The Watchmaker', written to accord with *Chambers's* warnings against the demon drink, Robert Chambers had issued a caution with his note of appreciation:

> It is really a droll sketch, and you have given it a somewhat moral turn at the end, though I fear your humorous genius is apt to make rather a wry face when attempting anything of that kind, and is disposed to put its tongue waggishly in one cheek, while attempting to look very serious with the other.

Hogg may also have felt at times that the economics of such publications, where huge sales were needed to offset a low selling price, worked against him as an author. When a portrait and notice of himself was prefixed to volume 21 of Limbird's twopenny weekly paper *The Mirror* he was pleased by the publicity and requested extra copies for visitors to Altrive, but also commented crossly that literature had been 'knocked on the head' by 'your cheap publications [...] and we will soon all be beggars'.[28]

During Hogg's stay in Edinburgh negotiations had been opened up with the Glasgow 'numbers' publishing firm of Blackie and Son for a multi-volume collection of Hogg's prose tales, when a letter intended for Archibald Fullarton had been received instead by the firm's Edinburgh agent, Mr Martin. The firm sold standard works with handsomely engraved illustrations in sections to subscribers who could not afford the price of such volumes except in instalments. Hogg was undoubtedly tempted by the prospect of huge sales, perhaps up to twenty thousand copies, but dismayed at the small percentage of the selling-price offered to him as the author, only one-twelfth where he expected a fifth or a sixth part. Since the Glasgow firm normally printed, published, and distributed their books themselves, Hogg would not be able to choose his own printer or allocate a part of the edition to an Edinburgh or London firm as he had done previously. Blackies also preferred to purchase the copyright in the works they published, or at least to receive the entire work before production commenced, since regularity of publication was essential to the successful completion of part-works. When Hogg returned to Altrive in February 1833 the matter was effectively put on hold, with Hogg declaring himself willing to accept some reduction in his author's share if the publication was to include plates and inviting the firm's principals to visit him at Altrive. The start of the 'reading season' in early November, he considered, would be the best time to begin this publication.[29]

On his return from Edinburgh Hogg set to work to finish recording his thirty-year friendship with Sir Walter Scott for John Macrone. In a letter of 13 January 1833 announcing the legal commencement of the new publishing partnership Cochrane had reminded Hogg of Macrone's work, adding 'Any materials which you may have, & report speaks largely on the subject, will be doubly valuable to him & honourable & profitable to us all'. Macrone's *Notices of the Life of Sir Walter Scott* was variously advertised as 'interspersed with numerous original and characteristic Letters and Anecdotes', and with anecdotes collected 'among the shepherds of Tweed and Yarrow'. Hogg's reminscences of Scott were a hot publishing property, for his hint of biographical intentions in *Altrive Tales* had been noted even as far away as America. When on 1 March Hogg made another attempt at a reconciliation with Blackwood, he could not resist mentioning what splendid copy they would have made for forty pages of *Blackwood's*

Edinburgh Magazine had they not been sent to London. Possibly Blackwood alerted Lockhart, directly or indirectly, to the fact that Hogg was to contribute to Macrone's Scott biography, since no advertisements specifically naming Hogg have been located. At any rate, Lockhart now intervened, informing Cochrane that Scott's executors would interfere to prevent the inclusion of his letters in Macrone's biography, and Macrone subsequently called on Lockhart with Hogg's manuscript. Lockhart, with his strong sense of propriety and as Scott's son-in-law and official biographer, after a cursory glance at it 'could not restrain his indignation, and poured out his indignation against Hogg in such unmeasured terms that his poor auditor was quite dumbfoundered'.[30] Hogg, wishing to retain Lockhart's friendship, felt he had no alternative but to ask Macrone for the immediate return of his manuscript.

At the same time, however, Hogg's letter to Lockhart expressed a wish to see his reminiscences of Scott published somehow. He had been partly paid, he admitted, and, Macrone having taken a copy, they 'will no doubt see the light some time'. Lockhart ignored such hints, accepting Hogg's assurance that 'they shall not as long as I live'. Hogg, however, could not really afford to lose such a marketable work. A number of American gentlemen had visited at Altrive, and several Hogg works had been reprinted in America. Hogg was 'most proud of being valued so highly by my transatlantic brethren'. He had received an offer for his Scott anecdotes 'from a place called Albion in America', and Lockhart and Scott's surviving family might not even be aware of a publication issued thousands of miles away.[31]

Albany, the state capital of New York, had a thriving cultural centre in the Albany Institute and an interest in Scotland. During the year following Scott's death, for instance, a six-feet square tablet in his memory was placed in the rotunda of the new City Hall. The Rev. William B. Sprague, minister of the Second Presbyterian Church in Albany and a noted autograph-collector, applied to Hogg for his autograph that summer, receiving a charming recollection of Hogg's shepherding days in Dumfriesshire in reply. He had visited Britain in 1828, forming a friendship with Dr Raffles, minister of a dissenting congregation in Liverpool, and his *Hints Designed to Regulate the Intercourse of Christians,* was to be advertised in Edinburgh by Waugh & Innes in 1834. The Albany lawyer and literary man Simeon de Witt Bloodgood, who had been Secretary to the Albany Institute in 1831, had previously requested Hogg's Scott anecdotes. On 22 June Hogg sent a revised version to him through Dr Raffles of Liverpool. Bearing Lockhart's disapproval in mind Hogg made it clear that he would prefer it if publication were confined to America, 'But if you cannot effect this and if it is contrary to the rule of nations then be sure to send every sheet as it comes from the press to Messrs Cochrane & Co 11 Waterloo Place London'.[32]

The families of Hogg's two younger brothers, Robert and David, were emigrating to America. A letter of 11 June 1832 in the *New North Briton* stated that a nephew of the Ettrick Shepherd was among the would-be emigrants to Quebec who had advanced money for their passage only to find that the ship-owners had taken deposits from almost four hundred passengers for a ship that would carry only one hundred and twenty. Twenty-one-year-old Samuel Hogg, the son of Hogg's brother Robert, was going to America to join his elder brothers, William and James, who had emigrated from Harris in 1830. The letter-writer called on the Ettrick Shepherd to 'awaken the Forest' to this fraudulent behaviour and prevent any more emigrants being similarly deceived. After hearing from his nephew Hogg wrote to the *Edinburgh Evening Post* on 2 April 1833 urging emigrants never to 'pay a sixpence until they are on board, and have received their berths' since that party 'what with board before sailing' on another vessel and their advance payments 'lost upwards of L.100'. He concluded by requesting 'that this notice may be copied into all the papers in the west of Scotland'. In America Robert's son James, a spirited lad in his late teens, was fortunate enough to attract the attention of a prosperous American landholder, Dr Robert Rose of Silver Lake in the north-west corner of Susquehanna county, Pennsylvania, bordering New York State. Dr Rose

> went out one day to see his workmen thirty of whom were working at some rural work and among them he percieved a very handsome young man plying away. He asked him where he came from and what was his name? He answered that he came from Scotland and that his name was James Hogg. "Why man" said Rose "that is the name best known to us here of all the names in the world That is the name of the Ettrick Shepherd" Yes said James he is my uncle and I am his namesake. "Then my man" said the laird "you and I shall never part as long as we live. He immediately offered him a farm stocked with 1000 sheep which James declined until he wrote to his father to come to his assistance.

Robert Hogg emigrated on that basis from Arran during the summer of 1833, leaving Hogg with no precise idea of his brother's destination. In sending his *Familiar Anecdotes of Sir Walter Scott* to Bloodgood on 22 June Hogg enquired where Silver Lake was and 'if it can be reached either by post steam or carrier', asking him to let his brother know 'that we are all well and that I will long with the most ardent impatience to hear' from him. Could Bloodgood help to transmit letters between them perhaps? After many weeks news eventually reached Scotland that Robert, the youngest of Hogg's brothers, had died on the voyage and a notice was duly inserted in the *Edinburgh Evening Courant* of 16 September 1833. Measles had broken out among the three hundred and sixty emigrants aboard the *Romulus*, and Robert developed pneumonia, died, and was buried at sea. Fortunately, Rose was kind to the bereaved family and clearly wrote Hogg a reassuring letter soon after their arrival. From Hogg's reply Rose had urged the emigration of the remaining Hogg brothers:

> The one has been head shepherd to Sir James Montgomery for about thirty years, and the other to Sir Walter Scott for the last twenty years. And were it not that I am the very man that I am, 'the Ettrick Shepherd,' I should be in America the first of them all, for I have long viewed, with wonder and amazement, the resources of that astonishing country. But my name has now been so long identified with Scotland and Ettrick Forest, that I cannot leave them. [...] I am, however, happy to hear from every corner of the great community of the west that I am more read there, and oftener reprinted, than any other living author.[33]

Writing to William Laidlaw's wife that November, Hogg told her, 'David I am perswaded will go to America and so I think will Will. old as he is'. Robert Hogg's sons Samuel and James tenanted the farm Rose had promised their father, while their older brother William possessed another in Pennsylvania. As Margaret Fraser has shown, Hogg acted from time to time as an emigration agent to William Dickson of Galt and New Dumfries township in Canada, who also offered to stock a farm for him there but was answered that 'The Yarrow couldna want him'. William Hogg also remained in Scotland, but David Hogg went to join his brother's family at Silver Lake in 1834, accompanied by Mr Jardine, a presbyterian minister who had gone out as pastor to the Scots congregation forming in the settlement. His first reports of America it seems were far from favourable, though William Laidlaw felt this was due more to 'his habitual love of sarcasm & satire' than the nature of his reception there. Eventually the families of David and Robert Hogg moved to Broome County in New York state and founded a settlement there known as

Mount Ettrick. The emigration of Hogg's brothers must have increased his awareness of his own popularity as a writer in the United States. 'I have got most strenous [*sic*] requests for copy-rights from the United States' he told Fullarton in September 1833. 'I am a greater favourite there than in any part of the world'.[34]

In June 1833 John Macrone paid another visit to Altrive and came away with three manuscript tales for a new Hogg work for the firm of Cochrane and Macrone, 'Genuine Tales of the days of Montrose'. 'Some Remarkable Passages in the Life of An Edinburgh Baillie', 'The Adventures of Colonel Peter Aston', and 'A Few Remarkable Adventures of Sir Simon Brodie' had all been composed originally in the mid-1820s for another collection, 'Lives of Eminent Men', though Hogg had clearly rewritten them since.[35] He also hoped that the firm might continue *Altrive Tales*, perhaps in conjunction with Blackie and Son of Glasgow.

In March, when he had hoped for a reconciliation with William Blackwood, Hogg had set about writing a *Noctes* of his own for *Blackwood's Edinburgh Magazine*. He afterwards completed it for *Fraser's Magazine* and sent it to London, where Fraser set it up in type and allowed Maginn to use it as the basis for an article of his own entitled 'The Shepherd's Noctes, and the Reason Why they do not Appear in Fraser's Magazine' published in the July issue. (A second *Noctes* authored by Hogg was returned to him in manuscript.) James Fraser undoubtedly meant well, but the publication of part of his work out of context was a great cause of embarrassment to Hogg. He had written his *Noctes* partly to showcase the poetry and music of his young Scottish protégés, such as Robert Gilfillan, George Allan and John Imlah, and instead their work was published as his own. Peter M'Leod evidently wrote to complain about this appropriation, for Hogg replied that 'instead of being an error of heart it was exactly the reverse. I am exceedingly vexed about it'. Hogg, evidently angry with James Fraser, did not apparently write to him again until November. Unlike Blackwood, who, Hogg said, 'will never once confess that he is in the wrong', Fraser was conciliatory:

> I knew your goodness of heart would sooner or later forgive a little indiscretion I might have been guilty of—and believe me it gave me great pleasure to receive once more a letter in your own hand & in the same kind strain as ever—Now there's an end of that unpleasant affair—it is one of the few I have had to bear for I do not *willingly* give offence to any one & I hate quarrelling.

In concluding his article, Maginn had declared, 'One series of the true and genuine *Epistolae Hoggi* would be worth an acre of the imitative *Noctes Ambrosianae*', and Fraser now endorsed this suggestion.[36] Perhaps this was the origin of Hogg's *A Series of Lay Sermons*, a volume publication brought out by Fraser in April 1834, for internal evidence suggests that it was not written before 1833. On 25 January 1834 Hogg mentioned 'a volume of Sermons on good principles and good breeding now in the London press' to an American correspondent, and a sentence about the Ettrick Shepherd having 'commenced preacher' also appeared in *The Athenaeum*. In this highly personal and often autobiographical work, Hogg reclaims the Noctean Shepherd and portrays him as the Sage of Ettrick, a Man of the Mountains, the sober family man of Altrive, partly retired from his career as a poet but a firm advocate of both bodily and mental exercise to ensure a vigorous and happy old age. The Shepherd's foibles such as vanity are united with a disarming self-mockery, and in pushing the lay sermon towards a more colloquial oral discourse Hogg accompanies sage advice to his young friends of both sexes with some amusing anecdotes. The naïve sincerity of the Shepherd is favourably contrasted with the affectation and falsehood all too common in polite society, and Hogg invites the reader to join him in an intimacy that is like a conversation. Read without envy, Hogg instructs, but 'read to be pleased, and it is more than probable you will be so'.[37]

When Hogg's *Lay Sermons* was published in April 1834 reviewers praised 'the strong sense and keen acuteness which they display' and the 'originality and mother-wit of Ettrick'. Hogg's anecdotal Man of the Mountains persona was generally liked, though one orthodox Calvinist took exception to Hogg's remarking that young ladies should not read the biblical book of Leviticus since 'there are many of the injunctions so disgusting, that they cannot be read even by men'.[38] Hogg was rebuked for his presumption in censoring holy writ in a Glasgow pamphlet entitled *The Pope of the Border* (1834), an indication of how far Hogg's work was still criticised in Scotland for its occasional failure to conform to religious orthodoxy.

In April 1833 Hogg asserted in person what he had so often asserted in his written work, the right of Borders folk to share in the representation of Scottish history. The Selkirk silver arrow had originally been a competition prize designed to stimulate archery practice among local men, but its purpose had almost been forgotten when in 1818 Scott as county Sheriff invited the Royal Company of Archers to visit Selkirk to shoot for it. The Company then appear to have kept this historic object at their headquarters in Edinburgh (where it still is) and to have regarded it as a prize of their own, returning with the arrow to compete in Selkirk and socialise with the town magistrates again in 1823, 1828, 1830 and 1833 and taking the arrow back to Edinburgh with them afterwards on each occasion. Hogg, as an active and probably a founding member of the St Ronan's Bowmen of the Border, intervened on this last occasion. He had gone to the Selkirk magistrates and argued a case for the local ownership of the arrow, but been told that they were unwilling to take away the exclusive privilege granted to the Royal Company of Archers some years previously. Hogg then presented himself bow in hand on the ground where the competition was held but was informed that no-one but a member of the Royal Company could shoot for the Selkirk arrow. Wanting to persuade William Steuart of Glenormiston, Captain of the St Ronan's Bowmen of the Border, to take the matter up on behalf of the local archery club, Hogg argued:

> The silver arrow of Selkirk is quite an antique and presented to the Bowmen of the Border to shoot for annually. There are actually many shepherds' names and farmers' names on it more than 140 years ago so that the Edin[r] gentry have no more right to shoot for it than the archers of Hindoostan.

Hogg proposed a challenge match between the Royal Company ('jovial fine fellows') and the St Ronan's Bowmen, at which local talent would be vindicated and fellowship created between the two bodies. Although Hogg received no immediate satisfaction it is possible that his voice was heard, for two years later the Royal Company did return the arrow temporarily in response to the magistrates' decision 'to throw open the competition for the prize to persons who were not members of the Royal company'.[39]

Hogg's health that summer appears to have been variable. Although he told Steuart that his left hand was now too 'nervish and unsteady' for him to improve as an archer, he won the sweepstakes at the St Ronan's Border Games on 2 August. His memory failed him, however, in singing his own songs at the dinner that closed the first day of the games, his head 'not being very clear that evening'. Sir John Hay, in proposing Hogg's health turned this into a neat compliment when he said that it was an honour to the Ettrick Shepherd 'that he could never be at fault without finding two or three prompters'. Margaret Hogg now began to filter his extensive correspondence, as Hogg told John Macrone: 'It is very seldom that I read a letter now and far seldomer that I write one but Margaret reads them and then she say[TEAR] there are such and such letters that I *must* answer and then what can one do?'[40]

Financially, Hogg could now describe himself as 'fighting my way equally, though poorly', and for a time at least he left payments for copies of the subscription edition of *The Queen's Wake* in Lockhart's hands, hoping that eventually it might be possible to purchase him a small annuity. An urgent appeal to Lockhart to send him the money to avoid a multiple poinding at Altrive was the result of his having guaranteed a loan of £91 for one of his wife's nephews some six years previously. Young James was now twelve years old and since students entered Scottish universities in their early to mid-teens, the Hoggs were now considering the possibility of giving him a college education. The master of the little Mount Benger school who lived in Hogg's family and supervised his own children's education, Mr Park, was off to university himself in November and Hogg wondered whether to get a governess for his daughters and send young James to Edinburgh University. He was, however, very young, and Hogg admitted, 'I cannot bear to part with him nor do I think he could live in Edin^r without me'.[41]

William Laidlaw left Kaeside on the Abbotsford estate on 27 May, to spend a day or two with his relations in Yarrow before taking up his new post in the Highlands as a factor to Lord Seaforth. Though they might not often meet, Hogg wrote, 'we knew we had it in our power to see each other when we listed and the blank that Laidlaw's departure has left is one that cannot be made up to me'. Now he might never see his friend of more than forty years again. Lord Napier also abandoned Thirlestane Castle towards the end of the year when appointed chief superintendent of trade in China. At a dinner held at the Tushielaw Inn on 14 November to mark Lord Napier's birthday, Hogg with his songs, 'shrewd sayings, and good nature' officiated as croupier, and like all those present was 'much interested by the manly and becoming manner' in which Napier's fourteen-year-old son, Francis, returned thanks on behalf of his absent father.[42] Lord Napier did not return, dying of fever at Macau the following year.

Another cause of depression was the fate of George Bryden of Crosslee, son to the childhood benefactor whose death in 1799 Hogg had commemorated in his first publication of *Scottish Pastorals*. 'Such a curse hanging over such a good man's family', Hogg wrote, 'is a thing that can hardly be contemplated with resignation'. Bryden had got into financial difficulties by 1831, when an eight-year lease of the farm was issued to trustees for his mother. One of the trustees, James Bryden of Moodlaw, was a grasping man who marked the farm-stock with his own brand and allowed George nothing, telling him, 'Ye hae no right to gang like a gentleman thir. Ye sood gang like a beggar ath ye ir'. Hogg feared at times for his friend's sanity, but could not get the other two trustees, John Grieve and his half-brother, another George Bryden, to intervene. Hogg's heart was 'like to break about the Brydens of Crosslee'.[43]

Hogg's nephew Robert had suffered from a 'leaching throat' as early as December 1830. Now a married man with a baby daughter, Mary, who had been born in March 1833, Robert was no longer able to work as a corrector of the press in Edinburgh and had retired to his father's house at Stobohope in Peeblesshire. At the end of October he described his symptoms of 'constant expectoration and occasional vomiting of blood' to Hogg, the classic signs of tuberculosis, then termed consumption. Hogg thought him in 'a hopeless state' by November, even though from time to time he was well enough to be employed in occasional journalism for his friend Robert Chambers. Sadly, Robert Hogg died on 9 January 1834, only thirty-one years old, and Hogg went over to his brother's at Stobohope for the funeral. Hogg tried to find a publisher for an anthology entitled *Beauties of the Scottish Poets of the Present Day* that Robert had worked on, so that the proceeds should go to his young widow and child, but was not successful.[44]

Hogg's own literary fortunes were mixed that year. No progress seems to have been made by Fullarton towards publication of the edition of Burns that Hogg had prepared for the beginning of the year, and a paragraph in *The Athenaeum* of 17 August 1833 announced a comparable edition of Burns's works in six volumes, edited by Allan Cunningham and published by the Cochrane firm. Hogg alerted Fullarton in early September, urging prompt publication of his own edition. However, John Blackie Junior came to Altrive around the end of October, and an agreement was finally concluded with Blackie and Son for the publication of Hogg's prose tales, a project which eventually resulted in *Tales and Sketches by the Ettrick Shepherd* of 1836–37. Hogg had proposed sixteen volumes, which Blackies 'declined contrary to every rule of Grammar' and the set was to consist of six volumes only. On 11 November Hogg sent off a copy of *The Brownie of Bodsbeck; and Other Tales* of 1818 marked with his revisions and corrections, promising a similar copy of *Winter Evening Tales* within a month.[45] If the new series was to be advertised as *Winter Evening Tales*, Cochrane and Macrone might continue the old *Altrive Tales* series in London.

Hogg was well aware that he had long been a popular author in North America, and that, in the absence of an international copyright agreement, many of his works had been published there in pirated editions. His recent American visitors and correspondence with Robert Rose had increased that impression, and made him more aware of the American literary market. He 'expressed a desire to have a copy of each work' of his own that had been published in America, and even showed some interest in American authors such as Fitz-Greene Halleck (1790–1867), whom he termed 'a fine poet' and whose 'Burns' he included in his edition of Burns's works. Hogg heard that William Gowan of Chatham Street in New York wanted to publish his work, and through his communication with Bloodgood of Albany the first edition of Hogg's *Familiar Anecdotes of Sir Walter Scott* was published by the New York firm of Harper & Brothers in April 1834.[46]

Postal communications between Britain and America were still slow and uncertain. There was no Universal Postal Union until 1875, which meant that each of the three stages of a letter's journey must be assessed and paid for separately—to the coast of Britain, by ship across the Atlantic, and from the point of arrival on the North American coast. In both countries during Hogg's lifetime postage was calculated on the distance and the number of sheets of paper in the letter, and though postage was generally paid by the recipient, letters for America would need to be pre-paid as far as the coast to be conveyed at all. The official postal packets were hopelessly slow, expensive, and inefficient, and between 1826 and 1840 did not even land their letters in America but in Canada, from where they were generally forwarded in closed bags through Halifax in Nova Scotia. Communications had improved markedly, however, after 1818 with the start of regular packet services run by private shipping companies between New York and Liverpool. The Black Ball Line ships sailed to a schedule, with or without full cargoes, and were advertised as taking twenty-three days on the eastward voyage and forty-one going west against the prevailing winds, though actual journey times would be rather longer in the winter. By the 1830s scheduled transatlantic crossings were made by many rival companies sailing from Boston, New York, or Philadelphia, and there were crossings from New York to Liverpool leaving regularly on four days of every month in the year.[47] Hogg's Albany contacts, Sprague and Bloodgood, clearly gave him the address of an agent in Liverpool who would receive his letters and arrange for them to be taken aboard ship, and they presumably had adequate arrangements for the collection of his letters at New York and their onward transmission by the newly-installed steamboats on the Hudson River up to Albany.

Under these improved conditions Hogg felt that it might now be possible for him to write specifically for American periodicals, and on

25 January 1834 he sent Bloodgood some magazine contributions with a letter:

> I shall enclose you a tale and one or two ballads for your periodical and I think you may depend on the one or the other every month. But you have done wrong in not sending me your agent's name in Liverpool for I have lost both your's and Dr. Sprague's and I little wot whether this parcel will reach you or not. I have just finished No 1 of "Tales of father's and daughters" which I think I shall send you. No 2 you may expect the week following at which time I shall write again. [...] Let only one thing of mine appear in your periodical at once and if I am in health I shall try to keep going

Hogg's willingness to test the waters for American periodical publication of his work may also have been partly motivated by his wish to obtain news of family members in America or to provide them with useful contacts there. This letter to Bloodgood coincided with the emigration of Hogg's nephew-by-marriage James Gray to the United States just as his earlier transmission of his Scott anecdotes had coincided with his request for news of his brother Robert and his family. It continues virtually as a character reference for Gray, giving his employment history as a head clerk and expressing a wish that 'I could get him engaged in some respectable house amongst you'. A subsequent letter enclosing articles for Bloodgood of 24 March was largely concerned with the emigration prospects of the bearer, 'Mr James Gray the nephew whom I wrote so earnestly to you about lately'.[48]

In other respects Hogg's experiment was comparatively unsuccessful. Despite Bloodgood's eagerness to secure Hogg as a periodical contributor he does not seem to have been particularly efficient in getting his articles into print and most of them have never been discovered. The second of Hogg's 'Tales of Fathers and Daughters' was not published in Albany for well over a year after leaving Altrive, when it appeared in three instalments in the July to September 1835 issues of a new literary paper, *The Zodiac*. News of progress of the publishing of Hogg's Scott anecdotes was also slow in reaching Britain. Hogg commented to James Cochrane on 1 March 1834, 'It is strange that there is no word to you from Albany for there is something going on there', while Macrone reported on 23 June, 'We have heard nothing of Bloodgood since his first packet'.[49]

Hogg seems to have sent several pieces of his work to the United States during 1834, but to have been totally ignorant of their fate. On 5 February 1834 he described himself as having been 'very busy all

winter though to little purpose mostly writing for the American press'.
In November he told Alexander Blackwood that he had sent articles
rejected for *Blackwood's Edinburgh Magazine* 'off directly two to London
two to Dublin and two to America all of which will soon be followed
by others'. But by 5 September 1835 Hogg had largely abandoned his
attempt to write for the American market as unworkable:

> I find my literary correspondence with the United States so
> completely uncertain that I have resolved to drop it altogether.
> I learned from many sources that my brethren beyond the
> Atlantic were sincere friends and admirers of mine and I tried
> to prop several of their infant periodicals but I never yet could
> learn if any of my pieces reached their destination and I am
> convinced the half of them never did.

Hogg's experiment lasted for less than two years, and an extensive
and painstaking trawl of American periodicals by Janette Currie has
revealed only a handful of Hogg items that were not simply pirated
reprints from British periodicals or editions of Hogg's work. Moreover some of this handful appear to be based on manuscripts obtained
as souvenirs by American visitors to Hogg at Altrive rather than on
copy sent by Hogg for American publications.[50]

The real transatlantic trade was still in pirated reprints. Popular
authors found their British publications quickly reissued in pirated
American editions, and the process also worked in the other direction. Although Hogg had expressed a hope that publication of his
Scott anecdotes could be confined to America, Cochrane warned him
on 9 August 1833 that 'the work is sure to be imported—or reprinted
here within two months of its appearance in America'. His estimate
proved accurate, for *Familiar Anecdotes of Sir Walter Scott* was published in
New York in April 1834, and by June a pirated reprint had been produced in Glasgow under the title of *The Domestic Manners and Private
Life of Sir Walter Scott*.[51]

Lockhart had written to Hogg on 23 September 1833 regretting
his quarrel with William Blackwood, stating 'friends are dropping
so fast into the grave that we had need to think well before we suffer
estrangement to arise among those that survive'. He did not follow
his own advice, however, when he learned of the publication of
Hogg's Scott anecdotes in contradiction to the promise Hogg had
given to suppress them. Nothing has apparently survived of the no
doubt painful exchanges between the two men at this time, but
Lockhart made no secret of his angry feelings generally. 'He has
drawn his own character', Lockhart told Blackwood, 'not that of his

benevolent *creator*, and handed himself down to posterity—for the subject will keep *this* from being forgotten—as a mean blasphemer against all magnanimity'. Lockhart's anger unfortunately had an adverse effect on his portrayal of Hogg in his own Scott biography, where he tended to portray him as a lout graciously tolerated by Scott rather than as a devoted friend and admirer. While terming Hogg 'perhaps, the most remarkable man that ever wore the *maud* of a shepherd', Lockhart with great bitterness also wrote that 'he did not follow his best benefactor until he had insulted his dust'. Where Lockhart led the way, others undoubtedly followed, notably William Maginn in *Fraser's Magazine*. Cleverly, he realised that the Glasgow *Domestic Manners* enjoyed no copyright protection in Britain, and advertisements for the August 1834 issue of *Fraser's* indicated that the whole of 'the Shepherd's book' was reprinted in the magazine's review of it. *Fraser's* would not wish to denigrate its free gift of a very marketable Hogg work, but the previous month Maginn had mercilessly ridiculed another recent Hogg publication, *Lay Sermons*, even though it was published by the magazine's proprietor, James Fraser. Lockhart's letter to Blackwood notes that 'Dr Maginn has handled Hogg in his own way in "Fraser's Mag."'.[52]

A prospectus for Hogg's edition of the works of Robert Burns finally appeared in the Edinburgh newspapers in March 1834, and was accompanied by publication of the first of the twelve two-shilling parts of the new edition. The parts would eventually form five volumes costing five shillings apiece. Two engravings (the frontispiece and engraved title-page for the first volume) accompanied the first part, as an earnest of the twelve engravings that were to be included in all. Hogg's biographical essay was another key selling-point, a 'concise, luminous, and singularly interesting Memoir of the Poet's Life, from the pen of the Ettrick Shepherd, than whom there is not, perhaps, another to be found within the whole length and breadth of Scotland, better qualified to appreciate the character, sympathise with the feelings and associations, and to do justice' to Burns.[53]

There was however another such in England, Hogg's fellow peasant-poet Allan Cunningham, who was simultaneously engaged in publishing a rival edition of Burns in five-shilling volumes for Hogg's own London publishers, Cochrane and Macrone. Both editions sought to construct a poetic tradition leading from Burns to the present editors. Allan Cunningham's eighth and final volume included a section of poems in honour of Burns, and Hogg followed his biographical essay on Burns with a similar section of 'Poems Written in Memory of Burns' that concluded with his own 'Robin's Awa!'.[54]

The Scotsman, reviewing Cunningham's third volume and the first part of Hogg's projected edition on 26 March, argued that 'although Allan Cunningham has had the start of the Ettrick Shepherd, we have no doubt there is mental appetite enough in the country for the works now publishing by *both* these gifted individuals'. However, the influential *Fraser's Magazine* attacked Hogg's egotism, remarking that the first part of the edition had satisfied the reviewer entirely that 'Hogg has a complete contempt for Burns; and [...] as lofty an opinion of the Ettrick Shepherd as even our own warm partiality could have wished to see him expressing on such an occasion'. Cunningham's edition soon outpaced Hogg's. It was well advertised and reviewed, particularly through *The Athenaeum* in which Cunningham had an interest, and the volumes also appeared more regularly. The six advertised volumes of Cunningham's Burns were published mid-month in January, February, March, April, May, and June 1834, and were afterwards followed by two volumes of supplementary material on 30 September and 3 December 1834 respectively. In sharp contrast to the month-by-month advertisements in prominent journals for the rival Cunningham edition, the intervals at which Hogg's edition appeared are now unknown. Hogg's edition was still incomplete when sets of the eight-volume Cunningham edition were being advertised as 'prepared in every variety of elegant binding' as suitable gifts for Christmas 1834. Moreover, Cunningham's son Peter followed up his father's Burns with a two-volume companion work, *The Songs of England and Scotland*, published in a uniform binding. The second volume, relating to Scotland, was published in July 1835 and placed Cunningham rather than Hogg at the centre of the recording and creation of a Scottish song tradition.[55]

Criticism of Hogg as an unduly egotistical editor may have led Archibald Fullarton to appoint William Motherwell as co-editor of the edition of Burns he was publishing during 1834. While the prospectus and wrappers for the initial instalments name Hogg as sole editor, wrappers for later parts and the 'Address' prefacing the first volume specify the editors as the Ettrick Shepherd and William Motherwell. On 23 September 1834 Hogg forwarded to Motherwell 'all the papers belonging to Burns that I can find' following them up on 3 November with others sent to him by Sir Cuthbert Sharp of Sunderland. 'My coadjutor little Motherwell a genuine fellow has left out two thirds of all that I wrote for not being orthodox', Hogg grumbled, 'and I am sure there never were more honest notes put to a work in the world'.[56] For one reason or another publication of Fullarton's edition was not completed until 1836, after the deaths of both editors.

Both Hogg's projected series of collected prose fiction were also subject to frustrating delays during 1834. On 25 March he sent the Glasgow firm his fantastic tale of a man and his polar bear, 'The Surpassing Adventures of Allan Gordon', hoping 'you will allow that Robinson Crusoe is a mere joke to it', and commented on a sample page layout for what became *Tales and Sketches by the Ettrick Shepherd* but there was no indication of when publication would commence. Cochrane and Macrone seemed similarly reluctant to continue with *Altrive Tales*, and James Cochrane was now suggesting an edition of only 750 copies much to Hogg's indignation. He had plenty of unpublished stories, he told Cochrane on 1 March, 'but as for bereaving a dozen volumes of all the original matter for a poor shabby edition of 750!! O lord that will never go down with the old Shepherd! In one word', he added, 'The Altrive Tales must either go on as you and I commenced them with a vol every two or three months and an original tale to begin each vol. one sixth part of the clear profits to be mine else against my will I must change my publishers'. Whether Hogg knew it or not the remaining copies of the first volume of *Altrive Tales* were remaindered that summer, Stillies' Library on Edinburgh's High Street advertising copies of *Altrive Tales* from the London firm of F. J. Mason at three shillings and sixpence. Cochrane and Macrone were also stalling the production of the series of Montrose tales they had agreed to publish for Hogg during the preceding summer, probably because Cochrane was pressing Hogg to extend what had been a one-volume collection to two or even three volumes.[57]

The renewal of friendly relations with the Blackwood firm must indeed have been welcome. John Wilson reported to Hogg on 30 April that without 'asking either you or Mr. Blackwood, I have written a *Noctes*, in which my dear Shepherd again appears'. Hogg would be paid five guineas per sheet for the series in future, a sum which ought to bring him in fifty pounds a year besides what he might earn by his own contributions to the magazine. Wilson added, 'Let the painful in the past be forgotten, and no allusion ever made to it'. In the joyous 'Noctes Ambrosianae No. LXV' of May 1834 the Shepherd arrives at a meeting of the magazine's contributors at the Fairy's Cleuch and is gleefully and sentimentally welcomed back into the Blackwoodian fold. In real life it was not so easy to turn the clock back and return to the status quo of 1831. William Blackwood was now mortally ill, in severe and exhausting pain from cancer that summer, and incapable of attending to his business for months before his death on 16 September. The publishing firm and the conduct of the magazine was effectively in the hands of his elder sons, Alexander and Robert Blackwood, who had been gradually assuming control and establishing their own preferences and ways of doing business during the period of Hogg's estrangement from the firm. To them he was a figure from the past, an old-fashioned author they had known in childhood and adolescence. When reminded by Hogg, they were willing to continue providing the services that their father had done—sending paper, obtaining his shooting licence and so on—but Hogg soon became painfully aware that his own tales and poems were largely unacceptable as contributions to *Blackwood's Edinburgh Magazine*. 'I am exactly like an actor' he told Alexander Blackwood in November, 'who is engaged at a certain salary and yet performs by a substitute claiming the half of the real actor's profits. When I returned into your service I expected that one of my pieces should appear in Maga every month for the most part as usual'. In July 1835, still wistfully looking back to his former position as a valued contributor, Hogg declared, 'Though I am now excluded from the pages of Maga perhaps I may get a corner by and by'.[58]

While he was beginning to feel that his best days as a writer were behind him, however, Hogg had never been so pursued by celebrity hunters. That summer saw one of his rare explosions of temper when he received a long and expensive letter from a Liverpool autograph-hunter:

> As I think you must be a great green goose to make me pay double postage for such a foolish request I wont send you one of Sir Walter's letters nor the letters of any other body save your own ridiculous one which you shall pay for as dearly as I did. I had the postage of nine letters to pay this morning not one of them worth one farthing to me

Apart from some temporary anxiety about the health of his son, who was confined to bed for more than a week in May with pain and swelling in his joints, that summer was an unusually pleasant one. John Wilson rented Thirlestane Castle, eight miles off, from the absent Lord Napier and Hogg consequently enjoyed a great deal of his company, and that of his older children and their friends. Wilson, his twenty-two year old son of the same name, and his nephew James Ferrier (who was to marry Wilson's daughter Margaret in 1837) often joined Hogg in angling and other country sports. They would also call at Altrive en route from Edinburgh to Thirlestane. The Altrive tutor, Charles Marshall, recalled that when

Wilson heard on one such occasion that he had been preceded by an unwelcome visitor to Thirlestane he said, 'I wont go home to-night' and sat up with Hogg and his young assistant until midnight, drinking toddy and talking. Visits were frequently exchanged. On 3 July, for example, Hogg reported to Alexander Blackwood that the 'Professor and other three of them were here the day before yester-day. I am going over on Saturday to stay a few days'. The Hoggs also made one of their now rare joint visits to Edinburgh, to attend the wedding of Dr William Gray who had eventually found the wife he wanted in his seventeen-year-old cousin, Margaret Phillips. The couple were married on 22 July, shortly before the end of his furlough, at St James Episcopal Chapel in Broughton Place in Edinburgh.[59] It seems a brave decision for a teenage girl to marry a man twice her own age and leave familiar Edinburgh for Bombay.

Hogg's visits to Edinburgh were becoming infrequent now, and social occasions increasingly centred on the local towns of Peebles and Innerleithen. In January 1834 Hogg had attended a commemo-rative dinner on Robert Burns's birthday at Cameron's hotel in Peebles, not in Edinburgh. Cameron had created an artificial curl-ing rink at his Innerleithen establishment, by oiling a board surface, and that year's St Ronan's Border Games included a curling compe-tition as well as the usual athletics and archery contests. A dinner in Hogg's honour was held at his Peebles establishment on 19 August, stage-managed and organised by John Wilson. Acting as Chairman to a party consisting of Hogg's friends among the local gentry, Edin-burgh's professional class, and Dumfriesshire cronies such as John McDiarmid, Wilson proposed Hogg's health as a gifted individual who 'by the strength of his genius alone, had raised himself to emi-nence and fame, as one of the brightest of the Sons of Song', and 'begged to drink that length of days might gild the evening of life among the peaceful hills of [Hogg's] native Yarrow, whose classic stream had at his hands received a *second* immortality'. The song written for the occasion by Robert Gilfillan followed, portraying Hogg as Burns's successor. The Muse of Scotia lighting down in Ettrick laments that 'Robin Burns has fled awa" before taking up with Hogg, who sings of Mary, Queen of Scots 'Ere woe had dimm'd her face sae fair; | What Mary's Palace would hae been | Had tyrants never linger'd there'.[60]

Cameron also invited all those present to his other establishment at Innerleithen on the following day to curl on his artificial rink for a silver medal presented by himself. Hogg, of course, took part in the contest, watched 'by a great number of visitors, with whom this delightful village is at present very full', and sang some of his best songs at the dinner which succeeded it. He was clearly by this time something of a tourist attraction in the locality, as the canny Mr Cameron realised. He frequently sent Hogg home in a chaise to Altrive free of charge.[61]

John Macrone from London visited Scotland again that autumn, but Margaret Hogg would not allow him in the house at Altrive in the wake of the September break-up of his publishing partnership with James Cochrane. Mary Cochrane was generally thought to be a very beautiful woman, with dark eyes and hair and a graceful bearing, but while Hogg shared the general admiration of her he seems to have had reservations about her behaviour. When W. H. Harrison, who had met her on the stairs in calling on Hogg at Waterloo Place in London in 1832, remarked on her grace and beauty, Hogg had replied, 'Ou, ay, she is a douce, ladylike, and bonnie creature, but I dinna ken hoo it is, but she does not keep her maids for three days; she has changed them five times since I have been here'. Hogg may also have been aware of marital disputes, since in his farewell poem to her on his departure from London he urged her to 'let gratitude move | Your soul for the peace of the man that you love!' After Hogg had introduced John Macrone to Cochrane everyone noticed the attention the young man paid to Cochrane's wife, but as his manners to ladies generally were ingratiating no-one thought anything of it. Hogg, sending his compliments to the Cochrane family in a letter to Macrone of 12 May 1833, had joked, 'I would like to kiss Mrs Cochrane myself but I wont depute you so all that you have to do is to give my kindest love to her'. Allan Cunningham 'set down the attentions of Mac. to a sort of forwardness for which he was something conspicuous', and was therefore taken aback to receive a call one Sunday afternoon from a distracted James Cochrane who told him that 'Macrone the villain [...] had seduced his wife'. He had found fourteen letters from Macrone stitched into his wife's petticoats that made the adulterous relationship quite explicit.[62]

The aftermath of Cochrane's discovery exemplifies the sexual double standard. Cochrane obviously repudiated his wife who disappears from his correspondence altogether, his household in future consisting of his teenage daughter and younger sons alone. What became of her? Did she have a family to take in their disgraced relation or would she join the ranks of London's prostitutes? John Macrone, on the other hand, was to marry the daughter of Professor Bordwine of the East India Company's college at Addiscombe in Surrey the following January, which Allan Cunningham thought

would 'help his character a little for the family is very respectable'.
The bride was in all likelihood ignorant both of his adultery with
Mrs Cochrane, and the fact that the publishing business he set up in
nearby St James's Square after the ending of his partnership with
James Cochrane was partly financed by a five-hundred-pound loan
from Sophia Sala, an older woman whom he had been courting simultaneously. Cochrane and Macrone were now rivals for ownership of books they had published together and for the most saleable
authors on the previous firm's list. The acrimony on both sides was
such that Allan Cunningham in his letter to Macrone of 23 February
1835 told him, 'I think indeed that matters have been pushed quite
far enough, and that it would be well for both sides to let byganes be
byganes. [...] I *am resolved to be neutral* were it but for my own peace'.[63]
Hogg stuck by the injured husband, James Cochrane, and in doing
so lost the services of the more enterprising publisher. John Macrone
went on to publish the early works of Charles Dickens before his
untimely death in 1837.

As the year drew to a close Cochrane prepared to publish Hogg's
Tales of the Wars of Montrose, which was now to be a three-volume
work. Hogg had added two more tales, 'Julia M'Kenzie and 'Wat
Pringle o' the Yair' to his original collection of June 1833, and on 13
December he sent Cochrane a final story, 'Mary Montgomery'. As
'A Genuine Border Story' this had been set in the 1680s rather than
the 1640s when rejected by the Blackwood firm a few weeks previously. Cochrane wrote to Hogg on 26 December 1834, with evidence that progress was now being made, informing him that three
sheets had already been printed and that Allan Cunningham was
busy correcting the proofs on Hogg's behalf. It was finally published
at the end of March 1835.[64]

This late work, set in the Scottish civil wars of the 1640s, seems to
reflect Hogg's growing unease with political developments in the
early 1830s. It portrays a fragmented world of partisan intrigue and
civil unrest that all but destroy traditional social values. Archibald
Sydeserf, the eponymous protagonist and narrator of 'Some Remarkable Passages in the Life of an Edinburgh Baillie', reveals an incrimi-
nating intimacy with the sordid and calculating side of men and of
public events, and his religious principles undercut rather than rein-
force personal integrity. As factions manoeuvre Scotland is 'getting
into a state of perfect anarchy and confusion'. Hope for the future
nation lies not in public measures but in individual actions motivated by Christian principles. In saving a Royalist lady with her
helpless baby and nurturing them in his own family the hero of 'Wat

Pringle of the Yair' eventually effects a reconciliation between peasant and aristocrat, Covenanter and Royalist, since the baby nursed
by his daughter Jenny continues the affectionate relations thus established. He eventually marries one of Wat's grand-daughters and thus
becomes 'Jenny's son, in reality'.[65]

Although the magisterial *Times* pronounced the collection 'totally
unworthy of the reputation which from [Hogg's] former productions
it might be expected he should still support', other critics found much
to praise. The *Edinburgh Evening Post* pronounced, 'He has written
some of the best, and a few perhaps of the coarsest, fictions in the
language—fictions so like reality that we are apt to think them matters of plain fact. But this is genius, and Hogg is a genius of a high
order'. To the *Literary Gazette* the tales were 'national, picturesque,
and animated'. While Hogg's fiction was criticised for coarseness
and for failing to achieve a standard set by Sir Walter Scott, many
reviews evidence real enjoyment in reading it. Sales, however, were
poor, probably because Cochrane had over-priced it at a guinea and
a half. Hogg himself echoed the complaint of *The Times* that it had
been 'spun out into three volumes'. 'I think the wars of Montrose is
far too dear a work just now when cheap publications are all the
rage' he told Cochrane on 15 June, urging him to 'bring down the
price to the Trade'. He received an advance of fifty pounds in December 1834, and another twenty-five pounds subsequently. By June
1835, however, sales had stuck at about three hundred copies.[66]

Throughout his literary career Hogg had utilised old-fashioned
patronage as well as manipulating new developments in publishing.
A temporary revival in the fortunes of the Tory party now occurred
that might open up the possibility of official patronage for him. The
post-1832 Liberal government, led firstly by Earl Grey and then by
Lord Melbourne, had been threatened by barely-suppressed contentions between those who felt sufficient reform had now been delivered and those who understood the Reform Act to be the precur-
sor of further change. One effect of these divisions within the Liberal party had been to throw an unprecedented level of power into
the hands of the Irish nationalist politician Daniel O'Connell, whose
position as M.P. for County Clare was maintained by the 'Irish rent'
of penny membership fees from the Catholic Association, a body
whose ultimate goal was the dissolution of the 1801 Act of Union
and the creation of an independent Irish nation. O'Connell, as someone who had forced his way into the exclusive world of British politics by invoking the power of the masses and was dependent for his
income on public subscriptions, was anathema to the Tory party and

probably to many aristocratic Whigs as well. But by identifying himself with reform in general, O'Connell became the effective leader of a group of thirty-nine M.P.'s in the new parliament, and as the government was increasingly obliged to placate him Lord Melbourne's situation was difficult.[67]

Rumour credited Queen Adelaide with influencing the King on behalf of the Tories, and Hogg had published a little poem in her honour in the *Newcastle Journal* of 1 March 1834 terming her the 'Queen o' Hearts' and lamenting supposed attacks on her by leading government politicians. When Lord Melbourne was dismissed by William IV *The Times* of 15 November cited a private letter, which declared 'The Queen has done it all', a phrase subsequently placarded all over London. Sir Robert Peel, as Tory leader of the House of Commons, hastened back from a visit to Italy to try to form a new government. On 19 December he published his famous Tamworth Manifesto, promising moderate reform and outlining a new conservatism.[68] His new Tory ministry, however, could hardly work well with a parliament triumphantly elected in the aftermath of the passage of the 1832 Reform Act, and a general election was to be held early the following year.

At the general election held in January and February 1835 Hogg saw some of his own local Tory friends restored to seats they had lost in 1832. Alexander Pringle of Whytbank ousted Robert Pringle of Clifton as M.P. for Selkirkshire, while the Duke of Buccleuch's younger brother, Lord John Scott, took Roxburghshire from the reformer Captain George Elliot. Shortly after the elections Hogg heard gossip through a London correspondent that Pringle might even be invited to join Peel's new government. Tory gains in rural counties, however, were not reflected in the country as a whole, since the towns were on the whole solidly Liberal. Peel's majority had only increased by about a hundred, and the Tories were still in a minority in the House of Commons. Significantly, the election had further strengthened the negotiating position of Daniel O'Connell, who had stood for re-election on an anti-Tory platform of supporting reformers of every type except where they were in direct competition with his fellow repealers of the Irish Act of Union. He was now the leader of around sixty M.P.'s and held the balance of power in the House of Commons, a tremendously strong bargaining position as regards any future Liberal government and a serious threat to Peel's ability to remain in office. Hogg regarded him simply as a traitor, writing to Allan Cunningham on 9 March, 'I augur very bad things for our country my dear Allan but God grant that I may be mistaken I wonder that none of them ever think of impeaching O'Connal for high treason'.[69]

Peel's short-lived ministry, however, brought Hogg some direct financial gain. The Tory politicians with whom he had gaily socialised during his London visit three years previously remembered him kindly, and the Prime Minister himself sent a hundred pounds on 9 March. In his accompanying letter Peel wrote:

> I am afraid from what I hear, indeed from what I have heard I think from yourself, that you have not turned your Intellectual Labours to any great account in a pecuniary point of view—If this be the case, and if the inclosed will relieve you from one moment of Embarrassment or anxiety, you may accept it without incurring the slightest obligation to any one but to the King from whom no one can refuse a favour.

It was rumoured that Peel intended to turn this one-off donation into an annual pension, and he did in fact send Hogg a further sum (probably of £40) before Lord Melbourne returned to office that summer. Hogg returned thanks in one of his most entertaining letters. He admitted that though he had 'made a great deal all things considered' by his writing yet '"the sum of saving knowledge" or rather common sense seems to have been withheld'. He confided, 'as I have a fine family whom I dearly love and am straining every nerve to give them a proper education at no time of my life could your remembrance of me have chanced so opportunely for real benefit'. Hogg's interest now reinforced his political convictions in a sincere wish to keep the Tory ministry in office. In his letter of thanks he urged Peel, 'For God's sake keep hold of the helm and if his Majesty is obliged to appeal once more to his people the bare mention of the destructionists and *Catholicks* forcing themselves into the control of both Church and state will secure every true Englishman to your side'. Meantime Hogg determined to put the money he had received beyond his own control for the benefit of his family, and in April he took a trip to Edinburgh to place both 'nest-eggs in the nests' in the name of his fourteen-year-old son, James.[70]

Hogg's constitution was now weakening and he had passed the winter quietly at Altrive, even spending the gala anniversary of Robert Burns's birth of 25 January at home. John Forbes, on behalf of the Canongate Kilwinning Lodge of Freemasons, wrote to invite Hogg to become their poet laureate in succession to Burns, and to visit Edinburgh at their expense for the purpose of being intiated into the mysteries of the order. In his reply Hogg described himself as 'long past the age of enjoying Masonic revels' though proud to become 'nominally the Poet-Laureate of the Lodge', and he promised to write them 'some poetical trifle annually'. He was also absent from a dinner held in Innerleithen on 27 January to mark the birthday of the Earl of Traquair, when his health was drunk 'with the most rapturous applause, all expressing their deepest anxiety that he might be long spared to enjoy his favourite pastime of angling in the Ettrick and the Yarrow'. At the beginning of March Hogg was so ill with toothache that the painful swelling kept him to his bed for more than a week, and although the Yarrow Games were held at Mount Benger on 17 March newspaper reports fail to mention Hogg's participation as they generally did, so he may well have been absent. When he made his April visit to Edinburgh he was accompanied by Charles Marshall, the teacher and literary assistant who lived in his family. Marshall recalled many years later that during this visit they had 'walked through the great thoroughfares together, but so long a period had elapsed since he had been much in the metropolis, that with the exception of Robert Chambers, John Johnstone, and a few others, no one recognised him'. From David Watson's Harrow Inn in Candlemaker Row, Hogg wrote to Peel on 25 April to thank him for his kindness in sending him financial help ('it is past twelve and they keep devilish bad pens at my inn here'), concluding his letter with a charming 'rather tipsy But your's most affectionately' above the signature.[71]

'A Screed on Politics' was published in *Blackwood's Edinburgh Magazine* for April, only the second article by Hogg to appear in the magazine since his reconciliation with the Blackwood firm the previous May. Hogg continues his old pleas for kindliness and mutual respect between opposing parties and the dislike of fiery zeal he had expressed in many previous works, including *The Private Memoirs and Confessions of a Justified Sinner*, but his old trust in the common sense of the common people now seems strained. He alludes to 'the insolence of the many-headed monster' and appears to regret the universal obsession with political matters that properly concern only an elite:

> In most other countries there are not above ten or twelve persons of choice genius and long experience concerned in the management of the public affairs, while all the rest mind their business. But now in this country there is scarcely that number who mind their business, the bill having given them far higher matters to mind. [...] I believe, if children under two years of age could be understood by signs and syllables,

that every soul in the realm is at this day a politician.

With another dig at O'Connell as a fearsome demagogue, Hogg also regrets that in the eyes at least of his own party the 'most arrant traitor is at this period an ornament to the state and the age'. When writing his reminiscences of Sir Walter Scott two years previously Hogg had declared his belief that Scott 'entertained an oppressive dread on his mind of an approaching anarchy and revolution'. He may partly have expressed his own rising fear. Writing to Peel in April Hogg owned that he had 'thought these many years that you were the only man who stood between us and anarchy and confusion', a key phrase used also in his recently-published *Tales of the Wars of Montrose*.[72]

Although Hogg was no longer an important contributor to *Blackwood's* the appearances of the Noctean Shepherd ensured that many people thought that he was. James Cochrane, for instance, had requested Hogg on 26 December 1834 to see that *Tales of the Wars of Montrose* was 'announced in the Noctes forthwith, & while you are about it you might just say a kind word on our edition of Burns'. A mention in the Noctes, according to Cochrane, was 'worth all the advertisements in Scotland'.[73] He (presumably like others) was unaware that Hogg's part in the *Noctes* had always been limited to contributing a few songs.

Hogg continued, however, to be a valued contributor to *Fraser's Magazine*, where his own work was still appearing regularly. Writing to James Fraser on 14 September Hogg described the magazine as 'a capital work', stating that after comparing articles on a similar political topic in issues of the three leading Tory periodicals, the *Quarterly Review*, *Blackwood's Edinburgh Magazine*, and *Fraser's Magazine* he had adjudged 'the palm to Fraser'. Hogg's sense of membership of a coterie was also fostered by the engraving of Maclise's sketch of 'The Fraserians' accompanying the number for January 1835. This included Hogg at a party of the magazine's contributors, seated at a round table wearing his plaid and draining his glass with the rim wedged firmly over his nose. Although the portrait of Hogg is far from flattering, he was amused rather than offended by it:

> The Fraserians are a part of them capital. You are rather too black and burly. Why do you always make me such a demon? Damn the fellow! with the exception of old greasy deranged Coleridge I am the best looking old fellow of the whole group nay either young or old.

Any Tory buoyancy resulting from Peel's new government, however,

THE FRASERIANS.

was to be short-lived. The Liberals quickly reached an informal agreement with O'Connell in February known as the 'Lichfield House compact'. In return for supporting a Liberal government and suspending agitation for the repeal of the Irish Act of Union, O'Connell's views would be heeded with regard to Irish appointments and legislation affecting Ireland. Peel, no longer able to command a majority in the House of Commons, resigned on 8 April 1835. Hogg seems to have mistakenly regarded this as only a temporary reverse. On 14 May he told Peel, 'I have no dread of the motely and heterogeneous batch remaining in power but then heaven knows what evil they may do in a short space!' As late as September he wondered, 'Why do not all the Torys in the kingdom join in petitioning the King to call Peel to the helm? Without that measure we are ruined'.[74] In fact with his resignation of office in April 1835 Peel had entered a period of opposition that lasted up to 1841. Hogg's chance of an annual government pension had evaporated.

With the return of summer, however, Hogg's health improved and he resumed some of his social activities. The Canongate Kilwinning Lodge invited Hogg, since he would not come to Edinburgh, to join them and be appointed their poet laureate at a specially-constituted meeting at the Cleikum Inn in Innerleithen instead. Two of Hogg's friends among the lodge members fetched him by carriage to Innerleithen in May and returned with him on the following day. After his initiation there was a convivial dinner at which Hogg sung 'When the Kye comes Hame' and other favourites among his songs. In his speech of thanks Hogg declared himself deeply touched by the kindness of his friends in having travelled from Edinburgh to enroll him in succession to Robert Burns. He added, 'I have experienced great kindness from literary friends; indeed, I will do Burns the justice to say, that he had to struggle through far greater difficulty than myself, and, consequently, is entitled to higher praise'.[75]

Evidently Hogg was well enough for his wife to take Harriet into Edinburgh in June, partly for a consultation with Dr Crighton about the little girl's lameness but also to visit her friends and relations there. Writing to her the day after her departure, Hogg declared that he had had no heart to go to the annual meeting of the Pastoral Society of Selkirkshire in Yarrow after she had left him, but he evidently did go to a local wedding shortly after finishing his letter. On the following day he was fishing in St Mary's Loch and Yarrow, and on the next day again his friend Robert Boyd and one or two more members of the St Ronan's Club were at Altrive to dinner. Three-year-old Mary asked Hogg to tell her mother to 'bring her some sweet biksets' from Edinburgh, and insisted on sleeping with him and her brother James at night. Midsummer's Day saw Hogg over at Innerleithen to compete with fifteen other gentlemen for a St Ronan's Club curling medal on the artificial rink of Cameron's Inn among 'an immense concourse' of spectators, a match which was won by the innkeeper himself. A succeeding contest between 'the men of Auld Reekie and those of Tweeddale' was won by a single shot by the Edinburgh men, and Hogg begged for the replay at which the local men restored their lost honours. Hogg, supporting the chairman at the dinner that followed, took nine or ten tumblers of toddy before the party went outside again, to take advantage of prolonged daylight by fitting in another bout of curling, and then 'a few additional tumblers' were taken.[76] While his wife was away, Hogg was plainly inclined to forget his recent ill-health and indulge in late hours and convivial drinking.

At the St Ronan's Border Games held on 3 and 4 August, Hogg was one of the judges of the athletics as usual, acted as croupier at the dinners which succeeded each day's games and was re-elected to the Club's committee of management. He joined in the archery and curling matches as usual, and obviously was kept in a bustle of busy excitement since he lost his hat on the ground and had to write in to the Edinburgh hatter's firm of Grieve and Oliver shortly afterwards for a replacement. He also ordered two gallons of whisky from Selkirk to be sent up to Birkhill for his usual August shooting expedition and wrote to Walter Boa to expect him on the evening of 12 August, the first day of the season. Young James would accompany him to carry his bag for him. His son would not need a separate bed, but Hogg warned Boa that 'it is not unlikely that some gentleman or other may palm himself on me for a day or two'.[77]

Father and son set out from Altrive in the afternoon of 11 August for Birkhill, walking along St Mary's Loch as far as the little cottage at Cappercleuch where they spent the night. To Hogg's delight there was a terrific thunderstorm from about eight in the evening until one the following morning, and while it lasted Hogg lay on his side in bed looking out across the water, entranced. He told his son he would not have missed it for a good deal, for even as a child he loved to watch the lightning and listen to the thunder. According to the recollections of his teenage son, Hogg was often in this nostalgic frame of mind that summer. In July his father had asked for his company one day on horseback up to the heights that separate Douglas Burn from Traquair, past the old tower and farm of Blackhouse where he had served as James Laidlaw's shepherd for ten of the best years of his life. On their return from Birkhill in August, he sat down on a spot where he could see Ettrick church through an opening in the hills and remained there silently for about half an hour. In retrospect his son felt that the poet was taking a last look at the scenes of his childhood and youth.[78]

Though declaring that 'the fire of genius is beginning to flag' Hogg still sent his contributions to *Fraser's Magazine*, and he continued to express his anger and bewilderment at recent political developments. In September 1835 Daniel O'Connell spoke at a series of mass meetings in northern England and in Scotland urging reform of the House of Lords that had acted to frustrate reform so many times in recent years, particularly in connection with the rejection of two Irish bills concerning tithes and municipal reform. 'Had Sir Robert continued at the helm', Hogg wrote to Fraser, 'I was safe; but damn the insolent, scoundrelly Whigs, Papists, and Radicals!'[79]

He was also working on a 'small religious work', *The Young Lady's Sabbath Companion*, that he had proposed to James Cochrane in June. Designed to appeal to the purchasers of annuals and gift-books, it was to comprise three equal parts of hymns, religious poems, and prose lessons or prayers. Cochrane had promised to prepare it 'in the first style—suitable for the Drawing Room & Cabinet of every young lady in Britain' and had promised Hogg fifty pounds for an edition of one thousand copies. (The work was not, however, completed.) William Motherwell and Archibald Fullarton also came to Altrive to discuss the only partly-published edition of the life and works of Robert Burns.[80]

When Hogg visited Robert Boyd, however, for a few days' fishing in and around Innerleithen he had a sharp attack of illness. After dinner on the last evening of his stay, Hogg declared that he intended to drink no more than one tumbler of whisky toddy and would then call on Mr Cameron. While they waited for him to return from his Peebles to his Innerleithen establishment they began to play bagatelle. Suddenly 'poor Hogg was seized with a most violent trembling' and though a couple of glasses of brandy steadied him a little he could not write his name to an order on the Commercial Bank in Edinburgh that he wanted to send in by the carrier, and he returned home as soon as the Altrive caravan arrived for him at dusk. Like Hogg's son, Boyd too felt that Hogg may have realised that his days were numbered. When the caravan arrived, Boyd recollected, Hogg 'shook hands with me, not at all in his usual way, and at the same time stated to me, that a strong presentiment had come over his mind that we would never meet again', as indeed they never did.[81]

It soon became plain that Hogg was suffering from liver failure, though he was not quite sixty-five years old and came from a family of long-livers. Although Hogg had portrayed himself in later works such as *Lay Sermons* as an old man, he had lived as a young one and his age was often taken to be ten or twelve years less than it really was. After being kept to the house for some weeks, by 20 October Hogg was confined to bed with a bilious fever that greatly exhausted him and this was accompanied by fits of hiccuping that continued until he was almost senseless. Dr Thomas Anderson of Selkirk came, but could do little to relieve this distressing symptom. With his old habit of jesting at his misfortunes, Hogg remarked that it was a reproach to the medical faculty 'that they could not cure the hiccup'. Alexander Laidlaw of Bowerhope visited him daily from the time he was confined to bed and Tibbie Shiel helped Margaret Hogg to nurse him. Tibbie had been a maidservant to Hogg's mother decades earlier and (it was sometimes rumoured) one of his own early loves. In his final days he gave her a very personal keepsake, his silver pocketwatch. As he lay in bed in a state of weakness his mind must have reverted often to the early days of his youth and vigour, for one day he said to his son (despite the college education that had been planned for him), 'James, I would like to see you a shepherd, as your father was before you. You might be happier in that than in any other profession'.[82]

Before mid-November his family had begun to fear the worst, but though Hogg was aware of his danger he was reluctant to have his friends informed of it. The bilious fever had turned to jaundice and on 12 November Alexander Laidlaw sent a notice to the *Glasgow Courier*, which announced five days later:

> With deep regret we announce that our National Bard, the Ettrick Shepherd, has for some time been in a very delicate state of health. For the last three weeks he has been constantly confined to bed, and at this moment his health is considered to be still in a very perilous state.

At the time this paragraph appeared Hogg was incapable of speech, and two days later Alexander Laidlaw decided not to return to Bowerhope: his old friend's death was expected hourly, and he barely left the room where Hogg's life was slowly ebbing.[83] James Hogg the Ettrick Shepherd died at noon on Saturday, 21 November.

Epilogue

It is hardly surprising that even with his robust constitution Hogg should have worn himself out at a relatively early age, for neither his nature nor his life were tranquil ones.

Hogg considered 'a certain keenness of disposition, prompting to the most active exertions, as the first ingredient in the happiness of man' and he defined happiness as 'the mind and the object in full possession of one another. A man's life will be always pleasant, if he enter with all his heart and soul into the concerns of it'.[1] He rightly described his own disposition as ardent, tending to pour energy and concentration into the moment and to become absorbed in a favourite pursuit to the exclusion of all other considerations. He would be the life and soul of the party, mixing jugs of toddy, laughing, telling stories, and performing his songs for hours on end. If he played his fiddle for the dancing at a wedding the dancers would be hard put to it to keep time with the motions of his bow, and he would wake the next morning in a state of dehydration. When pursuing his favourite sports he would be in the water and over rough ground, competing with young men half his age, eager to win the prize at archery, curling, or angling. A fierce determination underlay this ability to focus. As a boy, Hogg was not discouraged by frequent defeats in races with older and stronger boys or by the difficulties of mastering a violin with no teacher and few opportunities to practice, and as an adult he asserted his own talent and persistence as a writer against those of men of education and means until he had achieved the fame he knew he merited.

Hogg never acquired the self-preservation that generally grows with age and was inclined to be reckless both with his money and his health, leaning on the staying-power of his talent and his robust constitution to the end. At his death his wife and five children were left destitute, but were protected from the worst hardships by the legacy of his fame. The Duke of Buccleuch allowed Hogg's widow an annual sum in lieu of the house at Altrive, and a committee of concerned friends organised a public subscription to provide for her maintenance and the education of Hogg's children, followed years afterwards by a modest public pension.

Hogg's life took place between worlds, that of the labouring-class community into which he had been born and that of the professional literary men where his talent and determination placed him. He was born into a traditional oral culture and lived to see the beginnings of a mass culture, of a widening franchise and cheap penny papers. He told of ancient superstitions and social customs by means of the latest developments in print culture and publishing, and died only shortly before the age of the photograph. Of his many friends perhaps only Allan Cunningham, Dumfriesshire stone-mason turned professional author, shared this experience precisely. It was a life of contradictions, the friend of radicals like James Gray becoming a mainstay of Toryism, a man who was proud to declare himself a shepherd clinging to a middle-class lifestyle while failing to conserve the funds to support it, an apparently careless soul whose determination was so powerful that it can even appear slightly deranged.

His writing was the natural expression of this double vision, with its multiple viewpoints and rapid and unpredictable shifts of tone. His contemporaries read it with enjoyment but also with puzzlement or frustration and following his death and the successive appearance of increasingly bowdlerised editions, it fell into obscurity though it was never entirely obscured. Within Scotland his songs, his covenanting tale of *The Brownie of Bodsbeck* and the mysterious and other-worldly 'Kilmeny' of *The Queen's Wake*, continued to be read and enjoyed. That redoubtable Edinburgh schoolmistress of the 1930s, Miss Jean Brodie, for example, reads 'Kilmeny' to her pupils. A revival of Hogg's reputation occurred in the totalitarian twentieth century, with the publication of a new edition of *The Private Memoirs and Confessions* in 1947 introduced by André Gide. (All mankind had recently been reminded what inhumanities we are capable of when in thrall to an idea.) New and unbowdlerised editions of Hogg's work began to follow this, gradually at first and then, with the publication of the Stirling/South Carolina Research Edition of the Collected Works, regularly and systematically. The instabilities and uncertainties of Hogg's work, so unsettling to the Victorians, are now increasingly attractive and interesting though no more comfortable than ever they were. He is now viewed as one of the most important Scottish Romantics but also inspires the work of living writers. Among this creative family is one writer who also shares some of his genes: Alice Munro's *The View from Castle Rock* commemorates the emigration to North America in 1818 of James Laidlaw, her own ancestor and Hogg's first cousin.

Sources and Abbreviations

Detailed sources for this biography will be found in the Reference Notes, where the following abbreviations are used for frequently quoted sources. Wherever possible Hogg's own writings are referred to in the multi-volume Stirling/South Carolina Research Edition of the Collected Works of James Hogg (S/SC), of which nineteen volumes have been published by Edinburgh University Press since 1995.

Hogg's letters are in process of publication in three volumes as *The Collected Letters of James Hogg*, of which two volumes have now been published, covering the period to 1831. Wherever possible references to Hogg's correspondence are to this edition, but for the final four years of his life letters have been referenced individually from original manuscripts or first printings.

I owe a considerable debt to previous biographical works on Hogg, by his descendants Mary Gray Garden and Norah Parr, and also to Alan Lang Strout, whose *The Life and Letters of James Hogg, The Ettrick Shepherd: Volume 1 (1770–1825)* was published by Texas Technological College Press in 1946 and whose unpublished typescript for a second volume survives in NLS, MS 10495. Karl Miller's wonderfully-written, *Electric Shepherd: A Likeness of James Hogg* (Faber and Faber, 2003; paperback, 2005), gives an unrivalled picture of Hogg's dealings with literary Edinburgh.

Abbreviations for Works by Hogg

1802 HJ 'A Journey Through the Highlands of Scotland, in the Months of July and August 1802', *SM*, 64 and 65 (October, December 1802; February, April, May, and June 1803), 813–18, 956–63; 89–95, 251–54, 312–14, 382–86, and the previously unpublished portion edited by Hans de Groot in *SHW*, 6 (1995), 55–66

1803 HJ 'Unpublished Letters of James Hogg, the Ettrick Shepherd', *Scottish Review*, 12 (July 1888), 1–66, and the previously unpublished transcript of another portion edited by Hans de Groot as 'Hogg in the Hebrides in 1803', *SHW*, 13 (2002), 143–80

1804 HJ 'A Journey Through the Highlands and Western Isles, in the Summer of 1804', *SM*, 70 and 71 (June, August, September, October, November, and December 1808; January, February and March 1809), 423–26, 569–72, 672–74, 735–38, 809–11, 889–92; 14–17, 99–101, 181–84

Anecdotes *Anecdotes of Scott*, edited by Jill Rubenstein (S/SC, 1999) [paperback, 2004]

Annuals *Contributions to Annuals and Gift-Books*, edited by Janette Currie and Gillian Hughes (S/SC, 2006)

AT *Altrive Tales*, edited by Gillian Hughes (S/SC, 2003) [paperback 2005]

Brownie *The Brownie of Bodsbeck; and Other Tales*, 2 vols (Edinburgh, 1818)

Burns *The Works of Robert Burns*, edited with William Motherwell, 5 vols (Glasgow, 1834–36)

Confessions *The Private Memoirs and Confessions of a Justified Sinner*, edited by P. D. Garside (S/SC, 2001) [paperback 2002]

Dogs 'Further Anecdotes of the Shepherd's Dog', *Blackwood's Edinburgh Magazine*, 2 (March 1818), 621–26

FMinstrel *The Forest Minstrel*, edited by P. D. Garside and Richard D. Jackson, with Peter Horsfall (S/SC, 2006)

Frasers 'The Frasers in the Correi', *Fraser's Magazine*, 9 (March 1834), 273–78

G&A 'Anecdotes of Ghosts and Apparitions. I. David Hunter and Phemie. II. Robert Armstrong and Kennedy', *Fraser's Magazine*, 11 (January 1835), 103–12

Highlander 'A Tale of An Old Highlander', *The Metropolitan*, 3 (February 1832), 113–20

JR1 *The Jacobite Relics of Scotland. [First Series]*, edited by Murray G. H. Pittock (S/SC, 2002)

JR2 *The Jacobite Relics of Scotland. Second Series*, edited by Murray G. H. Pittock (S/SC, 2003)

Letters, I *The Collected Letters of James Hogg Volume 1 1800–1819*, edited by Gillian Hughes. Associate Editors Douglas S. Mack, Robin MacLachlan, and Elaine Petrie (S/SC, 2004)

Letters, II *The Collected Letters of James Hogg Volume 2 1820–1831*, edited by Gillian Hughes. Associate Editors Douglas S. Mack, Robin MacLachlan, and Elaine Petrie (S/SC, 2006)

LS *A Series of Lay Sermons on Good Principles and Good Breeding*, edited by Gillian Hughes with Douglas S. Mack (S/SC, 1997)

Mador *Mador of the Moor*, edited by James E. Barcus (S/SC, 2005)

MB1807 *The Mountain Bard* (Edinburgh, 1807)

MB1821 *The Mountain Bard* (Edinburgh, 1821)

Napier 'The Honourable Captain Napier and Ettrick Forest', *Blackwood's Edinburgh Magazine*, 13 (February 1823), 175–88

NM Lantern 'Nature's Magic Lantern', *Chambers's Edinburgh Journal*, 28 September 1833, 273–74

Peasantry 'On the Changes in the Habits, Amusements, and Conditions of the Scottish Peasantry', *Quarterly Journal of Agriculture*, 3 (1831–32), 256–63

Pilgrims *The Pilgrims of the Sun; A Poem* (London and Edinburgh, 1815)

PW *The Poetical Works of James Hogg*, 4 vols (Edinburgh, 1822)

QB *A Queer Book*, edited by P. D. Garside (S/SC, 1995)

QH *Queen Hynde*, edited by Suzanne Gilbert and Douglas S. Mack (S/SC, 1998)

QW *The Queen's Wake A Legendary Poem*, edited by Douglas S. Mack (S/SC, 2004) [paperback, 2005]

SC *The Shepherd's Calendar*, edited by Douglas S. Mack (S/SC, 1995) [paperback, 2002]

SG *The Shepherd's Guide: Being a Practical Treatise on the Diseases of Sheep* (Edinburgh, 1807)

Songs 1831 *Songs by the Ettrick Shepherd* (Edinburgh, 1831)

SP *Scottish Pastorals Poems, Songs, &c. Mostly Written in the Dialect of the South*, edited by Elaine Petrie (Stirling: Stirling University Press, 1988)

Spy *The Spy: A Periodical Paper of Literary Amusement and Instruction*, edited by Gillian Hughes (S/SC, 2000)

Stats. 'Statistics of Selkirkshire', *Prize Essays and Transactions of the Highland Society of Scotland*, 9 (1832), 281–30

TPW *The Three Perils of Woman*, edited by David Groves, Antony Hasler, and Douglas S. Mack (S/SC, 1995) [paperback, 2002]

TWM *Tales of the Wars of Montrose*, edited by Gillian Hughes (S/SC, 1996) [paperback, 2002]

VR Sermon 'A Very Ridiculous Sermon', *Fraser's Magazine*, 11 (February 1835), 226–31

WET *Winter Evening Tales*, edited by Ian Duncan (S/SC, 2002) [paperback 2004]

Abbreviations for Other Printed Sources

1791 SA *The Statistical Account of Scotland 1791–1799*, edited by Donald J. Withrington and Ian R. Grant, 20 vols (Wakefield: EP Publishing, 1973–1983)

1845 SA *The New Statistical Account of Scotland*, 15 vols (Edinburgh, 1845)

BibP Douglas S. Mack, *Hogg's Prose: An Annotated Listing* (Stirling: The James Hogg Society, 1985)

BibV Gillian Hughes, *Hogg's Verse and Drama: A Chronological Listing* (Stirling: The James Hogg Society, 1990)

Anderson William Anderson, *The Scottish Nation*, 3 vols (Edinburgh, 1865)

Brock Michael Brock, *The Great Reform Act* (London: Hutchinson, 1973)

Chambers *Memoir of Robert Chambers with Autobiographic Reminiscences of William Chambers* (Edinburgh, 1872)

Corson James C. Corson, *Notes and Index to Sir Herbert Grierson's Edition of the Letters of Sir Walter Scott* (Oxford: Clarendon Press, 1979)

Cosh Mary Cosh, *Edinburgh: The Golden Age* (Edinburgh: John Donald Publishers, 2003)

Craig-Brown T. Craig-Brown, *The History of Selkirkshire or Chronicles of Ettrick Forest*, 2 vols (Edinburgh, 1886)

Dibdin James C. Dibdin, *The Annals of the Edinburgh Stage* (Edinburgh, 1888)

Garden Mary Gray Garden, *Memorials of James Hogg, the Ettrick Shepherd* (Paisley, n. d.)

Gillies 'Some Recollections of James Hogg', *Fraser's Magazine*, 20 (October 1839), 414–30

GilliesLV R. P. Gillies, *Memoirs of a Literary Veteran*, 3 vols (London, 1851)

Goldie George Goldie, *A Letter to a Friend in London* (Edinburgh, 1821)

Gordon Mary Gordon, *'Christopher North': A Memoir of John Wilson*, 2 vols (Edinburgh, 1862)

Grierson *The Letters of Sir Walter Scott*, edited by H. J. C. Grierson and Others, 12 vols (London, 1932–37)

Groves David Groves, *James Hogg and the St Ronan's Border Club* (Dollar: Douglas S. Mack, 1987)

Harris Stuart Harris, *The Place Names of Edinburgh Their Origins and History* (Edinburgh: Gordon Wright Publishing, 1996)

Howitt William Howitt, *Homes and Haunts of the Most Eminent British Poets*, 2 vols (London, 1847)

Johnson Edgar Johnson, *Sir Walter Scott: The Great Unknown*, 2 vols (London: Hamish Hamilton, 1970)

Lockhart John Gibson Lockhart, *Memoirs of the Life of Sir Walter Scott, Bart.*, 7 vols (Edinburgh, 1837–38)

Miller Karl Miller, *Electric Shepherd: A Likeness of James Hogg* (London: Faber and Faber, 2003) [paperback 2005]

Minstrelsy Walter Scott, *Minstrelsy of the Scottish Border*, second edition, 3 vols (Edinburgh, 1803)

Morrison John Morrison, 'Random Reminiscences of Sir Walter Scott, of the Ettrick Shepherd, Sir Henry Raeburn, &., &c.', *Tait's Edinburgh Magazine*, 10 (September and October 1843), 569–78, 626–28

Oliphant Margaret Oliphant, *William Blackwood and His Sons: Their Magazine and Friends*, 2 vols (Edinburgh, 1897)

Parr Norah Parr, *James Hogg At Home: Being the Domestic Life and Letters of the Ettrick Shepherd* (Dollar: Douglas S. Mack, 1980)

PL John Gibson Lockhart, *Peter's Letters to His Kinsfolk*, 3 vols (Edinburgh, 1819)

Particulars 'Some Particulars Relative to the Ettrick Shepherd', *New Monthly Magazine*, 46 (February, March, and April 1836), 194–203, 335–42, 443–46

Riddell Henry Scott Riddell, 'James Hogg, the Ettrick Shepherd', *Hogg's Weekly Instructor*, 7, 14, and 21 August 1847, pp. 369–74, 386–92, and 403–09

Rogers Charles Rogers, *The Modern Scottish Minstrel*, 6 vols (Edinburgh, 1855–57)

Russell James Russell, *Reminiscences of Yarrow* (Edinburgh, 1886)

Stoddart Thomas Tod Stoddart, *An Angler's Rambles and Angling Songs* (Edinburgh, 1866)

T & B William B. Todd and Ann Bowden, *Sir Walter Scott: A Bibliographical History 1796–1832* (Newcastle, DE: Oak Knoll Press, 1998)

Trotter *East Galloway Sketches: or Biographical, Historical, and Descriptive Notices of Kirkcudbrightshire* (Castle Douglas, 1901)

Z 'Z.', 'Farther Particulars of the Life of James Hogg, the Ettrick Shepherd',

Scots Magazine, 67 (July and November 1805), 501–03 and 820–23

Abbreviations for Periodicals and Newspapers

BEM *Blackwood's Edinburgh Magazine*

CM *Caledonian Mercury*

D & GC *Dumfries and Galloway Courier*

EEC *Edinburgh Evening Courant*

EEP *Edinburgh Evening Post*

ELJ *Edinburgh Literary Journal*

EWJ *Edinburgh Weekly Journal*

FM *Fraser's Magazine*

PE & T *Prize Essays and Transactions of the Highland Society of Scotland*

QJA *Quarterly Journal of Agriculture*

QR *Quarterly Review*

SHW *Studies in Hogg and his World*

SM *Scots Magazine*

Abbreviations for Manuscript Sources

ATL Alexander Turnbull Library, Wellington, New Zealand

Beinecke Beinecke Rare Book and Manuscript Library, Yale University (Unless any other collection is noted, reference is to the James Hogg Collection, GEN MSS 61.)

BL British Library

EUL Edinburgh University Library

Laidlaw Manuscript reminiscences of Scott by William Laidlaw, in EUL Special Collections, MS Laing II. 281/2. A not entirely accurate transcript was published in the *Transactions of the Hawick Archaeological Society* for 1905, pp. 66–74

NLS National Library of Scotland

NRA(S) National Register of Archives for Scotland

OPR Old Parish Register

SUL Stirling University Library

WH Two letters by William Hogg to James Gray, in the James Hogg Collection, Beinecke Rare Book and Manuscript Library, Yale University, GEN MSS 61, Box 1, Folder 19. The first of 20 November 1813 is the original (referred to as A), and the second a copy of a follow-up letter (referred to as B). They were edited and reprinted by a Gray relative in Particulars, pp. 445–46, where the second is dated 12 December 1813.

Reference Notes

Chapter One: The Days of Vision

1. *1791 SA*, III, 678.
2. Alexander Laidlaw, see Garden, p. 4.
3. See Hogg's account of Ettrick Forest in NLS, Acc. 11232, p. 3.
4. *Letters*, I, 48; *MB1807*, pp. 50–67; *QW*, pp. 183–84.
5. Birth, marriage and death information from the OPRs of the places mentioned, substantially researched by Hogg's descendant David Parr for family notes on 'James Hogg and his Descendants' in June 2000; WH, A, fol. 1; Russell, p. 20.
6. Laidlaw, p. 23; *SC*, p. 18.
7. WH, A, fol. 1; *WET*, pp. 183, 98–99.
8. *SC*, pp. 103–12; WH, A, fol. 1.
9. Ettrick OPR; WH, A, fol. 1.
10. *MB1807*, p. 164.
11. The grave of Hogg's parents in Ettrick churchyard, according to the headstone, includes 'three of their sons', none of the four known children being buried there; *SC*, p. 111; *WET*, p. 144.
12. *Annuals*, p. 217; Robert Hogg married Elizabeth Oliver on 11/1/1807, and David Hogg married Elinor Oliver on 14/1/1810 (Yarrow OPR); WH, B, fol. 1.
13. WH, A, fols 1–2; *AT*, p. 13.
14. WH, A, fol. 1; *AT*, p. 12.
15. *SC*, p. 40.
16. *AT*, pp. 12–13; Z, p. 501; Gillies, p. 415.
17. *AT*, p. 12; *SP*, pp. 25, 27; JH to Janet Laidlaw, 4/11/1833, Queen's University Archives, Kingston, Ontario, Miscellaneous Collection, Locator #2999, James Hogg *fonds*.
18. *SC*, pp. 35–36, 41–43; VR Sermon, pp. 226–27.
19. *AT*, pp. 13–14; *Brownie*, II, 228.
20. *WET*, pp. 500, 508.
21. *JR1*, pp. 283–84; *EWJ*, 24/11/1819; *MB1807*, p. xii; *JR2*, p. 357; *Annuals*, p. 65.
22. WH, B, fol. 1; *SG*, pp. 59–60, 79–80; Z, p. 502; *Annuals*, p. 63.
23. Letter from James Hogg junior to Alexander Laidlaw, in Laidlaw's Scrapbook, p. 110, owned by Mrs Doreen Mitchell; JH to Unknown, 27/10/1833, *Notes and Queries*, fifth series, 10 (1878), p. 386; *LS*, p. 62; Dogs, pp. 622–23.
24. Peasantry, pp. 261–62; Z, p. 501; Riddell, p. 372.
25. Craig-Brown, I, 368; William Scott's settlement registered on 17/6/1816 (Peebles Commisary Court Records, National Archives of Scotland, CC/18/4/8, pp. 46–54; information from Richard Jackson).
26. Peasantry, pp. 258–59; Z, pp. 501–02; *MB1807*, p. vii; WH, B, fol. 1; *SP*, p. 1.
27. *LS*, p. 74; *EEC*, 26/3/1818; 'On the Hiring Markets in the Counties of Northumberland, Berwick, and Roxburgh', *QJA*, 5 (1834–35), 379–

86 (p. 382); Sir George Steuart Mackenzie, *A Treatise on the Diseases and Management of Sheep* (Edinburgh, 1809), pp. 110, 112, 113; *Songs 1831*, pp. 224–27.

28. *SC*, pp. 43–44.
29. *Letters*, I, 70, 367–68; *AT*, p. 25; Peasantry, p. 262. James Laidlaw's surviving accounts in NLS, Acc. 9084/8 include a note of sums paid to 'James Hogg my Servant' for lambs on 18 December 1793 and 27 December 1794.
30. *SC*, pp. 96–97; *LS*, p. 74; Z, p. 502; *SC*, p. 119; NM Lantern, p. 274.
31. Highlander, p. 113; Peasantry, pp. 262, 257; *WET*, p. 197.
32. Garden, pp. 21–22; *Letters*, I, 426; *WET*, pp. 166–228.
33. *TPW*, p. 128; Stats., pp. 295–96; *Anecdotes*, p. 38.
34. Napier, pp. 178–79; Stats., pp. 295–96.
35. *AT*, p. 16; WH, B, fol. 1.
36. WH, B, fol. 1; *AT*, p. 16; William Laidlaw (by T. W. Baynes rev. Gillian Hughes) in *Oxford DNB*; Garden, p. 24; Chambers, pp. 60–62.
37. *SC*, pp. 5, 15–19; John MacQueen, *The Rise of the Historical Novel* (Edinburgh: Scottish Academic Press, 1989), pp. 207–08.
38. Garden, p. 328; *SG*, pp. 168, 50; Dogs, p. 625.
39. JH, 'On the Preservation of Salmon', *QJA*, 3 (1831–32), 441–49 (pp. 444–45); see *Letters*, I, 2 for information on Alexander Laidlaw; William John Napier acknowledges information received from 'a most intelligent shepherd, Alexander Laidlaw of Bowerhope' in his Dedication to *A Treatise on Practical Store-Farming* (Edinburgh, 1822), p. vii; *1845 SA*, III, 41; Stats., pp. 304–05.
40. NM Lantern, p. 273; *SC*, p. 10; JH, 'Aunt Susan', *FM*, 3 (July 1831), 720–26 (p. 724); *MB1807*, p. 26.
41. Dogs, pp. 623, 626.
42. Z, pp. 502–03; *AT*, p. 17; *MB1807*, pp. xi, xii–xiii.
43. John Ballantyne, 'Hogg's Role in *The Scotch Gentleman*', *SHW*, 16 (2005), 131–33.
44. Z, pp. 820–21; *AT*, p. 19.
45. *Burns*, I, 203. There is another account of the same episode in *AT*, p. 17–18; *Autobiography of John Younger* (Kelso, 1881), p. 121.
46. Riddell, p. 372; *MB1807*, p. xiii; *AT*, p. 18.
47. Cosh, pp. 3–14; Harris, pp. 287, 462–64; *SC*, pp. 85, 87.
48. WH, B, fol. 2; *LS*, p. 106; Frasers, p. 273; 1802 HJ, p. 813; G&A, pp. 111–12.
49. Z, p. 821; *AT*, p. 20.
50. *AT*, p. 16; birth and marriage details from Ettrick OPR.
51. *SC*, pp. 116–17; 'Account of Mr Bryden', *PE & T*, 3 (1807), 533–35, and *Letters*, I, 450–51; *WET*, pp. 402, 406–09.
52. *Letters*, I, 5–6; Z, p. 821.
53. *WET*, pp. 166–228; *Songs 1831*, p. 191; *SC*, p. 61.
54. *SC*, p. 62.
55. See *Letters*, I, 6–11 for Hogg's literary confidants; *MB1807*, p. xix; *SP*, pp. 56, and Petrie's Introduction, especially pp. xi–xiii; *AT*, p. 21.
56. *SP*, pp. 35, 2, vii.
57. *The Oxford Companion to Scottish History*, ed. by Michael Lynch (Oxford:

Oxford University Press, 2001), pp. 249–50; *SP*, pp. 8–9; Dogs, pp. 625–26.

58. *Letters*, I, 9–11, 13, 39; *EEC*, 5/2/1801 and 9/2/1801.

Chapter Two: The Broken Ground

1. Andrew Mercer to Robert Anderson, 22/5/1801, NLS, Adv. MSS 22. 4. 11, fols 52–53.
2. Peter Garside, 'Editing *The Forest Minstrel*: The Case of "By a Bush"', *SHW*, 13 (2002), 72–94 (pp. 74–75); Mercer to Laidlaw, [5]/6/1802, NLS, Acc. 9084/9.
3. Garside, 'Editing *The Forest Minstrel*'; for 'Sandy Tod' see Miller, pp. 42–55; David Stuart M. Imrie, 'The Story of "The Scots Magazine"', *SM*, 30 and 31 (January, February, March, April and June 1939), pp. 269–74, 341–49, 445–52, 51–58, 141–50 (pp. 348–49); T & B, p. 19.
4. Johnson, I, 190, Laidlaw, pp. 4–8, 15.
5. *Letters*, I, 15; 1802 HJ, pp. 961, 313.
6. Garside, 'Editing *The Forest Minstrel*', pp. 74–77; Richard D. Jackson, 'Sir Walter Scott's "First" Meeting with James Hogg', *SHW*, 17 (2006), 5–18.
7. For Hogg's account see *AT*, pp. 60–65, based on 'Reminscences of Former Days. My First Interview with Sir Walter Scott', *ELJ*, 27 June 1829, pp. 51–52, and subsequently modified in *Anecdotes*, pp. 37–40.
8. Laidlaw, pp. 20–22; 'Lines to Sir Walter Scott, Bart.', *PW*, IV, 133–40 (p. 137); *AT*, pp. 60–61.
9. Laidlaw, p. 24; *AT*, pp. 62–63.
10. 'The Cutting o' My Hair', *BEM*, 28 (August 1830), 406; *SC*, p. 104; Riddell, pp. 374, 407–08; 'Letter from the Ettrick Shepherd', *BEM*, 6 (March 1820), 630–32.
11. Grierson, I, 182; *Letters*, I, 20–31; NLS, MS 877, fols 243–50.
12. NLS, MS 877, fol. 250; *Minstrelsy*, III, 73–74.
13. *Minstrelsy*, III, 1, 9–10; *Letters*, I, 16.
14. *Letters*, I, 24–26; Garside, 'Editing *The Forest Minstrel*', pp. 77–78.
15. 1802 HJ, pp. 961, 95, 312, 58; *Letters*, I, 26, 32, 37.
16. 1802 HJ, pp. 56, 314, 253, 94, 252; Anderson, II, 141.
17. 1802 HJ, pp. 383–84.
18. *Letters*, I, 31–32.
19. 1803 HJ, pp. 9–10, 27, 51, 47, 32.
20. 1803 HJ, p. 45, 57, 61.
21. 1803 HJ, p. 145; *SG*, p. 315; NLS, Charter 413; information from Bill Lawson.
22. See Hans de Groot's notes in 1803 HJ, pp. 167, 169–70.
23. 1803 HJ, p. 162.
24. 'Jamie's Farewell to Ettrick', *SM*, 66 (May 1804), 377.
25. Rogers, II, 37; *FMinstrel*, pp. 348–49; *AT*, pp. 72–73; Hans de Groot, 'When did Hogg meet John Galt?', *SHW*, 8 (1997), 75–76.
26. Lockhart, I, 408–09; *Letters*, I, 39–40.
27. *MB1807*, pp. xxii–xxiii; Riddell, p. 387; 1804 HJ, pp. 423, 424, 672, 809–10, 15–16, 99–100, 183.
28. *Letters*, I, 76–77; NLS, D/H.P 298 'Minute Books of the Court of Session', 24 (1805), pp. 221, 261, 302; 25 (1806), p. 395; and 28

(1808–09), pp. 464, 586 (information from Janette Currie and Richard Jackson); Z, p. 822.

29. *Letters*, I, 71, 77–78; information from Bill Lawson.

30. *AT*, p. 22; *EEC*, 27/2/1817; *Letters*, I, 42; Walter Scott, *Minstrelsy of the Scottish Border*, third edition, 3 vols (Edinburgh, 1806), I, 15.

31. *Songs 1831*, pp. 26, 4–5; *AT*, p. 66.

32. *Letters*, I, 42, 48, 44; Lockhart, II, 9; *Anecdotes*, p. 8; *QW*, p. 172.

33. 'Historical Register', *North British Magazine*, 1 (March 1804), 187; Walter Scott, note to *The Antiquary*, in *Waverley Novels*, 48 vols (Edinburgh, 1829–33), VI, 338–40.

34. See Peter Garside, 'The Origins and History of James Hogg's "Donald Macdonald"', *Scottish Studies Review*, 7 no. 2 (Autumn 2006), 24–39; 'R. G.', 'The Ettrick Shepherd's First Song', *ELJ*, 8 May 1830, pp. 275–76; *AT*, p. 20.

35. SG, pp. 252–323; *SM*, 67 (August 1805), 616–17.

36. *AT*, p. 21 ; *Letters*, I, 42, 48; *SM*, 66 (May and November 1804), 378–79 and 855–56; *Anecdotes*, p. 43.

37. *MB1807*, pp. 49, 64, 66.

38. *Letters*, I, 44, 46–47; Rogers, III, 43; *SM*, 67 (April 1805), 295.

39. *PE & T*, III (1807), 339–535 (pp. 339–43).

40. *Letters*, I, 43–44, 48.

41. *Burns*, V, 246, 177–80, 182.

42. Robert Wodrow, *The History of the Sufferings of the Church of Scotland from the Restauration to the Revolution*, 2 vols (Edinburgh, 1721–22), II, 448, 375–76; R. M. F. Watson, *Closeburn* (Glasgow, 1901), pp. 170–71.

43. 'A Tale of the Martyrs', *BEM*, 26 (July 1829), 48–51; Watson, *Closeburn*, pp. 169–70.

44. *1845 SA*, IV, 86; Watson, *Closeburn*, p. 171; JH to Rev. William Buell Sprague, 20/6/1833, Beinecke, GEN MSS 61, Box 1, Folder 46.

45. *Letters*, I, 50, 55.

46. *SM*, 67 (August 1805), 617; *Letters*, I, 50; *AT*, p. 22; Andrew Livingston to Walter Scott, 28/4/1806, NLS, MS 3875, fols 164–65.

47. *Letters*, I, 55, 58–60, 77, 40; see Suzanne Gilbert, 'Two Versions of "Gilmanscleuch"', *SHW*, 9 (1998), 92–128; Lockhart, II, 101.

48. *Letters*, I, 54–55, 60.

49. *Letters*, I, 57, 63–64. Suzanne Gilbert's forthcoming S/SC Edition volume of *The Mountain Bard* will discuss Scott's influence in further detail.

50. *MB1807*, pp. 103, 110, 115–16; *Letters*, I, 64, 61; *D & GC*, 26 December 1826.

51. Garside, 'Editing *The Forest Minstrel*', pp. 78–79; *Letters*, I, 57, 60, 64, 67–68; *FMinstrel*, pp. xxii–xxiii; Morrison, p. 572.

52. *FMinstrel*, p. xxiii, referring to a 'short' copy in Stirling University Library; *Letters*, I, 77.

53. 'Jock an' Samuel. A Scots Pastoral', *SM*, 68 (January 1806), 53–55. For the *SM* versions of the *MB1807* poems see *BibV*; 'Scottish Literary Intelligence', *SM*, 68 (June 1806), 444.

54. *Letters*, II, 485–89; 'To Mr T. M. C. London', *SM*, 67 (August 1805), 621–22; 'Answer to the Ettrick Shepherd', *SM*, 68 (March 1806), 206–08; 'To J– H–', *SM*, 69 (June 1807), 447–48.

55. *AT*, p. 69; Cunningham to JH, 16/2/1826, NLS, MS 2245, fols 90–91; Trotter, pp. 191–97.
56. Trotter, pp. 54–61; Morrison, pp. 572–73.
57. Morrison, p. 573; 'The Harp of the Hill', edited by Richard D. Jackson, *SHW*, 13 (2002), 134–42.
58. *SM*, 69 (February 1807), 112; *SM*, 69 (March 1807), 200; *SG*, p. 176; *AT*, p. 22.
59. Sir George Steuart Mackenzie, *A Treatise on the Diseases and Management of Sheep* (Edinburgh, 1809), p. 90.
60. *Dumfries Weekly Journal*, 9/9/1806; *Letters*, I, 71; *AT*, p. 23.
61. Information on the Harknesses from Closeburn OPR; *Dumfries Weekly Journal*, 21/10/1806; *Letters*, I, 73, 75, 79–80.
62. *Letters*, I, 73, 79–80.
63. Eskdalemuir OPR; for Hogg's relationship with Catherine Henderson see Gillian Hughes, 'James Hogg and the "Bastard Brood"', *SHW*, 11 (2000), 56–68; Yarrow OPR for Robert Hogg's marriage on 11/1/1807 and Ettrick OPR for the baptism of his eldest son William on 27/7/1807; *Letters*, I, 314.
64. Closeburn Kirk Session Papers, cited in Hughes, 'Bastard Brood', pp. 57–59.
65. *AT*, p. 23; *Spy*, p. 32; Grierson, II, 100; *Letters*, I, 92, 85–86; Rogers, II, 12.
66. *Letters*, I, 463; *D & GC*, 11 January 1820.
67. *Letters*, I, 78; *QW*, pp. 145, 147.
68. *Letters*, I, 84–88.
69. *Letters*, I, 98; JH to unknown correspondent, 21/4/1834, Robert H. Taylor Collection, Manuscripts Division, Rare Books and Special Collections, Princeton University Library.
70. *Letters*, I, 83, 93, 91, 98.
71. *Letters*, I, 102; *The Spy*, pp. 562–64.
72. *Letters*, I, 92, 90, 457–60; see also Janette Currie, 'James Hogg's Literary Friendships with John Grieve and Eliza Izett', in *Mador*, pp. xliii–lvii; *Songs 1831*, pp. 26, 242, 253; *FMinstrel*, pp. xxiv–xxv.
73. *The Spy*, p. 564; *Letters*, I, 94–96; Richard Jackson has identified the verse as from the version of 'The Bonny Lass of Deloraine' in *SM*, 69 (August 1807), 607–08.
74. *AT*, p. 23; *BibP* and *BibV*; 1804 HJ was written during the winter of 1804–05.
75. *Letters*, I, 98, 102–03; *FMinstrel*, p. 245.
76. Morrison, p. 574.
77. Morrison, p. 574; *Letters*, I, 101; *Spy*, pp. 32–34.
78. *AT*, p. 23; Hughes, 'Bastard Brood', pp. 59–61.
79. Riddell, p. 389; *AT*, p. 23.

Chapter Three: The Cause of Liberty

1. Robert Tannahill to James King, 1/4/1810, Glasgow University Library, Dept. of Special Collections, MS Robertson 1/37; *Letters*, I, 110, 116.
2. JH, 'On the Surest Means of Improving the Breeds of Sheep and the Quality of Wool', *Farmer's Magazine*, 13 (June 1812), 173–76; JH, 'On

the Cause, Prevention, Symptoms, and Cure, of a Destructive Malady among Sheep', *Farmer's Magazine*, 13 (August 1812), 306–12; JH, 'On the Diseases of Sheep', *Farmer's Magazine*, 13 (November 1812), 475–80.

3.　1802 HJ, p. 961; *Spy*, pp. 384–85.
4.　*Letters*, I, 102; *AT*, p. 27.
5.　Cosh *passim*; for the emptiness of Edinburgh in summer and the water shortage see *Spy*, pp. 118, 154, 588.
6.　*Spy*, p. 284; *PL*, II, 172, 175.
7.　Gillian Hughes, 'James Hogg and the Theatre', *SHW*, 15 (2004), 53–66; *AT*, p. 28; Dibdin, p. 263.
8.　*FMinstrel*, p. 5; Dibdin, pp. 500–02, 264, 267.
9.　GilliesLV, II, 123; *Letters*, I, 134, 121; *CM*, 25/1/1812.
10.　*Spy*, pp. 5, 157, 573–74, 595; Valentina Bold, 'The Magic Lantern: Hogg and Science', SHW, 7 (1996), 5–17; Annuals, pp. xlii–xliv.
11.　*AT*, p. 50; *PL*, II, 230–33; Robert Chambers, *Walks in Edinburgh* (Edinburgh, 1825), pp. 71–78.
12.　Robert Tannahill to James King, 1/4/1810, Glasgow University Library, Dept. of Special Collections, MS Robertson 1/37; James A. Kilpatrick, *Literary Landmarks of Glasgow* (Glasgow, 1898), p. 125.
13.　Garden, p. 307; *FMinstrel*, p. 7.
14.　*AT*, pp. 23–24; 'Literary Intelligence', *SM*, 72 (April 1810), 286.
15.　See *FMinstrel*, pp. xxxix, 7–8, and Garside and Jackson's Introduction *passim*; *AT*, p. 24.
16.　Introduction to *FMinstrel* and pp. 7, 90–91, 201.
17.　Lockhart, II, 377; 'Literary Intelligence', *SM*, 72 (October 1810), 767.
18.　GilliesLV, III, 55–56; *AT*, p. 18.
19.　*Spy*, pp. 562–64, 473.
20.　*Burns*, V, 246, 197, 364–65, and IV, 291.
21.　*Letters*, II, 360–64.
22.　*Burns*, V, 152; *Spy*, pp. 115–16, 333; Francis Place to Edward Wakefield, 16/1/[1814], BL, Add. MS 35,152, fols 29r–30v (information from Peter Jackson); Peter Jackson, 'William Wordsworth, James Gray, and the *Letter to a Friend of Robert Burns*: Some Unpublished Correspondence', *Notes and Queries*, n. s. 50 no. 3 (2003), 293–97.
23.　*Sketch of the Life of James Gray, M. A.* (Edinburgh, 1859), p. 6; William Steven, *The History of the High School of Edinburgh* (Edinburgh, 1849), pp. 161–62.
24.　Particulars, p. 202; *Letters*, I, 112.
25.　*Spy*, pp. 130, 589, 163, 376; *Letters*, I, 122; 'Love Pastoral', *SM*, 74 (March 1812), 216.
26.　*Letters*, I, 112.
27.　*EEC*, 2/7/1810; *Edinburgh Star*, 31/5/1811; Gillian Hughes, 'A Tory Memorial for the Newspapers', *SHW*, 11 (2000), 84–86.
28.　For 'Epitaphs on Living Characters' see *SM*, 72 (June 1810), 447, *The Spy*, pp. 19–20, 52–53, 105–06, and Trotter, p. 61.
29.　*AT*, pp. 24–26; *Anecdotes*, pp. 19–20, 58–59; *Letters*, I, 105.
30.　*AT*, p. 24; *Spy*, pp. 1, 2–3, 4–5.
31.　*Spy*, p. 516; *AT*, p. 25.
32.　*Letters*, I, 105, 109; *AT*, p. 25; *Spy*, pp. xxv–xxvii, 152; *EEC*, 1/12/1810.

33. Aikman's statement of 2/5/1832 appeared in James Browne's anonymous *The "Life" of the Ettrick Shepherd Anatomized* (Edinburgh, 1832), pp. 16–18; *Spy*, p. 272.
34. See 'Notes on Contributors', *Spy*, pp. 557–71.
35. *Spy*, pp. 514–15.
36. *Spy*, pp. 12–19, 44–51, 96–104 (pp. 15–16, 96, 104).
37. *AT*, p. 30; *Edinburgh Star*, 5/2/1813; *Letters*, I, 116, 120.
38. Gillian Hughes, 'James Hogg and the Forum', *SHW*, 1 (1990), 57–70 (p. 58), citing *EEC* 21/9/1811 and *Edinburgh Star* 13/11/1812.
39. *AT*, p. 27; Hughes, 'Forum', p. 58.
40. Hughes, 'Forum', pp. 59–60; *EEC*, 30/3/1811 and 6/4/1811; *Edinburgh Star*, 21/6/1811.
41. *Edinburgh Star* 21/6/1811; *AT*, p. 27; *Spy*, p. 440.
42. *AT*, p. 28; '"What's a' the hurry?" A Reminiscence of the Ettrick Shepherd', *ELJ*, 10/4/1830, p. 220.
43. Hughes, 'Forum', p. 63, citing *Edinburgh Star*, 21/6/1811, 25/2/1812, 3/4/1812, and 26/6/1812.
44. Hughes, 'Forum', pp. 63, 64–67 citing *Edinburgh Star* 13/11/1812 and 24/11/1812; *Letters*, I, 127.
45. *Edinburgh Star*, 8/12/1812, and 15/12/1812; Goldie, p. 12.
46. *Letters*, I, 119–20; *AT*, p. 28.
47. Harris, pp. 227–28; GilliesLV, II, 121; VR Sermon, p. 229.
48. *AT*, p. 28; *QW*, pp. xx.
49. *Spy*, pp. 209–12, 402–05; for discussion of the manuscripts of 'Earl Walter' and 'Glen-Avin' see *QW*, pp. 399–400; *Letters*, I, 118.
50. *QW*, pp. xxviii–xxxiii.
51. *QW*, pp. 62, 168–69; *Edinburgh Review*, 24 (November 1814), 157–74 (p. 160).
52. *QW*, pp. 7, 9, 15, 16, 163, 173, 406–07.
53. *QW*, pp. 38, 107–08, 129–30, 134–35, 144–45, 147, and notes.
54. *QW*, pp. 63, 170–72 and notes.
55. *QW*, pp. xx, 29; *Letters*, I, 125; *AT*, p. 33.
56. *AT*, pp. 28–29.
57. *Letters*, I, 125–26; *AT*, p. 29.
58. *AT*, pp. 29–30; *Letters*, I, 127.
59. T & B, p. 257; Johnson, I, 407; *Letters*, I, 131.
60. *EEC*, 23/1/1813; *AT*, p. 30.

Chapter Four: Of Minstrel Honours

1. *AT*, p. 30; the review in the extinct issue 9 of the *Scottish Review* published in August 1813 was reprinted in the American *Analectic Magazine*, n. s. 3 (February 1814), 104–25 (p. 109); advertisement for 'O Lady Dear' in *EEC* for 1/7/1813; see, for instance, Hogg's 'Macgregor' in John Stagg, *Magazine of the Muses* (Manchester, 1815), pp. 375–79; *QW*, p. liii.
2. *Letters*, I, 132, 161; Peter Garside, 'Hogg, Eltrive, and *Confessions*', *SHW*, 11 (2000), 5–24; 'Tam Wilson', *SM*, 76 (April 1814), 296; *AT*, p. 34.
3. Earl of Buchan to William Kerr, 16/7/1814, NLS, MS 2245, fols 6a–6b; *Edinburgh Star*, 13/12/1814; Musomanick Society of Anstruther certificate no. 13 for JH dated 24 September 1813, Mitchell Library,

Glasgow, MS 15/15.

4. Gillies, pp. 419, 425; Cosh, p. 7.
5. Gillies, pp. 421, 422; *LS*, p. 35.
6. Gillies, p. 422; *LS*, p. 48.
7. NLS, MS 4887, fol. 6; *PL*, III, 120–21.
8. *AT*, pp. 32–33; Gillies, p. 419.
9. John Wilson (by David Finkelstein) in *Oxford DNB*; Gordon, I, 198.
10. Gillian Hughes, '"Native Energy": Hogg and Byron as Scottish Poets', *The Byron Journal*, 34 no. 2 (2006), 133–142; *QW*, pp. 1, 394.
11. *Letters*, I, 136, 143, 147.
12. *Letters*, I, 136, 140, 145; *AT*, p. 33.
13. *Letters*, I, 150, 161; 'A Last Adieu', *BEM*, 1 (May 1817), 169.
14. *Letters*, I, 154, 155, 157, 166–67, 170–72, 175–76; *QW*, p. 1; *EEC*, 20/1/1814; *AT*, pp. 34–35; *Mador*, pp. xii–xiv.
15. *Letters*, I, 170; *Selections from the Poems and Letters of Bernard Barton Edited by His Daughter* (London, 1849), pp. xiv–xv; Gillies, p. 424; Roscoe to JH, undated draft, Liverpool Record Office, Liverpool Libraries and Information Services: 920 Ros 2047; *The Hunting of Badlewe* (Edinburgh, 1814), pp. v–viii; *AT*, p. 42.
16. Gillian Hughes, 'James Hogg and Edinburgh's Triumph Over Napoleon', *Scottish Studies Review*, 4 no. 1 (Spring 2003), 98–111; *EEC*, 11/4/1814.
17. *AT*, p. 35; 'Connel of Dee', *WET*, pp. 410–25; *Pilgrims*, title-page motto and pp. 23, 62; *Letters*, I, 211.
18. *AT*, p. 35; *Pilgrims*, pp. 117, 119, 122.
19. William Nicholson, *Tales in Verse, and Miscellaneous Poems* (Edinburgh, 1814), title-page and p. vii; *EEC*, 30/4/1814; *QW*, p. 82; Longmans to JH, 19/1/1814, in Reading University Library, Longman Archives, Part 1 Item 98 (Letter-Book 1812–1814), fol. 120.
20. *WET*, p. 560; see the advertisement leaf in NLS, ABS. 1.78.23, which lists among the volume editors of the series 'James Hogg, Esq. Author of the Queen's Wake, &c.' (information from Richard Jackson).
21. *Letters*, I, 136; Goldie to Barton, 28/10/1813, NLS, MS 1002, fols 85–86.
22. *Letters*, I, 173–74; *AT*, p. 31.
23. Lockhart, III, 99; *Letters*, I, 179, 188, 192; *AT*, pp. 36–37.
24. Hughes, 'Native Energy'; *Letters*, I, 139, 178, 181–82.
25. GilliesLV, II, 140; *AT*, pp. 66–67; Mary Moorman, *William Wordsworth A Biography: The Later Years 1803–1850* (Oxford: Clarendon Press, 1965), pp. 258–60; Sara Hutchinson, 'Notes for a Journal of a Tour of Scotland, 1814', The Wordsworth Trust, DCMS 77, fols 17–18.
26. Mrs Hughes (of Uffington), *Letters and Recollections of Sir Walter Scott*, ed. by Horace G. Hutchinson (London, 1904), p. 291; Duchess Harriet died on 24/8/1814, Corson, p. 390; Gillian Hughes, 'Hogg's Poetic Responses to the Unexpected Death of his Patron', *SHW*, 12 (2001), 80–89 (pp. 82–83), citing *EEC*, 3/9/1814.
27. Sara Hutchinson, 'Notes', fol. 18; Moorman, pp. 259–60; *The Letters of Sara Hutchinson from 1800 to 1835*, ed. by Kathleen Coburn (London: Routledge & Keegan Paul, 1954), pp. 78–79.
28. *AT*, pp. 65–67; *Letters*, I, 201.

29. *Songs1831*, p. 118; GilliesLV, II, 148; *Letters*, I, 200–02.
30. 'Celestial Phenomenon', *EEC*, 15/9/1814; *The Letters of William and Dorothy Wordsworth: Volume V. Part II 1829–1834*, second edition, ed. by Ernest de Selincourt, rev. by Alan G. Hill (Oxford: Clarendon Press, 1979), pp. 517–18.
31. *AT*, p. 68.
32. *Songs1831*, pp. 117–18; *Pilgrims*, pp. 132, 133, 141.
33. *Letters*, I, 201; *The Metropolitan*, 3 (March 1832), 65–68 (p. 66); *Songs1831*, p. 118.
34. *Letters*, I, 176, 201, 203, 205; *AT*, p. 37.
35. *Letters*, I, 217–18; *AT*, pp. 31–32; *QW*, p. lxiii; *Edinburgh Review*, 24 (November 1814), 157–74, advertised in *EEC*, 22/12/1814.
36. *Letters*, I, 198, 205; *PL*, II, 177–79.
37. *Letters*, I, 205, 209–10, 211; Blackwood to Murray, 21/1/1815, in NLS, John Murray Archive, Blackwood Box 2.
38. *Pilgrims*, pp. 126, 127.
39. *Letters*, I, 216; see also Hughes, 'Native Energy'.
40. *Letters*, I, 206, 213–14, 212; *AT*, p. 40.
41. Blackwood to Murray, 11/12/1814 mentions his intention to publish 'to morrow', NLS, John Murray Archive, Blackwood Box 2; *Letters*, I, 219, 220–21; *EEC*, 14/1/1815 and 23/1/1815.
42. Gillies, pp. 424–25; *AT*, p. 47.
43. *AT*, pp. 47–48; Gillies, p. 425; *Letters*, I, 227, 228, 230, 231–32.
44. *Letters*, I, 231, 234; *EEC*, 15/12/1814 and *Morning Chronicle*, 13/1/1815.
45. *EEC*, 28/1/1815 and 30/1/1815, which prints Hogg's song; *Letters*, I, 236.
46. William Nicholson (1781–1844) moved to Edinburgh in 1814. For Hogg's sitting to him see *Letters*, I, 235–36, 239. The now-missing picture is described in *EEC*, 19/6/1815.
47. Duke of Buccleuch to JH, 26/1/1815, NLS, MS 2245, fols 13–14; *Letters*, I, 236; the farm appears to have consisted of sixty acres in 1810–see Peter Garside, 'Hogg, Eltrive, and *Confessions*', *SHW*, 11 (2000), 5–24 (p. 10). But a letter to Walter, Duke of Buccleuch from his Chamberlain Charles Riddell of 1/9/1832 states, 'The ground possessed by Mr Hogg at Eltrieve contains about 41 acres'–see National Archives of Scotland, GD 224/581/4.
48. Roger S. Kirkpatrick, *A Register of Monumental Inscriptions in the Original Area of Yarrow Churchyard* (Hawick, 1933), p. 11; Gordon, I, 186; Garden, p. 86; Blackwood to Murray, 5/2/1815, NLS, John Murray Archive, Blackwood Box 2.
49. *AT*, pp. 48–49; Gillies, p. 425; *Letters*, I, 240.
50. *Letters*, I, 242, 244.
51. *Letters*, I, 246, 248–49; Murray to JH, 10/4/1815, NLS, MS 2245, fols 15–16; Johnson, I, 492–93; *EEC*, 4/5/1815.
52. *Letters*, I, 250–51, 299.
53. *Letters*, I, 253–55; summary of Thomson's letter to JH of 18/10/1815 in BL, Add. MS 35,267, fols 160v–161r.
54. *Letters*, I, 336–38, 339; Thomson to Hogg, 18/3/1818 and 30/11/1821, BL, Add. MS 35,268, fols 20r–21v, 72r–74v.
55. *Letters*, I, 343–45; *Songs1831*, p. 224.

56. *Letters*, I, 264, 274; Alexander Campbell, 'Notes of My third Journey to the Border', EUL Special Collections, MS La. II. 378, fols 16–17; Alexander Campbell, *Albyn's Anthology*, 2 vols (Edinburgh, 1816–18), II, 8–9.
57. Johnson, I, 496–503; T & B, p. 377; *Letters*, I, 250.
58. *Letters*, I, 256, 258–59; only a fragment of this first version of 'The Field of Waterloo' survives in NLS, MS 582, fol. 182; *PW*, II, 281–323.
59. *Letters*, I, 256, 258–59; JH, 'To the Ancient Banner of the House of Buccleuch', *The Ettricke Garland* (Edinburgh, 1815), pp. 6–8; *EEC*, 9/12/1815; *Morning Chronicle*, 27/12/1815.
60. *Letters*, I, 263; *AT*, p. 49; Blackwood to Murray, 20/12/1815 and 22/12/1815, in NLS, John Murray Archive, Blackwood Box 2.
61. GilliesLV, II, 241–42.
62. *Mador*, pp. xiv–xviii; *EEC*, 22/4/1816; Letters, I, 276; Blackwood to Murray, 27/4/1816 and 6–7/6/1816 in NLS, John Murray Archive, Blackwood Box 2; *British Lady's Magazine*, 4 (October 1816), 251–55 (p. 252), cited from *Mador*, p. xvi.
63. Blackwood to Murray, 6–7/6/1816, in NLS, John Murray Archive, Blackwood Box 2; *Letters*, I, 277–78; *Songs1831*, p. 68; JH, 'On the Present State of Sheep-Farming in Scotland', *Farmer's Magazine*, 18 (May 1817), 144–49 (pp. 145–46).
64. Gordon Willis, 'Hogg's Personal Library: Holdings in Stirling University Library', *SHW*, 3 (1992), 87–88; 1802 HJ, p. 59.
65. See *QH*, pp. xiv, xxx, lxvi, 238–44 ('Appendix: Beregonium'); *AT*, p. 42.
66. *Letters*, I, 277.
67. *Letters*, I, 280, 320–21; *AT*, pp. 40–41; *EEC*, 12/10/1816; John Ballantyne to JH, 10/10/1816, NLS, MS 2245, fols 23–24.
68. *EEC*, 16/12/1816; Ballantyne to JH, 10/10/1816, NLS, MS 2245, fols 23–24; *QR*, 15 (July 1816), 468–75.
69. *AT*, pp. 41–42; Blackwood to Murray, 19/5/1817, NLS, John Murray Archive, Blackwood Box 3.
70. Blackwood to Murray, 19/2/1817, NLS, John Murray Archive, Blackwood Box 3; *EEC*, 24/5/1817; *AT*, p. 42; *Monthly Review*, 88 (February 1819), 183–85 (pp. 183, 185).

Chapter Five: Ingenious Lies

1. Cosh, pp. 330–31, 542; Harris, p. 541; *Anecdotes*, p. 30.
2. *AT*, p. 43; *The Institute* (Edinburgh, 1811) is Pringle's mock-heroic account of the founding of the Edinburgh Institution—see also *Letters*, I, 466–68.
3. NLS, MS 4002, fols 69–70; Oliphant, I, 98–99.
4. *Letters*, I, 300–01; Oliphant, I, 106; Gillies, p. 427; *AT*, p. 44.
5. Carol Polsgrove, 'They Made it Pay: British Short-Fiction Writers, 1820–1840', *Studies in Short Fiction*, 11 (1974), 417–21; NLS, MS 30,001, fols 49–50; *EEC* and *CM*, 20/9/1817 give a prospectus for *Blackwood's*, and *EEC* and *CM*, 27/9/1817 for the *Edinburgh Magazine*; *Letters*, I, 300.
6. *Letters*, I, 295; NLS, MS 4807, fols 2–4.
7. *AT*, p. 73; Johnson, I, 620.

8. Andrew Lang, *The Life and Letters of John Gibson Lockhart*, 2 vols (London, 1897), I, 157; 'Translation from an Ancient Chaldee Manuscript', *BEM*, 2 (October 1817), 89–96; Gillies, p. 428.

9. *Letters*, I, 305, 356.

10. *Letters*, I, 377; *Burns*, V, 156.

11. 'Life and Writings of James Hogg', *Edinburgh Magazine*, 2 (January, February, and March 1818), 35–40, 122–29, 215–23; for Tickler's letters to Hogg see *BEM*, 2 (February and March 1818), 501–04 and 654–56; *Letters*, I, 368, 369.

12. *Glasgow Chronicle*, 12/5/1818; *To the Editor of the Glasgow Chronicle* (Edinburgh, 1818), NLS, HH. 4/2.40 (17); Grierson, V, 154–56.

13. *Letters*, I, 383–84, 386–87.

14. Oliphant, I, 145–48; Blackwood to Laidlaw, 2/1/1818, NLS, Acc. 9084/ 9; *Letters*, I, 323–24.

15. *Letters*, II, 494–500 (on Grieve).

16. *Letters*, I, 323–24; *BEM*, 2 (October 1817, January and March 1818), 82–86, 417–21, 621–26.

17. *Letters*, I, 345, 356, and II, 177, 509–10 (on Napier).

18. *Letters*, I, 361, 365, 376, 395; Peter Garside, 'Hogg, Eltrive, and *Confessions*', *SHW*, 11 (2000), 5–24.

19. Frasers, p. 273.

20. *JR1*, pp. xix–xx.

21. *WET*, pp. 98–99; *MB1807*, p. xii; *EWJ*, 24 November 1819; *JR2*, p. 307; *Letters*, II, 29–30, 142.

22. *JR1*, p. v; *AT*, p. 50.

23. *Letters*, I, 358, 379; *Burns*, V, 24; *JR2*, pp. 269, 338, 350, 480.

24. Grierson, V, 252, 316 and VI, 69.

25. For Hogg's payment of £50 on 6/3/1819 see *Letters*, I, 355–56, citing NLS, Deposit 268/43; *JR2*, pp. xvi–xvii.

26. *JR2*, pp. xvi–xvii; *Confessions*, p. 169.

27. Gillian Hughes, 'The Ettrick Shepherd's Nephew', *SHW*, 16 (2005), 20–35; *Letters*, II, 46, 55–56.

28. *Letters*, I, 145, 289, 312, 326, 351; *AT*, pp. 45–46; see also *The Brownie of Bodsbeck*, ed. by Douglas S. Mack (Edinburgh and London: Scottish Academic Press, 1976), pp. xiii–xvii; *Anecdotes*, p. 23; Johnson, I, 565.

29. Sharon Ragaz, '"Gelding" the Priest in *The Brownie of Bodsbeck*: A New Letter', *SHW*, 13 (2002), 95–103; Blackwood to Murray, 29/5/1818, John Murray Archive, Blackwood Box 3; Grierson, V, 140; *Letters*, I, 362; Peter Garside, 'Three Perils in Publishing: Hogg and the Popular Novel', *SHW*, 2 (1991), 45–63 (pp. 54–55).

30. Blackwood to JH, 25/11/1820, NLS, MS 30,002, fol. 15; *Letters*, I, 409–10, 432; SUL, MS 25 Box 4, Item 24; *WET*, pp. xviii–xix, xxvi.

31. *QW*, pp. lxvii–lxxi, 395–96, and Meiko O'Halloran, 'Hogg, Mary, Queen of Scots, and the Illustrations to *The Queen's Wake*', in *QW*, pp. lxxxvii–cxiii.

32. Douglas S. Mack, 'The Body in the Opened Grave: Robert Burns and Robert Wringhim', *SHW*, 7 (1996), 70–79; *EEC* for 9/1/1819, 18/ 2/1819, and 15/3/1819; *The Works of Mrs Hemans; With a Memoir of Her Life by Her Sister*, 7 vols (Edinburgh, 1839), I, 31–32; JH, 'Wallace', in *PW*, IV, 143–60 (p. 160).

33. *EEC*, 3/2/1817 and 25/2/1819; *D & GC*, 29/1/1822; Garden, pp. 253–55; *PL*, I, 120–21, 129, 140.

34. Aitken to David Laing, 10/4/1819, EUL Special Collections, La. IV. 17, fols 123–24; *Letters*, I, 440–42 (on Aitken); *Songs1831*, pp. 87, 112.

35. *EEC*, 3/2/1817; Gillian Hughes, 'Hogg, Art, and the Annuals' in *Annuals*, pp. xlii–liv; 'Letter to the Committee of Dilettanti', *BEM*, 3 (August 1818), 524–27 (pp. 525–26).

36. *Letters*, I, 207, 249, 426; Grierson, V, 257; JH to Hannah Lamont, 5/5/1833, Beinecke, Osborn MSS, Folder 7419.

37. *Letters*, I, 406, 413–14; Margaret Phillips to JH, 20/7/1819 and [3/8/1819], SUL, MS 25 Box 4, Items 19 and 20.

38. *Letters*, I, 411, 415, 425–26; Margaret Phillips to JH, [3/8/1819] and 26/10/1819, SUL, MS 25 Box 4, Items 18 and 20; *Letters*, II, 39.

39. *Letters*, I, 426, 433–34; Margaret Phillips to JH, 24/11/1819 and 30/12/1819, SUL, MS 25 Box 4, Items 22 and 23; Parr, p. 18; marriage contract of 27/4/1820, in SUL, MS 25 Box 2, Item 7.

40. Wilson to Aitken, 21/9/1819, NLS, Acc. 12430; 'Horae Scoticanae. No. I. The Bondspiel of Closeburn and Lochmaben', *BEM*, 6 (February 1820), 568–73 (pp. 569–70); *Letters*, II, 18–19.

41. *Letters*, II, 20–21, 23, 26–27; Margaret Phillips to JH, 25/3/1820, SUL, MS 25 Box 4, Item 26.

42. For details of the wedding see *Letters*, II, 22–23, 25, 26–27; Margaret Phillips to JH, [April 1820?], SUL, MS 25 Box 4, Item 29; marriage contract in SUL, MS 25 Box 2, Item 7; *D & GC*, 2 May 1820.

43. 'Extracts from Mr. Wastle's Diary', *BEM*, 7 (June 1820) 317–23 (pp. 321–22); *The Scotsman*, 29/4/1820; *Caledonian*, 1 (1820–21), 25–27; Aitken to Laing, 26/9/1820, EUL Special Collections, MS La. IV. 17, fols 133–34; Blackwood to JH, 21/7/1820, NLS, MS 2245, fols 38–39.

44. Elsie Swann, *Christopher North <John Wilson>* (Edinburgh, 1934), pp. 127–42; 'Professorship of Moral Philosophy', *CM*, 24/7/1820; for Gray's printed testimonials see EUL, P. 35/3; Blackwood to JH, undated, NLS, MS 30,002, fols 14–15; *Letters*, II, 30, 39, 54.

45. Parr, p. 9; *Letters*, II, 34–35, 36, 39-40; Scott to JH, 30/4/[1820], owned by Mrs Margaret Gilkison; *Anecdotes*, pp. 16, 56; *CM*, 25/9/1820; *PL*, II, 332.

46. *Letters*, I, 423, 425, 428; George Taylor, *A Memoir of Robert Surtees, Esq.*, ed. by James Raine, Surtees Society, 24 (Durham, 1852), p. 157; *Letters*, II, 2, 43.

47. *Letters*, II, 4, 33, 45, 57, 58–59; *MB1821*, p. 289.

48. Queensberry to JH, 26/9/1820, NLS, MS 2245, fols 46–47; *Letters*, II, 46, 54; *D & GC*, 31 October 1820.

49. *Letters*, II, 49–50; *Edinburgh Review*, 34 (August 1820), 148–60; 'Letter from James Hogg to his Reviewer', *BEM*, 8 (October 1820), 67–76; Blackwood to JH, undated, NLS, MS 30,002, fols 14–15.

50. Corson, p. 389; Scott to JH, 30/4/[1820], owned by Mrs Margaret Gilkison.

51. *Farmer's Magazine*, 18 (May 1817), 144–49 (pp. 144, 146, 148); *Letters*, II, 39–40; Laidlaw to Scott, 1/12/[1829], NLS, MS 3911, fols 101–03; *AT*, p. 54.

52. *Letters*, II, 57, 62, 76.
53. *WET*, pp. 434, 438, 440–41; NLS, MS 4887, fol. 6; *Letters*, II, 69, 72–73, 76, 88; Parr, p. 72.
54. *Letters*, II, 88, 101; *D & GC*, 19/6/1821; MH to JH, [27/8/1821] and 29/9/1821, ATL, James Hogg Papers (Item 110), MS-Papers-0042-12.
55. Riddell, p. 405; John Chisholm, *Sir Walter Scott as a Judge* (Edinburgh, 1918), p. 100; *Letters*, II, 84; NLS, MS 30,301, pp. 176–78; *AT*, p. 55.
56. *AT*, pp. 31, 32–33; Laidlaw to Blackwood, 10/7/[1821], NLS, MS 4007, fols 61–62; *Edinburgh Monthly Review*, 5 (June 1821), 662–72 (p. 671); Grierson, XII, 447.
57. *Letters*, II, 88, 91, 111; Goldie, p. 11; *AT*, p. 53.
58. *Letters*, II, 75–76.
59. *Letters*, II, 79, 84; Peter Garside, 'James Hogg's Fifty Pounds', *SHW*, 1 (1990), 128–32; Blackwood to JH, 12/6/1821, NLS, MS 30,969, fols 25–26.
60. *Letters*, II, 75–76; Boyd to JH, 6/3/1821, in NLS, Acc. 5000/188.
61. *Letters*, II, 88, 91–92.
62. *Letters*, II, 99–101; Grierson, VI, 487, 488–89 and X, 185; 'The Steam-Boat. No. VI', *BEM*, 10 (August 1821), 4–26 (pp. 14–26); 'Account of a Coronation-Dinner at Edinburgh', *BEM*, 10 (August 1821), 26–33 (information from Tom Richardson).
63. Blackwood to JH, 18/5/1821, NLS, MS 30,301, pp. 174–75.
64. Blackwood to JH, 14/8/1821 and 23/8/1821, NLS, MS 30,301, pp. 196–97, 197–201; *Letters*, II, 104–05.
65. Oliphant, I, 338; NLS, MS 30,002, fols 16–17; MS 30,301, pp. 197–201; NLS, MS 4887, fol. 6; *BEM*, 10 (August 1821), 43–52.
66. *Letters*, II, 109, 111, 120.
67. *Letters*, II, 110, 112.
68. *Letters*, II, 116; Grierson, XII, 446–47.
69. Goldie, p. 3; Howitt, II, 60–61; *Letters*, II, 114; Cadell to JH, 27/9/1821, NLS, MS 791, fol. 210.
70. *Letters*, II, 143–45, 150–51; *Edinburgh Magazine*, 9 (September, October, and November 1821), 219–25, 356–61, 439–43, 443–52; *AT*, p. 57.
71. Longman Archive, Reading University Library: Part 1 Item 101 (Letter-book 1820–25), fol. 174C; *Letters*, II, 123–25.
72. *Letters*, II, 130, 136; Cadell to JH, 2/2/1822 and 16/2/1822, NLS, MS 2245, fols 74–75, 76–77.
73. *Letters*, II, 160–61, 162; *D & GC*, 25 June 1822.
74. T & B, pp. 742–72.
75. *Anecdotes*, p. 52; *BEM*, 13 (May 1823), 592–611 (p. 609); *Letters*, II, 179, 183.
76. *Letters*, II, 159, 164; Blackwood to JH, 24/5/1822 and 18/6/1822, NLS, MS 30,305, pp. 329, 341–44.
77. For detailed accounts of the *Noctes* and their treatment of Hogg see *The Tavern Sages: Selections from the Noctes Ambrosianae*, ed. by J. H. Alexander (Aberdeen: ASLS, 1992), pp. vii–xvi (p. viii); Miller, pp. 158–84; Mark Parker, 'Introduction', *Blackwood's Magazine, 1817–25: Selections from Maga's Infancy*, ed. by Nicholas Mason and others, 6 vols (London: Pickering and Chatto, 2006), III, vii–xxxvi.
78. Oliphant, II, 75; Gillies, p. 429; *Songs1831*, p. 28.

79. *BEM*, 13 (May 1823), 592–611 (p. 595); *Letters*, II, 186; *BEM*, 28 (November 1830), 831–55 (p. 853).

80. Lockhart to JH, 13 July 1821, NLS, MS 2245, fols 58–59; John Prebble, *The King's Jaunt* (London: Collins, 1988); Johnson, II, 789; *Letters*, II, 169–70, 333.

81. Review of *The Royal Jubilee*, *BEM*, 12 (September 1822), 344–54 (p. 344); Gillies LV, III, 71.

82. Valentina Bold, '*The Royal Jubilee*: James Hogg and the House of Hanover', *SHW*, 5 (1994), 1–19; Garden, pp. 148–49.

83. Gillies to Lockhart, 28/1/1822, NLS, MS 934, fols 192–93; *CM*, 25/9/1820, 26/12/1822, and 28/12/1822; *EEC*, 1/2/1823; *Letters*, II, 186.

84. *Letters*, II, 173, 174, 191, 192.

85. *Letters*, II, 179; *TPW*, p. xiv.

86. *Letters*, II, 179, 180; *TPW*, pp. 128, 153–54.

87. *Letters*, II, 205, 224; *WET*, pp. 169–70, 174, 194.

88. Lockhart to O'Neill, 21/7/1824, NLS, Acc. 9714; Laidlaw to Lockhart, 12/[1/1826], NLS, MS 934, fols 258–59.

89. Notes by Mary Inglis, sister to Christian Phillips, in a scrapbook of Duncan family history, Ruthwell Savings Bank Museum, SBM 01/08/01/07; *Letters*, II, 203, 269.

90. *AT*, p. 55; *Confessions*, pp. xvii, 80, 90, 166, 168.

91. *BEM*, 11 (March 1822), 361; *BEM*, 14 (October 1823), 490.

92. Longman Archive, Reading University Library: Part 1 Item 101 (Letter-book 1820–25), fols 388B, 396C, 406C; *Confessions*, p. lxxi.

93. Longman Archive, Reading University Library: Part 1 Item 101 (Letter-book 1820–25), fol. 426B; *BEM*, 15 (March and April 1824), 359, 368; *Letters*, II, 196, 202, 205.

94. *QH*, pp. xv, 221–22, citing Longmans to Blackwood, 28/10/1824; *Letters*, II, 215–16.

95. *QH*, pp. xvi–xxxviii, 91, 163, 202.

96. *AT*, pp. 42–43; 'Scotch Poets, Hogg and Campbell, Hynde and Theodric', *BEM*, 17 (January 1825), 109–13, and 'Noctes Ambrosianae. No. XVIII', pp. 114–30 (pp. 123, 128, 130).

97. *QH*, pp. xvi, xlvii–lix; *Letters*, II, 236, 258; *AT*, p. 42.

Chapter Six: The Hard-Earned Sma' Propine

1. Juliet Barker, *The Brontës* (London: Weidenfeld and Nicolson, 1994), p. 149; *Letters*, II, 220, 276, 331.

2. *AT*, p. 58; JH to David Imrie, 23/2/1835, National Archives of Scotland, RH1/2/527.

3. *TWM*, pp. xi–xvii; *Letters*, II, 287; 'Love's Legacy or The Parting Gift', ed. by David Groves, *Altrive Chapbooks*, 5 (1988), 1–53 (p. 47).

4. *Letters*, II, 215–16; Blackwood to JH, 9/3/1826 and 19/1/1827, NLS, MS 30,309, pp. 134–35 and NLS, MS 30,310, pp. 13–15.

5. NLS, MS 30,310, pp. 88–90.

6. *Letters*, II, 188–89, 261, 271, 297, 299, 341, 345, 368, 380, 395, 449, 456, 462.

7. As recalled in Mr Purdie's lecture of 1931 incorporating family and local reminiscences, SUL, MS 98; Scott to Laidlaw, [15]/1/1821, NLS, MS 970, fols 26–27; *Letters*, 139, 292, 314, 340, 403, 414–15; 'A Living

Link with Scott, Hogg, and Wilson', *Chambers's Edinburgh Journal*, 1/5/
1897, pp. 280–82 (p. 282).

8. *Letters*, II, 248, 250, 256.
9. Johnson, II, 968.
10. *EWJ*, 23/4/1828; Isabel Quigly, *The Royal Society of Literature: A Portrait*
     (London: RSL, 2000), p. 43; 'Laws and Regulations', *Transactions of the
     Royal Society of Literature*, 1 (1829), vii–xxi.
11. Lockhart to JH, 23/9/1833, NLS, MS 2245, fols 232–33; 'Edinburgh
     Literary News', *Dumfries Monthly Magazine*, 1 (December 1825), 519–
     20; *AT*, p. 75; *Letters*, II, 242.
12. Lockhart to JH, 9/2/1827, and Jerdan to JH, 30/4/1827, NLS, MS
     2245, fols 92–96, 98–99; minutes of meeting of 30/5/1827, Archives
     of the Royal Literary Fund, 1790–1918, BL, Microfilm 1077/18/File
     594 (James Hogg). Permission was kindly granted by the Royal Lit-
     erary Fund.
13. *AT*, p. 55; Howitt, II, 60; Laidlaw to Scott, 1/12/[1829], NLS, MS
     3911, fols 101–03; 'A Living Link with Scott, Hogg, and Wilson', *Cham-
     bers's Edinburgh Journal*, 1/5/1897, pp. 280–82 (p. 281); Riddell, p. 406;
     NLS, MS 4854, fols 29–30; *D & GC*, 4/12/1827.
14. *Letters*, II, 348; 'Ane Waefu' Scots Pastoral', *Annuals*, pp. 28–30; JH to
     W. T. Mackenzie, 7/9/1832, Beinecke, GEN MSS 61, Box 3, Folder 51.
15. Stoddart, pp. 185–86, 210.
16. *Letters*, I, 393; JH to Allan Cunningham, 4/11/1832, Rare Books &
     Special Collections, Thomas Cooper Library, University of South
     Carolina; Michaela Reid, *The Forest Club 1788–2000* (Kelso: The For-
     est Club, 2003), pp. 84–99; entry for 13/2/1826, 'Minute Book of the
     Crookwelcome Club', owned by Mrs Doreen Mitchell.
17. Groves, pp. 13–14, citing *EWJ*, 2/4/1828.
18. James Walter Buchan and Henry Paton, *A History of Peeblesshire*, 3 vols
     (Glasgow, 1925–27), II, 430–33, 412.
19. *Letters*, II, 452, 482–83; *EWJ*, 10/4/1833; 'List of Post Towns and
     Postmasters in Scotland', *Edinburgh Almanack for 1832*.
20. Groves, pp. 1, 14, and *passim*; *CM*, 20/7/1833; 'Border Games', *EEP*,
     17/8/1833.
21. *EWJ*, 22/4/1829; *EEC*, 12/8/1830; *Letters*, II, 398–99.
22. 'Innerleithen Mineral Wells', *EEC*, 10/5/1834.
23. *Annuals*, pp. xiii–xix, xxxii–xxxvi, 3–6; *Letters*, II, 224.
24. *Marianne, The Widower's Daughter; A Christmas Tale* (Edinburgh, 1823),
     pp. 49–50; [Sarah Greene], *Scotch Novel Reading; or, Modern Quackery*, 3
     vols (London, 1824), I, 10; Blackwood to JH, 24/5/1828, NLS, MS
     30,310, pp. 490–92; *Letters*, II, 295–96, 300; *Letters and Recollections of
     Sir Walter Scott by Mrs Hughes (of Uffington)*, ed. by Horace G. Hutchinson
     (London, 1904), pp. 289–97.
25. *Letters*, II, 346–47; Blackwood to JH, 8/8/1829 and David Low to
     Blackwood, 29/7/1830, ATL, James Hogg Papers (Items 76 and 86).
     MS-Papers-0042-09; *BEM*, 23 (January 1829), 112–36 (p. 133);
     Gilfillan to JH, 9/9/1831, NLS, MS 2245, fol. 176; Gillian Hughes,
     'James Hogg and *The Picture of Scotland*', *SHW*, 14 (2003), 88–93.
26. Laidlaw to Scott, [February 1828], NLS, MS 3907, fols 333–34; cop-
     ies of drafts of Peter Phillips's will of 1812, owned by Liz Milne;

National Archives of Scotland, RS23/79, pp. 244–47 (information from Richard Jackson).

27. National Archives of Scotland, CS231/C/11/7 (information from John Ballantyne).
28. *Annuals*, p. 27; *D & GC*, 5/6/1827; *Letters*, II, 273.
29. *Letters*, II, 267, 271, 292–93; Blackwood to JH, 14/7/1827, NLS, MS 30,310, p. 182; *EWJ*, 28/5/1828.
30. James Gray (by Peter Jackson) in *Oxford DNB*; Mary Gray Garden, *Margaret Phillips (Wife of the Ettrick Shepherd)* (Privately printed, 1898), pp. 13–14; *Annuals*, pp. 124–26; Geoffrey Clarke, *The Post Office of India and Its Story* (London, 1921), pp. 16–17; *Letters*, II, 273.
31. *Confessions*, p. 156; *Letters*, II, 280, 282; *Annuals*, pp. 48–56 (p. 49).
32. JH to Chalmers Forest, 14/5/1832, Cornwall Record Office, Truro: RP 17/141; *Letters*, II, 302, 306–07.
33. *Letters*, II, 302, 303, 306–07.
34. *Letters*, II, 301, 302, 304 306; Russell, pp. 319–20; 'Hogg Monument Inauguration', *Border Magazine*, 40 (December 1935), 191–92.
35. *Anecdotes*, pp. 15–16; *Letters*, II, 309; 'A Living Link with Scott, Hogg, and Wilson', *Chambers's Edinburgh Journal*, 1/5/1897, pp. 280–82 (p. 281).
36. *EWJ*, 29/10/1828; *BEM*, 24 (November 1828), 640–76 (p. 676).
37. *SC*, pp. xv–xvi; *Letters*, II, 294, 326; JH to Blackwood, 2/3/1832, NLS, MS 4033, fols 125–26.
38. *ELJ*, 15/11/1828, pp. 9–10 and 29/10/1831, p. 260; 'A Letter from Yarrow. The Scottish Psalmody Defended', *ELJ*, 13/3/1830, pp. 162–63.
39. *Letters*, II, 368.
40. *Letters*, II, 342–43; Blackwood to JH, 6/6/1829, NLS, MS 30,311, pp. 271–72.
41. Garden, pp. 168, 299; *Letters*, II, 334; *Annuals*, pp. 138–39.
42. *EWJ*, 5/12/1827; 'A Living Link with Scott, Hogg, and Wilson', *Chambers's Edinburgh Journal*, 1/5/1897, pp. 280–82 (p. 281); *Letters*, II, 355.
43. Riddell, p. 405; *SG*, pp. 126, 134; Laidlaw to Scott, 19/4/1830, NLS, MS 3913, fols 39–40.
44. *Letters*, I, 92; *Letters*, II, 334, 370.
45. *CM*, 17/9/1835; *Edinburgh Weekly Chronicle*, 12/11/1831; Grierson, X, 404–05.
46. Laidlaw to Scott, 1/12/[1829], NLS, MS 3911, fols 101–03.
47. *Letters*, II, 369–70; National Archives of Scotland, GD224/1125/13, entry 30.
48. *Letters*, II, 377; Grierson, XI, 338.
49. *Letters*, II, 379, 381, 465; Blackwood to JH, undated, NLS, MS 30,311, p. 402.
50. 'To Our Readers', *ELJ*, 26/6/1830, p. 63; 'Portraits of the Ettrick Shepherd', *Border Magazine*, 36 (April 1931), 55; Lockhart, VII, 276.
51. Groves, p. 19; *Letters*, II, 381, 385.
52. *Edinburgh Weekly Chronicle*, 21/4/1830.
53. *Letters*, II, 384–85, 428.
54. *Letters*, II, 384–85, 395; JH to MH, 17/1/1832, SUL, MS 25B, Item 8; Jane Millgate, *Scott's Last Edition: A Study in Publishing History* (Edin-

burgh: Edinburgh University Press, 1987); *AT*, pp. xxxiv–xliii.

55. *AT*, pp. xvii–xviii; *Letters*, II, 401, 405.
56. *Letters*, II, 391; Oliphant, II, 97–100.
57. *EEC*, 12/8/1830; *Letters*, II, 394–95.
58. *EWJ*, 3/11/1830; *Edinburgh Weekly Chronicle*, 1/12/1830.
59. *Anecdotes*, pp. 17–18; *Letters*, II, 401, 403; Oliphant, I, 249.
60. *Letters*, II, 389, 417–18.
61. *Letters*, II, 405, 407–08, 413–14, 415.
62. *Letters*, II, 419, 421; *Edinburgh Weekly Chronicle*, 5/1/1831; MH to JH, 12/1/1831, ATL, James Hogg Papers (Item 110). MS-Papers-0042-12.
63. *EWJ* and *Morning Chronicle*, 12/1/1831; Blackwood to JH, 26/2/1831 and 17/3/31, NLS, MS 30,312, pp. 154–56, 163–64; Blackwood to JH, 12/3/1831, NLS, MS 2245, fol. 165.
64. *QB*, pp. xii–xv; Blackwood to JH, 26/2/1831 and 17/3/31, NLS, MS 30,312, pp. 154–56, 163–64; Blackwood to JH, 12/3/1831, NLS, MS 2245, fol. 165.
65. *QB*, pp. xi, xxi–xxii.
66. Blackwood to JH, 13/2/1832, NLS, MS 30,312, pp. 331–32.
67. Brock, pp. 25, 31–32, 76.
68. Brock, pp. 57, 391–92.
69. *JR1*, p. vi; 'A Screed on Politics', *BEM*, 37 (April 1835), 634–42 (pp. 634, 638); *Letters*, II, 265.
70. 'Will and Sandy. A Scots Pastoral', *QB*, pp. 175–79.
71. 'The Last Stork', *QB*, pp. 180–88; Blackwood to JH, 9/1/1830, NLS, MS 30,311, pp. 484–85.
72. 'The Magic Mirror', *BEM*, 30 (September 1831), 650–54; for Hogg's manuscript see NLS, MS 4805, fols 24–25; Lockhart to Blackwood, 22/9/1931, NLS, MS 4030, fol. 80; *Letters*, II, 458.
73. Oliphant, II, 104; NLS, MS 30,312, pp. 200–01; *EWJ*, 11/5/1831.
74. *Letters*, II, 385, 412, 442, 445–46; JH to Allan Cunningham, 8/11/1834, Beinecke, GEN MSS 61, Box 1, Folder 7; for a description of the extended house see 'A Visit to the Ettrick Shepherd', *American Monthly Magazine*, 3 (April 1834), 85–91, and Howitt, II, 59, 64.
75. *Letters*, II, 453, 458, 463.
76. NLS, MS 2245, fol. 156; *FM*, 6 (September 1832), 255.
77. Blackwood to JH, 17/9/1831, NLS, MS 30,312, p. 225; 'On the Separate Existence of the Soul', *FM*, 4 (December 1831), 529–37; Blackwood to JH, 11/10/1828, NLS, MS 30,311, pp. 71–73; 'A Remarkable Egyptian Story', *FM*, 7 (February 1833), 147–58; 'The Ettrick Shepherd's Last Tale. Helen Crocket', *FM*, 14 (October 1836), 425–40 (p. 426).
78. *Letters*, II, 387, 400, 401, 442.
79. 'Ballad of the Lord Maxwell', *Royal Lady's Magazine*, 2 (October 1831), 219–24; Blackwood to JH, 10/9/1831, ATL, James Hogg Papers (Item 79). MS-Papers-0042-09; *Letters*, II, 456.
80. *QR*, 44 (January 1831), 52–82 (p. 82); Blackwood to JH, 26/2/1831, NLS, MS 30,312, pp. 154–56; *Letters*, II, 426–27.
81. Cochrane to JH, 18/6/1835, NLS, MS 2245, fols 262–63; *Letters*, II, 442; *AT*, p. xx; unpublished paper by Richard D. Jackson, 'Two John Andersons, Edinburgh Publishers and Booksellers'.
82. Sir Richard Phillips to Hogg, 27/4/1832, photocopy owned by David

Parr; *The Letters of Charles Dickens: Volume One 1820–1839*, ed. by Madeline House and Graham Storey (Oxford: Clarendon Press, 1965), p. 83.

83. *AT*, p. xxii; *Letters*, II, 450, 465.
84. *Letters*, II, 452, 454–55, 463, 465.
85. *Letters*, II, 410, 416, 458, 460–61, 462–63, 468; 'The Deer-Stalkers of Glenskiach', *The Club-Book*, 3 vols (London, 1831), II, 205–314 and III, 1–123 (p. 208); *The Atlantic Club-Book* (New York: Harper and Brothers, 1834).
86. Moir to Blackwood, undated, NLS, MS 4030, fol. 212; Blackwood to Hogg, 15/10/1831 and 29/10/1831, NLS, MS 30, 312, pp. 242–43, 255–56; *Letters*, II, 469–70, 472.
87. *Letters*, II, 473, 474–75; MH to JH, 8/1/[1832], in Mary Gray Garden, *Margaret Phillips (Wife of the Ettrick Shepherd)* (Privately printed, 1898), pp. 40–42.
88. *Letters*, II, 475, 476.

Chapter Seven: The Glee of the City

1. *Letters*, II, 476; *Atlas*, 1/1/1832; Corson, p. 678; *Edinburgh Annual Register*, 14 (1821), 103; Grierson, VI, 487.
2. *Letters*, II, 467; *Letters*, I, 114; JH to Blackwood, 2/1/[1832] and 4/1/1832, NLS, MS 4033, fols 119–20, 121–22; JH to MH, 1/1/1832, Garden, pp. 242–43.
3. JH to MH, 1/1/1832, Garden, pp. 242–43; *The Athenaeum*, 7/1/1832, p. 19; JH to [Jerdan], 8/1/[1832], SUL, MS 95.
4. Edward Irving (by Stewart J. Brown) in *Oxford DNB*; JH to MH, 1/1/1832, Garden, pp. 242–43; JH to Blackwood, 2/1/[1832] and 4/1/1832, NLS, MS 4033, fols 119–20, 121–22; *Morning Advertiser*, 3/1/1832; Johnson, I, 640 and II, 794–95.
5. JH to MH, 10/1/1832, Garden, pp. 247–48; *Annuals*, pp. 351–57; *The Athenaeum*, 4/2/1832, p. 78; MH to JH, 11/2/1832, ATL, James Hogg Papers (Item 110). MS-Papers-0042-12.
6. JH to Cochrane, undated, NLS, MS 14,836, fol. 40; JH to [Jerdan], 8/1/[1832], SUL, MS 95; JH to MH, 5/2/1832, SUL, MS 25B, Item 7.
7. JH to MH, 10/1/1832, Garden, pp. 247–48; MH to JH, 22/1/1832, ATL, James Hogg Papers (Item 110). MS-Papers-0042-12; Riddell, pp. 406–07; JH to unknown, 27/10/1833, *Notes and Queries*, fifth series, 10 (1878), 386; *Annuals*, p. 39.
8. 'Noctes Ambrosianae New Series No 2', ed. by Douglas S. Mack and Gillian Hughes, *Altrive Chapbooks*, 2 (1985), 30–54 (p. 44); *The Athenaeum*, 4/2/1832, p. 82.
9. JH to James Robert Hogg, 18/1/1832 (Hogg Letters Project Papers, University of Stirling); Mary Anne Cochrane was baptised at St Martin's Ludgate on 2/9/1822 (*International Genealogical Index*); Cochrane to JH, 26/12/1834, NLS, MS 2245, fols 251–52; NLS, MS 2245, fols 230–31; JH to Cochrane, 4/11/1832, Beinecke, GEN MSS 61, Box 1, Folder 6; JH to Cochrane, 1/3/1834, Autograph File, H (By permission of the Houghton Library, Harvard University).
10. JH to MH, 10/1/1832, Garden, pp. 247–48; *AT*, pp. 200–03.

11. JH to MH, 10/1/1832, Garden, pp. 247–48; 'Abbotsford', *Athenaeum*, 13/8/1831, p. 520.
12. JH to MH, 17/1/1832, SUL, MS 25B, Item 8; JH to Blackwood, 5/2/ 1832, NLS, MS 4033, fols 123–24.
13. JH to MH, 21/1/1832, Garden, pp. 251–52; *Morning Chronicle*, 23/1/ 1832.
14. *Morning Advertiser*, 26/1/1832, 28/1/1832, and 30/1/1832; JH to MH, [26]/1/1832, Garden, pp. 254–56.
15. *Morning Chronicle*, 26/1/1832; *Spectator*, 28/1/1832, pp. 80–81; *Atlas*, 29/1/1832; 'Dinner to Burns', *Athenaeum*, 28/1/1832, pp. 66–67; *AT*, p. 27; MH to JH, 11/2/1832, ATL, James Hogg Papers (Item 110). MS-Papers-0042-12.
16. JH to MH, [26]/1/1832, Garden, pp. 254–56; *Burns*, V, 275, 287–88; William Jerdan, *Autobiography*, 4 vols (London, 1852–53), IV, 297; *Literary Gazette*, 28/1/1832, pp. 59–60; *The Times*, 26/1/1832.
17. *Morning Chronicle*, 31/1/1832; Garden, p. 246; JH to MH, 26/1/1832, Garden, pp. 254–56; Murray to JH, 30/1/1832, NLS, MS 2245, fol. 186; *The Times*, 26/1/1832; JH to MH, 5/2/1832, SUL, MS 25B, Item 7.
18. JH to MH, 17/2/1832, ATL, James Hogg Papers (Item 75b). MS-Papers-0042-08; S. C. Hall, *Retrospect of a Long Life*, 2 vols (London, 1883), II, 288–89; JH to MH, 5/2/1832, SUL, MS 25B, Item 7.
19. Mary L. Pendered, *John Martin, Painter. His Life and Times* (London, 1923), p. 177 (information from Meiko O'Halloran); William Jerdan, *Men I Have Known* (London, 1866), p. 251; Howitt, II, 37; JH to Picken, 16/[1–3/1832], Surrey Historical Centre: The Nichols Archive Project (Private Collection 1).
20. Saltoun to JH, 3/3/1832, NLS, MS 2245, fol. 190; 'Noctes Ambrosianae New Series No 2', pp. 36–38; Walter Arnold, *The Life and Death of the Sublime Society of Beef Steaks* (London, 1871), pp. 2–3, 6–11.
21. 'Noctes Ambrosianae New Series No 2', p. 38; JH to MH, 17/2/1832, ATL, James Hogg Papers (Item 75b). MS-Papers-0042-08; *Morning Chronicle*, 23/2/1832.
22. Hogg's London invitations are in Jessie Phillips Hogg's album, owned by David Parr; *Morning Advertiser*, 10/3/1832.
23. JH to MH, 17/2/1832, ATL, James Hogg Papers (Item 75b). MS-Papers-0042-08; MH to JH, 24/2/1832, Garden, p. 259; JH to Alexander Elder, 14/1/1833, Beinecke, GEN MSS 61, Box 1, Folder 8.
24. Murray to JH, 30/1/1832, NLS, MS 2245, fol. 186; JH to Blackwood, 5/2/1832 and 2/3/1832, NLS, MS 4033, fols 123–24, 125–26; Blackwood to JH, 13/2/1832 and 7/3/1832, NLS, MS 30,312, pp. 331–32, 371; JH to Murray, 17/2/1832, NLS, John Murray Archive, Box 37; JH to Cadell, 13/3/[1832], from the Miscellaneous Manuscripts Collection (Collection 100), Department of Special Collectins, Charles E. Young Research Library, UCLA.
25. JH to MH, 5/2/1832, SUL, MS 25B, Item 7; MH to JH, 11/2/1832, in ATL, James Hogg Papers (Item 110). MS-Papers-0042-12.
26. JH to Lockhart, 9/2/1832, British Library, Add. MS 70,949, fols 135– 36; Meiko O'Halloran, 'Hogg, Mary, Queen of Scots, and the Illustrations to *The Queen's Wake*', *QW*, pp. lxxxvii–cxiii (pp. c–civ).

27. John Murray III to JH, 26/6/[1832], NLS, John Murray Archive, Box 37; *Athenaeum*, 11/2/1832, p. 97 and 28/1/1832, p. 72; JH to MH, 5/2/1832, SUL, MS 25B, Item 7; see dust-jacket for Maclise's sketch.

28. *The Metropolitan*, 3 (February 1832), 51; JH to Lockhart, 24/2/1832, NLS, MS 924, no. 85; JH to MH, 14/3/1832, Garden, p. 262; *AT*, pp. xxiv–xxv.

29. *The Chappell Story, 1811–1961*, compiled by Carlene Mair (London: Chappell & Co., 1961), pp. 10, 13–14, 15; *The Chappell Centenary, 1811–1912* (London, [1912]), pp. 13–14, 27; JH to Peter M'Leod, 27/2/1832, NLS, MS 2208, fols 39–40.

30. *Athenaeum*, 14/1/1832, p. 40; Bond to JH, 24/3/1832, NLS, MS 2245, fols 199–200; *Monthly Magazine*, 17 (January and February 1834), 41, 181; JH to Bloodgood, 25/1/1834, The Historical Society of Pennsylvania, Philadelphia: British Poets Case 10 Box 39; Beinecke: Hogg C3.

31. JH to Laidlaw, 2/11/1832, Beinecke, GEN MSS 61, Box 1, Folder 40; JH to Macrone, 23/3/1832, The Huntingdon Library, San Marino, California, Rare Book 320006, v. 1 (fol. 54); James Cochrane to Sir Egerton Bridges, 13/10/1834, in Beinecke, MSS Osborn Files, Folder 3446.

32. *The Athenaeum*, 7/1/1832, p. 8; *Annuals*, p. 301; JH to Alexander Elder, 14/1/1833, Beinecke, GEN MSS 61, Box 1, Folder 8; *Letters*, II, 470; Gillian Hughes, 'James Hogg and *The Metropolitan*', *The Bibliotheck*, n. s. 1 no. 2 (2004), 7–23.

33. Joan McCausland, 'James Hogg and the 1831–32 Cholera Epidemic', *SHW*, 10 (1999), 40–47 (p. 40); MH to JH, 11/2/1832, ATL, James Hogg Papers (Item 110). MS-Papers-0042-12; JH to MH, 5/2/1832, SUL, MS 25B, Item 7; 'Some Terrible Letters from Scotland', *The Metropolitan*, 3 (April 1832), 422–31.

34. *The Athenaeum*, 25/2/1832, p. 134; *The Metropolitan*, 3 (March 1832), 65–68; *Letters*, II, 384.

35. J. A. Froude, *Thomas Carlyle. A History of the First Forty Years of His Life, 1795–1835*, 2 vols (London, 1882), II, 233–34.

36. *LS*, p. 35; William Jerdan, *Men I Have Known* (London, 1866), pp. 251–52.

37. Brock, p. 392; 'Noctes Ambrosianae New Series No 2', pp. 43–44.

38. *LS*, p. 12; MH to JH, 24/2/1832, Garden, p. 260; JH to MH, 10/3/1832, Buccleuch Heritage Trust; Lord Montague to JH, 6/3/1832, NLS, MS 2245, fols 193–94; MH to JH, 15/3/1832, ATL, James Hogg Papers (Item 110). MS-Papers-0042-12; JH to MH, 14/3/1832, Garden, p. 262.

39. MH to JH, 15/3/1832 and JH to MH, 23/3/1832, ATL, James Hogg Papers (Item 110). MS-Papers-0042-12; *The Times*, 19/3/1832.

40. MH to JH, 22/1/1832, ATL, James Hogg Papers (Item 110). MS-Papers-0042-12; JH to [Roscoe and Richie], 19/3/1832, Beinecke, GEN MSS 61, Box 1, Folder 17; *Annuals*, p. 360.

41. *Atlas*, 18/3/1832.

42. Blackwood to JH, 7/3/1832, NLS, MS 30,312, p. 371; JH to Alexander Blackwood, [29/4/1832], SUL, MS 94; JH to Cochrane, 1/4/1832, NLS, MS 2956, fols 159–60.

Chapter Eight: Man of the Mountains

1. JH to Hastie, 2/4/1832, NLS, MS 1809, fols 83–84; information about Hogg's musical box from David Parr; '75th Anniversary of a Border Newspaper', *Border Magazine*, 36 (August 1931), 126–27.
2. JH to Lord Mahon, 2/5/1832, Centre for Kentish Studies, Maidstone, Kent: C343 497/7 (Stanhope Papers).
3. JH to Alexander Elder, 14/1/1833, Beinecke, GEN MSS 61, Box 1, Folder 8; JH to Cunningham, 4/11/1832, Rare Books & Special Collections, Thomas Cooper Library, University of South Carolina; *EEC*, 11/6/1832; *CM*, 6/8/1832; Groves, pp. 26–28.
4. JH to Peter Muir, 31/10/1832, NLS, Acc. 8579; 'Abbotsford', *Athenaeum*, 13/8/1831, pp. 520–21; Sir Charles Gordon to JH, 2/10[1832], Royal Highland and Agricultural Society of Scotland Letter-Book 1832, p. 44 (information from Willie Johnston).
5. JH to Walter Phillips, 7/12/1832, Beinecke, Osborn MSS, Folder 7420; JH to Peter Muir, 26/12/1832, private collection.
6. *1845 SA*, IV, 123; Boa family website at http://www.hunterboa.com/ettrick.html, consulted on 21/1/2007; 'The Ettrick Shepherd and his "One Pound Note"', *CM*, 8/2/1836.
7. JH to Jerdan, 27/12/1832, NLS, MS 20,437, fols 42–43; William Jerdan, *Men I Have Known* (London, 1866), p. 253.
8. *Letters*, II, 425–26, 434–35; Stoddart, pp. 211–13.
9. JH to Chalmers Forest, 14/5/1832, Cornwall Record Office, Truro: RP 17/141; Garden, pp. 210, 276–77; JH to Hannah Lamont, 23/6/1834, NLS, Acc. 9430, no. 107.
10. *EEC*, 3/5/1832; JH to Alexander Blackwood, 15/6/[1832], NLS, MS 4719, fols 160–61.
11. *AT*, pp. xxvi–xxviii; *Fraser's Magazine*, 5 (May 1832), 482–89 (p. 487).
12. Sir Richard Phillips to JH, 27/4/1832, photocopy owned by David Parr; JH to Cochrane, 3/5/1832, Beinecke, GEN MSS 61, Box 1, Folder 6; JH to Lockhart, 3/5/1832 and 4/10/1832, NLS, MS 924 nos. 86, 83; JH to Elder, 14/1/1833, Beinecke, GEN MSS 61, Box 1, Folder 8; JH to Jerdan, 27/12/1832, NLS, MS 20,437, fols 42–43; JH to Oliver & Boyd, 7/7/1832, NLS, Acc. 5000/188; JH to Fullarton, 14/9/1932, NLS, MS 3813, fols 66–67.
13. JH to Fullarton, 23/4/1832, Beinecke, GEN MSS 61, Box 1, Folder 47; JH to Lockhart, 3/5/1832, NLS, MS 924, no 86; *Literary Gazette*, 16/6/1832 and 15/12/1832, pp. 381 and 797; Lockhart to JH, 21/6/1832, Special Collections, University of Otago Library, Dunedin; John Murray III to JH, 26/6/[1832], NLS, John Murray Archive, Box 37.
14. 'A Visit to the Ettrick Shepherd', *American Monthly Magazine*, 3 (April 1834), 85–91 (p. 85); Howitt, II, 59; 'Biographical Sketch of James Hogg, the Ettrick Shepherd', *Mirror*, 21 (January to June 1833), v–viii (p. viii).
15. Johnson, II, 1263–65; *Anecdotes*, p. 75; JH to Joseph Snow, 21/7/1832, Archives of the Royal Literary Fund, 1790–1918: BL, Microfilm 1077/18, File 594 (James Hogg). Permission was kindly granted by the Royal Literary Fund.
16. *EEC*, 31/5/1834 and 8/12/1834; JH to Lockhart, 4/10/1832, NLS,

MS 924 no 83; JH to Lockhart, 17/9/1833, NLS, MS 934, fols 219–20; JH to Cunningham, 4/11/1832, Rare Books & Special Collections, Thomas Cooper Library, University of South Carolina.

17. *AT*, p. 64; *Anecdotes*, pp. xxxvi–xxxviii; JH to Cochrane, 4/11/1832, Beinecke, GEN MSS 61, Box 1, Folder 6; Hogg's Burns with an inscription to Macrone of 30/10/1832, Beinecke, Tinker 453 (information from Janette Currie).

18. JH to Fullarton, 14/9/1832 and 14/11/1832, NLS, MS 3813, fols 66–67, 69; JH to Fullarton, 14/10/1832, Beinecke, GEN MSS 61, Box 1, Folder 36.

19. JH to Duke of Buccleuch, 7/12/1832, NRA(S) 162 (Ogilvie of Chesters Papers), published with grateful thanks to the Ogilvie family.

20. Brock, p. 392; Michael Lynch, *Scotland: A New History* (London: Century, 1991), pp. 391–92; JH to Duke of Buccleuch, 21/7/1832, National Archives of Scotland, GD224/33/3; T. Wilkie, *The Representation of Scotland* (Paisley, 1895), pp. 233, 260.

21. Charles Riddell to Duke of Buccleuch, 1/9/1832, National Archives of Scotland, GD224/581/4; Peter Garside, 'Hogg, Eltrive and *Confessions*', *SHW*, 11 (2000), 5–24; Laidlaw to George Laidlaw, 22/9/1832, NLS, Acc. 9084/9; Particulars, p. 339; Scottish Borders Council Museums and Galleries Service, ETLMS 9962; JH to Peel, 7/4/1835, BL, Add. MS 40,419, fols 162–63.

22. JH to Jerdan, 27/12/1832, NLS, MS 20,437, fols 42–43; JH to Cunningham, 4/11/1832, Rare Books & Special Collections, Thomas Cooper Library, University of South Carolina.

23. JH to Walter Phillips, 7/12/1832, Beinecke, Osborn MSS, Folder 7420; Robert Chambers, *The Picture of Scotland*, 2 vols (Edinburgh, 1827), I, 230.

24. JH to Peter Muir, 26/12/1832, private collection; JH to Elder, 14/1/1833, Beinecke, GEN MSS 61, Box 1, Folder 8; JH to MH, 16[1/1833], ATL, James Hogg Papers (Item 110). MS-Papers-0042-12; *EEP*, 19/1/1833; *EEC*, 26/1/1833; JH to Fullarton, [30]/1/1833, NLS, MS 3813, fol. 71.

25. JH to MH, 5/2/[1833], ATL, James Hogg Papers (Item 110). MS-Papers-0042-12; JH to Elder, 14/1/1833, Beinecke, GEN MSS 61, Box 1, Folder 8; JH to Elizabeth Hogg, 25/7/1833, Beinecke, Osborn MSS, Folder 7414, 'H'.

26. JH to Peter Cunningham, 17/6/1833, Walter B. Beale Papers, University of Washington Libraries, Special Collections; JH to Elizabeth Hogg, 25/7/1833, Beinecke, Osborn MSS, Folder 7414, 'H'; JH to Macrone, 3/8/1833, Brooks Collection. Volume VI, fol. 83A (Courtesy of the Society of Antiquaries of Newcastle-upon-Tyne); JH to Lockhart, 17/9/1833, NLS, MS 934, fols 219–20; Garden, p. 309; Howitt, II, 62–63.

27. JH to MH, 5/2/[1833], ATL, James Hogg Papers (Item 110). MS-Papers-0042-12; Gordon, II, 215–23; JH to Lockhart, 17/9/1833, NLS, MS 934, fols 219–20.

28. Chambers to JH, 4/10/1832 and 17/5/1833, NLS, MS 2245, fols 214–15, 220–21; 'Popular Information on Literature. Second Article', *Chambers's Edinburgh Journal*, 19/5/1832, p. 122; *Mirror*, 22 (1833), 405.

29. Gillian Hughes and Peter Garside, 'James Hogg's *Tales and Sketches* and the Glasgow Numbers Trade', *Cardiff Corvey: Reading the Romantic Text*, 14 (Summer 2005) at http://www.cf.ac.uk/encap/corvey/articles/cc14_n02.html; JH to Lockhart, 17/9/1833, NLS, MS 934, fols 219–20.

30. Cochrane to JH, 13/1/1833, NLS, MS 2245, fol. 218; *EEC*, 18/3/1833; *Athenaeum*, 12/1/1833, p. 27; *Anecdotes*, pp. xxxvii–xliii.

31. JH to Lockhart, 20/3/1833, NLS, MS 1554, fols 75–76; JH to unknown American, 7/3/[1833], in *The Domestic Manners and Private Life of Sir Walter Scott* (Glasgow, 1834), pp. 53–54.

32. *EEC*, 29/8/1833 and 2/10/1834; 'William Buell Sprague' in *Dictionary of American Biography*; private letter, 6/9/2001, from Coreen Hallenbeck, Research Assistant, Albany Institute of History and Arts; W. B. Sprague, *Letters from Europe, in 1828* (New York, 1828), p. 132; JH to W. B. Sprague, 20/6/1833, Beinecke, GEN MSS 61, Box 1, Folder 46; JH to Bloodgood, 22/6/1833, Beinecke, GEN MSS 61, Box 1, Folder 3; JH to Thomas Raffles, 22/6/1833, The John Rylands University Library, The University of Manchester, English MS 353/111.

33. Claude Howard with Nancy Armstrong, 'The Emigration of Hogg's Brothers', *Newsletter of the James Hogg Society*, nos. 5 and 6 (1986 and 1987), pp. 11–13 and 7–10 respectively; letter cited in 'Upper Canada. By a Backwoodsman', *Blackwood's Edinburgh Magazine*, 32 (August 1832), 238–62 (pp. 248–49), information from David Groves; 'The Ettrick Shepherd's Advice to Emigrants', *EEP*, 6/4/1833; JH to Janet Laidlaw, 4/11/1833, Queen's University Archives, Kingston, Ontario, Miscellaneous Collection, Locator #2999, James Hogg *fonds*; JH to Bloodgood, 22/6/1833, Beinecke, GEN MSS 61, Box 1, Folder 3; JH to Rose, 24/9/1833, *Journal of Belles Lettres*, 16/2/1835, unpaginated.

34. JH to Janet Laidlaw, 4/11/1833, Queen's University Archives, Kingston, Ontario, Miscellaneous Collection, Locator #2999, James Hogg *fonds*; Margaret Fraser, 'Ettrick Shepherd: Emigration Agent', *SHW*, 5 (1994), 96–101; *EEC*, 20/9/1834; Laidlaw to Hogg, 22/2/1835, NLS, MS 2245, fols 256–57; JH to Fullarton, 5/9/1833, NLS, MS 3813, fols 72–73.

35. *TWM*, pp. xi–xiii; JH to Macrone, 17/6/[1833], Beinecke, GEN MSS 61, Box 1, Folder 34; Cochrane to JH, 24/7/1833, NLS, MS 2245, fols 228–29.

36. JH to John Wilson, 16/3/1833, NLS, MS 2530, fols 3–4; Fraser to JH, 26/6/1833 and 18/11/1833, NLS, MS 2245, fols 224–25, 234; *Fraser's Magazine*, 8 (July 1833), 49–54; JH to Peter M'Leod, 25/7/1833; NRA(S), OA75, Papers of the Society of Antiquaries of Scotland, VI, 349; *AT*, p. 58.

37. *LS*, p. xii, 104; JH to Bloodgood, 25/1/1834, Historical Society of Pennsylvania, Philadelphia, British Poets, Case 10, Box 39; *Athenaeum*, 25/1/1834, p. 71.

38. *British Critic*, 16 (July 1834), 244; *Johnstone's Edinburgh Magazine*, 1 (May 1834), 534–38 (p. 535); *LS*, p. 26.

39. JH to Steuart of Glenormiston, 24/4/1833, NRA(S) 180/147 (private collection); Sir James Balfour Paul, *The History of the Royal Company of Archers* (Edinburgh, 1875), pp. 133, 157, 198, 348–49.

40. 'Border Games', *EEP*, 17/8/1833; JH to Macrone, 12/5/1833, Bodleian Library, University of Oxford, MS. Autogr. d. 11, fols 321–22.
41. JH to Lockhart, 17/9/1833, NLS, MS 934, fols 219–20; JH to Janet Laidlaw, 4/11/1833, Queen's University Archives, Kingston, Ontario, Miscellaneous Collection, Locator #2999, James Hogg *fonds*.
42. Laidlaw to Anne Scott, 27/5/1833, NLS, Dep. 253/16; JH to Janet Laidlaw, 4/11/1833, Queen's University Archives, Kingston, Ontario, Miscellaneous Collection, Locator #2999, James Hogg *fonds*; William John Napier (by J. K. Laughton rev. Andrew Lambert) in *Oxford DNB*; *EWJ*, 30/10/1833.
43. JH to Janet Laidlaw, 4/11/1833, Queen's University Archives, Kingston, Ontario, Miscellaneous Collection, Locator #2999, James Hogg *fonds*; information from John Ballantyne.
44. Gillian Hughes, 'The Ettrick Shepherd's Nephew', *SHW*, 16 (2005), 20–35; JH to Boyd, 22/11/1834, NLS, Acc. 5000/188; William Jerdan, *Autobiography*, 4 vols (London, 1852–53), IV, 299–300; JH to Fullarton, 15/5/1835, NLS, MS 3649, fols 219–20.
45. *Athenaeum*, 17/8/1833, p. 556; JH to Fullarton, 5/9/1833, NLS, MS 3813, fols 72–73; JH to Janet Laidlaw, 4/11/1833, Queen's University Archives, Kingston, Ontario, Miscellaneous Collection, Locator #2999, James Hogg *fonds*; JH to Blackie and Son, 11/11/1833, NLS, MS 807, fol. 20.
46. Stephanie Anderson-Currie, 'Preliminary Census of Early Hogg Editions in North American Libraries', South Carolina Working Papers in Scottish Bibliography, 3 (Department of English, University of South Carolina, 1993); 'A Visit to the Ettrick Shepherd', *American Monthly Magazine*, 3 (April 1834), 85–91 (pp. 87, 88–89); *Burns*, V, 278–81; *Anecdotes*, p. 1.
47. Malcolm Beresford Montgomery, *The Postage Rates of the North Atlantic Mails (1635–1950)* (Southhampton: M.B. Montgomery, 1991), pp. 1–7; Wayne E. Fuller, *The American Mail: Enlarger of the Common Life* (Chicago: University of Chicago Press, 1972), pp. 191–94; Frank Staff, *The Transatlantic Mail* (London: George G. Harrap & Co., 1956), pp. 61–62.
48. JH to Bloodgood, 25/1/1834, Historical Society of Pennsylvania, Philadelphia: British Poets, Case 10, Box 39; JH to Bloodgood, 24/3/1834, Department of Rare Books & Special Collections, University of Rochester Library.
49. 'Tales of Fathers and Daughters No 2', ed. by Douglas S. Mack, *SHW*, 15 (2004), 126–62 (p. 146); JH to Cochrane, 1/3/1834, Autograph File, H (By permission of The Houghton Library, Harvard University); Macrone to JH, 23/6/1834, NLS, MS 2245, fols 243–44.
50. JH to 'John', 5/2/1834, NLS, Acc. 11000; JH to Alexander Blackwood, 17/[11]/1834, NLS, MS 4039, fols 33–34; JH to Shelton Mackenzie, 5/9/1835, Historical Society of Pennsylvania, Philadelphia: Simon Gratz Collection, Case 12 Box 3; Janette Currie is preparing a full list of original and reprinted Hogg items in American periodicals—meantime see her 'From Altrive to Albany: James Hogg's Transatlantic Publications' at http://www.star.ac.uk/Archive/Papers/Currie.pdf

and "'The Banshee" and "The Rose of Plora'", ed. by Janette Currie, *SHW*, 17 (2006), 145–65.

51. Cochrane to JH, 9/8/1833, NLS, MS 2245, fol. 230; *Anecdotes*, p. 1.
52. Lockhart to JH, 23/9/1833, NLS, MS 2245, fols 232–33; *Anecdotes*, p. li; Lockhart, I, 329 and VII, 419; *EEC*, 4/8/1834; *Fraser's Magazine*, 10 (July and August 1834), 1–10, 125–56.
53. *EEC*, 24/3/1834.
54. *Burns*, V, 287–88.
55. *The Scotsman*, 26/3/1834; *Fraser's Magazine*, 10 (July 1834), 1–10 (p. 10); *Athenaeum*, 6/12/1834, p. 895; *CM*, 20/7/1835.
56. JH to Motherwell, 23/9/1834, NLS, MS 3649, fol. 217; JH to Motherwell, 3/11/1834, Beinecke, GEN MSS 61, Box 1, Folder 42; JH to Cunningham, 8/11/1834, Beinecke, GEN MSS 61, Box 1, Folder 7.
57. JH to Blackie and Son, 25/3/1834, Beinecke, GEN MSS 61, Box 1, Folder 30; JH to Cochrane, 1/3/1834, Autograph File, H (By permission of the Houghton Library, Harvard University); *EEP*, 23/8/1834; *TWM*, pp. xiv–xv.
58. Wilson to JH, 30/4/1834, *Tales and Sketches by the Ettrick Shepherd*, 6 vols (Edinburgh, 1878), I, xxxix–xl; Oliphant, II, 127; JH to Alexander Blackwood, 17/[11]/ 1834, NLS, MS 4039, fols 33–34; JH to Messrs Blackwood, [July] 1835, NLS, MS 4040, fol. 289.
59. JH to William Saunders, 9/8/1834, Beinecke, MSS 61, Box 1, Folder 45; JH to Wilson, [May] 1834, NLS, MS 4039, fols 35–36; Gordon, II, 224–28; NLS, MS 4885, fol. 5; Garden, p. 301; JH to Alexander Blackwood, 3/7/1834, NLS, MS 4039, fols 31–32; Edinburgh St Cuthberts OPR.
60. *EEP*, 1/2/1834; *EEC*, 10/5/1834 and 11/8/1834; 'Dinner to the Ettrick Shepherd', *The Scotsman*, 23/8/1834.
61. 'Dinner to the Ettrick Shepherd', *The Scotsman*, 23/8/1834; Howitt, II, 63.
62. W. H. Harrison, 'Notes and Reminiscences', *University Magazine*, 1 (June 1878), 698–712 (pp. 703–04); *Annuals*, p. 273; JH to Cochrane, 13/ 10/1834, NLS, MS 10,998, fol. 178; Cunningham to JH, 15/11/1834, NLS, MS 2245, fols 249–50; JH to Macrone, 12/5/1833, Bodleian Library, University of Oxford, MS Autogr. d. 11, fols 321–22.
63. John Macrone (by Robert L. Patten) in *Oxford DNB*; *The Life and Adventures of George Augustus Sala* (London, 1896), pp. 141–43; Cunningham to Macrone, 23/2/1835, Beinecke, Osborn MSS, Folder 17157.
64. *TWM*, pp. 240–41; 'A Genuine Border Story', ed. by Gillian Hughes, *SHW*, 3 (1992), 95–145; *Athenaeum*, 14/3/1835, p. 213; Cochrane to JH, 26/12/1834, NLS, MS 2245, fol. 251.
65. *TWM*, pp. 65, 222.
66. *The Times*, 9/5/1835; *Literary Gazette*, 21/3/1835, pp. 179–80; *EEP*, 25/ 4/1835; JH to Cochrane, 15/6/1835, Beinecke, GEN MSS 61, Box 1, Folder 6; Cochrane to JH, 26/12/1834 and 18/6/1835, NLS, MS 2245, fols 251, 262–63.
67. Daniel O'Connell (by R. V. Comerford) and Sir Robert Peel (by John Prest) in *Oxford DNB*; Brock, pp. 316–17.
68. 'The Ettrick Shepherd's Last Song', *Newcastle Journal*, 1/3/1834 (infor-

mation from Janette Currie and Meiko O'Halloran); Sir Robert Peel (by John Prest) in *Oxford DNB*.

69. T. Wilkie, *The Representation of Scotland* (Paisley, 1895), pp. 233, 260; JH to Alexander Pringle, 9/2/1835, The W. Hugh Peal Collection, Special Collections and Digital Programs, University of Kentucky Libraries; JH to Cunningham, 9/3/1835, Historical Society of Pennsylvania, Philadelphia: British Poets Case 10, Box 39.

70. Peel to JH, 9/3/1835, NLS, MS 2245, fol. 316; 'Mr Hogg, the Ettrick Shepherd', *Gentleman's Magazine*, n. s. 5 (January 1836), 94–98 (p. 97); JH to Peel, 7/4/1835, BL, Add. MS 40,419, fols 162–63; JH to Peel, 25/4/1835, BL, Add. MS 40,420, fols 64–65.

71. John Forbes to JH, 17/1/1835, NLS, MS 2245, fols 252–55; JH to Forbes, 25/1/1835, R. Borland, *James Hogg, The Ettrick Shepherd: Memorial Volume* (Selkirk, 1898), pp. 47–48; *CM*, 5/2/1835 and 30/3/1835; *EEP*, 28/3/1835; Garden, p. 305; JH to Peel, 25/4/1835, BL, Add. MS 40,420, fols 64–65.

72. 'A Screed on Politics', *BEM*, 37 (April 1835), 634–42 (pp. 635, 637, 642); *Anecdotes*, p. 15; JH to Peel, 25/4/1835, BL, Add. MS 40,420, fols 64–65.

73. Cochrane to JH, 26/12/1834, NLS, MS 2245, fol. 251; JH to Alexander Blackwood, [February 1835], NLS, MS 4719, fol. 187.

74. JH to Fraser, 14/9/1835, Beinecke, Osborn MSS, Folder 7416; JH to Peel, 14/5/1835, BL, Add. MS 40,420, fol. 166.

75. *Freemason's Quarterly Review*, 2 (June 1835), 220–22 (p. 221).

76. JH to MH, undated and 19/[6]/1835, ATL, James Hogg Papers (Item 110). MS-Papers-0042-12; 'Innerleithen.–Summer Curling', *CM*, 29/6/1835.

77. *CM*, 8/8/1835; Groves, pp. 36–37; JH to Grieve and Oliver, [September 1835], *Border Magazine*, 36 (August 1931), 127; JH to William Brockie, 7/8/1835, Beinecke, GEN MSS 61, Box 1, Folder 33; JH to Walter [Boa], 10/8/[1835], Canterbury Caledonian Society, Christchurch, New Zealand.

78. Garden, pp. 323–24; James Hogg junior to Alexander Laidlaw, in Laidlaw's Scrapbook (p. 110), owned by Mrs Doreen Mitchell.

79. JH to Fraser, 17/9/1835, *Fraser's Magazine*, 14 (October 1836), 425.

80. *Annuals*, pp. 357–58; JH to Cochrane, 15/6/1835, Beinecke, GEN MSS 61, Box 1, Folder 6; Cochrane to JH, 18/6/1835, NLS, MS 2245, fols 262–63; Garden, pp. 301–02.

81. Howitt, II, 63–64.

82. Garden, pp. 326–27; information from Doreen Mitchell, who has the watch and Alexander Laidlaw's scrap-book (letter from James Hogg junior to Laidlaw, p. 110).

83. Garden, p. 327; *Glasgow Courier*, 17/11/1835; intimation of death to George Boyd, 24/11/1835, NLS, Acc. 5000/188.

Epilogue

1. *LS*, p. 87.

Index

As the theme of this biography is James Hogg there is no separate entry for him in this Index: subjects relating to him are distributed throughout, and his works are entered under their titles. The names of peers are entered under their peerage titles, and entries for married women are given under the surname of the husband, following English practice, except where the woman continued to be generally known by her surname at birth when this Scots practice is followed.